PAPERS

RELATING TO

THE TREATY OF WASHINGTON.

VOLUME V.—BERLIN ARBITRATION.

CONTAINING THE MEMORIAL OF THE UNITED STATES ON THE CANAL DE HARO AS ITS BOUNDARY-LINE; CASE OF THE GOVERNMENT OF HER BRITANNIC MAJESTY; REPLY OF THE UNITED STATES THERETO; SECOND AND DEFINITIVE STATEMENT OF THE GOVERNMENT OF HER BRITANNIC MAJESTY; AND CORRESPONDENCE.

WASHINGTON:
GOVERNMENT PRINTING OFFICE.
1872.

NOTE.

The figures in brackets denote the pages of the editions presented at Berlin, and the references occurring are to those pages.

CONTENTS.

I.

MEMORIAL ON THE CANAL DE HARO AS THE BOUNDARY-LINE OF THE UNITED STATES OF AMERICA, AS PRESENTED BY THE AMERICAN PLENIPOTENTIARY, GEORGE BANCROFT.

II.

CASE OF THE GOVERNMENT OF HER BRITANNIC MAJESTY SUBMITTED TO THE ARBITRATION AWARD OF HIS MAJESTY THE EMPEROR OF GERMANY, ETC.

III.

REPLY OF THE UNITED STATES TO THE CASE OF THE GOVERNMENT OF HER BRITANNIC MAJESTY.

IV.

SECOND AND DEFINITIVE STATEMENT ON BEHALF OF THE GOVERNMENT OF HER BRITANNIC MAJESTY.

V.

CORRESPONDENCE.

I.

MEMORIAL

ON

THE CANAL DE HARO

AS

THE BOUNDARY LINE OF THE UNITED STATES OF AMERICA,

PRESENTED IN THE NAME OF

THE AMERICAN GOVERNMENT

TO

HIS MAJESTY WILLIAM I,

GERMAN EMPEROR AND KING OF PRUSSIA,

AS ARBITRATOR,

BY THE AMERICAN PLENIPOTENTIARY,

GEORGE BANCROFT.

MEMORIAL.

The treaty of which the interpretation is referred to Your Majesty's arbitrament was ratified more than a quarter of a century ago. Of the sixteen members of the British cabinet which framed and presented it for the acceptance of the United States, Sir Robert Peel, Lord Aberdeen, and all the rest but one, are no more. The British minister at Washington who signed it is dead. Of American statesmen concerned in it, the minister at London, the President and Vice-President, the Secretary of State, and every one of the President's constitutional advisers, except one, have passed away. I alone remain, and after finishing the three-score years and ten that are the days of our years, am selected by my country to uphold its rights.

Six times the United States had received the offer of arbitration on their Northwestern boundary, and six times had refused to refer a point where the importance was so great and the right so clear. But when consent was obtained to bring the question before Your Majesty, my
country resolved to change its policy, and in the heart of Europe,
[4] before a tribunal from which no judgment but a just one can *em-
anate, to explain the solid foundation of our demand, and the principles of moderation and justice by which we have been governed.

The case involves questions of geography, of history, and of international law; and we are glad that the discussion should be held in the midst of a nation whose sons have been trained in those sciences by a Carl Ritter, a Ranke, and a Heffter.

The long-continued controversy has tended to estrange from each other two of the greatest powers in the world, and even menaced, though remotely, a conflict in arms. A want of confidence in the disposition of the British government has been sinking into the mind of the States of the Union now rising on the Pacific, and might grow into a popular conviction, not easy to be eradicated. After having secured union and tranquillity to the people of Germany, and attained a happiness never before allotted by Providence to German warrior or statesman, will it not be to Your Majesty a crowning glory now, in the fullness of years and in the quiet which follows the mighty struggles of a most eventful life, to reconcile the two younger branches of the great Germanic family?

THE POINT FOR ARBITRATION.

The point submitted for arbitration is limited with exactness. By Article I of the Treaty concluded at Washington on the 15th of June, 1846, between the United States and Her Britannic Majesty, it was stipulated that the line of boundary between the territories of the United States and those of Her Britannic Majesty, from the point on the forty-ninth parallel of north latitude up to which it had already been ascertained, should be continued westward along the said parallel of north latitude "to the middle of the channel which separates the continent from Vancouver's Island, and

Appendix No. 1, p. 3.

[5] thence *southerly, through the middle of the said channel and of Fuca's Straits to the Pacific Ocean." The British Government claim that the water-line here referred to should run through a passage which they have thought proper to name the straits of Rosario, and which the United States, for the purpose of this reference, permit to go by that name. The United States claim that the water-line runs through the canal de Haro. The arbitrator is to say finally and without appeal which of those claims is most in accordance with the true interpretation of the treaty of June 15, 1846. That is the point submitted, and that alone; nothing more and nothing less.

Appendix, p. 4, l. 20, 21.

If the United States can but prove their claim to be most in accordance with the true interpretation of the treaty, it is agreed that the award shall be in their favor; how much more, then, if they prove that their interpretation is the only one which the treaty admits!

HOW THIS DISCUSSION WILL BE CONDUCTED.

In conducting this discussion I shall keep in mind that the restoration of friendship between the two powers which are at variance is the object of the arbitration. Nothing that has been written since the ratifications of the treaty were exchanged can alter its words or affect its interpretation. I shall, therefore, for the present at least, decline to examine all communications that may have taken place since that epoch, except so far as is necessary to explain why there is an arbitration, and shall thus gain the advantage of treating the subject as simply an investigation for the ascertainment of truth.

Since the intention of the negotiators must rest on the knowledge in their possession at the time when the treaty was made, I shall use the charts and explorations which have advanced, or profess to have
[6] advanced, our knowledge of the *country in question, and which are anterior to that date. Of such charts I have found six, and six only; and though they are of very unequal value, yet for the sake of impartiality and completeness I present photographic copies or extracts of every one of them. Of charts of explorations of a later date, it was my desire to make no use whatever; but then, as will appear in the sequel, there would be not one map on which the channel claimed by the British government could be found with the name of "the straits of Rosario;" I am therefore compelled to add a later chart, on which that name is placed, as required for the arbitration. This chart also shows the length and breadth and depth of the respective channels.

My task is an easy one; for I have only to deduce the intentions of the negotiators of the treaty from its history, and to interpret its words according to the acknowledged principles of international law.

PARALLELS OF LATITUDE THE CUSTOMARY BOUNDARIES OF ENGLISH COLONIES IN NORTH AMERICA.

A parallel of latitude extending from the Atlantic to the Pacific was a usual boundary established by England for its colonies in North America. The charter granted in 1620 by James I, to the company of Plymouth for New England, bounded its territory by the parallels of 48° and of 40° north latitude "in length and breadth throughout the mainland from sea to sea." The charter granted by Charles I to Massachusetts in 1628 had in like manner for its northern and southern boundaries parallels of latitude running from sea to sea. So, too, had the old patent of Connecti-

Appendix, p. 6, l. 14-17.

P. 6, l. 24-27.

cut; so too had the charter to Connecticut, granted by Charles II, in 1662. The charter granted in 1663 by Charles II, to the Lords Proprietors of Carolina, adopted as their northern boundary the parallel of six and thirty degrees, and as their southern boundary the parallel of "one and thirty de-
[7] grees of *northern latitude, and so west in a direct line as far as the South seas." The precedent was followed by George II, in the charter granted in 1732 for Georgia; and in 1761 George III officially described that colony as extending by parallels "westward in direct lines" to the Pacific.

P. 7, l. 7-10.
P. 7, l. 16-18.
Appendix, p. 7, l. 29-21.

THE SAME RULE CONTINUED IN THE TREATY OF PEACE OF 1872.

In the first convention between the United States of America and Great Britain, signed at Paris on the 30th of November, 1782, the northern boundary line of the United States was carried by the two powers through the great upper lakes to the most northwestern point of the Lake of the Woods. If from that point the line was to be continued, the treaty, adopting the precedent of the past century of colonization, and foreshadowing the rule of the future, prescribed "a due west course."

Appendix No. 4, p. 8.

THE SAME RULE APPLIED TO THE BOUNDARY OF LOUISIANA.

By the treaty of April 30, 1803, between the United States of America and the French Republic, the United States came into possession "forever and in full sovereignty" of the colony and Territory of Louisiana.

Appendix No. 5, p. 8.

No sooner had the United States made this acquisition than they sent out an exploring expedition, which made known to the world the Rocky Mountains and the branches of the river of Oregon, the mouth of which an American navigator had been the first to enter.

By the acquisition of Louisiana the Republic of America and Great Britain, as sovereign over the territory of Hudson Bay, became neighbors still further to the west; and the two powers took an early opportunity to consider their dividing line west of the Lake of the Woods. The United States might have demanded, perhaps should have
[8] demanded, under *the treaty of 1782, that the line "due west" should proceed from "the most northwest point of the Lake of the Woods." That point is near the parallel of 50°; the United States consented to the parallel of 49°. But with regard to the continuation of the line, while Mr. Madison, the American Secretary of State, was desirous not to advance claims that could be "offensive to Spain," both parties, adopting the words of the treaty of 1782, agreed as between themselves that the line should proceed on that parallel "in a due west course" to the Rocky Mountains. In 1807 this agreement would have been ratified; but the maritime decrees of the Emperor Napoleon, dated at Berlin and at Milan, disturbed the peace of the oceans, and orders in council in Great Britain, which finally provoked war with the United States, interposed delay.

Appendix No. 6, p. 9.
Appendix No. 7, p. 9, 10.
Appendix No. 6, p. 9, l. 1, 2.

When, in 1815, the terms of peace were to be adjusted, the American plenipotentiaries were instructed by their Government as to the northwestern boundary, to consent to no claim on the part of Great Britain to territory in that quarter south of the forty-ninth parallel of latitude; and they implicitly adhered to their instructions.

Appendix No. 50, p. 56.

Convention with G. Britain Oct. 20, 1816. Art. 1, 2, 3.

In due time the negotiations, which had effected an agreement in 1807, were renewed; and, on the 20th of October, 1818, the parallel of 49° was adopted as the boundary line between the two countries as far as the Stony, or, as we now more commonly call them, the Rocky Mountains. From that range of mountains to the Pacific, America, partly from respect to the claims of Spain, was willing to delay for ten years the continuance of the boundary line.

THE UNITED STATES ACQUIRE THE CLAIMS OF SPAIN NORTH OF 42°.

The ocean chivalry of Spain were the first to explore the northern coast of the Pacific. Hernando Cortes began the work. The
[9] straits of Fuca take their name from a Greek *navigator who was
in the Spanish service in 1592. Perez, a Spaniard, whose explorations extended as far to the north as 54°, discovered Nootka Sound in 1774. In the next year Bodega y Quadra reached the fifty-eighth degree, and Heceta, on the 15th of August, 1775, returning from Nootka, noticed, though he did not enter, the mouth of the river Oregon. In 1789, 1790, 1791, before a British keel had entered the straits of Fuca, a succession of Spanish navigators, Martinez and de Haro, Eliza, Fidalgo, Quimper, and others, had explored and draughted charts of the island which is now called Vancouver, and the waters which lie to the east of it. When Vancouver, on the 29th of April, 1792, passed through the straits of Fuca and entered those waters, he encountered, to his mortification, Spanish navigators who had already explored them and who produced before him a chart of that region made by Spanish officers the year before.

Appendix No. 12, p. 13.

Tratado de Limites Entre S. M. Ca. y los Estados unidos de America. Art. 3.

By the treaty of Spain with the United States, of the 22d of February, 1819, "His Catholic Majesty ceded to the United States all his rights, claims, and pretensions to any territories north of the parallel of latitude 42°, from the Arkansas River to the Pacific."

Thus did the custom of boundaries by a parallel of latitude receive a new confirmation; and thus did the United States become sole heir to all the pretensions and rights which Spain had acquired in North America, north of the parallel of 42°, and beyond that of 49°.

MR. HUSKISSON OBJECTS TO THE DIVISION OF VANCOUVER ISLAND.

Appendix No. 8, p. 10.

When the ten years' limitation of the treaty of 1818 drew near, Mr. Canning, secretary of state for foreign affairs in Great Britain, on the 20th of April, 1826, invited the American Government to resume negotiations (attempted in vain in 1824) for settling the boundary upon the northwest coast of America.

[10] *At that time John Quincy Adams was President of the United
States, with Henry Clay for Secretary of State; and the nego tiation on the American side was conducted in London by Albert Gallatin. Re-enforced as were the United States of America by the titles of both France and Spain, in addition to their own claims from contiguity and discovery, they remained true to their principle of moderation, and again it was resolved not to insist on the territory to the north of 49° which Spain had ceded; and on the 19th of June, 1826, "in the spirit of concession and compromise, which he hoped Great Britain would recognise and reciprocate," Mr. Clay authorized Mr. Gallatin to propose "the extension of the line on the parallel of 49° from the Stony Mountains to the Pacific Ocean." "This" he wrote, "is our ultima-

Appendix No. 9, p. 11.

tum, and you may so announce it. We can consent to no line more favorable to Great Britain." In the following August Mr. Clay repeated to Mr. Gallatin: "The President cannot consent that the boundary on the northwest coast shall be south of forty-nine." Appendix No. 9, p. 12, l. 5-7.

On the 22d of November, 1826, Mr. Huskisson, one of the British plenipotentiaries, remarked on the straight line proposed by the United States, that its cutting off the lower part of Vancouver Island was quite inadmissible. Appendix No. 10, p. 12. Here is the first intimation of the boundary line of 49° to the Pacific, with just so much deflection as to leave the southern extremity of Vancouver Island to Great Britain.

To this Mr. Gallatin, nine days later, replied, that "to the forty-ninth parallel the United States would adhere as a basis." Yet as it seemed to cut Vancouver Island in an inconvenient Appendix No. 11, p. 13. manner, he had in view the exchange of that southern extremity for an equivalent north of 49° on the mainland. Here is the first intimation of the possibility, on the part of the United States, to vary from the line of 49°, but only so far as to yield to Great Britain the southern extremity of Vancouver Island, in return for a full equivalent.

[11] *But the interest of the Hudson Bay Company was better subserved by leaving the whole region open to the fur trade, and the United States on their part had no motive for hastening an adjustment. The American envoy, therefore, in 1827 consented to prolong the treaty of 1818, yet with the proviso that either party might abrogate it, on giving notice of twelve months to the other contracting party. Convention with Great Britain, August 6, 1827. Under this convention the question of jurisdiction and boundary remained in abeyance for nearly sixteen years.

LORD ABERDEEN AND MR. EVERETT DISCUSS THE NORTHWESTERN BOUNDARY.

In October 1822, the British foreign secretary, the Earl of Aberdeen, who through the agency of Lord Ashburton had just settled our northeastern boundary from the Lake of the Woods to the Atlantic, expressed to Mr. Everett, then American minister at London, a strong wish that he might receive instructions to settle the boundary between the two countries on the Pacific Ocean. Appendix No. 13, p. 14. No. 14, 15, p. 15.

American emigrants had already begun to find their way on foot across the continent. In 1843 a thousand emigrants, armed men, women, and children, with wagons and cattle, having assembled on the western frontier of Missouri, marched across the plains and through the mountain passes to the fertile valley of the Willamette in Oregon. The ability of America to enforce its rights by occupation grew with every year. But its increasing power did not change its policy of moderation, and to meet the wish of Lord Aberdeen, on the 9th of October, 1843, the Government of the United States sent to Mr. Everett the necessary powers, with this instruction: "The offer of the forty-ninth parallel may be again tendered, with the right of navigating the Columbia on equal terms." Appendix No. 16, p. 16.

On the 29th of November, 1843, soon after Mr. Everett's full powers

[12] had arrived, he and Lord Aberdeen had a very *long and important conversation on the Oregon question; and the concession of Lord Aberdeen appearing to invite an expression of the extremest modification which the United States could admit to their former proposal, Mr. Everett reports that he said: Appendix No. 19, p. 19. P. 20, l. 25-27. P. 20, l. 31-36.

I thought the President might be induced so far to depart from the forty-ninth

parallel as to leave the whole of Quadra and Vancouver's Island to England, whereas that line of latitude would give us the southern extremity of that island, and consequently the command of the straits of Fuca on both sides. I then
P. 21, l. 1-3. pointed out on a map the extent of this concession; and Lord Aberdeen said he would take it into consideration.

The next day Mr. Everett more formally referred to the subject in a
Appendix, p. 21, 22. note to the British secretary:

46 GROSVENOR PLACE, 30th *November*, 1843.

MY DEAR LORD ABERDEEN. * * * It appears from Mr. Gallatin's correspondence that * * * Mr. Huskisson had especially objected to the extension of the 49° to the Pacific, on the ground that it would cut off the southern extremity of Quadra and Vancouver's Island. My suggestion yesterday would obviate this objection. * * * A glance at the map shows its importance as a modification of the forty-ninth degree. * * * Edward Everett.

On the 2d of February, and on the 1st of April, 1844, Mr. Everett
Appendix No. 20, reports that he continuously insisted with Lord Aberdeen
p. 22-24. that the only modification which the United States could, in his opinion, be brought to agree to, was that they should waive their
P. 18, l. 32, 33. claim to the southern extremity of Vancouver Island, and that Lord Aberdeen uniformly answered: "he did not think
P. 23, l. 39, 40. there would be much difficulty in settling the question."

During the following months Mr. Everett and Lord Aberdeen, both wishing sincerely to settle the controversy, had further frequent conversations, and, as the result of them all, Mr. Everett reported that
[13] England would not accept the *naked parallel of 49° to the ocean, but would consent to the line of the forty-ninth degree, provided it could be so modified as to leave to Great Britain the southern ex-
Appendix No. 22, tremity of Vancouver Island. "I have spared no pains,"
p. 26, l. 23-27. wrote Mr. Everett on the 28th of February, 1845, "to impress upon Lord Aberdeen's mind the persuasion that the utmost which the United States can concede is the 49th parallel with the modification suggested, taking always care to add that I had no authority for saying that even that modification would be agreed to."

To one fact I particularly invoke the attention of the Imperial arbitrator: not the least room for doubt was left by Mr. Everett with regard to the extent of the modification proposed. He had pointed it out to Lord Aberdeen on the map, and had so often and so carefully directed his attention to it, that there could be no misapprehension on the limit of the proposed concession. Mr. Everett retired from office in the full persuasion that the northwestern boundary would be settled, whenever the United States would consent so far to depart from the parallel of 49° as to leave the whole of Vancouver Island to Great Britain.

THE PAMPHLET OF MR. STURGIS.

The subject attracted public attention. On the 22d of January, 1845,
Appendix No. 21, Mr. William Sturgis, a distinguished citizen of the United
p. 24, 25. States who had passed several years on the northwest coast of America, delivered in Boston a lecture on what was now generally called the Oregon question, in which, hitting exactly the idea of Mr. Everett, he proposed as the boundary: "a continuation of the parallel of 49° across the Rocky Mountains to tide-water, say to the middle of the Gulf of Georgia; thence by the northernmost navigable passage (not north of 49°) to the straits of Juan de Fuca, and down the middle of these straits to the Pacific Ocean; the navigation of the Gulf of
[14] Georgia and the Straits of Fuca to be forever *free to both parties; all the islands and other territory lying south and east of this line to belong to the United States, and all north and west to Great

Britain. By this arrangement we should yield to Great Britain the portion of Quadra and Vancouver's Island that lies south of latitude 49° * * * Will Great Britain accede to this? I think she will."

The pamphlet of Mr. Sturgis, accompanied by a map on which the proposed boundary is marked, was read by Lord Ashburton and by Lord Aberdeen. To one who eminently enjoyed the confidence of both governments Lord Aberdeen pronounced it "a clear and sensible view of the matter." Appendix No. 26, p. 30, l. 3. Lord Ashburton, whose opinion on the subject carried the greatest weight, wrote to Mr. Sturgis: Appendix No. 25, p. 28, l. 7-11.

Your treatise enables me every day to answer satisfactorily the questions put to me so often, where is the Oregon, and what is this dispute about? You have stated the case distinctly in a few pages, and, what is indeed uncommon, with great impartiality

MR. BUCHANAN NEGOTIATES WITH MR. PAKENHAM.

Meantime the negotiation on the Oregon question had been transferred to the new British minister at Washington. Offers of arbitration had been rejected; emigration across the plains gave promise of founding States on the Pacific; and the Congress of the United States teemed with propositions to prepare for establishing a territorial government in Oregon. When the administration of Mr. Polk entered upon office, all parties in America were unanimous in insisting on a boundary at the least as favorable as the parallel of 49°; while a very large number, and seemingly the largest number, thought the time had come for America, as the heir of Spain, to carry its claims beyond the parallel of 49°. But the new administration would not swerve from the moderation which had marked the policy of the country.

[15] Meantime both parties had received more accurate in*formation on the geography of that district. In July, 1841, Appendix No. 27, p. 31. Captain Wilkes had made a survey of the waters south of 49°, especially of the channel of Haro; and in the early part of 1845 his narrative and accompanying map had been published both in America and England. Believing now that Great Britain would accept the line of 49°, with the small modification for the southern end of Vancouver Island, the American administration, on the 12th of July, 1845, made to the British minister at Washington the proposal, "that the Oregon territory shall be divided between the two countries by Appendix No. 28, p. 31. the forty-ninth parallel of north latitude from the Rocky Mountains to the Pacific Ocean; offering at the same time to make free to Great Britain any port or ports on Vancouver's Island south of this parallel, which the British government may desire." A friendly spirit dictated the proposition, which it was sincerely hoped and expected might "prove the foundation of lasting peace and harmony between the two countries."

The proposition, which excited surprise by its moderation, was rejected by the British plenipotentiary at Washington, who, Appendix No. 29, p. 32. without even waiting to refer the subject to the ministry in England, suffered the negotiation on his part to drop, expressing his trust that the United States would offer "some further proposal for the settlement of the Oregon question." Appendix No. 30, p. 32, 33.

In consequence of receiving such an answer, the American Secretary of State withdrew the offer that he had made.

On hearing of this abrupt rejection of the American proposal, Lord Aberdeen invited Mr. MacLane, the new American minister at London, to an interview, of which Mr. MacLane made Appendix No. 31, p. 34. report:

Lord Aberdeen not only lamented but censured the rejection of our proposition by

Mr. Pakenham without referring it to his government. He stated that if Mr. Pakenham had communicated the American proposition to the government here, as he was expected to have done, he, Lord Aberdeen, would have taken it up as a basis of his
[16] action, and entertained little doubt that he would have been enabled * to propose modifications which might have resulted in an adjustment mutually satisfactory to both governments.

The conduct of Mr. Pakenham was not censured in private only. Lord
Appendix No. 34, p. 37-39. Aberdeen censured it in the House of Lords. In the House of Commons, on the night of Friday, the 23d of January, 1846, Lord John Russell condemned it as "a hasty proceeding." Sir Robert Peel was cheered, when on the same evening he observed:

It would have been better had he transmitted that proposal to the home government for their consideration; and, if found in itself unsatisfactory, it might possibly have formed the foundation for a further proposal.

And now that the re-opening of the negotiation was thrown upon his ministry, he was loudly applauded by the House, as he gave a pledge for his own future conduct in these words:

I think it would be the greatest misfortune, if a contest about the Oregon between two such powers as England and the United States, could not, by the exercise of moderation and good sense, be brought to a perfectly honorable and satisfactory conclusion.

FINAL PROPOSAL OF THE EARL OF ABERDEEN.

Lord Aberdeen confessed that it now fell to him to propose a peaceful solution of the long controversy. Mr. Everett had left him no doubt as to the utmost departure from the parallel of forty-nine degrees, which the United States, under the late administration, could have conceded. The only doubt was now, if the United States would still be willing to yield so much. The rude rejection of Mr. Buchanan's proposal had
Appendix No. 35, p. 39-41. roused and united their people. Mr. Calhoun, the late Secretary of State, and the ablest Senator from one section of the country, declared himself in the Senate for the forty-ninth degree as the boundary line. Mr. Webster, the former Secretary of State, who had settled with Lord Ashburton the northeastern boundary, re-
[17] peatedly "said as plainly as he could speak, or put down * words in writing, that England must not expect anything south of forty-nine degrees." All those members of Congress who were of a different
P. 40, l. 8-21. P. 40, l. 22-26, p. 41. mind, Mr. John Quincy Adams, a late President of the United States, Mr. Cass, afterward Secretary of State, Mr. Sevier, then the chairman of the Committee on Foreign Affairs, contended, not for less than the line of forty-nine degrees, but, under the heirship from
Appendix No. 36, p. 41. Appendix No. 33, p. 36. Spain, for very much more. The voice of England became loud for the line of the forty-ninth parallel. Mr. Bates, an American naturalized in Great Britain by act of Parliament, and much trusted by both governments, wrote from London:

The forty-ninth degree, to the strait, giving Vancouver's Island to Great Britain, is as much as any American, be he Bostonian or Carolinian, will, I think, consent to give up. If Great Britain is not satisfied with that, let them have war if they want it.

The British government sought anxiously to know what proposition
P. 35, l. 11, 12. the American Government would consent to receive, and the American Government proved its firmness by its moderation. To protect the rights of the country, Congress voted to give to Great Britain the twelve months' notice required by treaty, for terminating the convention of 1827, and thus open the region of the Northwest to the progress of American colonization. Meanwhile, on the 26th of Febru-
Appendix No. 37, 43 l. 7-9, 17. ary, 1846, Mr. Buchanan answered, that the President would consent to consult the Senate on the proposition, to divide

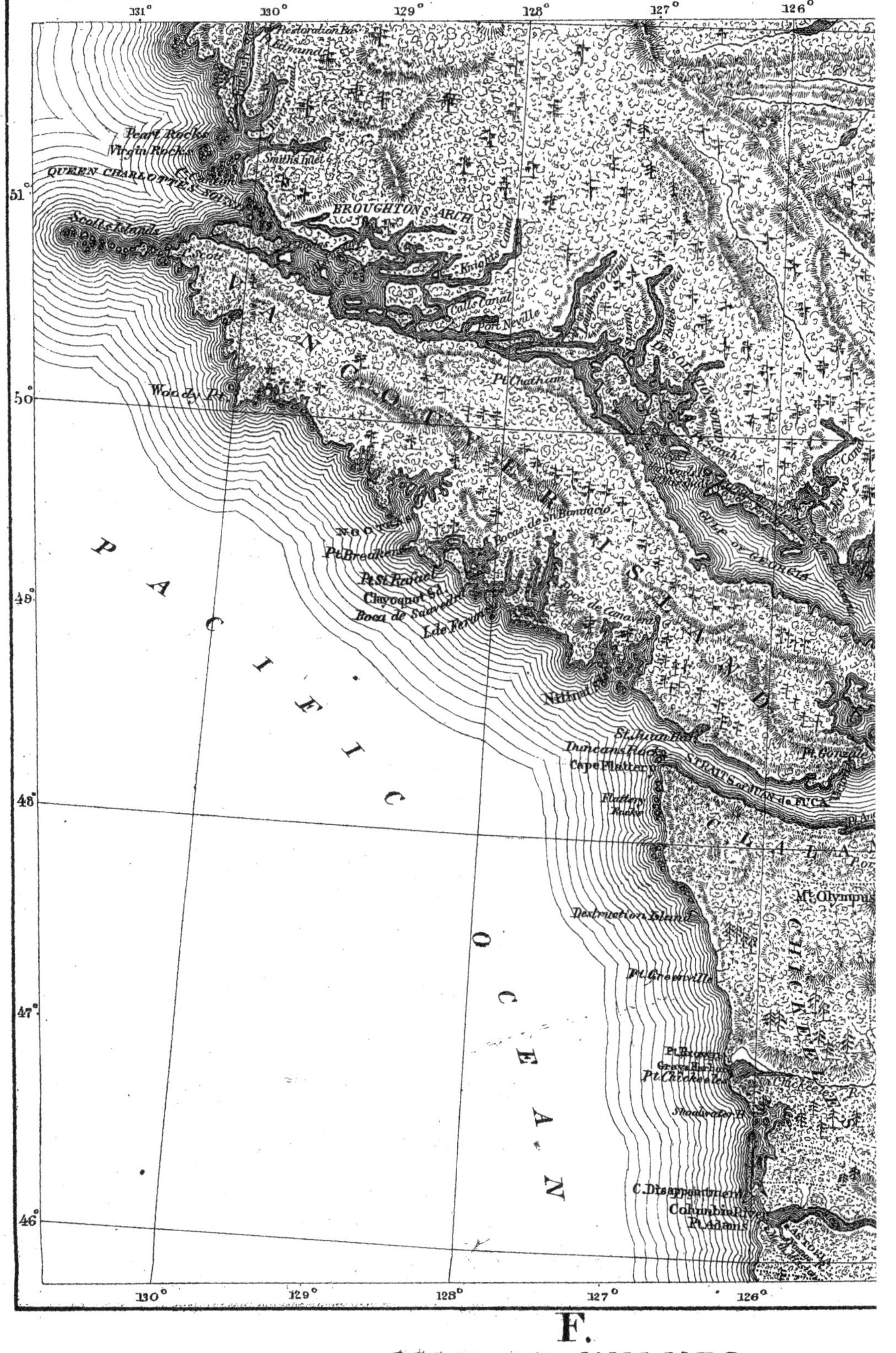

F.

MAP OF WILKES.

1845

the territory between the two countries "by the forty-ninth parallel and the straits of Fuca," so that "the cape of Vancouver's Island would be surrendered to Great Britain." This was exactly the proposition of Mr. Everett.

On the 15th of May, 1846, information of the notice for terminating the convention of 1827 was received by the British ministry in London. For four years Lord Aberdeen had been striving to close this question of boundary. Appendix No. 42, p. 46, l. 15-18, 24. He had privately and publicly censured his subordinate, Mr. Pakenham, at Washington,
[18] for rejecting the parallel of forty-nine. * He had taken pains to learn what deviation from that parallel the United States might accept. The Secretary of State for the United States, after minute inquiry concerning the probable vote of the Senate, had promised not at once to reject the offer of the line proposed by Mr. Everett, and not to listen to any demand for a larger concession. This had been formally communicated to the British Government by Mr. MacLane, the American minister at London. And now, within two days after receiving news of the termination of the convention of 1827, Lord P. 46, l. 23-27. Aberdeen held a lengthened conference with Mr. MacLane, in which the nature of the proposition he contemplated submitting for an amicable settlement of the Oregon question "formed the subject of a full and free conversation." P. 47, l. 1, 2. Mr. MacLane was a calm and experienced statesman, trained in business, exact in his use of words, careful especially in reporting what was said by others. Lord Aberdeen in the House of Lords publicly expressed his esteem for him, Appendix No. 45, p. 51, l. 30-33. founded on an acquaintance which dated from fifteen or sixteen years before.

With this knowledge of Mr. MacLane's character, and of the confidence reposed in him by Lord Aberdeen, I request the imperial arbitrator to take in hand the map of the Oregon territory by Wilkes, Map F. which had been published in England as well as in America in 1845, and which was the latest, most authentic, and best map of the Territory, as well as the only one recognized by the Appendix No. 41, p. 46, l. 6, 7. American Senate; and with this map in hand to read the following extract from Mr. MacLane's official report of the interview, made on the 18th of May, 1846:

> I have now to state that instructions will be transmitted to Mr. Pakenham by the steamer of to-morrow to submit a new and further proposition on the Appendix No. 42, p. 47, l. 3-11. part of this Government for a partition of the territory in dispute.
>
> The proposition, most probably, will offer substantially:
>
> First. To divide the territory by the extension of the line on the parallel of
> [19] forty-nine to the sea; that is to say, *to the arm of the sea called Birch's Bay, thence by the canal de Arro and straits of Fuca to the ocean.
>
> * * * * * * *

Here follow other clauses conceding to the Hudson Bay Company a temporary use of the Oregon River for navigation, with other advantages, P. 47. and protection to British subjects who would suddenly come under the jurisdiction of the United States. To these clauses the phrase "most probably" applies, for they were not precisely ascertained; but not to the boundary; on that point the further statement of Mr. MacLane in the same dispatch leaves no room for a doubt. His words are:

> During the preceding administration of our Government, the extension of the line on the forty-ninth parallel to the straits of Fuca, as now proposed by P. 48, l. 25-29. Lord Aberdeen, was actually suggested by my immediate predecessor, (Mr. Everett,) as one he thought his Government might accept.

Now what the proposal of Mr. Everett had been, we know from the citations which I have made from his dispatches; and I have already referred to the fact that he had drawn the line of demarkation upon the map, and specially directed the attention of Lord Aberdeen to it.

On the same day Lord Aberdeen sent the treaty which Mr. Pakenham
Appendix No. 43, was to invite Mr. Buchanan to sign. In the accompanying
p. 49. instruction to Mr. Pakenham he accepted the parallel of
No. 45, p. 51, l. 4-6. 49° as the radical principle of the boundary, and described the line as a line of demarkation "leaving the whole of
No. 43, p. 50, l. 6, 7. Vancouver Island with its ports and harbors in the possession of Great Britain."

A suspicion of ambiguity could not lurk in the mind of any one. Mr. Benton found the language so clear that he adopted it as his own. In his speech in the Senate on the day of the ratification of the treaty, he said:

> The first article of the treaty is in the very words which I myself would have [20] used, if the two governments had *left it to me to draw the boundary line between them. * * * The line established by Appendix No. 44, p. 50. the first article follows the parallel of 49° to the sea, with a slight deflection, through the Straits of Fuca, to avoid cutting off the south end of Vancouver's Island. * * * When the line reaches the channel which separates Vancouver's Island from the continent, it proceeds to the middle of the channel, and thence, turning south, though the channel de Haro, (wrongly written Arro on the maps,) to the Straits of Fuca, and then west, through the middle of that strait, to the sea. This gives us * * * the cluster of islands between de Haro's Channel and the continent.

The language of the treaty seemed perfectly clear to the Senate, to the President, to his Secretary of State, and to every one of his constitutional advisers, as departing from the line of the parallel of 49° only so far as to yield the southern extremity of Vancouver's Island, and no more. And so it was signed on the 15th of June, 1846, and returned to England for the exchange of ratifications.

In the House of Commons Lord Palmerston welcomed it as honorable
Appendix No. 5, p. 54, l. 13, 14. to both countries; Sir Robert Peel quoted from a dispatch which proved that he was aware of the three days' debate in the American Senate on the treaty before its approval. He cited every word of the article on the boundary, and interpreted it thus:

> Those who remember the local conformation of that country will understand that
> P. 53, l. 31-38. that which we proposed is the continuation of the forty-ninth parallel of latitude till it strikes the Straits of Fuca; that that parallel should not be continued as a boundary across Vancouver's Island, thus depriving us of a part of Vancouver's Island, but that the middle of the channel shall be the future boundary, thus leaving us in possession of the whole of Vancouver's Island, with equal right to the navigation of the straits.

[21] *MR. BUCHANAN AND SIR ROBERT PEEL BELIEVED THEY HAD CLOSED EVERY CAUSE OF DISSENSION.

It had been the special object of Mr. Buchanan to leave nothing in
Appendix No. 46, the treaty which could give occasion to future controversy.
p. 54, l. 25-28. And on the night before Sir Robert Peel retired from office, never again to resume it, he spoke of the treaty as having averted the dreadful calamity of a war between two nations of kindred origin and common language, and having at length "closed every cause of dissen-
P. 54, l. 34, 35. sion between the two countries." All Great Britain, all the
P. 55, l. 1-3. United States, were gladdened by the belief that at last every controversy between the two nations had come to a happy end.

THE MINISTRY OF LORD JOHN RUSSELL RENEWS DISSENSION.

And yet it was not so. My country has had no serious difficulties on its limits with any power but Great Britain. When its boundary on the

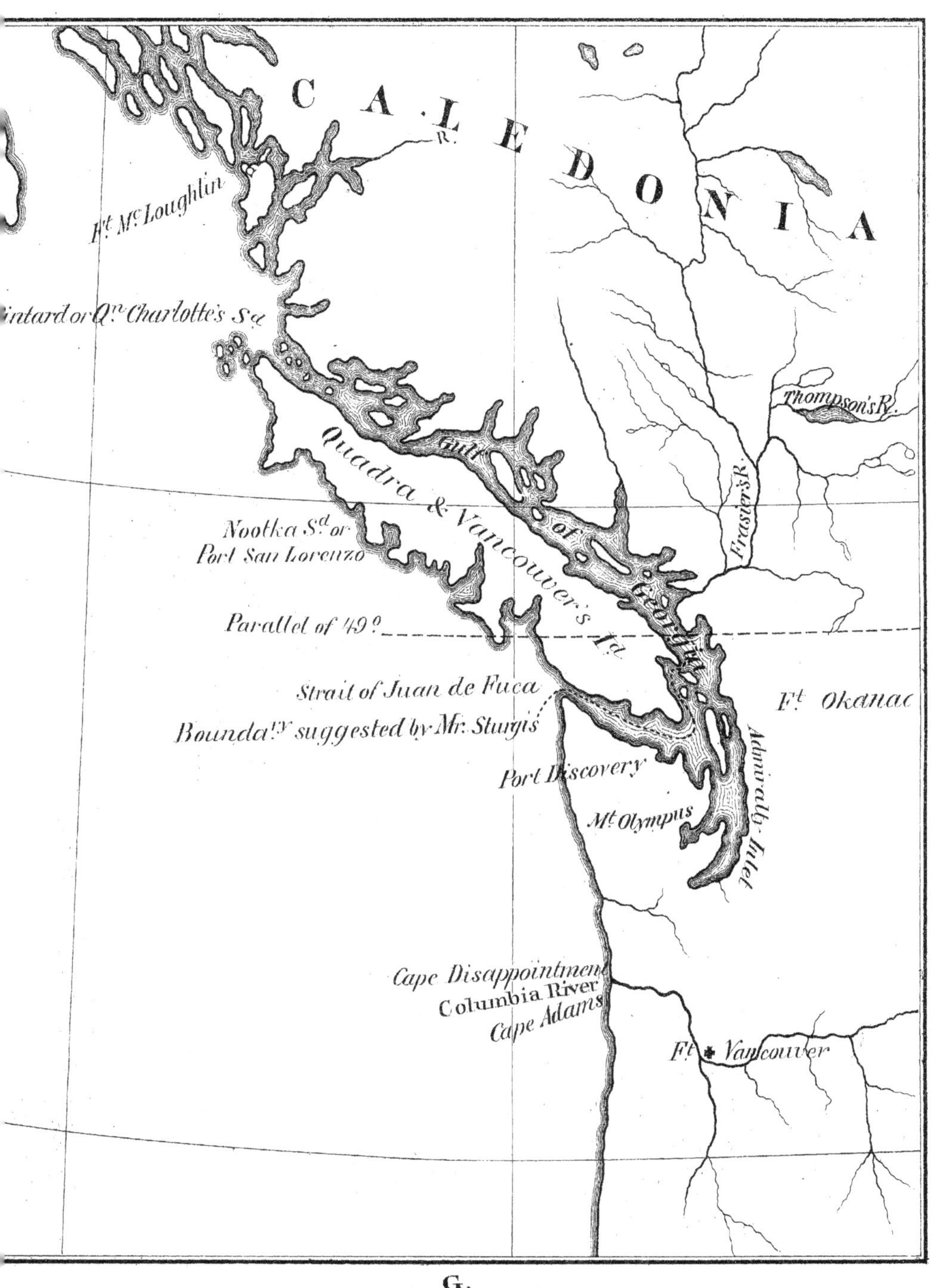

G.

MAP OF W. STURGIS.

1845

south with Spain was adjusted by treaty, not a difference arose, though the line extended from sea to sea. When, afterward, the southern boundary was regulated with Mexico under a treaty most imperfect in its descriptions, commissioners unrestrained by instructions promptly settled the line. It is with Great Britain alone that obstinate dissensions on boundaries, extending from the Gulf of Saint Lawrence to the Pacific, have exercised disturbing influences for sixty-four years. At last we thought ourselves assured of quiet on that side also by the treaty of 1846; and though its terms were not altogether satisfactory, the country, in the expectation of rest, accepted cheerfully and unanimously the action of its Government. Yet, after a pause of hardly two years, the strife was re-opened by the ministry which succeeded that of Sir Robert Peel. Under instructions from Lord Palmerston, the British min-
[22] ister at Washington on the *13th of January, 1848, in a proposed draught of instructions to commissioners for settling the boundary, indirectly insinuated a claim that the line of boundary should be drawn on the channel through which Vancouver in 1792 had sailed from Admiralty Inlet to Birch's Bay.

This insinuation took the American Government by surprise. The history of the negotiation shows that no such line was suggested by either side to the other. Vancouver was an explorer, who examined every inlet and bay and passage, not a merchant seeking the shortest, most natural, and best passage. Nothing justifies a reference to his course of sailing from one interior bay to another, as the line of the treaty. The suggestion is in open conflict with the law of nations. The draught of the treaty was made entirely, even to the minutest word, by the British ministry, and was signed by both parties without change. The British government cannot, therefore, take advantage of an ambiguity of their own, otherwise the draught of the treaty would have been a snare. Such is the principle of natural right, such the established law of nations. Hugo Grotius lays down the rule that the interpretation must be made against the party which draughted the conditions: "Ut contra eum fiat interpretatio, qui conditiones elocutus est." But no one has expressed this more clearly than Vattel, who writes:

Appendix, p. 51, l. 4-6, 22-25. P. 53, l. 16, 17. P. 54, l. 19, 20.

H. Grotius. De jure belli et pacis, III, 20, § 26.

Vattel, liv. II, § 264.

Voici une règle qui coupe court à toute chicane : Si celui qui pouvoit et devoit s'expliquer nettement et pleinement, ne l'a pas fait, tant pis pour lui : il ne peut être reçu à apporter subséquemment des restrictions qu'il n'a pas exprimées. C'est la maxime du droit romain : pactionem obscuram iis nocere, in quorum fuit potestate legem apertius conscribere. L'équité de cette règle saute aux yeux; sa nécessité n'est pas moins évidente. Nulle convention assurée, nulle concession ferme et solide, si on peut
[23] les rendre *vaines par des limitations subséquentes, qui devoient être énoncées dans l'acte, si elles étoient dans la volonté des contractans.

"Here is a rule which cuts short all chicanery: If he who could and should express himself plainly and fully, has not done so, so much the worse for him; he cannot be permitted subsequently to introduce restrictions which he has not expressed. It is the maxim of Roman law: An obscure contract harms those in whose power it was to lay down the law more clearly. The equity of this rule is self-evident; its necessity is not less obvious. There can be no assured convention, no firm and solid concession, if they can be rendered vain by subsequent limitations, which ought to have been announced in the act, if they existed in the intention of the contracting parties."

PLEA FOR THE INTEGRITY OF SIR ROBERT PEEL'S MINISTRY.

And can it be true, that Sir Robert Peel and Lord Aberdeen were insincere in their professions of an earnest desire to settle the boundary question in Northwest America? Did they put into the core of the treaty which they themselves framed, words interpreted in one way by all Americans and by themselves in public, and secretly interpreted by themselves in another? When Sir Robert Peel, on the last night of his official life, in the face of political enemies and friends, cast up the account of his ministry for the judgment of posterity, and declared, in the most public and solemn manner, that he "had closed every Appendix No. 52, p. 54, l. 33-35. P. 55, l. 1-3. cause of dissension between Great Britain and the United States," had he indeed planted the seed of embittered discord in the instrument that he and his associate minister claimed as their own work, and extolled as a convention of peace?

My respect for Sir Robert Peel and his administration forbids
[24] the thought that they put any ambiguity into the treaty *which they themselves draughted. There attaches to human language such imperfection that an acute caviller may dispute about the meaning of any proposition. But the words of the present treaty are so singularly clear that they may claim protection under the first general maxim Vattel, liv. II, 17, § 263. of international law on the subject of interpretation: "Qu'il n'est pas permis d'interpréter ce qui n'a pas besoin d'interprétation."

THE WORDS OF THE TREATY.

The words of the treaty are as follows:

From the point on the forty-ninth parallel of north latitude, where the boundary laid down in existing treaties and conventions between the United Appendix No. 1, p. 3. States and Great Britain terminates, the line of boundary between the territories of the United States and those of Her Britannic Majesty shall be continued westward along the said forty-ninth parallel of north latitude, to the middle of the channel which separates the continent from Vancouver Island, and thence southerly through the middle of the said channel, and of Fuca's Straits, to the Pacific Ocean: *Provided, however,* That the navigation of the whole of the said channel and straits south of the forty-ninth parallel of north latitude remain free and open to both parties.

THE WORDS OF THE TREATY, TAKEN TOGETHER.

The language of the treaty, taken as a whole, admits no interpretation but the American. The radical principle of the boundary is the forty-ninth parallel of north latitude, and the only reason for departing from that parallel was to yield the whole of Vancouver Island, and no more, to the power which would already possess the greater part of that island. To express this line concisely, in both countries it was described as the line of the "forty-ninth parallel and Fuca's Straits." This short
[25] form of expression occurs many times in the dispatches *of Mr. MacLane; in the instructions of Mr. Buchanan; in the letters of Mr. Bates from London; in an article in the London Quarterly Review, written in February, 1846, and published in March; and, finally, in the speech of Sir Robert Peel, on the 29th of June, 1846, which I have already quoted. The description of the line as that "of the forty-ninth parallel and Fuca's Straits" was not only the usage of the day; it was also well chosen for all time. The forty-ninth parallel can be found as long as the sun shall continue in the heavens; Fuca's Straits end at the southeast cape of Vancouver Island, and will end there till nature shall heave with a convulsion. If the name of Haro does not specially appear in the treaty, let it be borne in mind that neither does the name of the Gulf of Georgia.

THE CHANNEL.

The words of the description, considered collectively, establish the American interpretation of the treaty and exclude every other. The same result follows from the consideration of each separate word. When

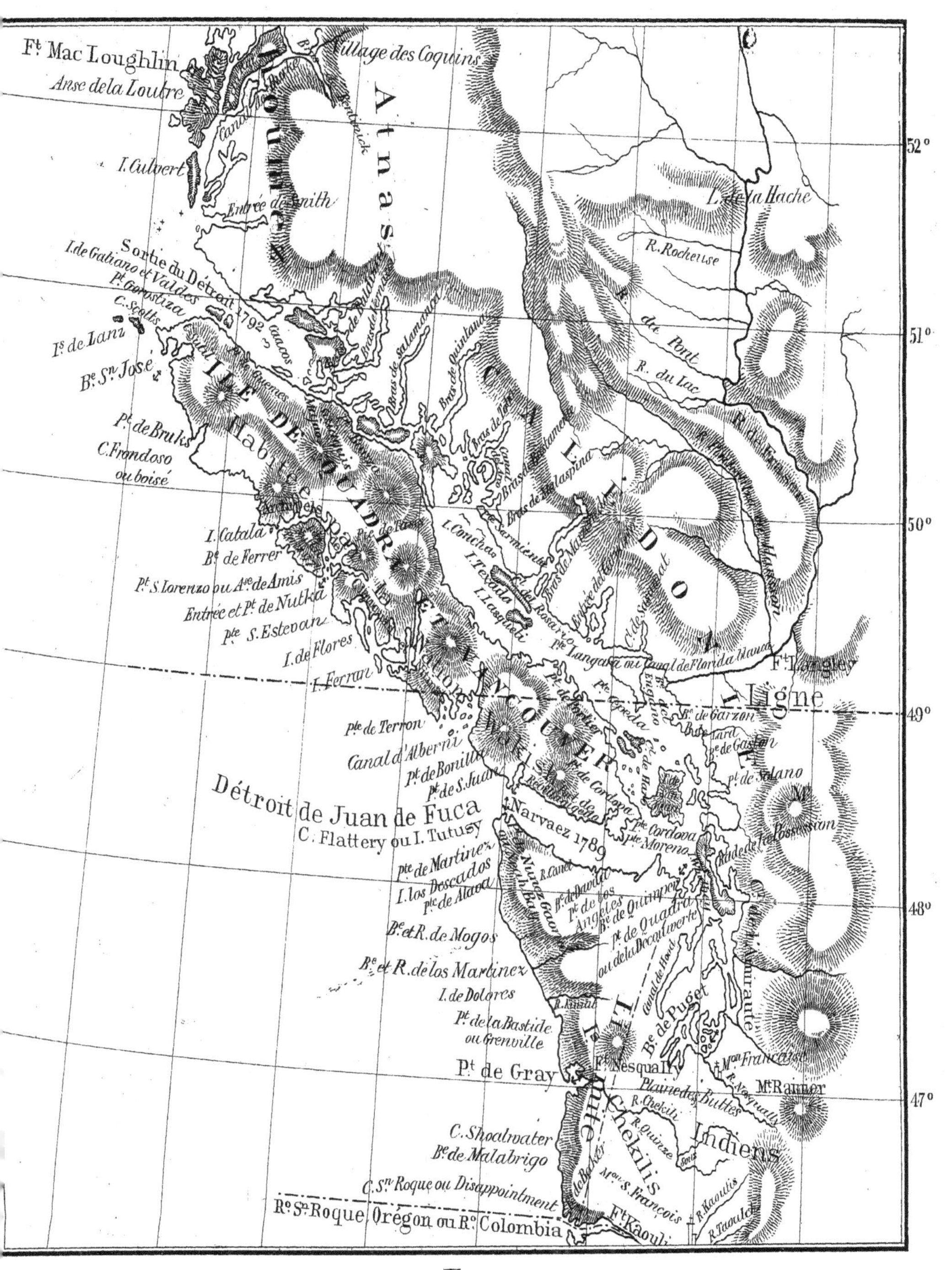

E.

MAP OF DUFLOT DE MOFRAS.

1844.

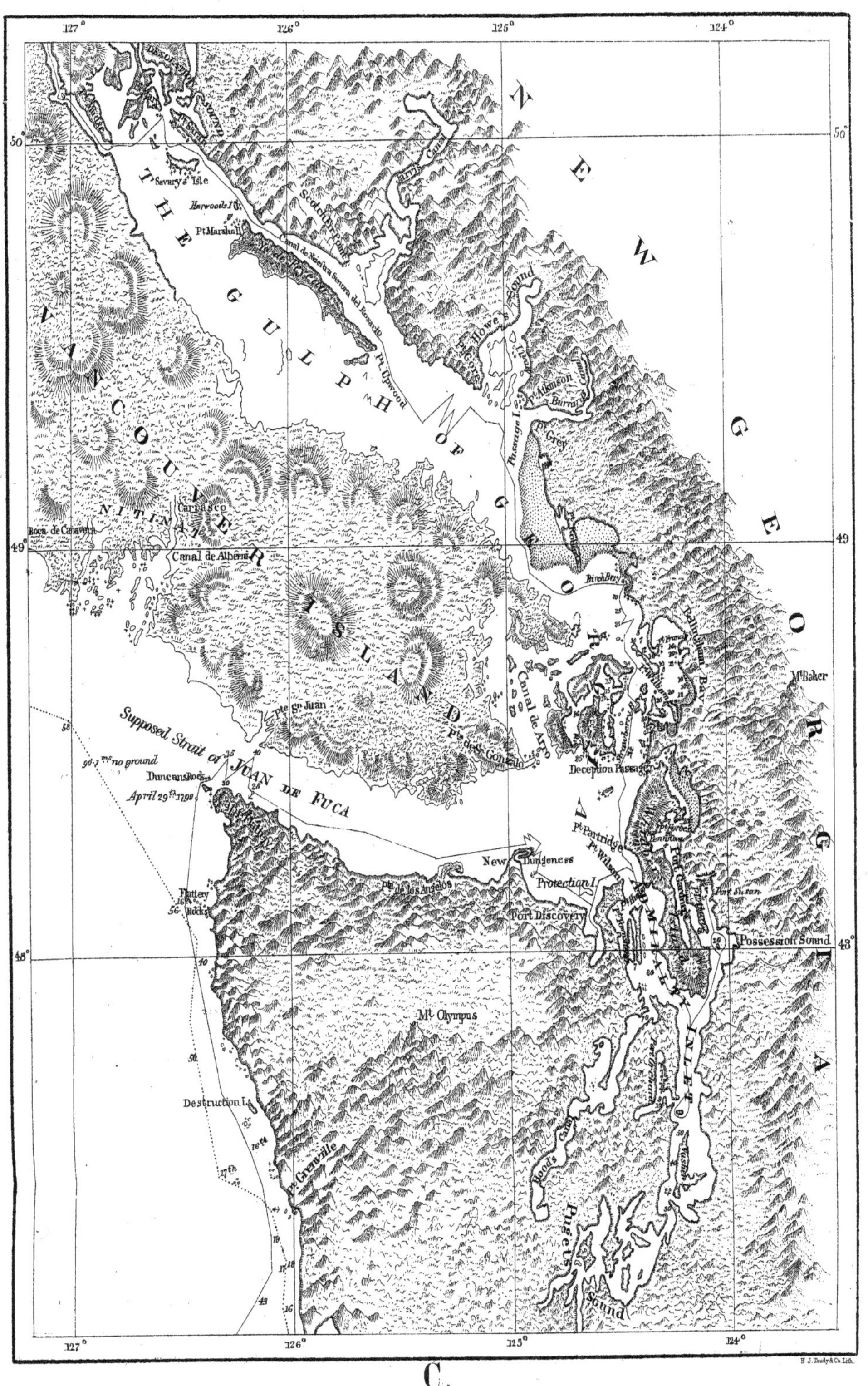

C.

MAP OF VANCOUVER.

1798

the treaty speaks of the "channel," for that part south and west of Birch's Bay, it must mean the channel of Haro, for no other "channel" was known to the negotiators. The channel of Haro was on the map of Vancouver, the highest English authority, and on the map of Wilkes, the highest American authority at the time when the treaty was signed; and no other channel is named on either of these maps, or on any map used by the negotiators. On the chart of those waters by Duflot de Mofras, published in 1844, under the auspices of Louis Philippe and the French ministry, the channel of Haro is named, and no other. In the collection of maps in the Royal Library at Berlin, not a single German or other map, anterior to June, 1846, names any other channel than that of Haro. How is it possible, then, that any other channel could have been intended, when
[26] no other was named on any map which it can be pretended *was known to Lord Aberdeen or Mr. MacLane, to Mr. Buchanan or Mr. Pakenham?

Map C. Map F. Map E.

Again, the word "channel," when employed in treaties, means a deep and navigable channel; and where there are two navigable channels, by the rule of international law, preference is to be given to the largest column of water. Now, compared with any other channel through which a ship could pass from the sea at the forty-ninth parallel to the Straits of Fuca, the channel of Haro is the broadest and the deepest, the shortest and the best. Its maximum width is six and a half English miles, and there is no other channel of which the maximum width exceeds four miles. The narrowest part of the channel of Haro is about two and a quarter English miles, and there is no other channel of which the minimum width exceeds about one and a quarter English miles. With regard to depth, the contrast is still more striking. A cross-section on the parallel of 48° 45′ shows the Canal de Haro to be there about a hundred and twenty fathoms deep, about twice as deep as any other; on the parallel of 48° 35′ the Canal de Haro is nearly a hundred and fifty fathoms deep, against thirty fathoms for any competitor; on the parallel of 48° 25′ the Canal de Haro has nearly a hundred and ten fathoms, while no other passage has more than forty.

Map H.

Not only is the volume of water in the Canal de Haro vastly greater than that in any other passage—a single glance at any map shows that it is the shortest and most direct way between the parallel of 49° and Fuca's Straits. Duflot de Mofras describes it as notoriously the best.

Appendix No. 48, p. 55, l. 17-19.

If the channel of Haro excelled all others only on one point—if it were the widest though not the deepest, or the reverse, or, if being the widest and deepest, it were not the shortest and best, there might be some degree of color for cavil; but since the channel of Haro is the broadest and the deepest, and the shortest and the best, how can any one venture to pretend that any other is "the channel" of the treaty?

[27] *"THE CHANNEL WHICH SEPARATES THE CONTINENT FROM VANCOUVER ISLAND."

The next words of the treaty are: "The channel which separates the continent from Vancouver Island," and this, from latitude about 48° 46′, can be no other than the Canal de Haro. It is the only one which from that latitude to "Fuca's Straits" separates the continent from Vancouver Island. There are other passages which divide islands from islands, but none other separates the continent from Vancouver Island.

In the statement the continent is properly named first, because it is far away in the interior of the continent that the line begins, and it is the continent that the line leaves in going toward Vancouver. But when a great continent like North America is spoken of as distinguished from a large island lying near it, the intervening cluster of smaller islands would, according to all geographical usage, be taken as included with the continent, and thus the channel of Haro divides the continent from Vancouver. But we will not waste words. Nobody can dispute that the Canal de Haro washes the eastern shore of Vancouver Island, and separates that island from the continent.

"AND THENCE SOUTHERLY."

The next words in the treaty are: "And thence southerly." The southerly deflection from the forty-ninth parallel is made to avoid cutting Vancouver Island, and must be limited to that object. The movement of the boundary line is steadily west to the Pacific. The treaty knows only two points of compass: "westward" and this "southerly" deviation from the due west course. The southern deflection, therefore, must always be accompanied with the idea of a western direction; and of two channels going in a "southerly" direction, that which least interrupts the general "westward" direction of the line must be chosen as the channel of the treaty.

[28] *"THROUGH THE MIDDLE OF THE SAID CHANNEL AND OF FUCA'S STRAITS TO THE PACIFIC OCEAN."

The next words of the treaty are: "Through the middle of the said channel and of Fuca's Straits to the Pacific Ocean." The treaty contemplates a continuous channel to the Pacific; the channel of Haro and Fuca's Straits form such a continuous channel, and a glance at the map will show that no other channel can pretend to do so.

So, then, the description of the treaty as a whole applies to no channel but that of Haro; and every single phrase, taken separately, points also to that channel, and to that channel alone.

"THE STRAITS OF ROSARIO."

And yet the British government ask the Imperial arbitrator to find the channel of the treaty in a passage for which, in January, 1848, they had no name and no other description than "the wide channel to the east of numerous islands, which is laid down by Vancouver," and which now, in 1871, they call by the name of "the Rosario Straits."

My first request is that the Imperial arbitrator will ascertain where on the 15th of June, 1846, the day when the treaty was signed, the negotiators supposed Rosario Straits to lie. On that day the name "Straits of Rosario" was, on every map used by the negotiators, placed upon the waters which divide the island of Texada from the continent, far north of the parallel of 49°. There it lies fast anchored on the
Map C.
map of Vancouver, published in 1798; it holds the same place in the atlas of the French translation of Vancouver. There, too,
Map E.
it is found on the French map of Duflot de Mofras, pub-
Map F.
lished in 1844; and also on the map of Wilkes, published in 1845; and there, too, on the British map of Vancouver Island, published by the geographer to the Queen, so late as 1848. Then,
[29] since all British and American maps, which in 1846 *had on them the name "Straits of Rosario," located those straits far to the

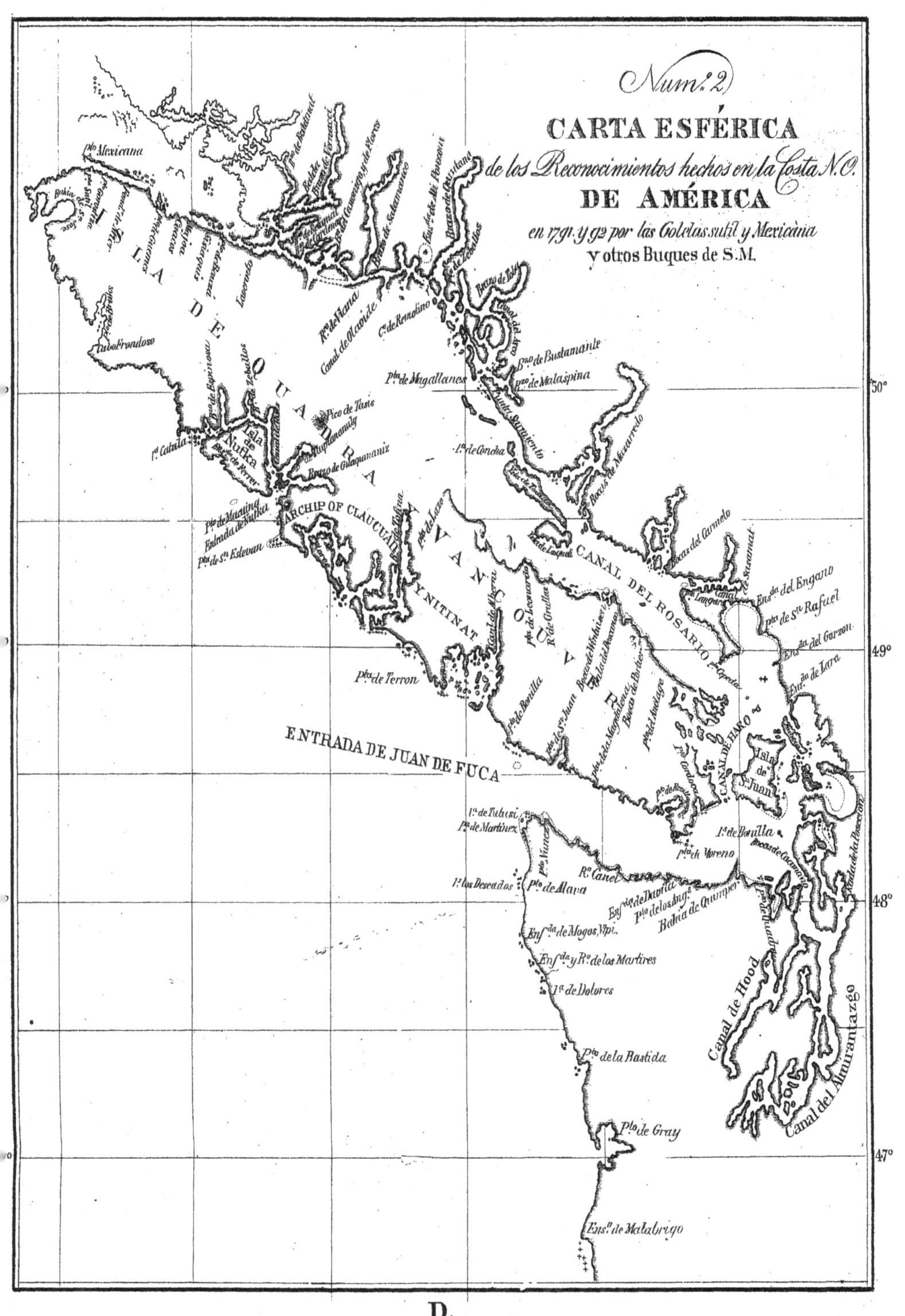

D.

MAP OF THE SUTIL Y MEXICANA.

1792.

(Published in 1802.)

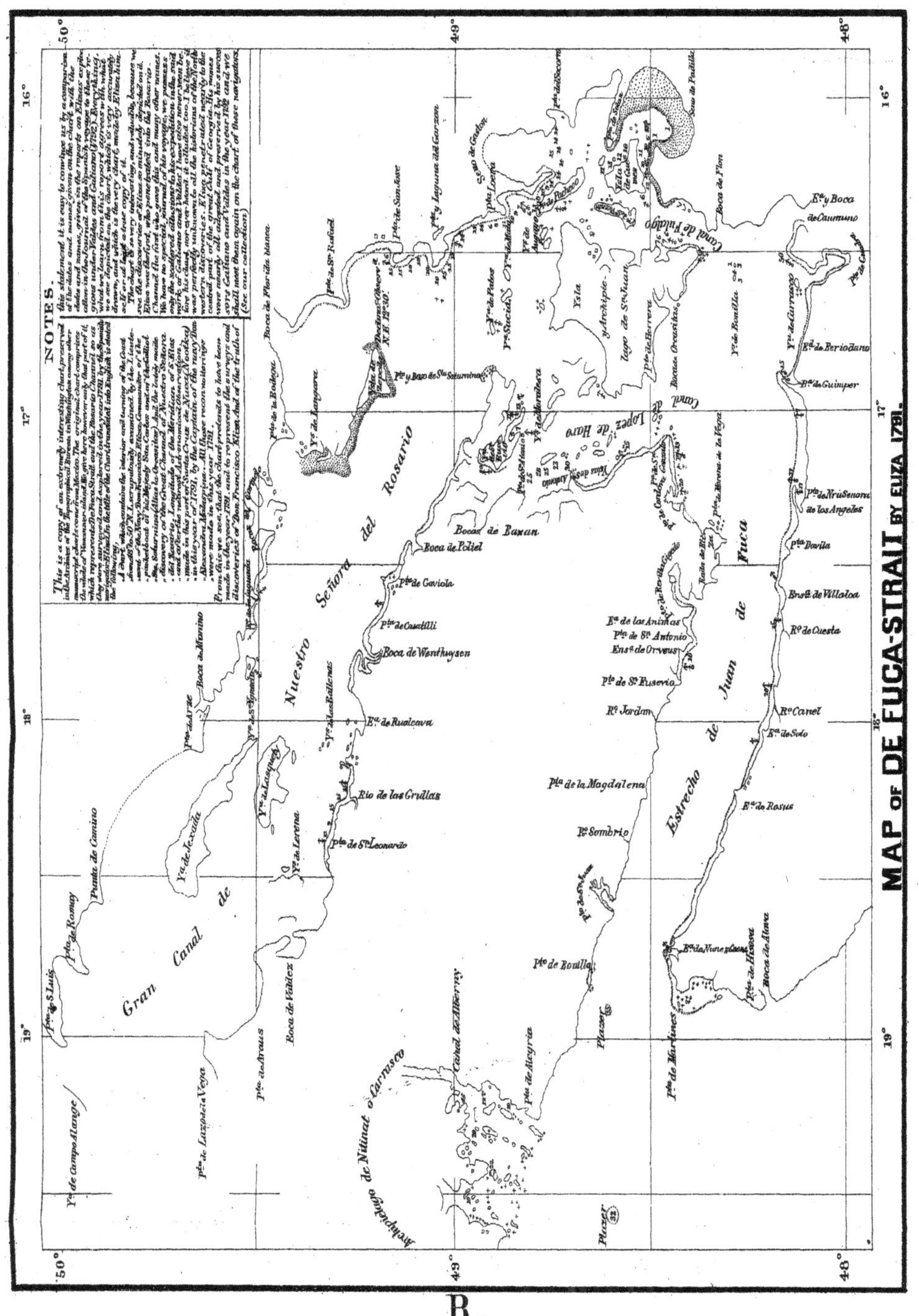

B.

MAP OF ELIZA.

1791

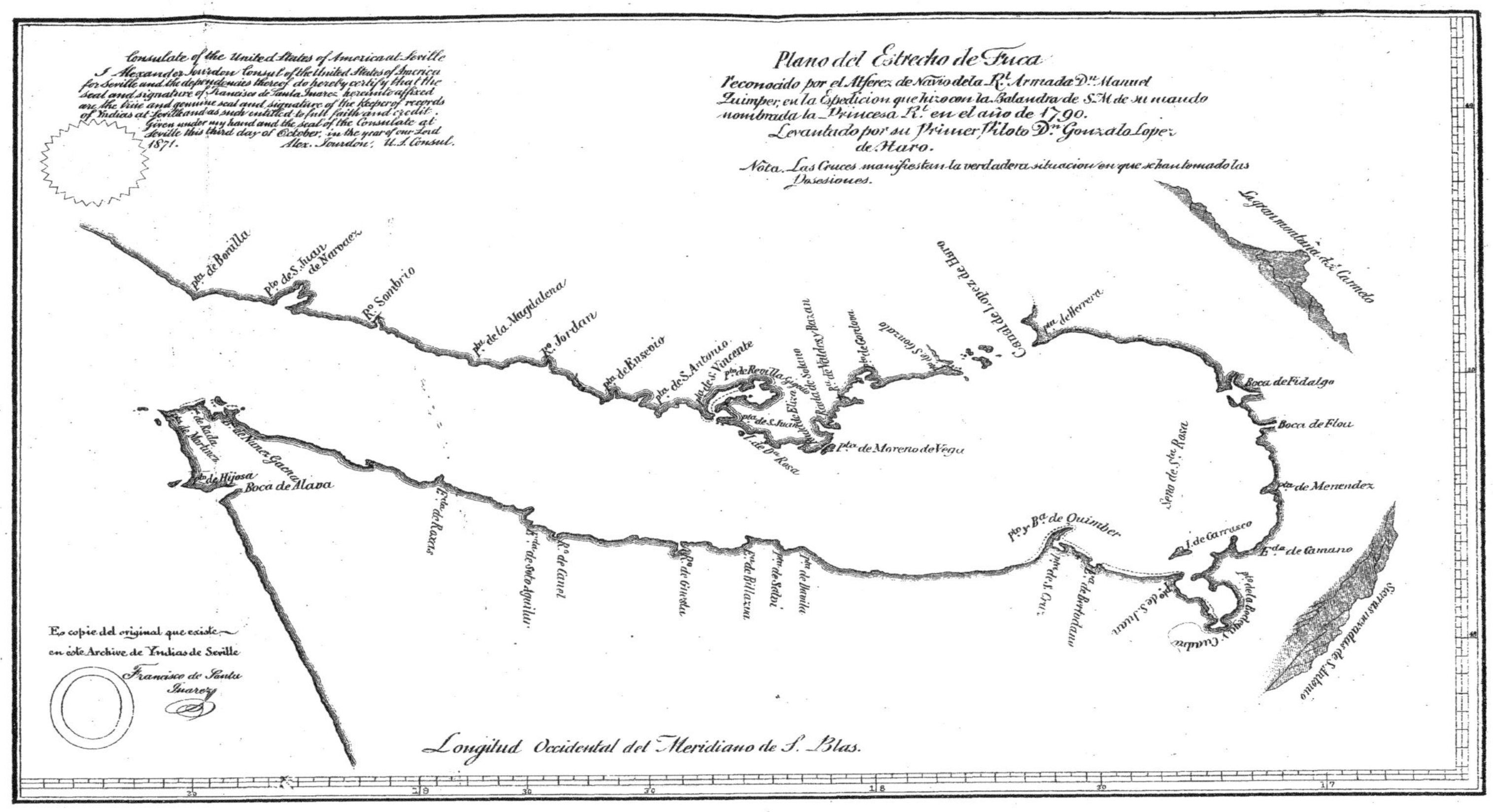

A.

MAP OF DE HARO

1790.

north of 49°, how can the British government invite Your Majesty to say that the straits of Rosario form the line of boundary established by British and American negotiators in that year between the United States and the British territory?

How and why the British unmoored the name from the waters to which they themselves had consigned it, and where it remained for just half a century, I leave them to explain and to justify. I remark only that they cannot produce a map, English, French, Spanish, or German, older than 1848, on which the passage which they now call the Straits of Rosario bears that name. On Spanish maps the name is applied only to the very broad channel lying north of the Canal de Haro and of the forty-ninth parallel of latitude. Map B. Map D.

Further: the so-called Straits of Rosario are not straits at all. It is the track of Vancouver on his way from Admiralty Inlet to the north, as his map shows; but it received from him no name whatever. On British maps it never bore a name till after the British government introduced a new interpretation of the treaty of June, 1846.

Again—and this remark is of conclusive importance, by itself alone sufficient to decide the question—the line of the treaty must run from the middle of "the channel which separates the continent from Vancouver Island." Now, the so-called Straits of Rosario neither touch the continent nor Vancouver Island. They divide small islands from small islands, and nothing else; they have no pretension to divide Vancouver from the continent, or the continent from Vancouver.

Moreover, the water-line of the treaty must be a channel which makes a continuous line with Fuca's Straits; for the words of the treaty are, "through the middle of the said channel and of Fuca's Straits." Now, the so-called Straits of Rosario lead only to a sound, which Spanish voyagers called the Bay of Santa Rosa; they Map A.
[30] do not connect with Fuca's Straits, *which cease at the south-eastern promontory of Vancouver Island. Reversing the track of Vancouver, and following the so-called straits of Rosario southerly, the mariner would enter Admiralty Inlet; he never would reach the Straits of Fuca.

Then, too, compared with the Canal de Haro, the so-called Strait of Rosario is, as we have seen, a narrower passage, a shallower passage, and a roundabout passage.

CONCLUSION.

But enough: the rights of America cannot be darkened except by an excess of words. The intention of the parties to the treaty is made plain by its history, and the boundary which we claim is clearly set forth in its words, taken collectively and taken separately. I will close by citing general principles of interpretation established by international law.

A party offering the draught of a treaty is bound by the interpretation which it knew at the time that the other party gave to it. Lord Aberdeen cannot have doubted how the treaty was understood by Mr. MacLane, by Mr. Buchanan, and by the Senate of the United States. "Where the terms of promise," writes Paley, whose work was long a text-book at Oxford, "admit of more senses than one, the promise is to be performed in the sense 'in which the promiser apprehended at the time that the promisee received it.' This will not differ from the actual intention of the promiser, where the promise is given without collusion or reserve; but we put the rule in the above Appendix No. 49, p. 56.

form to exclude evasion, wherever the promiser attempts to make his escape through some ambiguity in the expressions which he used."

Again: "Where a right admits of different degrees, it is only the smallest degree which may be taken for granted." "Ist ein Recht verschiedener Abstufungen fähig, so darf zunächst nur die geringste Stufe als zugestanden angenommen

Heffter's Volkerrecht, § 95, p. 176. Ed. 1867.

[31] *werden." This rule of Heffter fits the present case so aptly that
it seems made for it. There being degrees in the departure from the parallel of 49°, it must be taken that only the smallest degree was conceded.

Finally and above all: there is a principle which not only controls the interpretation of treaties, but the results of investigation in every branch of human knowledge. A theory which implies confusion and contradiction is at once to be rejected; of two rival theories, that which most nearly reconciles all phenomena is to be preferred; the theory that reconciles all appearances and all circumstances is to be received as true. The British interpretation of the treaty implies that the British, who exclusively draughted it, sowed the seeds of future dissensions in the very instrument by which they proposed to settle every boundary question forever; that among the negotiators of the treaty there were those who duped, and those who were dupes. Lord Aberdeen ceases to be the "straightforward" man of Mr. MacLane's report. On the American side the statesmen appear void of spirit and of common sense, and easily circumvented. The historical process by which the treaty was arrived at becomes incomprehensible. The names on maps must be changed; the conformation of islands and continents and the highways of the great deep are made to expand and contract so as to suit the cavils of a government which does not profess exactly to understand the true meaning of the treaty, for every word of which it is itself responsible. Take the other theory; interpret the treaty as the Americans accepted it, and there are no statesmen on the British side who attempted to dupe, and no dupes on the American side. The history of the negotiation becomes clear, and is consistent with its result. Mr. MacLane retains the reputation for prudence and clear perception and careful statement which has always been attributed to him. All words that fell from the pen or lips of every one concerned in framing, accepting,
[32] or approving the treaty, agree together and *bear the stamp of
good intention and uprightness. Everything that was uttered by Mr. Everett, Mr. MacLane, and Mr. Buchanan, by Lord Aberdeen, Mr. Benton, or Sir Robert Peel, is perfectly reconciled, without even the semblance of contradiction. The straits and channels may rest where nature has set them, and old names may be restored to their rightful places. The completion of the treaty does honor to the labors of honest and able statesmen, bent on establishing friendship and peace between "kindred nations." Persons and history, and reports of conversations and the words of the treaty, all chime together in the most perfect harmony, inviting an award which will command ready aquiescence, and leave nothing to rankle in the wound which it heals.

APPENDIX.

No. 1.

Extract from the treaty of Washington, of June 15, 1846.

Boundary established in 1846.

ARTICLE 1. From the point on the forty-ninth parallel of north latitude, where the boundary laid down in existing treaties and conventions between the United States and Great Britain terminates, the line of boundary between the territories of the United States and those of Her Britannic Majesty shall be continued westward along the said forty-ninth parallel of north latitude to the middle of the channel which separates the continent from Vancouver Island, and thence southerly through the middle of the said channel, and of Fuca's Straits, to the Pacific Ocean: *Provided, however*, That the navigation of the whole of the said channel and the straits south of the forty-ninth parallel of north latitude remain free and open to both parties.

No. 2.

Extract from the treaty of Washington, of May 8, 1871.

THE NORTHERN BOUNDARY.

Matter and form of arbitration.

ARTICLE 34. Whereas it was stipulated by Article 1 of the treaty concluded at Washington on the 15th of June, 1846, between the United States of America and Her Britannic Majesty,
[4] that the *line of boundary between the territory of the United States and those of Her Britannic Majesty, from the point on the forty-ninth parallel of north latitude, up to which it had already been ascertained, should be continued westward along the said parallel of north latitude "to the middle of the channel which separates the continent from Vancouver Island, and thence southerly through the middle of the said channel, and of Fuca Straits, to the Pacific Ocean;" and whereas the commissioners appointed by the two high contracting parties to determine that portion of the boundary which runs southerly through the middle of the channel aforesaid were unable to agree upon the same; and whereas the government of Her Britannic Majesty claims that such boundary-line should, under the terms of the treaty above recited, be run through the Rosario Straits, and the Government of the United States claims that it should be run through the Canal de Haro, it is agreed that the respective claims of the government of Her Britannic Majesty and of the Government of the United States shall be submitted to the arbitration and award of His Majesty the Emperor of Germany, who, having regard to the above-mentioned article of the said treaty, shall decide thereupon finally and without appeal which of these claims is most in accordance with the true interpretation of the treaty of June 15, 1846.

ARTICLE 35. The award of His Majesty the Emperor of Germany shall be considered as absolutely final and conclusive, and full effect shall be given to such award without any objection, evasion, or delay whatsoever. Such decision shall be given in writing and dated. It shall be in whatsoever form His Majesty may choose to adopt. It shall be delivered to the representatives or other public agents of the United States and Great Britain respectively, who may be actually at Berlin, and shall be considered as operative from the day of the date of the delivery thereof.

ARTICLE 36. The written or printed case of each of the two parties, accompanied by the evidence offered in support of the same, shall be laid before His Majesty the Emperor of Germany within six months from the date of the exchange of the ratification of this treaty, and a copy of such case and evidence shall be communicated by each party to the other through their respective representatives at Berlin. The high contracting parties may include in the evidence to be considered by the arbitrator such documents, official correspondence, and other official or public statements bearing on the subject of the refer-
[5] ence as they may consider necessary *to the support of their
respective cases. After the written or printed case shall have been communicated by each party to the other, each party shall have the power of drawing up and laying before the arbitrator a second and definitive statement, if it think fit to do so, in reply to the case of the other party so communicated, which definitive statement shall be so laid before the arbitrator, and also be mutually communicated in the same manner as aforesaid, by each party to the other, within six months from the date of laying the first statement of the case before the arbitrator.

ARTICLE 37. If in the case submitted to the arbitrator either party shall specify or allude to any report or document in its own exclusive possession, without annexing a copy, such party shall be bound, if the other party thinks proper to apply for it, to furnish that party with a copy thereof, and either party may call upon the other through the arbitrator to produce the originals or certified copies of any papers adduced as evidence, giving in each instance such reasonable notice as the arbitrator may require; and if the arbitrator should desire further elucidation or evidence with regard to any point contained in the statements laid before him, he shall be at liberty to hear one counsel or agent for each party in relation to any matter, and at such time and in such manner as he may think fit.

ARTICLE 38. The representatives or public agents of the United States and Great Britain at Berlin respectively shall be considered as the agents of their respective Governments to conduct their cases before the arbitrator, who shall be requested to address all his communications and give all his notices to such representatives, or other public agents, who shall represent their respective governments generally in all matters connected with the arbitration.

ARTICLE 39. It shall be competent to the arbitrator to proceed in the said arbitration, and all matters relating thereto, as and when he shall see fit, either in person, or by a person or persons named by him for that purpose, either in the presence or absence of either or both agents, and either orally or by written discussion, or otherwise. The arbitrator may, if he think fit, appoint a secretary or clerk for the purposes of the proposed arbitration, at such rate of remuneration as he shall think proper. This, and all other expenses of and connected with said arbitration, shall be provided for as hereinafter stipulated.

[6] *ARTICLE 41. The arbitrator shall be requested to deliver, together with his award, an account of all the costs and expenses which he may have been put to in relation to this matter, which shall forthwith be paid by the two governments in equal moieties.

ARTICLE 42. The arbitrator shall be requested to deliver his award in writing as early as convenient after the whole case on each side shall be laid before him, and to deliver one copy thereof to each of the said agents.

No. 3.

Extract from the patent granted by James I of England, November 3, in the eighteenth year of his reign, to the council of Plymouth.

English colonial charters bounded English colonies by parallels of latitude.

* * * * "Wee, therefore, of our especiall Grace, mere Motion, and certaine Knowledge, by the Aduice of the Lords and others of our Priuy Councell, have for Us, our Heyrs and Successors, graunted, ordained, and established, and in and by these Presents, Do for Us, our Heirs and Successors, grant, ordaine, and establish, that all that Circuit, Continent, Precincts, and Limitts in America, lying and being in Breadth from Fourty Degrees of Northerly Latitude from the Equinoctiall Line, to Fourty-eight Degrees of the said Northerly Latitude, and in Length by all the Breadth aforesaid throughout the Maine Land, from Sea to Sea." * *

Extract from the charter of Massachusetts Bay, granted by Charles I of England, March 4, 1628.

* * * * * "We do give and grant all the Landes and Hereditaments within the Space of Three English Miles to the southward of Massachusetts Bay: and all those Landes and Hereditaments within the Space of Three English Miles to the Northward of the River called Merrimack, all Landes and Hereditaments whatsoever, lying within the Lymitts aforesaide, North and South in Latitude and Bredth, and in Length and Longitude, of and within all the Bredth aforesaide, throughout the mayne Landes there, from the Atlantick and Westerne Sea and Ocean on the East Parte, to the South Sea on the West Parte."

* * * * * * *

---

[7] **Extract from the old patent for Connecticut.*

* * * "Robert, Earl of Warwick," * * "doth give" * * "the Space of forty Leagues upon a straight line near the Sea-Shore, toward the South-West, West-and-by-South or West, as the Coast lieth towards Virginia, accounting three English Miles to the League, and also all and singular the Lands and Hereditaments whatsoever, lying and being within the Lands aforesaid, North and South in Latitude and Breadth, and in Length and Longitude, of and within all the Breadth aforesaid, throughout the Main Lands there, from the Western Ocean to the South Sea;" * * * *

Extract from the charter granted by Charles II of England to the lords proprietors of Carolina, March 24, 1663.

* * * * "all that territory or tract of ground" * * * "extending from the North end of the Island called Lucke-Island, which lieth in the Southern Virginia Seas and within six and thirty degrees of the Northern Latitude, and to the West as far as the South Seas, and so southerly as far as the river St. Matthias, which bordereth upon the coast of Florida, and within one and thirty degrees of Northern Latitude, and so West in a direct line as far as the South Seas aforesaid;" * * * *

Extract from the commission of Governor Wright, of Georgia, of the 20th of January, 1764.

"George III, by the grace of God of Great Britain, France, and Ireland, King, Defender of the Faith, and so forth, to our trusty and well-beloved James Wright, esquire, greeting:
* * "We did, by our letters-patent, under our great seal of Great Britain, bearing date at Westminster, the 4th day of May, in the first year of our reign, constitute and appoint you, James Wright, esquire, to be our captain-general and governor-in-chief in and over our colony of Georgia, in America, lying from the most northern stream of a river there most commonly called Savannah, all along the sea-coast to the southward, unto the most southern stream of a certain other great water or river called Altamaha, and westward from the heads of the said rivers, respectively, in direct lines to the South Seas." * *

---

[8] *No. 4.

Articles between the United States of America and His Britannic Majesty, November 30, 1782.

ARTICLE II.

First treaty between the United States and Great Britain adopts for boundary a due west course.

"From the northwest angle of Nova Scotia" * * * "through Lake Superior" * * * "to the Long Lake; thence through the middle of said Long Lake, and the water-communication between it and the Lake of the Woods, to the said Lake of the Woods; thence through the said lake to the most northwestern point thereof, and from thence on a due west course." * * * * *

No. 5.

Extract from the treaty between the United States of America and the French Republic, April 30, 1803.

The United States acquire Louisiana.

ARTICLE I. Whereas, by the article the third of the treaty concluded at St. Ildelfonso, the 9th Vendémiaire, an 9 (1st October, 1800,) between the First Consul of the French and His

Catholic Majesty, it was agreed as follows: "His Catholic Majesty promises and engages on his part to cede to the French Republic, six months after the full and entire execution of the conditions and stipulations herein relative to his royal highness the Duke of Parma, the colony or province of Louisiana, with the same extent that it now has in the hands of Spain, and that it had when France possessed it; and such as it should be after the treaties subsequently entered into between Spain and other States."

And whereas, in pursuance of the treaty, and particularly of the third article, the French Republic has an incontestable title to the domain and to the possession of the said territory: The First Consul of the French Republic, desiring to give to the United States a strong proof of his friendship, doth hereby cede to the said United States, in the name of the French Republic, forever and in full sovereignty, the said territory, with all its rights and appurtenances, as fully and in the same manner as they have been acquired by the French Republic, in virtue of the above-mentioned treaty concluded with His Catholic Majesty.

---

[9] *No. 6.

Additional and explanatory articles, signed the — day of ———, 1807, to be added to the treaty of amity, commerce, and navigation, between His Britannic Majesty and the United States of America, signed at London, the 31st day of December, 1806.

[Inclosed in Messrs. Monroe and Pinckney's letter of the 25th April, 1807. From London.]

ARTICLE 5. It is agreed that a line drawn due west from the Lake of the Woods along the forty-ninth parallel of north latitude shall be the line of demarcation [division line] between His Majesty's territories and those of the United States to the westward of the said lake as far as the territories of the United States extend in that quarter; and that the said line shall to that extent form the southern boundary of His Majesty's said territories, and the northern boundary of the said territories of the United States; provided that nothing in the present article shall be construed to extend to the northwest coast of America, or to the territories belonging to or claimed by either party on the continent of America to the westward of the Stony Mountains.

The United States and Great Britain agree on the forty-ninth parallel as a division line.

No. 7.

Mr. Madison to Mr. Monroe and Mr. Pinckney.

[Extract.]

DEPARTMENT OF STATE, *July* 30, 1807.

GENTLEMEN: * * * * * *

1st. The modification of the fifth article (noted as one which the British commissioners would have agreed to) may be admitted in case that proposed by you to them be not attainable. But it is much to be wished and pressed, though not made an ultimatum, that the proviso to both should be omitted. This

The United States respect the claims of Spain on the Pacific.

[10] is in no view *whatever necessary, and can have little other effect than as an offensive intimation to Spain that our claims extend to the Pacific Ocean. However reasonable such claims may be compared with those of others, it is impolitic, especially at the present moment, to strengthen Spanish jealousies of the United States, which it is probably an object with Great Britain to excite by the clause in question.

No. 8.

Mr. Canning to Mr. King.

FOREIGN OFFICE, *April* 20, 1826.

The British government invite negotiations on the N. W. boundary.

The undersigned, His Majesty's Principal Secretary of State for Foreign Affairs, has the honor to request Mr. Rufus King, Envoy Extraordinary and Minister Plenipotentiary of the United States, to have the goodness to inform the undersigned whether Mr. King is provided with instructions for the resumption of the negotiations of last year, with respect to a settlement of boundaries upon the northwest coast of America.

The undersigned is particularly induced to make this inquiry by having received from Mr. Vaughan a copy of the communication, lately addressed by the President of the United States to the House of Representatives, of that part of Mr. Rush's correspondence of last year which relates to this important subject.

The undersigned has to add that the British plenipotentiaries, Mr. Huskisson and Mr. Addington, are perfectly prepared to enter into conferences with Mr. King thereupon; and either to renew the proposal brought forward by Mr. Huskisson and Mr. Stratford Canning in their conference of the 13th of July, 1824, and unanswered, or to bring forward another; to discuss any new proposal on the same subject, or which may be suggested on the part of the plenipotentiary of the United States. The undersigned has the honor to renew to Mr. Rufus King the assurance of his high consideration.

GEORGE CANNING.

RUFUS KING, Esq., *&c.*, *&c.*, *&c.*

---

[11] *No. 9.

Mr. Clay to Mr. Gallatin.

[Extract.]

June 19, 1826.

The parallel of 49° the ultimatum of the United States.

As by the convention of 1818 the forty-ninth parallel of north latitude has been agreed to be the line of boundary between the territories of the United States and Great Britain, east of the Stony Mountains, there would seem to arise, from that stipulation, a strong consideration for the extension of the line along the same parallel, west of them to the Pacific Ocean. In bringing themselves to consent to this boundary the Government of the United States feel that they are animated by a spirit of concession and compromise which, they persuade themselves, that of Great Britain cannot but recognize, and ought not to hesitate in reciprocating. You are then authorized to propose the annulment of the third article of the convention of 1818, and the extension of the line on the parallel of 49 from the eastern side of the Stony Mountains, where it now terminates, to the Pacific Ocean, as the permanent boundary between the territories of the two powers in that quarter. This is our ultimatum, and you may so announce it. We can consent to no other line more favorable to Great Britain.

Mr. Clay to Mr. Gallatin.

[Extract.]

LEXINGTON, *August* 9, 1826.

* * * * * * *

"He [the President] is very desirous of an amicable settlement of all the points of difference between Great Britain and the United States on just principles. Such a settlement alone would be satisfactory to the people of the United States or would command the concurrence of their Senate. In stating in your instructions the terms on which the President was willing that the several questions pending between the two governments might be arranged, he yielded as much to a spirit of concession as he thought he could consistently with the interests of this
[12] country. He is especially not *now prepared to authorize any stipulations involving a session of territory belonging to any State in the Union, or the abandonment, express or implied, of the right to navigate the St. Lawrence, or the surrender of any territory south of latitude forty-nine on the northwest coast." * * * * "II. The President cannot consent that the boundary between the territories of the two powers on the Northwest Coast should be south of forty-nine. The British Government has not been committed by a positive rejection of a line on the parallel of forty-nine; but if it had been, its pride may take refuge in the offer which, for the first time, you are to propose, of a right in common with us to the navigation of the Columbia River. There is no objection to an extension of the time to be allowed to British settlers to remove from south of forty-nine to a period of fifteen years if you should find that it would facilitate an arrangement."

No. 10.

Mr. Gallatin to Mr. Clay.

LONDON, *November* 25, 1826.

SIR: * * * * * * *

The latter part of our conversation was of a more conciliatory nature. Mr. Huskisson said that it would be lamentable that, in this age, two such nations as the United States and Great Britain should be drawn to a rupture on such a subject as the uncultivated wilds of the Northwest Coast. But the honor and dignity of both countries must be respected, and the mutual convenience of

Mr. Huskisson objects to dividing Vancouver Island.

both parties should also be consulted. He then objected to the straight line which we proposed, as having no regard to such convenience, and observed particularly that its cutting off the southern portion of Quadra and Vancouver's Island, (that on which Nootka Sound is situated,) was quite inadmissible. I told him that, taking only convenience into consideration, their proposal was far more objectionable. * * *

ALBERT GALLATIN.

Hon. HENRY CLAY,
Secretary of State.

---

[13] *No. 11.

Mr. Gallatin to Mr. Clay.

LONDON, *December* 2, 1826.

SIR: * * * * * * * *

Mr. Gallatin proposes to exchange Vancouver south of 49° for an equivalent on the mainland.

Mr. Huskisson then asked me whether I was authorized to deviate from the forty-ninth parallel of latitude as a boundary. I did not think that he had any right to ask the question; but, as it was only from courtesy, and to avoid, at the opening of the negotiation, expressions at all savoring of harshness, that I had used the words "whilst insisting on the forty-ninth degree," instead of the word "ultimatum;" and as, in fact, the United States had nothing to conceal, I answered the question: To the forty-ninth parallel of latitude the United States would adhere as a basis. If, on account of the geographical features of the country, a deviation founded on mutual convenience was found expedient, a proposal to that effect might be entertained, provided it was consistent with that basis; that is to say, that any deviation in one place to the south of the forty-ninth parallel should be compensated by an equivalent in another place to the north of that parallel. I must observe that what I had in view was the exchange of the southern extremity of Nootka's Island, (Quadra and Vancouver's,) which the forty-ninth parallel cuts in an inconvenient manner, for the whole or part of the upper branches of the Columbia River north of that parallel.

ALBERT GALLATIN.

Hon. HENRY CLAY,
Secretary of State.

No. 12.

Extract from Vancouver's "Voyage," vol. 1, page 312.

Spanish explorers preceded Vancouver.

"As we were rowing, on Friday morning, [June 22, 1792,] for Point Grey, * * * we discovered two vessels at anchor under the land. * * * These vessels proved to be a detachment from the commission of Señor Melaspina, who was himself employed in the Philippine Islands; that Señor Melaspina had, the preceding year, visited the coast; and that these vessels, His Cath-
[14] *olic Majesty's brig the Sutil, under the command of Señor Don D. Galiano, with the schooner Mexicana, commanded by Señor Don

C. Valdes, both captains of frigates in the Spanish navy, had sailed from Acapulco on the 8th of March, in order to prosecute discoveries on this coast. Señor Galiano, who spoke a little English, informed me that they had arrived at Nootka on the 11th of April, from whence they had sailed on the 5th of this month, in order to complete the examination of this inlet, which had, in the preceding year, been partly surveyed by some Spanish officers whose chart they produced.

"I cannot avoid acknowledging that, on this occasion, I experienced no small degree of mortification in finding the external shores of the gulph had been visited and already examined a few miles beyond where my researches during the excursion had extended." * * * *

No. 13.

Mr. Everett to Mr. Webster.

LONDON, *October* 19, 1842.

SIR: * * * * * * *

Lord Aberdeen, in the conference which ensued after the exchange of the ratifications, observed that his only subject of regret in connection with the treaty was, that the boundary between the two countries on the Pacific Ocean had not been provided for; and expressed a strong wish that I might receive instructions on that subject. * * * * * *

Lord Aberdeen wishes to settle the Oregon boundary.

EDWARD EVERETT.

DANIEL WEBSTER, Esq.,
Secretary of State.

---

[15] *No. 14.

Mr. Everett to Mr. Webster.

LONDON, *November* 18, 1842.

SIR: * * * * * * *

On arriving at the Foreign Office I was told that Lord Aberdeen wished to see me, and was conducted to his room. He informed me that he wished to read me a copy of a despatch which he had addressed to Mr. Fox, directing him to make known to the President the strong desire of Her Majesty's government to engage, without delay, in a negotiation for the settlement of the boundary between the two countries on the Pacific Ocean, and his wish that instructions should be sent to me for that purpose. * * * In the conversation which ensued, he dwelt with great earnestness on the danger to the good understanding between the two countries so happily established by the treaty of Washington, to be apprehended from leaving this question in its present unsettled state. * * * *

Lord Aberdeen wishes to negotiate on the boundary without delay.

EDWARD EVERETT.

DANIEL WEBSTER, Esq.,
Secretary of State.

No. 15.

Mr. Everett to Mr. Upshur.

[Confidential.]

LONDON, *August* 17, 1843.

DEAR SIR: * * * * * *

Mr. Everett thinks the negotiation can be best carried on at Washington.

When Lord Aberdeen spoke of instructing Mr. Fox on the Oregon question, he added an expression of his regret that the negotiation should fall into his hands. He has on many occasions expressed a wish that I should be charged with the negotiation. Could I hope to bring it to a successful issue, it would of course be very agreeable; but it seems to me out of the question to carry on such a negotiation anywhere but at Washington.

* * * * * * *

EDWARD EVERETT.

Hon. A. P. UPSHUR.

---

[16] *No. 16.

Mr. Upshur to Mr. Everett.

DEPARTMENT OF STATE,
Washington, October 9, 1843.

Full powers are sent to Mr. Everett to negotiate on the Oregon boundary.

SIR: The President directs that you take an early occasion to bring again to the attention of Her Majesty's government the subject of the claims of the two countries respectively to the territory west of the Rocky Mountains. The difficulties which the conflicting claims of Russia to a portion of this territory have heretofore interposed, are now happily removed by the treaty of April, 1824, which defines the limits within which that power engages to restrict its settlement; so that the questions now to be settled rest exclusively between Great Britain and the United States. * * *

The offer of the forty-ninth parallel of latitude, although it has once been rejected, may be again tendered, together with the right of navigating the Columbia upon equitable terms. Beyond this the President is not now prepared to go. * * * * *

You will receive herewith the necessary powers to negotiate upon the subject. If, however, the British government prefers that the negotiation shall be conducted in Washington, that arrangement will be perfectly agreeable to the President.

A. P. UPSHUR.

EDWARD EVERETT, Esq.

No. 17.

Mr. Everett to Mr. Upshur.

[Confidential.]

LONDON, *November* 2, 1843.

The negotiation transferred to Washington.

SIR: By the steamer of the 16th October, I had the honor to receive your despatch No. 62, inclosing a full power from the President to treat with this government for the adjustment of the Oregon boundary, and containing your instructions on that subject. I lost no time in applying for an interview with Lord Aber-

deen, and saw him the first day of his return to town. On appris-
[17] ing *him of the disposition of the President to open a negotiation
on this subject at London, Lord Aberdeen informed me that such an arrangement would have been altogether agreeable to him if somewhat earlier made, and reminded me that he had very often, in the course of the last winter, expressed the wish that the President would authorize me to treat on the subject. He had, however, lately come to a conclusion and taken a step that made it necessary to treat upon the subject at Washington: this was the recall of Mr. Fox and the appointment of a successor. Among the grounds for adopting this measure, was the belief that there would be decided advantage in putting the management of this subject into new hands, and consequently that had been and would be assigned as a leading reason for the contemplated change. This course, he said, had not been resolved upon till they had entirely given up the expectation that I should be authorized to treat on this subject.

* * * * * * *

EDWARD EVERETT.

A. P. UPSHUR, Esq.,
Secretary of State.

No. 18.

Mr. Everett to Mr. Upshur.

[Private and confidential.]

LONDON, *November* 14, 1843.

HON. A. P. UPSHUR: * * *

Mr. Everett argues for the parallel of 49°.

I had a long and, upon the whole, quite a satisfactory conversation with Lord Aberdeen at his dwelling-house on the 6th instant. He was on a visit to Windsor Castle, from which he wrote me a note requesting me to call upon him at Argyll House (his town residence,) and I believe he came to London principally for the purpose of holding this interview. He returned to the castle to dinner. He told me that he had communicated to Mr. Fox, by the steamer of the 4th, that his successor was appointed. * * He then led the way to a free and desultory but general and comprehensive conversation on the Oregon question, observing in the outset that it was chiefly in the hope of putting this question in a favorable train of adjustment
that Mr. Fox had been recalled and Mr. Pakenham appointed. *
[18] * * Lord Aberdeen assented also *to my remark that the
numerous stations which the Hudson's Bay Company had established south of the forty-ninth degree of north latitude since the year 1818, though they might and unquestionably would embarrass the British government in reference to that company, and through them in reference to public opinion, ought not to prejudice the claims of the United States. This I think a very important point, to be firmly kept in view. * * * In offering the forty-ninth degree of latitude as the boundary we make a very fair, equitable, and liberal offer, an offer founded on the obvious and natural principles of distribution; while they, in refusing this offer and insisting on the Columbia River, proceed upon no such principle, but simply insist upon a boundary very favorable to themselves. Our offer, I said, proceeded on the old principle of the

English charters of running northern and southern boundaries from sea to sea. If it be objected by Lord A. (as it was) that lines of latitude were arbitrary and might be very unnatural and inconvenient boundaries, I told him that this circumstance was as likely to be in their favor as ours; that lines of latitude had the advantage that they could always be ascertained by men of science; and that, in point of fact, the forty-ninth degree had proved a very convenient line for 1,000 miles. In fact the part of the boundary running on the parallel is the only part in reference to which no controversy has arisen or is to be feared. Another natural and obvious principle, I observed, connected with this, but not identical, was the extension of contiguous territory. * * *

This train of remark produced an obvious effect upon Lord Aberdeen, and after making some inquiry as to the course which things would probably take in Congress during the approaching session, in reference to this subject, and expressing a strong hope that no step would be taken by either House to embarrass the two governments in the negotiation, he said, if this can be avoided, "I do not think we shall have much difficulty;" and this remark he repeated. As not a syllable fell from me authorizing the expectation that the United States would be induced to run the line below the forty-ninth degree, I considered that remark, twice made, coupled with the tenor of my own observation on the reasonableness of that boundary, as authorizing the inference that Mr. Pakenham would be instructed to assent to it. The main difficulty in the way of this will be that the forty-ninth degree has twice been offered by the United States, or rather thrice, and declined by England. Lord *Aberdeen on former occasions has admitted as much. To meet this difficulty, it may deserve the President's consideration whether he would not agree to give up the southern extremity of Quadra and Vancouver's Island (which the forty-ninth degree would leave within our boundary) on condition that the entrance of the straits of Juan de Fuca should at all times be left open and free to the United States, with a free navigation between that island and the main land, and a free outlet to the north. * *

Lord Aberdeen thinks there will not be much difficulty in settling the boundary.

[19]

Mr. Everett suggests that a deflection from 49° would leave to Great Britain the whole of Vancover Island.

If there is any reliance in appearance and professions, Mr. Pakenham will go to America with the best feelings for an honorable adjustment of the matter in discussion.

EDWARD EVERETT.

No. 19.

Mr. Everett to Mr. Upshur.

[Confidential.]

LONDON, *December* 2, 1843.

SIR: I had a long and important conversation with Lord Aberdeen on the 29th ultimo, which I now beg leave to report to you confidentially for the information of the President.

Mr. Everett and Lord Aberdeen discuss the boundary.

I have observed to you in a former communication that, though the negotiation relative to the Oregon boundary had, in consequence of the recall of Mr. Fox and the appointment of Mr. Pakenham, been transferred to Washington, I should use my best efforts to produce such an impression on Lord Aberdeen's mind, as to the prominent points of the question, as might have a favorable influence in the preparation of the instructions to be given to Mr. Pakenham. With this end in view I had, in a former interview, as I have already informed you, gone over the ground generally in support of our claim, particularly urging, and as I thought with some effect, the reasonableness of the terms on which the United States have uniformly offered to adjust the boundary. In my interview with Lord Aberdeen on the 29th I pursued the same line of argument.

* * * * * * *

I first made some remarks on the claim of the United States, as
[20] the representatives of Spain, to an extension on the north*western coast of America, originally indefinite, and limited only by the compacts with Russia, to which Spain and the United States are parties. * * * * * *

Passing from this topic I urged with all the force in my power the extreme reasonableness of the proposal of the United States to run the line on the forty-ninth parallel to the sea, on the grounds of extension of contiguous territory; of giving to each power the tract due west of its acknowledged territory; and on the ground that in a final appropriation of a region at present unappropriated (assuming for the sake of argument that Oregon territory is in that condition) that the United States certainly were entitled, besides their own share, to two other shares, in the right of France and Spain, whose title they had combined with their own. * * * * * *

After considerable discussion of these points, Lord Aberdeen finally said that these were grounds which, in the main result, had been long ago taken by the United States, and rejected by England; that the question was quite different from what it would have been if now presented for the first time; and that it was impossible for the present ministry to accept what had been rejected in 1824 and 1826; that they did not suppose that we, any more than themselves, could now agree to terms which we had declined then; and that, consequently, there must be concession on both sides; that they were willing to act on this principle, and that we must do the same.

I regarded this observation, now made to me for the first time, although the Oregon boundary since my residence in England has been the subject of very frequent conversation between Lord Aberdeen and myself, as very important. I told Lord Aberdeen that I thought it would be very difficult for the United States to make any modification of their former proposal, except in one point, which I did certainly regard as very important to England, if she entertained any views to the future settlement of the country. I thought the President might be induced so far to depart from the forty-ninth parallel as to leave the whole of Quadra and Vancouver's Island to England, whereas that line of latitude would give us the southern extremity of that island, and consequently, the command of the straits of Fuca on both sides. If the country is to be occupied by a dense population, as there is no reason to doubt would one day be the case, this would be a valuable concession to England, without implying a great sacrifice on our part. I observed, I was not au-
[21] thorized to say this would be agreed to; I could only *say I thought and wished it might be. I then pointed out on a map the extent of this concession, and Lord Aberdeen said he would take it into consideration.

Mr. Everett points out on a map the deflection from 49° that would leave Vancouver to Great Britain.

He then asked me if I was confident of the accuracy of the statement which I had made relative to the offer in 1826, on the part of Great Britain, to give us a port within the straits of Fuca, with an adjacent territory. * * * * * * *

I accordingly considered his inquiry to proceed from some anxiety lest

I should be mistaken, and a wish to have the fact established that they had then offered us a territory north of Columbia, in order now to facilitate the way for an abandonment of the Columbia as the boundary.

I may be in an error in this view of the subject; but it is the result of the closest consideration I have been able to give it, that the present government, though of course determined not to make any discreditable sacrifice of what they consider their rights, are really willing to agree to reasonable terms of settlement. * * * *

I spoke with considerable earnestness in reprobation of the conduct of the Hudson's Bay Company in multiplying and pushing their posts far to the south of the Columbia, and said I trusted that the government would not allow itself to be embarrassed by this circumstance. Fair warning had been given to the company in 1818, that no settlements after that date should prejudice the rights of either party. He said he did not consider the existence of those settlements as a very serious matter, but the navigation of the Columbia was a serious one. * * *

EDWARD EVERETT.

A. P. UPSHUR, Esq.,
Secretary of State.

[Inclosure B to the above.]

Mr. Everett to Lord Aberdeen.

[Private.]

46 GROSVENOR PLACE, *November* 30, 1843.

Mr. Everett presents his proposition to Lord Aberdeen in writing.

MY DEAR LORD ABERDEEN: The proposition relative to a port within the straits of Fuca and an adjacent tract of country was made by Mr. Huskisson and Mr. Addington to
[22] Mr. Gallatin, on the 1st December, 1826, and will *be found recorded in the protocol of the third conference, which was held on that day.

It appears from Mr. Gallatin's correspondence that at a former conference Mr. Huskisson had especially objected to the extension of the forty-ninth degree to the Pacific, on the ground that it would cut off the southern extremity of Quadra and Vancouver's Island.

My suggestion yesterday would obviate this objection. I ought, however, to repeat, in thus alluding to that suggestion in writing, that though it would have been within my competence to propose it, (subject to the approbation of my Government,) had the negotiation remained in my hands, it would have been so only under the general authority to propose and receive terms of compromise. The suggestion itself is not specifically alluded to in my instructions.

A glance at the map shows its importance as a modification of the forty-ninth degree, and I should be truly rejoiced if, in regarding it in that light, your lordship would permit it to become the basis of a final settlement of this serious difficulty.

EDWARD EVERETT.

The EARL OF ABERDEEN, *&c., &c.*

No. 20.

Mr. Everett to Mr. Nelson.

LONDON, *April* 1, 1844.

SIR: * * * * * *

Mr. Everett and Lord Aberdeen continue the discussion.

The principle of running the forty-ninth degree of latitude to the sea and leaving to each party west of the Rocky Mountains the continuation of its territory east was in all other respects the most natural and equitable basis of settlement.

I had on previous occasions pursued substantially this line of argument with Lord Aberdeen, and I received from him now the same answer to it as formerly, viz, that Great Britain could not now accept terms which she had distinctly refused before; that he felt that we were under the same necessity; that he did not expect the United States to agree to what they had already rejected; and that consequently it must, he thought, be assumed as the basis of negotiation that something
[23] must be yielded on each side. To *this I replied, that though as
a general principle of negotiation under such circumstances this might be admitted, it was impossible to leave out of view the substantial character of the former propositions on either side; and that in proportion as he (Lord Aberdeen) should, on reconsidering the subject, be inclined to think that the offer formerly made by the United States to continue the forty-ninth parallel to the sea was an equitable offer, and one founded on natural and reasonable principles of adjustment, he ought to be satisfied with but a moderate departure from that proposal; particularly if such a modification, without involving a great sacrifice to us, were eminently advantageous to them. In fact such a modification was the only one which the United States could, in my opinion, be brought to agree to. The modification which I had formerly suggested, viz, that the United States would waive their claim to the southern extremity of Quadra and Vancouver's Island, which would be cut off by the forty-ninth degree of latitude, was precisely of this kind.

It could be of no great importance to us to hold the southern extremity of an island of which the main portion belonged to England' while the entire possession of the island, and consequently the free entrance of the Straits of Fuca, would be a very important object to Great Britain. I repeated what I had often observed before, that I had no authority to say that this modification would be agreed to by the United States, but that I thought it might.

Lord Aberdeen did not commit himself on the point, whether or not this proposal, if made by the Government of the United States, would be accepted. He however stated (as I understood him) that he had caused a map to be colored as I suggested; that he was desirous to go as far as possible for the sake of settling the controversy; that Mr. Pakenham's original instructions were drawn up in this spirit; and that since he left home, he (Lord Aberdeen) had enlarged his discretionary powers. I confess from these facts, viz, that Lord Aberdeen does not expect us to agree to the Columbia as the boundary, not even with the addition of Port Discovery and an adjacent tract of country within the Straits of Fuca (which we refused in 1826,) that he has never negatived the idea of the forty-ninth degree with the suggested modification; that he has uniformly said that he did not think there would be great
[24] difficulty in settling the question, and this although I* have as
uniformly assured him that, in my opinion, the United States

Mr. Everett thinks that Great Britain will accept the line of 49° with the proposed deflection.

would not stop short of the 49th degree except in the point above stated; I draw the inference that this proposal would in the last resort be accepted. I am satisfied that the ministry sincerely wish to settle the controversy, and are willing to go as far as their views of consistency and the national honor will permit to effect that object.

They do not, therefore, I imagine, much regret the agitation of the subject in the United States, and are willing we should advance a claim to the 54° 40′; such a course on our part will make it easier for them to agree to stop at 49°. * * * * *

EDWARD EVERETT.

JOHN NELSON, Esq.,
Secretary of State ad interim.

No. 21.

Extract of a lecture delivered by Mr. William Sturgis before the Mercantile Library Association of Boston, January 22, 1845.

Views of Mr. Sturgis.

* * * I deem it very desirable that the question of boundary should be speedily adjusted, and that the limits and the rights of each party be so clearly established and defined as to prevent all danger of collision hereafter.

In this opinion I doubt not that the distinguished statesmen, Messrs. Pakenham and Calhoun, who now have charge of the negotiation, will cordially concur; and it seems to me that each party will attain their object, and justice be done to both, by adopting as the boundary a continuation of the parallel of 49° across the Rocky Mountains, to tidewater, say to the middle of the Gulf of Georgia; thence by the northernmost navigable passage (not north of 49°) to the Straits of Juan de Fuca, and down the middle of those straits to the Pacific Ocean; the navigation of the Gulf of Georgia and the Straits of Juan de Fuca to be forever free to both parties—all the islands and other territory lying south and east of this line to belong to the United States, and all north and west to Great Britain. By this arrangement we should yield to Great
[25] *Britain the portion of Quadra and Vancouver's Island that lies south of latitude 49°, which, in a territorial point of view, is of too little importance to deserve a moment's consideration; and both parties would secure, for a considerable extent, a well-defined natural boundary, about which there could hereafter be no doubt or dispute. Will Great Britain accede to this? I think she will. Up to the close of the last negotiation, in 1827, the free navigation of the Columbia was declared to be indispensable to Great Britain, by the British commissioners; but subsequent developments will probably render the British less pertinacious upon this point. The "summary" presented by the commissioners in 1827 shows that the Columbia was then supposed to be the most convenient, in fact the only, navigable channel of communication between the ocean and most of the numerous establishments of the Hudson Bay Company, west of the Rocky Mountains. Within a few years past, however, several rivers of considerable magnitude have been explored from the interior to the seas into which they empty, north of latitude 49°. These are "Frazer's River," which disembogues about that parallel; the river called by Harmon the "Nach-

aottatain," in about the latitude 53°; "Simpson's River," a little north of latitude 55°; and "Stickene River," in 55° 50′. All these would be within the British territory, or are so situated that the British, by their convention with Russia, would have the right of navigating them; and they would afford convenient communication with most of their establishments north of 49°; and if this adjustment should be made they would retain none south of that line. I should be reluctant to cede to Great Britain the free navigation of the Columbia, for there are serious objections to giving to any nation the unlimited right of using a stream where it flows wholly through the territories of another. For obvious reasons the exercise of such a right must endanger the harmony and peace of the parties; and, especially at such a remote point, would be a fruitful cause of jealousy, and very likely to occasion collision. But Great Britain will not relinquish the right to the free navigation and use of the Straits of Juan de Fuca, if she retains the territory north of 49°. The use of these straits would, in fact, be indispensable to her, for through them is the only convenient access to a considerable portion of this territory. * * * * * *

---

[26] *No. 22.

Mr. Everett to Mr. Calhoun.

LONDON, *February* 28, 1845.

SIR: * * * * * * *

I have anticipated in some degree another point to which Lord Aberdeen has given great prominence in all our conversations, viz, the entire impossibility that England should accept terms which she has already refused. I do not think I can be mistaken in saying that, unless it comes in the form of an award, she will never agree to the naked proposition of the forty-ninth degree. I have, however, a pretty confident belief that she would accept that line with the modification alluded to in my dispatches above mentioned, viz, the southern extremity of Quadra and Vancouver's Island, though cut off by the forty-ninth parallel, to be theirs. Lord Aberdeen has never told me they would agree to this; but I am still of the opinion expressed in my former dispatches, and for the reasons therein stated, that they would do so, and I am confident that this is the best boundary which we can get by negotiation. The concession of the southern end of the island, while of little importance to us, would be a great boon to them, as giving them a passage through the Straits of Fuca; and on the ground of this advantage, I am of opinion that they would consider themselves justified in acceding in other respects to the forty-ninth degree; but if the expectation prevails that they can be led by negotiation to agree to a boundary which we should regard as more favorable than this, I am confident that expectation will prove delusive. At the same time I have spared no pains to impress upon Lord Aberdeen's mind the persuasion that the utmost which the United States can concede is the forty-ninth parallel with the modification suggested, taking care always to add that I had no authority for saying that even that modification would be agreed to. * * *

Mr. Everett thinks that the line of 40°, deflected so as to give the whole of Vancouver to Great Britain, is all that either party will concede.

EDWARD EVERETT.

JOHN C. CALHOUN, Esq.,
Secretary of State.

[27] No. 23.

Mr. Everett to Mr. Calhoun.

LONDON, *March* 7, 1845.

SIR: * * * * * * *

I took an opportunity a few days since to explain to the Comte de St. Aulaire, the French embassador, at his request, the merits of the claim of the United States, and the present state of the controversy. I have since done the same thing in conversation with the Chevalier Bunsen, the Prussian minister, who, at my recommendation, has made himself acquainted with Mr. Greenhow's work.

Lord Ashburton thinks there will be not much difficulty in coming to an adjustment.

A day or two since I had a good deal of conversation with Lord Ashburton on the general question. Knowing that he is habitually consulted by the Government on American subjects, I thought it of some importance to endeavor to impress his mind with the reasonableness of the American pretensions. Having done this, I stated to him my confident opinion that the Government of the United States would never accept a boundary materially less favorable than the forty-ninth degree of latitude. He said he did not think there would be much difficulty in coming to an adjustment, unless steps were taken on our side which wore the appearance of defiance and menace. Any such step would put it out of the power of England, as a similar step on her part would put it out of the power of the United States, to compromise on any terms. I attach the greater importance to these remarks, because Lord Ashburton has lately conferred with Lord Aberdeen on the subject. * * * * *

EDWARD EVERETT.

JOHN C. CALHOUN, Esq.,
Secretary of State.

No. 24.

Mr. Everett to Mr. Calhoun.

[Confidential.]

LONDON, *April* 2, 1845.

SIR: * * * * * * *

Mr. Sturgis's pamphlet regarded by a friend of the British ministry as fair and candid.

A person very high in the confidence of the government, but not belonging to it, informed me a day or two since [28] that he con*sidered the view of the Oregon question lately delivered on the subject in Boston by Mr. William Sturgis as fair and candid.

EDWARD EVERETT.

JOHN C. CALHOUN, Esq.,
Secretary of State.

No. 25.

Lord Ashburton to Mr. Sturgis.

LONDON, *April* 2, 1845.

SIR: Your lecture on the Oregon question reached me last week, and as the subject itself interests me, and still more so everything connected with the maintenance of peace and friendly intercourse between our countries, I lost no time in reading it. I beg you will accept my very best thanks for your obliging attention. Your treatise enables me every day to answer satisfactorily the question put to me so often, where is the Oregon and what is this dispute about? You have stated the case distinctly in a few pages, and what is indeed uncommon, you have stated it with great impartiality. Your leaning is perhaps to the side of the American argument; but if those who have to settle the subject by negotiation treat it with the same fairness and candor you have done, there can be no danger of its leading to consequences which all honest men would deprecate. I have personally a high opinion of the future destinies of that portion of the coast of the Pacific. The Northern Pacific Ocean, and in the course of time probably the eastern shores of Asia, will find their masters in the country north of California. But I have a very low opinion of any interest either your country or mine are likely to have in any division of the territory. From the moment it becomes of any real importance, it will not be, and should not be, governed from either Washington or from Westminster. You do not, or should not want land, and we certainly do not want colonies, and least of all such as would be unmanageable from
[29] their distance, and only serve to embroil us with our *neighbors.

Lord Ashburton regards Mr. Sturgis's pamphlet as distinct and impartial.

I am not without a wish that this new Pacific republic should be founded by our own race, which with all their defects, are likely to spread the best description of Christian civilization; but to say the truth, I care little whether this be done from Old England directly, or intermediately through New England. What I do care about is that we should not quarrel about this or any other measure, and I really believe that we should all be better by leaving this question to sleep again for another half century.

Repeating my thanks for your obliging attention, I have the honor to be, sir, your very obedient,

ASHBURTON.

The Hon. WM. STURGIS.

No. 26.

Mr. Bates to Mr. Sturgis.

[Strictly confidential.]

LONDON, *May* 1, 1845.

MY DEAR SIR: I wrote you some weeks since to thank you for the pamphlets you were so kind as to send me on the Oregon question. Since the date of my letter the few copies of your address sent over have circulated pretty rapidly, and have been read by all the ministers, I have no doubt. I now inclose you an article cut from the Examiner of last week. It was written by my friend Senior, the political economist, as you will see, with your paper before

Lord Aberdeen pronounces Mr. Sturgis's pamphlet clear and sensible.

him. He showed it to me before it was printed, as he frequently does his articles for reviews, (I suppose for the purpose of getting a common-sense opinion,) and I advised him to send it to Lord Aberdeen, with a note to say, if he found anything amiss in it that it should not be published. Lord Aberdeen answered that it was all right, except an unimportant omission in regard to the negotiations of 1818–'19. A few days since Lord Aberdeen, among others, dined with Mr. Van der Weyer. After dinner Lord Aberdeen came to me, and talking on various
[30] matters, got to America and the Oregon *question. I carefully avoided leading the conversation, but he seemed desirous to talk Oregon. The sum of what he said was this: he complimented your paper as a clear and sensible view of the matter; that the declaration [of] the President required to be met by a declaration of some sort from this government; that what had been said he hoped would be taken in the sense it was given as meaning simply that the British government do not admit that the United States have a right to the whole of Oregon. I told him that the declaration of the President appeared to have excited very little attention in the United States. He seemed anxious to impress on my mind that this country was disposed for peace and an amicable settlement of the question. * * * * *

JOSHUA BATES.

The Hon. WM. STURGIS.

Extract from an article by Mr. —— Senior, in the [London] Examiner, No. 1943. *Saturday, April* 26, 1845.

The only real claim of the British rests on contiguity.

"If arbitration be unobtainable, the only mode of accommodation is mutual concession; and the terms which we suggest for that mutual concession are those which, if we were arbitrators, we should award, namely, that the boundary should be the forty-ninth parallel until it meets the Pacific, and then the sea. Our only real claim rests on contiguity, and this would give us more than mere contiguity entitles us to. This would give us the whole of Vancouver's Island, and it would give us an abundance of good harbors. It would also give us the country which is best for the purposes for which we use it, the fur trade. * * Whatever be Lord Aberdeen's policy, the Opposition will, we trust, not add to its difficulties. * * * We trust that the English negotiators will not deny every principle of law, however sacred, which they find opposed to them, and every fact, however notorious, that makes against them."

---

[31] *No. 27.

Narrative of the United States exploring expedition during the years 1838, 1839, 1840, 1841, 1842, *by Charles Wilkes, U. S. N., commander of the expedition, in five volumes and an atlas: Philadelphia,* 1845.

[VOLUME IV, CHAPTER XIV, 1841, PAGE 484.]

Wilkes surveys Canal de Haro in July 1841.

"A large boat expedition was also fitted out, of which I took charge in person, to proceed across the Straits of the Fuca, to complete the survey of the Canal de Arro, with the adjacent bays and harbors, and thence to the mouth of Fraser's river. * * * * * *

"On the morning of the 25th July, 1841, the brig parted company, and in the afternoon I set out, with seven boats, to cross the strait. * *

"On the 26th we began the survey of this labyrinth of islands, which was continued the next day, 27th. * * *

"On the 28th the duties of our surveyors were again resumed, and a finish made of those of the Canal de Arro. This was effected through the strenuous exertions of both officers and men, and the same night we reached the Vincennes. * * * We had completed all that was essential for the navigation of the Canal de Arro." * * *

No. 28.

Mr. Buchanan to Mr. Pakenham.

[Extract.]

DEPARTMENT OF STATE,
Washington, July 12, 1845.

Mr. Buchanan offers the line of 49° with free ports on Vancouver.

* * * He (the President) has, therefore, instructed the undersigned again to propose to the government of Great Britain that the Oregon Territory shall be divided between the two countries by the forty-ninth parallel of north latitude, from the Rocky Mountains to the Pacific Ocean; offering at the same
[32] time to make *free to Great Britain, any port or ports on Vancouver's Island, south of this parallel, which the British government may desire. * * * * * * *

JAMES BUCHANAN.

Rt. Hon. R. PAKENHAM, *&c., &c., &c.*

No. 29.

Mr. Pakenham to Mr. Buchanan.

[Extract.]

WASHINGTON, *July* 29, 1845.

Mr. Pakenham rejects Mr. Buchanan's offer.

* * * The undersigned, therefore, trusts that the American plenipotentiary will be prepared to offer some further proposal for the settlement of the Oregon question more consistent with fairness and equity, and with the reasonable expectations of the British government, as defined in the statement marked D, which the undersigned had the honor to present to the American plenipotentiary at the early part of the present negotiation.

R. PAKENHAM.

Hon. JAMES BUCHANAN, *&c., &c., &c.*

No. 30.

Mr. Buchanan to Mr. Pakenham.

[Extract.]

DEPARTMENT OF STATE,
Washington, August 30, 1845.

Mr. Buchanan withdraws his offer.

* * Such a proposition as that which has been made never would have been authorized by the President had this been a new question.

Upon his accession to office he found the present negotiation pending. It had been instituted in the spirit and upon the principle of compromise. Its object, as avowed by the negotiators, was not to demand the whole territory in dispute for either country; but, in the language of the first protocol, "to treat of the respective claims of the two
[33] countries to the Oregon territory, with a view to *establish a
permanent boundary between them westward of the Rocky Mountains to the Pacific Ocean."

Placed in this position, and considering that Presidents Monroe and Adams had, on former occasions, offered to divide the territory in dispute by the forty-ninth parallel of latitude, he felt it his duty not at once abruptly to arrest the negotiation, but so far to yield his own opinion as once more to make a similar offer.

Not only respect for the conduct of his predecessors, but a sincere and anxious desire to promote peace and harmony between the two countries, influenced him to pursue this course. The Oregon question presents the only intervening cloud which intercepts the prospect of a long career of mutual friendship and beneficial commerce between the two nations, and this cloud he desired to remove.

These are the reasons which actuated the President to offer a proposition so liberal to Great Britain.

And how has this proposition been received by the British plenipotentiary? It has been rejected without even a reference to his own government. Nay, more; the British plenipotentiary, to use his own language, "trusts that the American plenipotentiary will be prepared to offer some further proposal for the settlement of the Oregon question, more consistent with fairness and equity, and with the reasonable expectations of the British government."

Under such circumstances, the undersigned is instructed by the President to say that he owes it to his own country, and a just appreciation of her title to the Oregon territory, to withdraw the proposition to the British government which had been made under his direction; and it is hereby accordingly withdrawn.

In taking this necessary step, the President still cherishes the hope that this long pending controversy may yet be finally adjusted in such a manner as not to disturb the peace or interrupt the harmony now so happily subsisting between the two nations.

* * * * * * *

JAMES BUCHANAN.

Right Hon. RICHARD PAKENHAM, *&c., &c., &c.*

[34] *No. 31.

Mr. McLane to Mr. Buchanan.

LONDON, *October* 3, 1845.

SIR: I received, on the 29th ultimo, your dispatch No. 9, dated the 13th September, transmitting a copy of your last note (30th August, 1845) to Mr. Pakenham, relative to the Oregon question.

Lord Aberdeen censures the rejection of the American proposition by Mr. Pakenham.

On the day following I was invited by Lord Aberdeen, in the note hereto appended, to an interview at his house in Argyll street, which I granted accordingly. The object of the interview, as I had anticipated, related exclusively to the posture in which the negotiations between the two governments had been placed by your note of the 30th August to Mr. Pakenham, and the withdrawal of the proposition which the President had previously directed.

Lord Aberdeen not only lamented but censured the rejection of our proposition by Mr. Pakenham, without referring it to his government. * * He stated that if Mr. Pakenham had communicated the American proposition to the government here, as he was expected to have done, he, Lord Aberdeen, would have taken it up as the basis of his action, and entertained little doubt that he would have been enabled to propose modifications which might ultimately have resulted in an adjustment mutually satisfactory to both governments. * * *

I did not fail, however, to take the occasion to press upon Lord Aberdeen the great difficulties with which, in the present state of public sentiment in the United States, the President could concede even that which he had done in the position he had authorized. * * *

It was quite obvious to me that Lord Aberdeen had become convinced in his own mind, though in what way I do not pretend to conjecture, that the terms which it was his intention ultimately to propose or assent to would be accepted by the President, and that on this account he particularly regretted the interruption in the negotiation without affording an opportunity for that purpose.

* * * * * * *

LOUIS McLANE.

Hon. JAMES BUCHANAN,
Secretary of State.

---

[35] *No. 32.

Mr. McLane to Mr. Buchanan.

LONDON, *December* 1, 1845.

SIR: Although it is well understood here that in the present posture of the Oregon question my connection with it must be in a great degree informal, the Earl of Aberdeen occasionally makes it a subject of conversation.

Lord Aberdeen would have taken Mr. Buchanan's offer as the basis of negotiations.

At his request, I have recently had an interview with him, when he put in my hand, to read, two dispatches from Mr. Pakenham, one in explanation of his rejection without reference to his government of the President's proposition; the other containing a statement of his subsequent attempts to induce you to allow the President's proposition to stand as the basis of further negotiation, or to have some assurance of the answer which a new proposition from the British government would receive. * * * The principal object of Lord Aberdeen in seeking the interview, appeared to me to be to point out the embarrassment in which he thought the President's withdrawal of his proposition had placed this government. It was quite evident, indeed he expressly said, that he was not prepared to accept the President's proposition, but desired only to make it the basis of further negotiation and modified propositions from this government, which he would have done, notwithstanding the rejection of it by Mr. Pakenham, if it had not been withdrawn by direction of the President.

* * * Although I am quite sure that the Earl of Aberdeen has no idea at present of accepting the compromise contained in the President's proposition, it would not surprise me if an arrangement upon that basis should prove acceptable to large and important classes in this country, indeed complained of principally by the Hudson's Bay Company, and those in its interest.

That the ministry would find it difficult and hazardous to prefer war to such a settlement may well be imagined, although you may assume it to be certain that when war becomes inevitable it will receive the undivided support of the British people.

I believe the government and people here are quite prepared for the re-assertion in the message of the President's opinions expressed
[36] in his inaugural address, and, perhaps, for a recommendation *by him to terminate the joint occupation in the manner provided by the existing treaty.

And I also think that unless the recommendation in the message should be such as to discourage further negotiation, and to manifest a determination to insist upon our whole right, they would not lead to any immediate measures upon the part of this government, or materially add to the embarrassment in which the relations between the two countries appear to be at present involved. * * * * *

LOUIS McLANE.

JAMES BUCHANAN, Esq.,
Secretary of State.

No. 33.

Mr. Bates to Mr. Sturgis.

[Private.]

LONDON, *December* 2, 1845.

SIR: * * * * * * *

Hudson Bay company prevent settlement. No American will concede more than the line of 49° and Fuca's Straits.

Our relations with the United States.—When I last wrote to you on this subject, I gave you to understand that the negotiations were going well, but I soon after learned that there had been a hitch at Washington, and a very awkward one it is, for the British government must now make the first move, and whether they will make that move remains to be seen. One thing is consolatory, viz, that after the publication of Mr. Webster's speech here yesterday consols improved. The stock-jobbers say that "the 49° is about right, and there can be no difficulty." That will be the

feelings of nine-tenths of the people of Great Britain; but this has been refused by so many ministers previously, that Lord Aberdeen may hesitate; the western members of Congress will rail, and the merchants will be kept in hot water another year. The Hudson Bay Company prevent a settlement, I have no doubt—they might have twenty years' occupation and the right of pre-emption to their lands under cultivation, and to become Americans or not at the expiration of the time, as they may choose, always conforming to any laws the United States may establish for the government of the territory. This, with the 49° to the
[37] strait, giving Vancouver's Island to Great Britain, is *as much
as any American, be he Bostonian or Carolinian, will, I think, consent to give up. If Great Britain is not satisfied with that, let them have war if they want it. * * * * *

JOSHUA BATES.

Hon. WM. STURGIS.

No. 34.

Mr. McLane to Mr. Buchanan.

LONDON, *February* 3, 1846.

SIR: * * * * * * *

Mr. Pakenham's conduct strongly disapproved in England.

It will be perceived from the remarks of Lord John Russell, and Sir Robert Peel more particularly, that the observations I have heretofore made of the effect upon public opinion in this country of the President's proposition for compromise are fully confirmed, and that the rejection of the proposition by Mr. Pakenham, without sending it to his government, at least as the basis of negotiation, is strongly disapproved by both parties. I have reason to know, also, that there is an expectation with all classes here that this disapprobation should have its influence in disposing our Government to give a favorable and amicable reception to any future overtures which may be made for resuming the negotiation. * * *

On the subsequent night, Friday, the 23d of January, the subject was again introduced to the notice of the House of Commons by Lord John Russell. He said:

Lord John Russell calls Mr. Pakenham's rejection of the American offer a hasty proceeding.

It would appear that a proposition for a compromise had been made from the President to Her Majesty's government, and he (Lord John Russell) conceived that that proposition had changed the state of the question. The proposition itself might be satisfactory or not satisfactory; but, having been made, it did appear to him to require a statement from those in authority in this country of the terms on which they would be satisfied to settle this question. That proposition, he understood, had not been received by Her Majesty's government, but had been declared to be wholly inadmissible by our minister in America. He (Lord John Russell) confessed he thought that was a hasty proceeding on the part of the representative of Her Majesty in the United States, but what he wished to ask was, whether the negotiations had recommenced or were going on.

* * * * * * *

[38] *Sir Robert Peel observed:

Sir Robert Peel says that Mr. Pakenham ought to have referred the American offer to his government.

On the subject of the Oregon territory, I have to state that a proposal was made by Mr. Buchanan, with the authority of the President of the United States, to Mr. Pakenham, and that the proposal so made suggested a division of the territory. Whether or not that proposal ought to have been accepted, I cannot say. Mr. Pakenham thought that the terms proposed were so little likely to be acceptable, that he did not feel himself warranted in transmitting the proposal to the government at home; and, on signifying this to Mr. Buchanan, the latter immediately stated that the proposal was withdrawn. This is the state of the negotiation at present, so far as I am informed, respecting the proposal submitted by Mr. Buchanan. I have the highest opinion of Mr. Pakenham; I have the greatest respect for his talents, and the greatest confidence in his judgment; yet, I must say, that it would have been better had he transmitted that proposal to the home government for their consideration, and if found in itself unsatisfactory, it might possibly have formed the foundation for a further proposal. [Hear!] * * * * * *

Sir Robert Peel for a peaceable settlement of the Oregon question.

We have no hesitation in announcing our sincere desire for the interests of this country, for the interests of the United States, and for the interests of the civilized world, in continuing to strain every effort which is consistent with national honor for the purpose of amicably terminating those disputes. [Hear!] * * * *

I think it would be the greatest misfortune if a contest about the Oregon between two such powers as England and the United States could not, by the exercise of moderation and good sense, be brought to a perfectly honorable and satisfactory conclusion. [Cheers.] * * * * * *

Mr. McLane reports that the British government will accept the line of 49° and the Straits of Fuca.

After these observations, I owe it more particularly to myself to state that, believing from the history of our previous negotiations as to the Oregon question that it may now be settled upon the basis of a compromise, and, with reference to interests which have grown up during the joint occupation of the territory, without a violation of any duty which a public man owes to the rights and honor of his country, I would not be unwilling, taking the President's proposition of the 12th July as a basis, to urge a final adjustment of the question according to that proposition, but conceding to the Hudson Bay Company a continuance of the privileges of joint occupation, including the navigation of the Columbia, for a period
[39] of seven or ten years longer; and I hope that *I may be allowed
to add that I would be willing to assume the responsibility of assenting to an adjustment by extending the boundary to the Pacific by the forty-ninth parallel and the Strait of Fuca with free ports to both nations, or by extending the free navigation of the Columbia River for a longer period, provided similar advantages upon the Saint Lawrence could thereby be secured to the United States.

I believe that upon one of these grounds, perhaps upon either, an adjustment may be concluded, and I have a strong conviction that the first indicated is entirely practicable.

I am, however, constrained at the same time to state, from all that has come to my knowledge here, that I have no reason to believe that more favorable terms than those I have above adverted to would under any circumstances be consented to by this government. * * *

LOUIS McLANE.

Hon. JAMES BUCHANAN,
Secretary of State.

No. 35.

Extract from the speech of Mr. Calhoun, of South Carolina, in the Senate, March 16, 1846.

The line of 49° the only line admissible.

* * * "The past history of the affair, the fact that it had been frequently offered by us substantially as an ultimatum, added to the fact that 49° was the boundary on this side of the Rocky Mountains, left no doubt on my mind that, if settled by compromise, it must be on that basis." * * * *

Extract from the speech of Mr. Webster, of Massachusetts, in the Senate, March 30, 1846.

* * * I was not very far out when I took the precaution of reducing what I intended to say to writing. What I said was, (and I presumed not to dictate, or to speak as *ex cathedra*,) that in my judgment public opinion in both countries tended to a union on the general basis of the proposal made by this Government to that of England in 1826. * * *

Great Britain cannot expect anything south of 49°.

[40] * * * *What I meant, and what I said, was, that if 49° should be agreed on as a general basis, I was satisfied to negotiate about all the rest. But the gentleman from Ohio and the Senate will do me the justice to allow that I said, as plainly as I could speak or put down words in writing, that England *must not expect anything south of forty-nine degrees.* I said so in so many words. * *

Extract from the debate on the Oregon question, in the House of Representatives, February 9, 1846.

Mr. T. B. King: * * * "I should like, with all respect and deference to the learned and venerable gentleman from Massachusetts, (Mr. Adams,) to ask whether, in his judgment, our title to the entirety of the Oregon territory is 'clear and unquestionable?'"

John Quincy Adams regards America's title as clear to all territory on the Pacific south of 54° 40′.

Mr. John Quincy Adams. * * * "According to the construction we gave to 'clear and indisputable,' in relation to the question of right and wrong, I say that our title is clear and unquestionable." * * * * * * *

Extract from the speech of Mr. J. Q. Adams, in the House of Representatives, April 13, 1846.

* * * "I am not for settling the question at the line of 49°." * * * "If this House pass this, and instead of putting down 'south of the line of 49°,' as is proposed by this amendment, will say 'south of latitude 54° 40′,' I will vote for it." * * * "Great Britain had no claim whatever. I believe she has no pretensions to any now." * * * * * * *

Extract from the speech of Mr. Cass, of Michigan, in the Senate, June, 1846

* * * "We are seeking a doubtful good, at the certainty of a great sacrifice." * * * "Those who believe that our title to all Oregon is so 'clear and unquestionable' that no portion of it ought to be relinquished, may well contend for its whole extent, and risk the consequences." * * *

To accept the line of 49° regarded as a sacrifice.

[41] **Extract from the speech of Mr. Sevier, of Arkansas, chairman of the Committee on Foreign Relations, in the Senate, March 25, 1846.*

Many Americans claim 54° 40′ as the boundary, and would fight for 49°.

* * * Sir, I am not sure but that a majority of the people of the United States would rather fight Great Britain to-morrow than yield up to her any part of Oregon south of 54° 40′. I am not sure but that a majority of the people of the United States are now ready to assert the title of the United States to the whole of Oregon, believing, as that majority do, that the title of their country to the whole of it is unquestionable; and with this assertion of their title, I am not sure but that this majority are not now ready, upon the slightest intimation from those who have control of our public affairs, to maintain it at all hazards. * * * These people, with these impressions, are now looking and reading about Oregon, and are quietly and firmly forming their resolves upon the subject. 54° 40′ are chalked upon doors and windows, and upon walls, pillar, and post, everywhere. * * * These people are in no temper for unjust concessions, in the form of compromises. Is there, sir, a man in America, of any party or of any sect, that would not sooner fight Great Britain to-morrow than yield up any part of Oregon south of 49°? In support of our title, up to that line, and for everything south of it, we should find even our Quaker friends in uniform, with arms in their hands, crying aloud, in the highways and by-ways, "To your tents, O Israel!"

No. 36.

Extract from the [London] Quarterly Review for March, 1846, Vol. LXVII, page 603.

The Quarterly in favor of the line of 49° and Fuca's Straits.

* * * We believe that the proposition for a division by the forty-ninth degree and the Straits of Fuca—which we have hitherto called Mr. Dargan's, but of which we hear no more under that name—would have been at any time and under any circumstances received with as much satisfaction as now. We are more and more convinced by the advices which we have lately
[42] *received, that the American cabinet will not and—if it would—could not make any larger concession. It is, we believe, all that any American statesman could hope to carry, and we are equally satisfied, that on our part, after so much delay and complication, and considering it in its future effect on the tranquillity of the district itself, it is the best for our interests and sufficient for our honor. * * *

No. 37.

Mr. Buchanan to Mr. McLane.

DEPARTMENT OF STATE,
Washington, February 26, 1846.

SIR: * * * * * *

The President may consent to consult the Senate on any British proposition.

The President, since the date of his message, has seen no cause to change his opinion, either in regard to our title to Oregon, or to the manner in which it ought to be asserted. But the Federal Constitution has made the Senate, to a certain extent, a co-ordinate branch of the treaty-making power. Without their advice and consent no treaty can be concluded. This power could not be intrusted to wiser or better hands. Besides, in their legislative character, they constitute a portion of the war-making, as in their executive capacity they compose a part of the treaty-making power. They are the representatives of the sovereign States of this Union, and are regarded as the best index of the opinion of their constituents. A rejection of the British ultimatum might probably lead to war, and as a branch of the legislative power, it would be incumbent upon them to authorize the necessary preparations to render this war successful. Under these considerations, the President, in deference to the Senate, and to the true theory of the constitutional responsibilities of the different branches of the Government, will forego his own opinions so far as to submit to that body any proposition which may be made by the British Government not, in his judgment, wholly inconsistent with the right and honor of the country. Neither is the fact to be disguised that, from the speeches and proceedings in the Senate, it is probable that a proposition to adjust the Oregon question on the parallel of 49° would receive their favorable consideration. * * * *

[43] *The President is desirous so to adjust the Oregon question as not to leave open any source from which might proceed new difficulties and new dangers, again to threaten the peace of the two countries. * * * *

The President wishes not to leave open any source of new difficulties.

The President would also consent, though with reluctance, to submit to the Senate the second proposition suggested by you, dividing the territory in dispute between the two countries, "by extending the boundary to the Pacific by the forty-ninth parallel and the Straits of Fuca;" but without the superadded words "with free ports to both nations." These words are indefinite, and he cannot infer from them the extent of your meaning. In case the first proposition to which you refer should be made by the British government, the President would not object to the terms of his offer of the 12th July last, "to make free to Great Britain any port or ports on Vancouver Island south of this parallel, which the British Government may desire." If the cape of this island should, however, be surrendered to Great Britain, as would be the case under the second proposition, then he would consider the question in regard to free ports as terminated. I need not enlarge to you upon the inconvenience, not to say impossibility, under our system of government, after one or more States shall have been established in Oregon, (an event not far distant,) of making any of their ports free to Great Britain, or any other nation. Besides, our system of drawbacks secures to other nations the material advantages of free ports without their inconveniences.

The President would submit to the Senate the line of 49° and the Straits of Fuca.

There is one point which it is necessary to guard, whether the first or the second proposition should be submitted by the British government. The Strait of Fuca is an arm of the sea, and under the public law all nations would possess the same right to navigate it, throughout its whole extent, as they now have to the navigation of the British Channel. Still, to prevent future difficulties, this ought to be clearly and distinctly understood. * * * * * *

JAMES BUCHANAN.

LOUIS MCLANE, Esq., *&c., &c., &c.*

[44] *No. 38.

Mr. McLane to Mr. Buchanan.

LONDON, *March* 3, 1846.

SIR: * * * * * *

Mr. McLane reports that Great Britain will assent to no better partition than the line of 49° and Fuca's Straits.

I sought and obtained an interview with Lord Aberdeen on the 25th February. * * *

I have little or no expectation that this government will offer or assent to a better partition than the extension of a line on the forty-ninth parallel to the Straits of Fuca, and thence down the middle of the strait to the Pacific; and if the line of the forty-ninth parallel should intersect the Columbia, according to Mr. Gallatin's proposition, at a point from which it is navigable to the ocean, with the free navigation of that river, at least for such a period as may be necessary for the trade of the Hudson's Bay Company, they will also, I am quite sure, expect some arrangements for the protection of the present agricultural settlements of British subjects south of the forty-ninth degree of latitude, and north of the Columbia. If the Columbia River be not navigable from the point at which it would be intersected by the extension of a line along the forty-ninth parallel, I believe it quite certain that the navigation of the river would not be insisted on.

* * * * * * *

I must, however, repeat the opinion that, whatever may be the result of any present expectation, and according to any view it may take of the question, this government will not be likely to propose or assent to a basis of partition different from that I have already stated in the foregoing part of this dispatch. If there be a disposition on the part of our Government to treat upon that basis, I have great confidence that the negotiation would result in an amicable settlement of the question.

* * * * * * *

LOUIS McLANE.

Hon. JAMES BUCHANAN,
Secretary of State.

---

[45] *No. 39.

Mr. Bates to Mr. Sturgis.

LONDON, *April* 3, 1846.

The Oregon question sure to be settled on the American basis.

MY DEAR SIR: The Oregon question is now as good as settled, provided the Senate, by a good majority, pass their pacific resolutions. Your pamphlet, by fixing public attention on a reasonable mode of settlement, on both sides of the water has done more than all the diplomatic notes. I claim the merit of suggesting the mode of getting rid of the question of the Hudson's Bay Company and the navigation of the Columbia, by allowing the company to enjoy it for a fixed number of years. Mr. McLane and the Government had not thought of it. In the Quarterly is an article written by Croker, which adopts completely these views. * * *

JOSHUA BATES.

No. 40.

Mr. McLane to Mr. Buchanan.

LONDON, *April* 17, 1846.

SIR: * * * * * *

My dispatch of the 17th of March, after an opportunity had been afforded of seeing and reflecting upon your final answer to Mr. Pakenham's proposal to arbitrate, acquainted you that very soon after the date of the last note of the Earl of Aberdeen to Mr. Pakenham, I had positively ascertained that this government would take no further step toward renewing the negotiation until after Congress had finally acted upon the question of notice.

The British government wait for Congress to give notice of the abolition of the treaty for the non-occupation of Oregon.

* * * * * * *

LOUIS McLANE.

HON. JAMES BUCHANAN,
Secretary of State.

---

[46] *No. 41.

Extracts from the speech of Mr. Dix, of New York, in the Senate, February 19, 1846.

* * * "The historical facts are too well authenticated to be permanently misunderstood. They were so well known at the time, that even the rivalry—not to say the detraction—of the day conceded to Gray the merit of the discovery by designating the river by the name he gave it—the name of the vessel that first entered its waters." * * * "Look at the map of Oregon on your table, by Captain Wilkes, and you will find Gray's Bay, so named by Broughton, (see Vancouver's Journal, vol. 3, p. 92,) on the north side of the Columbia, and higher up than Astoria. According to Gray's own log, he anchored, the day he discovered and entered the river, ten miles above the entrance, and three days after he sailed twelve or fifteen miles higher up. He must, therefore, have been from six to fifteen miles above the site of the settlement at Astoria." * * *

Wilkes's map of Oregon the map used by the American Senate.

No. 42.

Mr. McLane to Mr. Buchanan.

LONDON, *May* 18, 1846.

SIR: * * * * * * * *

In my last dispatch, dated on the 3d instant, after an interview with Lord Aberdeen, I informed you that as soon as he received official intelligence of the Senate's vote upon the resolution of notice, he would proceed finally to consider the subject of Oregon, and direct Mr. Pakenham to submit a further proposition upon the part of this government; and also that it was understood that

Mr. McLane and Lord Aberdeen discuss the Oregon question.

he would not be prevented from taking this course by any disagreement between the two Houses as to the form of the notice.

I have now to acquaint you that, after the receipt of your dispatches on the 15th instant by the Caledonia, I had a lengthened conference with Lord Aberdeen; on which occasion the resumption of the negotiation for an amicable settlement of the Oregon question, and
[47] the nature of the proposition he contemplated *submitting for
that purpose, formed the subject of a full and free conversation.

I have now to state that instructions will be transmitted to Mr. Pakenham by the steamer of to-morrow, to submit a new and further proposition on the part of this government for a partition of the territory in dispute.

The proposition, most probably, will offer substantially—

The British government will offer to divide the territory by the parallel of 49°, Birch's Bay, Canal de Haro, and Fuca's Straits.

First. To divide the territory by the extension of the line on the parallel of forty-nine to the sea—that is to say, to the arm of the sea called Birch's Bay; thence by the Canal de Haro and Straits of Fuca to the ocean, and confirming to the United States—what indeed they would possess without any special confirmation—the right freely to use and navigate the strait throughout its extent.

Second. To secure to the British subjects occupying lands, forts, and stations anywhere in the region north of the Columbia and south of the forty-ninth parallel, a perpetual title to all their lands and stations of which they may be in actual occupation; liable, however, in all respects, as I understand, to the jurisdiction and sovereignty of the United States as citizens of the United States. Similar privileges will be offered to be extended to citizens of the United States, who may have settlements north of the forty-ninth parallel; though I presume it is pretty well understood that there are no settlements upon which this nominal mutuality could operate. I have no means of accurately ascertaining the extent of the present British settlements between the Columbia and the forty-ninth parallel. They are not believed by Lord Aberdeen to be numerous, however, consisting, as he supposes, of a few private farms and two or three forts and stations. I have already, in a previous dispatch, taken the liberty to remind you that by their charter the Hudson's Bay Company are prohibited from acquiring title to lands, and that the occupations to be affected by this reservation have been made either by the squatters of that company, or by the Puget's Sound Land Company, for the purpose of evading the prohibition of the Hudson's Bay charter.

They are, in point of fact, also, according to Captain Wilkes's account, cultivated and used chiefly by the persons employed in the service of the former company, and as auxiliary to their general business of hunting and trapping, rather than with a view, as it has been generally supposed, of colonizing or of permanent settlement.
[48] *Lastly. The proposition will demand for the Hudson's Bay
Company the right of freely navigating the Columbia River.

It will, however, as I understand, disclaim the idea of sovereignty or of the right of exercising any jurisdiction or police whatever on the part of this government or of the company, and will contemplate only the right of navigating the river upon the same footing and according to the same regulations as may be applicable to the citizens of the United States. * * * *

It is scarcely necessary for me to state that the proposition as now submitted has not received my countenance.

Although it has been no easy task, under all the circumstances, to lead to a re-opening of the negotiations by any proposition from this government, and to induce it to adopt the parallel of forty-nine as the basis of a boundary, nevertheless I hoped it would have been in my power to give the present proposition a less objectionable shape, and I most deeply lament my inability to accomplish it. I have, therefore, felt it my duty to discourage any expectation that it would be accepted by the President, or, if submitted to that body, approved by the Senate.

I do not think there can be much doubt, however, that an impression has been produced here that the Senate would accept the proposition now offered, at least without material modification, and that the President would not take the responsibility of rejecting it without consulting the Senate. * * * * *

It must not escape observation that, during the preceding administration of our Government, the extension of the line on the forty-ninth parallel to the Straits of Fuca, as now proposed by Lord Aberdeen, was actually suggested by my immediate predecessor, (Mr. Everett,) as one he thought his Government might accept. * * * * * * *

The above proposed boundary-line is that suggested by Mr. Everett.

I have myself always believed, if the extension of the line of boundary on the forty-ninth parallel by the Straits of Fuca to the sea would be acceptable to our Government, that the demand of a right freely to navigate the Columbia River could be compromised upon a point of time, by conceding it for such period as might be necessary for the trade of the Hudson's Bay Company, north or south of the forty-ninth parallel. * * * * *

[49] *I have not the least reason to suppose it would be possible to obtain the extension of the forty-ninth parallel to the sea, so as to give the southern cape of Vancouver Island to the United States.

* * * * * * *

LOUIS McLANE.

Hon. JAMES BUCHANAN,
Secretary of State.

No. 43.

The Earl of Aberdeen to Mr. Pakenham.

[Extract.]

MAY 18, 1846.

The boundary (said Lord Aberdeen) having been fixed by the convention of 1818, between the possessions of Great Britain and the United States, and the line of demarcation having been carried along the forty-ninth parallel of latitude for a distance of eight hundred or one thousand miles, through an unfrequented and unknown country, from the Lake of the Woods to the Rocky Mountains, it appeared to the Government of the United States that it was a natural and reasonable suggestion that this line should be continued along the same parallel for about half this distance, and through a country as little known or frequented from the Rocky Mountains to the sea. And, indeed, with reference to such a country, the extension of any line of boundary already fixed might equally have been suggested, whether it had been carried along the forty-ninth or any other parallel of latitude.

Lord Aberdeen offers the forty-ninth parallel, retaining the whole of Vancouver Island for England.

On the other hand, however, it may justly be observed that any division of territory in which both parties possess equal rights ought to proceed on a principle of mutual convenience rather than on the adherence to an imaginary geographical line; and in this respect it must be confessed that the boundary thus proposed would be manifestly defective. It would exclude us from every commodious or accessible harbor on the coast; it would deprive us of our long-established means of water-communication with the interior for the prosecution of our trade; and it would interfere with the possessions of British colonists resident in a district in which it is believed that scarcely an American citizen, as a settler, has ever set his foot.

[50] *You will accordingly propose to the American Secretary of State that the line of demarcation should be continued along the forty-ninth parallel, from the Rocky Mountains to the sea-coast, and from thence, in a southerly direction, through the center of King George's Sound and the Straits of Juan de Fuca, to the Pacific Ocean, leaving the whole of Vancouver Island, with its ports and harbors, in the possession of Great Britain.

No. 44.

Extract from the speech of Mr. Benton, of Missouri, in the Senate, June 18, 1846. Debate on the ratification of the Oregon treaty. Appendix to the Congressional Globe, first session Twenty-ninth Congress. 1845–'46. Page 867.

Mr. Benton finds that the boundary-line passes through the Canal de Haro.

"The first article of the treaty—and it is the main one, and almost the whole treaty—is in the very words which I myself would have used if the two governments had left it to me to draw the boundary-line between them. The line established by that article—the prolongation of the boundary on the east side of the Rocky Mountains—follows the parallel of 49° to the sea, with a slight deflection through the Straits of Fuca, to avoid cutting the south end of Vancouver Island. * * * * *

When the line reaches the channel which separates Vancouver Island from the continent, (which it does within sight of the mouth of Fraser's River,) it proceeds to the middle of the channel, and thence, turning south, through the channel De Haro, (wrongly written Arro on the maps,) to the Straits of Fuca; and then west through the middle of that strait to the sea." * * * * *

No. 45.

Extract from the speech of the Earl of Aberdeen in the House of Lords, Monday, June 29, 1846. (Hansard's Debates 87, 1038.)

Lord Aberdeen and Parliament are aware of the interpretation given to the treaty by the U. S. Senate.

When I saw that the Senate and the House of Representatives had adopted resolutions of such a conciliatory and friendly
[51] *description, I did not delay for a moment putting aside all ideas of diplomatic etiquette, which might have led me to expect that some steps would be taken on

the other side; but, without waiting a moment, I prepared the draught of a convention, which was sent by the packet of the 18th of May to Mr. Pakenham, to be proposed for the acceptance of the United States Government. I have brought with me a letter from Mr. Pakenham, which I received this morning, and from which I shall read an extract. The letter is dated the 13th of June, and Mr. Pakenham says:

In conformity with what I had the honor to state in my dispatch No. 68, of the 7th instant, the President sent a message on Wednesday last to the Senate, submitting for the opinion of that body the draught of a convention for the settlement of the Oregon question, which I was instructed by your lordship's dispatch, No. 19, of the 18th of May, to propose for the acceptance of the United States Government. After a few hours' deliberation on each of the three days, Wednesday, Thursday, and Friday, the Senate, by a majority of thirty-eight votes to twelve, adopted yesterday evening a resolution advising the President to accept the terms proposed by Her Majesty's government. The President did not hesitate to act on this advice; and Mr. Buchanan accordingly sent for me this morning, and informed me that the conditions offered by Her Majesty's government were accepted by the Government of the United States, without the addition or alteration of a single word.

Gratifying as this intelligence is, I feel it is but an act of duty and justice, as well as a pleasure, that I should bear the tribute of my testimony to the most friendly and conciliatory course which has been adopted by the United States minister in this country. That gentleman I have long known, and long had reason to esteem in official intercourse fifteen or sixteen years ago; and I am perfectly certain that, by every means in his power, he has contributed to this result. I am well assured that there is no person in this house or in this country who more cordially participates in the feeling of satisfaction which it is fitted to produce than Mr. McLane.

Lord Aberdeen's regard for Mr. McLane.

---

[52] *No. 46.

Extract from the speech of Sir Robert Peel in the House of Commons, Monday, June 29, 1846.

* * * Sir, if anything could have induced me to regret that decision on the part of the House which terminates the government, it would have been the wish that we should survive the day when intelligence might be received from the United States as to the result of our last attempt to adjust the differences with that country; differences which, unless speedily terminated, must probably involve both countries in the necessity of an appeal to arms. The House will probably recollect that after we had offered to leave the dispute respecting the territory of the Oregon to arbitration, and that offer had been rejected, the President of the United States sent a message to Congress, which led to discussions with regard to the termination of the convention entered into several years since, which provided for a temporary adjustment of our differences—at least, for a temporary avoidance of quarrel—and enabled the two countries jointly to occupy the territory of the Oregon. The two Houses of the American Congress advised the President to use his unquestionable power, and to signify to this country the desire of the United States to terminate, after the lapse of a year, the existing convention. They, however, added to that advice, which might, perhaps, otherwise have been considered of an unsatisfactory or hostile character, the declaration that they desired the notice for the termination of the convention to be given, in order that an amicable adjustment of the dispute

between the two countries might thereby be facilitated. It appeared to us that the addition of that conciliatory declaration—the expression of the hope that the termination of the convention might the more strongly impress upon the two countries the necessity of amicable adjustment—removed any barrier which diplomatic punctilios might have raised to a renewal by this country of the attempt to settle our differences with the United States. We did not hesitate, therefore, within two days after the receipt of that intelligence—we did not hesitate, although the offer of arbitration made by us had been rejected—to do that which, in the present state of the protracted dispute, it became necessary to do, namely, not to propose renewed and
[53] lengthy negotiations, but to specify frankly and *without reserve,
what were the terms on which we could consent to a partition of the country of the Oregon. Sir, the President of the United States met us in a corresponding spirit. Whatever might have been the expressions heretofore used by him, however strongly he might have been personally committed to the adoption of a different course, he most wisely and patriotically determined at once to refer our proposals to the Senate—that authority of the United States whose consent is requisite for the conclusion of any negotiation of this kind; and the Senate, acting also in the same pacific spirit, has, I have the heartfelt satisfaction to state, at once advised acquiescence in the terms we offered. From the importance of the subject, and considering that this is the last day I shall have to address the House as a minister of the Crown, I may, perhaps, be allowed to state what are the proposals we made to the United States for the final settlement of the Oregon question. In order to prevent the necessity for renewed diplomatic negotiations, we prepared and sent out the form of a convention, which we trusted the United States would accept. The first article of that convention was to this effect, that—

The words of the treaty were chosen by the British ministry.

From the point on the forty-ninth parallel of north latitude, where the boundary laid down in existing treaties and conventions between Great Britain and the United States terminates, the line of boundary between the territories of her Britannic Majesty and those of the United States shall be continued westward along the said forty-ninth parallel of north latitude to the middle of the channel which separates the continent from Vancouver's Island, and thence southerly, through the middle of the said channel, and of Fuca's Straits, to the Pacific Ocean; provided, however, that the navigation of the said channel and straits, south of the forty-ninth parallel of north latitude, remain free and open to both parties.

Those who remember the local conformation of that country will understand that that which we proposed is the continuation of the forty-ninth parallel of latitude till it strikes the Straits of Fuca; that that parallel should not be continued as a boundary across Vancouver's Island, thus depriving us of a part of Vancouver's Island, but that the middle of the channel shall be the future boundary, thus leaving us in possession of the whole of Vancouver's Island, with equal right to the navigation of the straits. * * * Sir, I will not occupy the attention of the House with the mere details of this convention. I have read the important articles. On this
[54] very day, *on my return from my mission to Her Majesty to offer
the resignation of Her Majesty's servants, I had the satisfaction of finding an official letter from Mr. Pakenham, intimating in the following terms the acceptance of our proposals, and giving an assurance of the immediate termination of our differences with the United States:

Sir Robert Peel's interpretation of the treaty.

WASHINGTON, *June* 13, 1846.

MY LORD: In conformity with what I had the honor to state in my dispatch, No. 68, of the 7th instant, the President sent a message on Wednesday last to the Senate, submitting for the opinion of that body the draught of a convention for the settlement of the Oregon question, which I was instructed by your lordship's dispatch, No. 19, of the 18th of May, to propose for the acceptance of the United States.

After a few hours' deliberation on each of the three days, Wednesday, Thursday, and Friday, the Senate, by a majority of thirty-eight votes to twelve, adopted yesterday evening a resolution advising the President to accept the terms proposed by Her Majesty's government. The President did not hesitate to act on this advice, and Mr. Buchanan accordingly sent for me this morning, and informed me that the conditions offered by Her Majesty's government were accepted by the Government of the United States, without the addition or alteration of a single word.

I have the honor to be, &c.,

R. PAKENHAM.

The Right Hon. the EARL OF ABERDEEN, K. T., &c.

Sir Robert Peel declares every cause of dissension between Britain and America at an end.

Thus, sir, the governments of two great nations, impelled, I believe, by the public opinion of each country in favor of peace—by that opinion which ought to guide and influence statesmen—have, by moderation, by mutual compromise, averted the dreadful calamity of war between two nations of kindred origin and common language, the breaking out of which might have involved the civilized world in general conflict. A single year, perhaps a single month, of such a war would have been more costly than the value of the whole territory that was the object of dispute. But this evil has been averted consistently with perfect honor on the part of the American Government, and on the part of those who have at length closed, I trust, every cause of dissension between the two countries. * * Sir, I do cordially rejoice that, in surrendering
[55] power at the feet of a majority of this House, I have the *opportunity of giving them the official assurance that every cause of quarrel with that great country on the other side of the Atlantic is amicably terminated.

No. 47.

Mr. McLane to Lord Palmerston.

JULY 13, 1846.

The American President regards the treaty of June, 1846, as establishing amity.

* * The treaty, as concluded and ratified by the President, appearing to be in all in respects identical with the project admitted of Her Majesty's Government, the ratification on the part of Her Majesty may be anticipated as not likely to occasion any hesitation; and the undersigned has been instructed to express a desire, on the part of the President, that he should be able, before the adjournment of Congress, to acquaint that body with the final consummation of an act which, he cherishes the hope, may be regarded as establishing the foundation of a cordial and lasting amity between the two countries. * * * * *

LOUIS McLANE.

38 HARLEY STREET, *July* 13, 1846.

No. 48.

Extract from Exploration du territoire de l'Orégon, etc., exécutée pendant les années 1840, 1841, *et* 1842, *par M. Duflot de Mofras, attaché à la légation de France à Mexique ; oüvrage publié par ordre du roi, sous les auspices de M. le Maréchal Soult, Duc de Dalmatie, presidént du conseil, et de M. le ministre des affaires etrangères. Paris,* 1844. *Tome II, p.* 135.

Mofras describes the channel of Haro as the best.

Dans l'espace qui s'étend de la terre ferme jusqu'à la partie est de la grande île de Quadra, il existe une foule de petites îles qui, malgré les abris sûrs qu'elles offrent aux navires, présentent à la navigation de grandes difficultiés. Le passage le plus facile est par le Canal de Haro, entre l'île de Quadra et Van Couver et celle de San Juan.

---

[56] *No. 49.

Paley's Works, edition of 1825, *vol. iv, page* 85.

II. In what sense promises are to be interpreted.

Ambiguity no escape from the proper sense of a promise.

Where the terms of promise admit of more senses than one, the promise is to be performed "in that sense in which the promiser apprehended at the time that the promisee received it."

* * * * * * *

This will not differ from the actual intention of the promiser, where the promise is given without collusion or reserve; but we put the rule in the above form, to exclude evasion in cases in which the popular meaning of a phrase, and the strict grammatical signification of the words, differ; or, in general, wherever the promiser attempts to make his escape through some ambiguity in the expressions which he used.

* * * * * * *

No. 50.

Secretary Monroe to the American commissioners for treating for peace with Great Britain.

DEPARTMENT OF STATE, *March* 22, 1814.

American commissioners instructed in 1814 to yield nothing south of 49°.

GENTLEMEN: Should a treaty be concluded with Great Britain, and a reciprocal restitution of territory be agreed on, you will have it in recollection that the United States had in their possession, at the commencement of the war, a post at the mouth of the river Columbia, which commanded the river, which ought to be comprised in the stipulation, should the possession have been wrested from us during the war. On no pretext can the British government set up a claim to territory south of the northern boundary of the United States. It is not believed that they have any claim whatever to territory on the Pacific Ocean. You will, however, be careful, should a definition of boundary be attempted, not to countenance, in any manner, or in any quarter, a pretension in the British government to territory south of that line.

JAMES MONROE.

II.

CASE

OF THE

GOVERNMENT OF HER BRITANNIC MAJESTY,

SUBMITTED TO THE

ARBITRATION AND AWARD

OF

HIS MAJESTY THE EMPEROR OF GERMANY,

IN ACCORDANCE WITH

ARTICLE XXXIV OF THE TREATY BETWEEN GREAT BRITAIN AND THE UNITED STATES OF AMERICA, SIGNED AT WASHINGTON, MAY 8, 1871.

TABLE OF CONTENTS

APPENDIX.

CHARTS.

No. II.

A chart showing part of the coast of Northwest America, with the tracks of His Majesty's sloop Discovery, and armed tender Chatham, commanded by George Vancouver, esq., and prepared under his immediate inspection by Lieutenant Joseph Baker, in which the continental shore has been traced and determined from latitude 50° 30′ north and longitude 236° 12′ east to latitude 52° 15′ north and longitude 232° 40′ east at the different periods shown by the tracks. (Published at London in 1798.)

No III.

North America, west coast.—Haro and Rosario Straits, surveyed by Captain G. H. Richards and the officers of Her Majesty's ship Plumper, 1858-'59; and the shores of Juan de Fuca Strait to Admiralty Inlet. (From Captain H. Kellett's survey, 1847.)

No. IV.

America, northwest coast.—Strait of Juan de Fuca, surveyed by Captain Henry Kellett, R. N., 1847; Haro and Rosario Straits, by Captain G. H. Richards, R. N., 1858; Admiralty Inlet and Puget Sound, by the United States exploring expedition, 1841; south coast of Cape Flattery, by the same, in 1853.

No. V.

Map of Oregon and Upper California, from the surveys of John Charles Frémont and other authorities. (Drawn by Charles Preuss, under the orders of the Senate of the United States. Washington City, 1848.)

CASE OF THE GOVERNMENT OF HER BRITANNIC MAJESTY.

His Majesty the Emperor of Germany having consented to accept the office of arbitrator between the Government of the United States of America and the Government of Her Britannic Majesty, under the provisions of Article XXXIV of the treaty concluded at Washington on the 8th May, 1871, between the United States and Her Britannic Majesty, the Government of Her Britannic Majesty submits to the consideration of His Majesty the Emperor of Germany, in pursuance of Article XXXVI of the said treaty, the following case:

THE QUESTION FOR DECISION.

The question submitted to the decision of His Imperial Majesty affects so much of the boundary-line between Her Britannic Majesty's possessions in North America and the territories of the United States as is comprised between the continent of America and Vancouver Island. Charts Nos. 3 and 4

The boundary-line is described in the treaty between the United States and Great Britain, of June 15, 1846, in the following general terms: Appendix No. 2.

TREATY OF JUNE 15, 1846.

From the point on the forty-ninth parallel of north latitude, where the boundary-line laid down in existing treaties and conventions Article I.
[2] between *Great Britain and the United States terminates, the line of boundary between the territories of Her Britannic Majesty and those of the United States shall be continued westward, along the said forty-ninth parallel of north latitude, to the middle of the channel which separates the continent from Vancouver Island, and thence southerly, through the middle of the said channel and of Fuca's Straits, to the Pacific Ocean; provided, however, that the navigation of the whole of the said channel and straits south of the forty-ninth parallel of north latitude remain free and open to both parties.

The question more immediately submitted to the decision of His Imperial Majesty is described in Article XXXIV of the treaty of 8th May, 1871, in the following terms: Appendix No. 1.

TREATY OF MAY 8, 1871.

Whereas it was stipulated by Article I of the treaty concluded at Washington on the 15th June, 1846, between Her Britannic Majesty and the United States, that the line of boundary between the territories of the United States and those of Her Britannic Majesty, from the point on the forty-ninth parallel of north latitude, up to which it had already been ascertained, should be continued westward along the said parallel of north latitude to the middle of the channel which separates the continent from Vancouver Island, and thence southerly through the middle of the said channel and of Fuca Straits to the Pacific Ocean; and whereas the commissioners appointed by the two high contracting parties to determine that portion of the boundary which runs southerly through the middle of the channel aforesaid were unable to agree upon the same; and whereas the government of Her Britannic Majesty claims that such boundary-line should, under the terms of the treaty above recited, be run through the Rosario Straits, and the Government of the United States claims that it should be run through the Canal de Haro, it is agreed that the respective claims of the government of Her Britannic Majesty and the Government of the United States shall be sub-
[3] mitted to the *arbitration and award of His Majesty the Emperor of Germany, who, having regard for the above-mentioned article of the said treaty, shall decide thereupon finally and without appeal which of those claims is most in accordance with the true interpretation of the treaty of June 15, 1846.

It will be observed by His Imperial Majesty, that whereas the treaty of June, 1846, speaks only of the channel which separates the continent from Vancouver Island, through the middle of which the boundary line is to be run, the treaty of 1871 speaks of the Rosario Straits and the Canal de Haro as if there was more than one channel between the continent and Vancouver Island through which the boundary line may be run and be continued through the middle of Fuca's Straits to the Pacific Ocean.

It will be convenient, therefore, to bring to the attention of His Imperial Majesty at once the hydrography of the entire space between the continent and Vancouver Island south of the forty-ninth parallel of north latitude, according to the best information which is in the possession of Her Majesty's government.

THE STRAIT OF GEORGIA.

The forty-ninth parallel of north latitude, continued westwardly, according to the provisions of the treaty of June 15, 1846, Chart No. 4. strikes the upper waters of the ancient Gulf of Georgia, designated by the Spaniards El Canal del Rosario, in Semiahmoo Bay. These waters are now termed, in British charts, the Strait of Georgia. Continued across that bay, the parallel line intersects a narrow peninsula, the extreme of which was named, by Vancouver, Point Roberts. This point extends about one and three-quarter miles (English) south of the parallel line. Continued across the Strait of Georgia, the parallel line strikes at an acute angle a line drawn southerly through the middle of the channel.

Respecting so much of the boundary-line as extends to the middle of the Strait of Georgia, there is no controversy between the high contracting parties to the treaty of June 15, 1846, that it terminates at a point on the parallel of 49° north latitude in the middle of the
[4] Strait of Georgia. It is with regard to the line to be *drawn southerly from the parallel of 49° north latitude through the middle of the channel that the commissioners of the high contracting parties have been unable to agree. The true direction of such a line drawn toward the Strait of Fuca would appear, from a survey of the waters, to be southeast by east for a distance of about nineteen miles, where the Strait of Georgia gradually expands to a width of nearly forty miles, and may be said to lose the characteristic features of a single strait.

The space now entered upon is encumbered by numerous islands, varying in size and character, among which are three navigable channels leading into Fuca's Straits.

The most eastern of the three channels has been of late termed in British charts the Rosario Straits, and in American charts Ringgold's Channel. The most western is termed in British charts the Haro Strait, and in American charts the Canal de Arro. The latter term has been borrowed from the Spaniards, who term the lower part of the strait the Canal de Lopez de Haro.

There are, besides, other narrow passages; but they may scarcely be considered as highways for ships passing from the Strait of Georgia into Fuca's Straits.

THE ROSARIO STRAIT.

From a point midway between Saturna Island and the continent and four miles (English) south of Point Whitehorn, on the shore Chart No. 4. of the continent, the waters of the Strait of Georgia merge on almost the same line of bearing (southeast by east) into those of the Rosario Strait, passing eastward of the small islands of Patos, Sucia, Matia, and Clark, thence between the large islands of Lummi and Orcas. At Point Lawrence, which is the eastward point of Orcas, the strait trends a little westward of south for three or four miles, (English,) and then leads by a due south course into the head-waters of the Straits of Fuca, the whose distance from the point above mentioned as where the Strait of Georgia merges in the Rosario Strait, being thirty miles, (English.)

The width of the Rosario Strait varies from six to one and one-third miles, (English.) At its northern entrance, between the Island of
[5] Sucia and Sandy Point, on the *continent, it is six miles (English) across; but the Alden Bank lies almost between those two points.

There is, however, a clear passage of four miles (English) eastward of the bank, and a passage of one and a half miles (English) westward. The least water on the shoal part is two and one-fourth fathoms (English.) The bank itself is an extensive patch, being two and a half miles (English) north and south, and more than one mile (English) east and west. On the greater part of it, anchorage may be had in from five to nine fathoms, (English.)

The bank is not really an impediment to the channel. The shoal part of it, which would be dangerous to a ship, is of small extent, and is easily avoided by good natural leading-marks during the day, and by the lead at night; while it is a manifest advantage to a sailing-vessel to be able to anchor in a moderate depth should calms, strong tides, or fogs render it desirable, and when it would probably be impossible to fetch a harbor. The width of the Rosario Strait, southward of the Alden Bank, soon decreases to three and a half miles and two miles, (English,) which latter is about its average breadth. Between Cypress and Blakely Islands it is as narrow as one and one-third miles; but soon opens out again to two and a half miles. The Bird and Belle Rocks lie almost in the center of the strait, three and a half miles (English) within its southern entrance. The former is an extensive rock, 15 feet above high water. The latter lies north-northeast of it, more than half a mile, (English,) and is covered until near low water. The tides, which sweep with considerable strength over these rocks, are calculated to render the passage between them dangerous to sailing-vessels in calms or fogs; but there is a good passage on either side of them; that to the eastward of them being one and three-fourths miles (English) wide, while the width of that to the westward is one and a half miles, (English.) The Williamson and Denis Rocks, which extend about one-third of a mile off the southwest side of Allan Island, are easily avoided. The former is 22 feet above high water; the latter awash at low spring tides.

The Davidson Rock, occasionally uncovering itself at low spring tides, lies three-fourths of a mile (English) east by south of Colville
[6] Island, *and is easily avoided, as it is marked by kelp. The only other hidden danger which has been discovered to exist in Rosario Strait is the Panama Reef, which extends one-third of a mile (English) off the northwest end of Sinclair Island. This reef is marked by kelp, and uncovers itself at low water. A rock, also, which is about the same distance west of Rock Islet, near the north end of Cypress Island, is also marked by kelp, and uncovers itself at low water.

The tides in Rosario Strait run with considerable strength. In the narrow part between Cypress and Blakely Islands they have been found, during spring tides, to exceed six miles (English) an hour; in other parts of the strait their velocity is from two to five miles, (English.) The depth of water, however, being from twenty-five to thirty-five fathoms over the greater part of the strait, admits of vessels anchoring anywhere, if it should be necessary; but the most desirable stopping-places are Fidalgo Bay, on the western side of the island of the same name; Walmouth Bight, on the southeast side of Lopez Island; the Guemes Passage and Strawberry Bay, on the west side of Cypress Island.

THE CANAL DE HARO.

Chart No. 4.

On the other hand, the Canal de Haro, from the point where the Strait of Georgia may be said to lose the characteristic features of a single strait, takes a direction about southwest and a half south between the east point of Saturna Island and the small Island of Patos, for a distance of eight miles, (English;) it then turns to the westward, and runs in a direction southwest by west for almost an equal distance, until between Stuart and Moresby Islands, where it turns to the southward, and runs for a farther distance of about twenty miles, (English,) trending to the southeast, when it strikes the Straits of Fuca.

The width of the Canal de Haro at its northern entrance, between East Point and Patos Island, is two and one-half miles, (English,) where, from the strong tides and irregularity of the bottom, heavy races occur; about the same width is carried for twelve miles, (English,) when,
[7] between Turn Point and Moresby *Island, it decreases to something less than two miles, (English,) and the narrowest part, which is between Stuart Island and Cooper's Reef, is one and three-fourths miles, (English.) After passing south of Henry Island, it gradually widens, and is more than six miles in breadth when it enters the Straits of Fuca.

The water is deeper and the depth is more irregular in the Canal de Haro than in the Rosario Strait, and though the tides run with about equal velocity in both, the former is more subject to irregularities and races.

The eastern or San Juan shore of the canal is bold and steep.

After passing San Juan, when northward of Henry Island, very strong and irregular tides are met with, and there are rocks off Spieden Island which must not be approached too close.

Off Turn Point, on Stuart Island, there are strong whirls and eddy tides; and, unless with a commanding breeze, a sailing-vessel is liable to be turned round by them and lose the power of her helm.

On the western side of the canal the principal dangers are—

The Zero Rock, and its neighboring shoals in Cormorant Bay; also the Kelp Reefs, which extend southward and eastward of Darcy Island.

Cormorant Bay, however, affords good anchorage. To enter it vessels may safely stand in midway between Gordon Head and Zero Rock, and anchorage in nine fathoms, where they will be free from any considerable tide. The Low and Bare Islands, northward of Sidney Island, should not be approached very close, and Cooper's Reef should be particularly avoided. The flood-tide sets strongly to the northwest through the Miner's Channel, and sailing-vessels would be very liable to be set into it during light winds.

Plumper Sound, on the northern side of the bend of the strait, between Stuart Island and the east point of Saturna Island, is a good anchorage, with a moderate depth of water for vessels seeking shelter, and one of the few among the group of islands, which is of easy access to a sailing-vessel.

[8] Cowlitz Bay, on the western side of Waldron *Island, is also an excellent stopping-place, easy of access or egress.

There are two small anchorages in Stuart Island, Reid and Prevost Harbors, but they are only suited to small vessels or steamers.

A vessel passing through the Canal de Haro may seek shelter in any of the above-mentioned anchorages, but the great depth and irregular nature of the bottom would render it impossible for her to anchor anywhere in the main channel.

Such is the most complete account which Her Majesty's Government is able to lay before His Imperial Majesty respecting the hydrography of the two channels which are in controversy.

ORIGIN OF THE NAMES OF THE TWO CHANNELS.

With regard to the origin of the respective names of the two channels there is some uncertainty. From an account published by Mr. Robert Greenhow, the librarian of the Department of State of the United States, in his "History of Oregon and California," (Boston, 1845,) it would appear that, in the summer of 1790, an attempt was made by the Spaniards to explore the waters supposed to be identical with a north-west passage leading into the Polar Sea, which, according to an ancient tradition, had been discovered in the sixteenth century by a Greek pilot, called commonly Juan de Fuca. For that purpose, to quote Mr. Greenhow's words, (History, p. 221,) "Elisa, the commandant of Nootka, detached Lieutenant Quimper, in the sloop Princess Royal, who traced the passage in an eastwardly direction, examining both its shores to the distance of about a hundred miles from its mouth, when it was observed to branch off into a number of smaller passages toward the south, the east, and the north, some of which were channels between islands, while others appeared to extend far into the interior. Quimper was unable, from want of time, to penetrate any of these passages; and he could do no more than note the positions of their entrances and of several harbors, all of which are now well known, though they are generally dis-
[9] tinguished by names *different from those assigned to them by the Spaniards. Among these passages and harbors were the Canal de Caamano, afterward named by Vancouver Admiralty Inlet; the Boca de Flon, or Deception Passage; the Canal de Guemes, and the Canal de Haro, which may still be found under those names in English charts, extending northward from the eastern end of the strait; Port Quadra, the Port Discovery of Vancouver, said to be one of the best harbors on the Pacific side of America, with Port Quimper near it on the west; and Port Nunez Gaona, called Poverty Cove by the American fur-traders, situated a few miles east of Cape Flattery, where the Spaniards attempted, in 1792, to form a settlement. Having performed this duty as well as possible, under the circumstances in which he was placed, Quimper returned to Nootka, where he arrived in the beginning of August."

It is probable that it was upon the authority of Quimper, who was an ensign of the royal navy of Spain, that the name of the *Canal de Haro* was given to the strait which separates Vancouver Island from the island of San Juan, in the Spanish chart of the discoveries made on the northeast coast of America, annexed to the narrative of the expedition of the Spanish exploring vessels, Sutil and Mexicana, which was published at Madrid in 1802, by order of the King of Spain. Chart No. 1.

A very brief allusion is made in the first chapter of that narrative to Appendix No. 4. Quimper's expedition. He is stated to have sailed from the Port of Nootka on May 31, 1790, to have reconnoitered the Port of Claucaud, (in Vancouver Island,) to have entered afterward into the Canal of Fuca, to have visited certain ports and part of the coast, to have taken surveys, and to have retired on the 1st of August, the weather not permitting him to continue his labors.

Mr. Greenhow cites, as his authority, the journal of Quimper's voyage, among the manuscripts obtained from the hydrographical department at Madrid.

On the other hand, the name of *Rosario Channel* appears, from the narrative of the Sutil and Mexicana, to have originated with
[10] Lieutenant *Elisa, who, prior to the arrival of those vessels, had penetrated into the upper waters, now called the Strait of Georgia, and had given to them the name of "El Canal del Rosario." Appendix No. 4. That name is accordingly given to those waters in the chart which represents the course of that expedition. Vancouver, on Chart No. 2. the other hand, in his chart, to which reference will be made hereafter, assigns that name to certain narrow waters farther north, which separate the continent from the island now called Texada. How the name has come to be applied in modern days to the waters of the Strait of Georgia, as they are traced southerly through the islands until they join the headquarters of the Straits of Fuca, does not appear. No name was in use at the time when the treaty of June 15, 1846, was concluded, to distinguish these waters from the upper waters. *The fact, however, is clear, that the name assigned by the Spaniards to the upper waters of the ancient Gulf of Georgia is used in the present day to denote the channel which Her Majesty's government maintains to be the true continuation of that strait.*

The expedition of the Sutil and Mexicana, in 1792, appears to have Appendix No. 4. Chart No. 1. ascended the Straits of Fuca to its headwaters, having touched first at Port Cordova, (now Esquimalt Harbor,) at the southern extremity of Vancouver Island. It thence proceeded between the Island of Bonilla (Smith's Island) and the southeast point of Lopez Island, at that time believed to be one and the same island with San Juan, until it reached the mouth of the Canal de Guemes, which separates the Island of Guemes from the continent. The expedition then passed up that strait into the "Seno de Gaston," now Bellingham Bay, and thence along the passage which separates the island of Pacheco (now Lummi Island) from the continent, into the upper waters now known as the Strait of Georgia. The two vessels continued their voyage onward in those waters past the promontory of Cepeda, afterward called Point Roberts by Vancouver, and were employed in reconnoitering the Boca de Florida, the first large inlet north of Point Roberts, when they were joined by Vancouver.

[11] The expedition under Vancouver, after making *a complete Chart No 2. survey of the Strait of Fuca up to its headwaters, had also passed onward through the channel between the the northeast point of Lopez Island and the continent; but instead of directing its course eastward, like the Sutil and Mexicana, on reaching Guemes Island, it continued its course northward along the main channel, which separates Blakely Island from Cypress Island, and anchored in Strawberry Bay.

Thence it pursued its course between Orcas Island and Lummi (Pacheco) Island, until it reached Birch Bay. Passing onward, it pursued a north and west course past Point Roberts, and fell in with the Spanish vessels Sutil and Mexicana, as already mentioned, off the first large inlet north of Point Roberts.

The narrative of Vancouver's expedition was made public in 1798, and there was annexed to it a chart, in which the course of the expedition is traced through the present Rosario Strait, and soundings are given at the entrance and in various parts of that strait, and in the upper waters of the ancient gulf in continuation of that strait.

The name of the Canal de Arro appears also in this chart, assigned to the lower part of the strait which separates Vancouver Island from San Juan; but the parts on the west and north shores of these waters are not shaded, intimating that Vancouver derived his information from Spanish authorities.

No soundings whatever are given of the Canal de Haro, either in Vancouver's chart or in the Spanish chart annexed to the narrative of the voyage of the Sutil and Mexicana.

The chart of Vancouver, in which the soundings, as above mentioned, are laid down, has been the guiding chart for all British vessels navigating the waters between the continent and Chart No. 2.
Vancouver's Island from 1798 until some time after 1847, when a more accurate survey was made of the Strait of Fuca by Captain Kellett; and there is evidence preserved in the logs of vessels in the service of the Hudson's Bay Company prior to that year that it was their invariable practice to use the Rosario Strait as the leading channel from Fuca's Strait into the upper waters now known as the Strait of Georgia.

[12] *Mr. Greenhow, in his "Memoir on the Northwest Coast of North America," (New York, 1840,) page 139, says that "the observations of Vancouver form the basis of our best maps of the west coast of America, from the thirtieth degree of latitude to the northern extremity of Cook's inlet, as also of those of the Sandwich Islands, which he surveyed with care. The maps contained in the atlas annexed to the journal of the voyage of the Sutil and Mexicana are nearly all copied from those of the British navigator."

EXTENT OF FUCA'S STRAIT.

It will have been observed by His Imperial Majesty that Her Majesty's Government, in speaking of Fuca's Strait, uses that expression to denote the inlet of the sea which extends from Chart No. 3.
Cape Flattery to Whidbey Island, which lies off the American continent. The utmost length of Fuca's Strait would thus extend over about 2° 5′ of longitude, equal, in that latitude, to about 80 miles, (English,) when it merges, at its southeast extremity, in Admiralty Inlet, and at its northeast extremity in Rosario Strait.

NAVIGATION OF FUCA'S STRAIT.

The Rosario Strait and the Canal de Haro are both of them connected immediately with Fuca's Strait, so that it is possible for a vessel setting out from a port on either side of the channel, Chart No. 4.
under the 49th parallel of north latitude, to pass by either of these intervening channels into Fuca's Strait, and thence to the Pacific Ocean; with this difference, however, that *a vessel passing down the Rosario Strait* would enter Fuca's Strait at its eastern end in about 122° 47′ west longitude, the proper and safe course for such a vessel being to the eastward of Davidson's Rock, at the distance of about 1 mile south of Cape Colville, and *so would have to navigate the whole of Fuca's Strait* on its

way to the Pacific Ocean, whereas *a vessel passing down the Canal*
[13] *de Haro* can keep a safe *course between Discovery Island and
the Middle Bank, and enter the Strait of Fuca in about 123° 10′ west longitude, and so *would only be obliged to navigate about two-thirds of Fuca's Strait* on its way to the Pacific Ocean. On the

Chart No. 3.

other hand, a vessel entering Fuca's Strait from the Pacific Ocean, and *bound up the Rosario Strait* by night, after making the light upon Race Island, would have to make the light upon New Dungeness, which is about 70 miles from Cape Flattery, and then the light upon Smith or Blunt Island, which lies almost in the centre of the eastern end of Fuca's Strait and about 6 miles from the entrance of the Rosario Strait. Having made Smith's Island, the vessel may pass safely either to the northward or the southward of it, according as the wind may allow. In the former case she would probably have to pass within 3 miles of Cape Colville before she can enter the Rosario Strait. On the other hand, if she is obliged to keep a course to the southward of Smith's Island, she would probably have to pass within 3 miles of Whidbey Island before she reaches the entrance of the Rosario Strait. She might thus be obliged, in one or the other case, to navigate within *the three miles limit.* On the contrary, a vessel entering Fuca's Strait from the ocean, and bound up the Canal de Haro, will not be under any necessity to pass within territorial waters on either side of the boundary line in order to reach the entrance of the Canal.

Having thus, in the first place, brought under the consideration of His Imperial Majesty the physical features of the waters through which the boundary line is be drawn, pursuant to the provisions of the Treaty of the 15th June, 1846, Her Britannic Majesty's Government proposes, in the second place, to submit to the consideration of His Imperial Majesty certain rules of interpretation which, in the opinion of jurists of the highest authority, are applicable to the interpretation of Treaties, and which, in the opinion of Her Britannic Majesty's Government, may be properly invoked to elicit the true interpretation of the treaty of the 15th June, 1846.

[14] *RULES FOR THE INTERPRETATION OF TREATIES.

There are certain admitted Rules to which Her Majesty's Government invites the attention of His Imperial Majesty, as proper to be observed in the interpretation of Treaties:

1. *The words of a Treaty are to be taken to be used in the sense in which they were commonly used at the time when the Treaty was entered into.*

In affirmatiom of this rule, Vattel (l. ii, chap. 17, sec. 271) writes: "In the interpretation of Treaties, compacts, and promises, we ought not to deviate from the common use of language unless we have very strong reasons for it;" and in illustration of what he means by "the common use of language," he goes on to say, in section 272, "The usage we here speak of is that of the time when the Treaty or the Deed, of whatever kind, was drawn up and concluded. Languages incessantly vary, and the signification and force of words changes with time."

Vattel, l. ii, chap. 17, sec. 271. London, 1811.

2. *In interpreting any expressions in a Treaty, regard must be had to the context and spirit of the whole Treaty.*

In affirmation of this rule, Vattel (ibid., sec. 285) writes as follows: Vattel, ibid., sec. 285.

It frequently happens that, with a view to conciseness, people express imperfectly, and with some degree of obscurity, things which they suppose to be sufficiently elucidated by the preceding matter, or which they intend to explain in the sequel; and, moreover, words and expressions have a different force, sometimes even a quite different signification, according to the occasion, their connection, and their relation to other words.

The connection and train of the discourse is, therefore, another source of interpretation. We must consider the whole discourse together, in order perfectly to conceive the sense of it, and to give to each expression not so much the signification which it may individually admit of, as that which it ought to have from the context and spirit of the discourse. Such is the maxim of the Roman law: "Incivile est, nisi totâ
[15] lege perspectâ, unâ aliquâ particulâ ejus propositâ, *judicare vel respondere."—(Digest, l. i, tit. iii, De Legibus, leg. 24.)

3. *The interpretation should be drawn from the connection and relation of the different parts.*

Upon this rule, Vattel (ibid., sec. 286) writes as follows: Vattel, l. ii, chap. 17, sec. 286.

The very connection and relation of the things in question helps also to discover and establish the true sense of the Treaty or of any other piece. The interpretation ought to be made in such a manner that all the parts may appear consonant to each other—that what follows may agree with what preceded, unless it evidently appear that, by the subsequent clauses, the parties intended to make some alteration in the preceding ones. For it is to be presumed that the authors of a deed had an uniform and steady train of thinking; that they did not aim at inconsistencies and contradictions, but rather that they intended to explain one thing by another; and, in a word, that one and the same spirit reigns throughout the same production or the same Treaty.

4. *The interpretation should be suitable to the reason of the Treaty.*

In illustration of this rule, Vattel (ibid., sec. 287) writes: Vattel, ibid., sec. 287.

The reason of the law or of the Treaty—that is to say, the motive which led to the making of it and the object in contemplation at the time, is the most certain clue to lead us to the discovery of its true meaning; and great attention should be paid to the circumstance whenever there is question either of explaining an obscure, ambiguous, indeterminate passage in a law or Treaty, or of applying it to a particular case. When once we certainly know the reason which alone has determined the will of the person speaking, we ought to interpret and apply his words in a manner suitable to that reason alone; otherwise, he will be made to speak and act contrary to his intention, and in opposition to his own views.

Pursuant to this rule, a prince who on granting his daughter in marriage has promised to assist his intended son-in-law in all his wars, is not bound to give him any assistance if the marriage does not take place.

[16] *But we ought to be very certain that we know the true and only reason of the law, the promise, or the Treaty. In matters of this nature it is not allowable to indulge in vain and uncertain conjectures, and to suppose reasons and views, where there are none certainly known. If the piece in question is in itself obscure—if, in order to discover its meaning, we have no other resource than the investigation of the author's views or the motives of the deed, we may then have recourse to conjecture, and, in default of absolute certainty, adopt as the true meaning that which has the greatest degree of probability on its side. But it is a dangerous abuse to go without necessity in search of motives and uncertain views in order to wrest, restrict, or extend the meaning of a deed, which is of itself sufficiently clear and carries no absurdity on the face of it. Such a procedure is a violation of that incontestable maxim, that it is not allowable to interpret what has no need of interpretation.

It may be observed, by the way, that the motive of the High Contracting Parties to the Treaty of 1846, and the object they had in view, are explicitly stated in the Preamble of the Treaty, so that it will not be necessary for His Imperial Majesty to travel out of the words of the Treaty itself, for the purpose of ascertaining the reason of it.

5. *Treaties are to be interpreted in a favourable rather than an odious sense.*

Vattel, l. ii, chap. 17, sec. 301.

In illustration of this rule Vattel (ibid., sec. 301) writes:

It will not be difficult to show in general what things are favourable, and what are odious. In the first place, everything that tends to the common advantage in Conventions, or that has a tendency to place the Contracting Parties on a footing of equality, is favourable. The voice of equity and the general rule of contracts require that the conditions between the parties should be equal. We are not to presume, without very strong reasons, that one of the Contracting Parties intended to favour the other to his own prejudice; but there is no danger in extending what is for the common advantage. If, therefore, it happens that the Contracting Parties have not made known their
[17] *will with sufficient clearness, and with all the necessary precision, it is certainly more conformable to equity to seek for that will in the sense most favourable to equality and the common advantage, than to suppose it in the contrary sense. For the same reason everything that is not for the common advantage, everything that tends to destroy the equality of a contract, everything that onerates only one of the parties, or that onerates the one more than the other, is odious. In a Treaty of strict friendship, union, and alliance, everything which, without being burdensome to any of the parties, tends to the common advantage of the Confederacy, and to draw the bonds of the union closer, is favourable. In unequal treaties, and especially in unequal alliances, all the clauses of inequality, and principally those that onerate the inferior ally, are odious. Upon this principle that we ought, in cases of doubt, to extend what leads to equality and restrict what destroys it, is founded that well-known rule—"Incommoda vitantis melior, quam commoda petentis, est causa." (Quinctilian, Inst. Orat., l. vii, ch. iv.) The party who endeavours to avoid a loss has a better cause to support than he who aims at obtaining an advantage.

6. *Whatever interpretation tends to change the existing state of things at the time the Treaty was made is to be ranked in the class of odious things.*

Vattel, l. ii, chap. 18, sec. 305.

Vattel, (ibid., sec. 305,) in illustration of this rule, observes that "the proprietor cannot be deprived of his right, except so far precisely as he relinquishes it on his part; and in case of doubt the presumption is in favour of the possessor. It is less repugnant to equity to withhold from the owner a possession which he has lost through his own neglect, than to strip the just possessor of what lawfully belongs to him. In the interpretation, therefore, we ought rather to hazard the former inconvenience than the latter. Here also may be applied in many cases the rule above-mentioned, (sec. 301,) that the party who endeavours to avoid a loss has a better cause to support than he who aims at obtaining an advantage."

---

[18] *Her Britannic Majesty's Government will now proceed to submit to the consideration of His Imperial Majesty, in the third place, their views as to the proper application of the above rules to the interpretation of the Treaty of 15th June, 1846.

THE FIRST RULE OF INTERPRETATION IN ITS APPLICATION TO THE TREATY OF 1846.

Chart No. 2.

The general use of the Rosario Strait before 1846.

In accordance with the first rule above mentioned, Her Majesty's Government submits to the consideration of His Imperial Majesty the following facts in support of the position that the narrow waters, now designated the Rosario Strait in British Charts, were the only channel between the Continent and Vancouver's Island *generally known and commonly used by sea-going vessels* at the time when the Treaty of 15th June, 1846, was made, and that the words "the Channel," in the signification which *common usage* affixed to them at that tim , denoted those waters.

(1.) Vancouver's expedition, in 1792, after exploring the head-waters of Fuca's Strait, passed on to the northward, along the narrow waters which separate Lopez Island from what was then believed to be the Continent, and followed those waters in their course between Blakely Island and Cypress Island into Birch Bay, and thence passed onwards to Point Roberts and the upper waters of the ancient Gulf now called the Strait of Georgia. Soundings were made throughout the passsage, which are stated in Vancouver's narrative, and are laid down in the chart annexed to it, sufficient to secure for future navigators a safe course from Fuca's Strait into the upper Gulf. Vancouver did not explore, nor does he give any soundings of the Canal de Haro. It is not mentioned in his narrative; the name of it, however, appears on the face of his Chart, distinguishing waters without soundings from the Channel through which Vancouver passed.

(2.) The Spanish exploring vessels Sutil and Mexicana, in the same year, appear, from the narrative of the expedition, to
[19] have pursued *a course to the southward of the San Appendix No. 4.
Juan Island until they reach the head-waters of Fuca's Strait. They then entered the same channel which Vancouver entered, and followed it as far as the Island of Guemes, when Chart No. 1.
they passed onwards, along the Canal de Guemes, into Bellingham Bay, ("El Seno de Gaston.") From Bellingham Bay they pursued a northerly course past Point Roberts into the upper waters of the ancient Gulf.

(3.) The Chart of Vancouver, which gives soundings only for navigating through the Rosario Channel, was the Chart in general use up to the end of 1846. Chart No. 2.

(4.) No Spanish chart of a date antecedent to the Treaty of 15th June, 1846, is known to Her Majesty's Government, in which soundings are given for navigating through the Canal de Haro.

(5.) When the Beaver, the first steam-vessel used by the Hudson's Bay Company, passed up from Fuca's Strait to Fort Langley, on the Frazer River, in 1837, she made use of what is known as the Rosario Channel. She explored the Canal de Haro for the first time in 1846.

(6.) When the United States exploring vessel Porpoise, under Lieutenant Ringgold, passed up to the northward, from Fuca's Straits into the upper Gulf, in 1841, she made use of what is now known as the Rosario Channel. The boats, on the other hand, of her consort, the Vincennes, which remained at New Dungeness, were dispatched to the Canal de Haro to make a survey of it. Lieutenant Wilkes, in his narrative, (vol. iv, p. 515,) states that they were so engaged for three days, by which time they "completed all that was essential to the navigation of it."

(7.) Her Majesty's steamer Cormorant. the first of Her Majesty's steamships which navigated the waters between the Continent and Vancouver's Island, in September, 1846, passed up Appendix No. 6.
the Rosario Channel to the northward, and returned to Fuca's Strait by the same channel.

(8.) The declarations of sea-captains and other persons in the service of the Hudson's Bay Company are conclusive that the only channel used and considered safe by them prior to 1846, was Appendix No. 5.
the Rosario Channel.

[20] * THE SECOND AND THIRD RULES OF INTERPRETATION.

It is conceived by Her Majesty's Government that the second and third rules for the interpretation of Treaties, already brought to the attention of His Imperial Majesty, as they are of a cognate character, may be conveniently considered together in their application to the question submitted to the arbitration of His Imperial Majesty.

These rules may be, then, briefly expressed:

(*a*) That *the context and spirit of a discourse is a source of interpretation*, where particular expressions are obscure from over-conciseness of statement.

(*b*) The interpretation of any part of a discourse ought to be made in such a manner that *all the parts may be consonant to one another.*

Appendix No. 2.

It may be observed, then, in the first place, that the only expressions in the Treaty of 15th June, 1846, respecting which any disagreement has arisen between the High Contracting Parties, are to be found in the second paragraph of the first article of it: "And thence southerly, through the middle of the said Channel, and of Fuca's Strait, to the Pacific Ocean;" and that the disagreement is limited to the words "the said Channel." It is considered, therefore, by Her Majesty's Government that, in order to arrive at the true interpretation of the above words, regard may properly be had, not merely to the context of the paragraph itself, but to the text of the preceding and following paragraphs of the 1st Article, which is the operative part of the Treaty as regards the settlement of the line of boundary.

The 1st Article, then, of the said Treaty, is divided into three paragraphs:

1. From the point in the 49th parallel of north latitude, where the boundary laid down in existing Treaties and Conventions between Great Britain and the United States terminates, the line of boundary between the territories of Her Britannic Majesty and the United States shall be continued westward along the said 49th parallel of north latitude to the middle of the Channel which separates the Continent from Vancouver's Island.

[21] *2. And thence southerly through the middle of the said Channel and of Fuca's Straits to the Pacific Ocean.

3. Provided, however, that the navigation of the whole of the said Channel and Straits south of the 49th parallel of north latitude remain free and open to both parties.

The context of the Treaty considered.

Looking now to the text of the first paragraph of this Article in connection with the second paragraph, Her Majesty's Government submits to His Imperial Majesty that the second paragraph may be read as if it were written *in extenso* thus: "And thence southerly through the middle of the Channel which separates the continent from Vancouver's Island, and through the middle of Fuca's Straits to the Pacific Ocean," the channel and the straits being so connected in the second paragraph as to be governed by the preceding words, "through the middle of."

Now, the extent of the waters here designated as Fuca's Strait is not in controversy. It is true, indeed, that by some writers, amongst whom may be mentioned Mr. Robert Greenhow, the Librarian to the Department of State of the United States, and the author of a Memoir, Historical and Political, on the North-west Coast of North America, published in 1840 by direction of the Senate, the term "Fuca's Strait" has been used prior to the Treaty of 1846 to denote the whole of the channel through which it was supposed that the Greek pilot, Juan de Fuca, found a passage into the Polar Sea in the sixteenth century. Thus Mr. Greenhow, in his "History of Oregon," (p. 29,) speaking of the three great groups of islands south of 54° 40′ north latitude, says, "The southernmost group embraces one large island, and an infinite number of smaller

ones, extending from the 49th parallel to the 51st, and separated from the continent on the south and east by the channel called the Strait of Fuca." There is a slight inaccuracy, it may be observed, in this passage as regards the latitude of the group of islands; but Mr. Greenhow, in a previous passage of the same work, (p. 22,) has described the channel which he has in view with greater accuracy, as running eastward
[22] about one hundred miles between the *48th and 49th parallels of latitude, and then turning to the north-west.

The view of Her Majesty's Government is, that the term "Fuca's Straits" is used in the Treaty of 1846 to signify the lower portion only of Mr. Greenhow's Channel, namely, the inlet of the sea which extends eastward from the Pacific Ocean to the entrance of the passage, through which Vancouver continued his voyage to the northward, and which he has laid down in his chart as a navigable channel, connecting Fuca's Strait with the upper waters of the ancient Gulf.

In accordance with this signification of Fuca's Straits, Her Majesty's Government submits to His Imperial Majesty that the term "Fuca's Straits" must be taken to have been inserted in the second paragraph of the first Article of the Treaty of 1846 for the sake of describing with greater precision the course of the boundary line, and that it is one of the necessary conditions of the boundary line that it should be drawn *through the middle of the inlet of the sea*, of which Cape Flattery may be regarded as the south-western extremity, and Deception Pass as the north-eastern extremity.

Now, a line may be properly said to be drawn through the middle of this inlet, if it be drawn in either of two ways, namely, if it be drawn lengthways, or if it be drawn breadthways. There can, however, be no doubt as to which of such alternative lines is required to satisfy the Treaty, as the line is to be drawn to the Pacific Ocean, and this can only be effected by *drawing the line through the middle of Fuca's Straits lengthways*. Upon this point in the case Her Majesty's Government submits to His Imperial Majesty that there can be no reasonable doubt.

The consonance of the second and third paragraphs of the Treaty.

Her Majesty's Government further submits to His Imperial Majesty, that in order that the second paragraph of the first Article of the Treaty of 1846 shall be consonant to the third paragraph—in other words, in order to account for and give reasonable effect to the third paragraph, whereby the navigation of *the whole of Fuca's Straits* is secured to both the High Contracting
[23] Parties—the second paragraph must be interpreted as *requiring the line to be drawn southerly *through the middle of a channel which will allow it to enter the head-waters of Fuca's Straits, and to be continued through the middle of the Straits in an uninterrupted line to the Pacific Ocean;* in other words, the boundary line, after it has entered Fuca's Straits, must divide the waters of the Straits in such a manner as to render the proviso necessary which is embodied in the third paragraph.

For the purpose of bringing this part of the case more completely before the mind of His Imperial Majesty, Her Majesty's Government will recapitulate briefly the characteristics of Fuca's Straits, as they bear upon the question.

Chart No. 4.

The breadth, then, of Fuca's Straits where they leave the Pacific Ocean between Cape Flattery on the Continent, their southern point, and Bonilla Point on Vancouver's Island, their northern point, is thirteen miles. Within these points they soon narrow to eleven miles, and carry this width on an east course for forty miles. They then take an east-north-east direction to the shore of Whidbey Island. Between Race Islands and the Southern shore is the narrowest part of the Straits. Their least breadth, however, in this part is not less than eight miles, after which the Straits expand immediately to seventeen miles, a width which they maintain more or less in the part where the Canal de Haro enters them. On the other hand, it is difficult to define precisely the place where the waters of Fuca's Straits merge in those of the Rosario Strait, but Fuca's Straits gradually contract as they approach the entrance of the Rosario Strait, which is only five miles wide. A provision which thus secures to the vessels of either nation the right of free navigation on either side of the boundary line *throughout the whole of the channel and Fuca's Straits*, would be perfectly intelligible, and, in fact, would be a requisite precaution, if the line is to pass through Rosario Strait, dividing the head-waters of Fuca's Straits; but it would not be in any such sense a *necessary precaution*, if the line of boundary is to be drawn through the Canal de Haro.

[24] *On the former supposition it would be reasonable to secure to either party the free navigation of the whole of Fuca's Straits equally as of the Rosario Channel, inasmuch as the *medium filum aquæ* in the uppermost part of Fuca's Straits would be within the "three miles limit" of either shore; on the other hand, the part of Fuca's Straits, where the Canal de Haro strikes them, are of so great a breadth that there would be an ample margin of common navigable water for vessels on either side of the *medium filum aquæ*, and no necessity for vessels passing to and from the Pacific Ocean *to navigate within the jurisdictional waters* of either of the High Contracting Parties.

Reason of the third paragraph.

If it should be said on behalf of the United States Government that the proviso in the third paragraph of the first Article of the Treaty of 1846 was not inserted by way of *precaution*, but rather by way of *comity*, to preserve to both the High Contracting Parties a liberty of navigation hitherto enjoyed by them in common, Her Majesty's Government submits that considerations of *comity* would equally have required the extension of the proviso to the waters of the Channel, which separates the continent from Vancouver's Island *north of the forty-ninth parallel of north latitude*, as both parties had heretofore enjoyed in common the free navigation of those waters; but no such precaution has been taken in the Treaty to limit the exercise of exclusive sovereignty north of the forty-ninth parallel.

Again, it would have been an unreasonable thing to have provided by the Treaty that both parties should retain the free enjoyment of the navigation of *the whole of Fuca's Straits*, unless the Treaty is to be interpreted as requiring the boundary line to be drawn through the middle of those Straits, and continued through the Rosario Channel, in which case the free navigation of the whole of Fuca's Straits to the eastward of the Canal de Haro would be at times a condition essentially necessary to enable British or American vessels, as the case may be, to enter or leave the channel connecting Fuca's Straits with the waters of

[25] the upper Gulf. *To contend, indeed, that this provision of the Treaty would be consonant to an interpretation of the Treaty which would continue the boundary line through the Canal de Haro, is to deprive the proviso of any rational meaning, as American vessels would possess the right of navigating the Straits to the eastward of the Canal de Haro without any such proviso, and British vessels would not require any such liberty to enable them to enter or leave the Channel through which the boundary line is to pass from Fuca's Straits into the waters of the upper Gulf.

THE FOURTH RULE OF INTERPRETATION.

The fourth of the rules to which Her Britannic Majesty's Government has invited the attention of His Imperial Majesty is, that *the interpretation should be suitable to the reason of the Treaty*, that is to say, the motive which led to the making of it, and the object in contemplation at the time.

"We ought," says Vattel, (section 287,) "to be very certain that we know the true and only reason of the law, or the Treaty. In matters of this nature it is not allowable to indulge in vague and uncertain conjectures, and to suppose reasons and views where there are none certainly known. If the piece in question is in itself obscure; if, in order to discover its meaning, we have no other resource than the investigation of the author's views or the motives of the deed, we may then have recourse to conjecture, and in default of absolute certainty adopt, as the true meaning, that which has the greatest degree of probability on its side. But it is a dangerous abuse to go without in search of motives and uncertain views in order to wrest, restrict, or extend the meaning of the deed, which is of itself sufficiently clear, and carries no absurdity on the face of it."

The motive of the Treaty.

Now, the motive of the Treaty, as recited in the Preamble of it, was to terminate a state of doubt and uncertainty, which had hitherto prevailed respecting the sovereignty and government of the territory on the north-west coast of America, lying
[26] westward of the Rocky Mountains, by an *amicable compromise of the rights mutually asserted by the two parties over the said territory.

It is a reasonable presumption from this Preamble that Her Britannic Majesty's Government, which drew up the paragraph of the Treaty of 1846, the meaning of which is in controversy, *had a definite boundary line in view*, which would terminate all doubt and uncertainty as to the limits within which the respective Parties to the Treaty were henceforth to exercise rights of sovereignty.

The Treaty of 1846, it should also be borne in mind, was not an ordinary Treaty of friendship or alliance, in which a paragraph respecting mutual boundaries was inserted amongst paragraphs relevant to other matters; but it was a Treaty, of which *the primary object was the settlement of a boundary line*, and it would be unreasonable to attach a vague and uncertain meaning to any words descriptive of the boundary line, if such words are susceptible of a *definite and certain meaning.*

The object of the Treaty.

It is not too much to say, and it will probably not be disputed—for it has been so stated by one of the most eminent of American statesmen—that the great aim of the United States in 1846 was to establish the 49th parallel of north latitude as the line of boundary on the western side of the Rocky Mountains, "*not to be departed from for any line further south on the Continent;*" and that with regard to straits, sounds, and islands in the neighbouring seas, they were subjects of minor importance, to be dealt with in a spirit of fairness and equity. (Speech of Mr. Webster before the Senate of the United States, March 30, 1846.)

On the other hand, it is notorious, and it is also patent on the face of the Treaty itself, that the great aim of Her Britannic Majesty's Government was to meet the views of the United States Government in regard to the 49th parallel of north latitude with *as little sacrifice as possible of the rights heretofore enjoyed by the Hudson's Bay Company and other British subjects in the waters south of that parallel.*

Now, it is a remarkable feature of the Treaty that *no name is*
[27] *given to the Channel*, to the *middle of which the 49th parallel of north latitude was to be continued after leaving the Continent, and through the middle of which it was to be drawn southerly after being deflected from that parallel. The Channel is described as "the Channel separating the continent from Vancouver's Island," and the line is simply directed to be drawn "southerly through the middle of the said Channel and of Fuca's Straits." The presumption arising from this description of it is that *the Channel intended by the Treaty was the only Channel then used by sea-going vessels, and that it had no distinguishing name*, but that upon the face of the charts then in use it would readily answer the description given of it in the Treaty, and would admit of the boundary line being deflected and continued through the middle of it and of Fuca's Straits to the Pacific Ocean.

No name is given to the Channel.

It will be seen by His Imperial Majesty, on an examination of Vancouver's Chart, which was the most accurate chart known to Her Britannic Majesty's Government at the time when the Treaty was made, and which was the Chart under the consideration of Her Britannic Majesty's Government when they framed the first Article of the Treaty, that the name of the Gulf of Georgia is assigned in that Chart *to the whole of the interior sea*, which separates the Continent from the group of islands, the chief of which is called Quadra and Vancouver's Island, such being the name of the largest island at the time when the chart was constructed, and that *no distinguishing name* is assigned either to the *channel* up which Vancouver sailed to the northward, or to the portion of the Gulf in the 49th parallel of north latitude. Her Majesty's Government accordingly contends, (1,) that the boundary line, which is directed by the Treaty to be continued westward along the 49th parallel of north latitude to the middle of a channel without any distinguishing name, and thence southerly through the middle of the said channel and of Fuca's Straits, is intended by the words of the Treaty to be drawn through the middle of a channel which had, at that time, no distinguishing name;
[28] and (2) that, as the channel now called the Rosario *Strait is found in the charts of the period (1846) without any distinguishing name assigned to it, and in other respects corresponding with the requirements of the Treaty, such channel ought to be preferred to the Canal de Haro, which bore a distinguishing name at that period.

Chart No. 2.

Her Britannic Majesty's Government contends, on this part of the case, that to draw the line through the middle of the waters distinguished in Vancouver's Chart from the Channel, through which he sailed, by the name of the "Canal de Arro," and which waters are represented in that chart as unsurveyed, would be to continue the line not through "the said Channel"—that is, a Channel without any distinguishing name—but through a channel which, at the time the Treaty was made, was distinguished by name from the channel surveyed by Vancouver. No reason can well be assigned, if such a channel was contemplated by both parties, why it should not have been designated by its distinguishing name to prevent all uncertainty.

But it may be said that there is evidence that the Canal de Haro was contemplated by the United States Government, and that they had charts in their possession which satisfied them that it was a navigable and safe channel, equally as the channel along which Vancouver sailed. The reply to such an argument is not far to seek. If it can be established that one of the parties to the Treaty had knowledge only of one navigable Channel corresponding to the provisions of the Treaty, the fact that the other party was aware of another navigable Channel could never justify such an interpretation being given to the Treaty as should bind the former to accept the Treaty in a sense of which it did not know it to be capable, when the Treaty may be interpreted in a sense in which both parties were aware that it was capable of being interpreted. *The reason of the thing* is against such an interpretation as has been proposed to be given to the Treaty on the part of the United States Government.

There is a further reason why the Canal de Haro does not satisfy the language of the Treaty.

The commencement of the boundary line, which is to be drawn
[29] southerly, is described in *the Treaty as being in a Channel
under the 49th parallel of north latitude; but a glance at the chart will satisfy His Imperial Majesty that the Canal de Haro cannot, in any proper sense of the words, be held to commence under that parallel. It has a distinct commencement between Saturna Island and Patos Island, under a lower parallel. *It has, therefore, not only a distinguishing name, but it has its physical characteristics which distinguish it* from the channel described in the Treaty of 1846 as identical with the channel under the 49th parallel of north latitude.

THE FIFTH RULE OF INTERPRETATION.

The fifth rule of interpretation, to which Her Britannic Majesty's Government has invited the attention of His Imperial Majesty, is, that *Treaties are to be interpreted in a favourable rather than in an odious sense.*

A favourable interpretation to be preferred to an odious interpretation.

"We are not to presume," says Vattel, (sec. 30,) "without any strong reasons, that one of the Contracting Parties intended to favour the other to his own prejudice, but there is no danger in extending what is for the common advantage. If, therefore, it happens that the Contracting Parties have not made known their will with sufficient clearness and with all the necessary precision, it is certainly more conformable to equity to seek for that will in the sense most favourable to equality and the common advantage."

The Charts in use in 1846.

Chart No. 2.

Now, it may be stated by Her Majesty's Government without fear of contradiction, that, at the time when the Treaty of 1846 was signed at Washington, no charts were in use by those who navigated the interior sea between the Continent and Vancouver's Island, but Vancouver's Chart and possibly a Spanish Chart, purporting to be constructed in 1795 upon the surveys made by the Sutil and Mexicana. Of the latter chart, indeed, Her Britannic Majesty's Government had no certain knowledge in 1846, for the only Spanish chart of those waters, which is to be found in the archives of the British Admiralty at Whitehall, did not come into
its possession until 1849. In neither, however, of those Charts are
[30] *there are any soundings of a navigable passage through the
Canal de Haro. It is true, indeed, that in the Spanish Chart some soundings are given of Cordova Channel, in which the boats of the Sutil and Mexicana appear to have crept close along the shore; but there are no soundings to guide a vessel out of the Canal de Haro into any part of the upper waters, which are south of 49° parallel of north latitude. An interpretation, therefore, of the Treaty, which would declare the Canal de Haro to be the channel down which the boundary line is to be carried, would be to declare that Her Britannic Majesty's Government, when it concluded the Treaty of 1846, *intended to favour the United States Government to its own prejudice;* for it would be to

declare that Her Britannic Majesty's Government intended *to abandon the use of the only channel leading to its own possessions* which it knew to be navigable and safe, and to confine itself to the use of a channel respecting which it had no assurance that it was even navigable in its upper waters for sea-going vessels; nay, respecting which it is not too much to say that Her Britannic Majesty's Government *had a firm belief that it was a dangerous strait.* On the other hand, an interpretation which would declare Vancouver's Channel, now distinguished by the name of the Rosario Strait, to be the common boundary, will give to both Parties the use of a Channel, which was known to both Parties at the time when the Treaty was made to be a navigable and safe channel. The two Parties in respect of such an interpretation would be placed in a position of equality.

THE SIXTH RULE OF INTERPRETATION.

The presumption is in favour of the possessor of a thing.

The sixth Rule of Interpretation, which is a corollary to the next preceding Rule, and which is also submitted to the attention of His Imperial Majesty, is that, *in case of doubt, the presumption is in favour of the possessor of a thing;* in other words, the party who endeavours to avoid a loss has a better cause to support than he who aims at obtaining an advantage.

It has been already said that the Channel in use in 1846, and
[31] the only Channel in use by *British vessels navigating from the
Straits of Fuca to the stations of the Hudson's Bay Company on Frazer's River, and elsewhere north of the 49th parallel of north latitude, was the channel surveyed by Vancouver, and of which soundings are given in his Chart.

Chart No. 2.

The Government of the United States contends for an interpretation of the Treaty *which will dispossess British vessels of the use of this channel.* There is no evidence, on the other hand, that the Canal de Haro was used by vessels of the United States prior to the Treaty of 1846.

Her Britannic Majesty's Government, on the other hand, is not contending for an interpretation of the Treaty which will deprive the citizens of the United States of any right habitually exercised by them prior to the Treaty. If, indeed, the United States Government had knowledge from unpublished surveys or otherwise, prior to the Treaty of 1846, that the Canal de Haro was a navigable and safe channel, it cannot be denied that citizens of the United States, if they used any channel at all prior to 1846, made use of the channel now called the Rosario Strait. It is submitted accordingly to His Imperial Majesty, that an interpretation of the Treaty, which declares the Rosario Strait to be the channel, through the middle of which the boundary line is to be drawn, will continue to American citizens the full enjoyment of such rights of navigation as were exercised by them prior to the Treaty, whilst a declaration in favour of the claim of the United States will strip British subjects of corresponding rights. *Wherever there is doubtful right,* it is less *repugnant to equity to withhold from a claimant the enjoyment of a thing, which he has never possessed, than to strip the possessor of a thing of which he has habitually had the enjoyment.*

The question whether any third channel, other than the Rosario Strait or the Canal de Haro, would satisfy the requirements of the Treaty of 1846, has not been touched upon by Her Britannic Majesty's Government for these reasons—amongst others, that the existence of any intermediate navigable channel was unknown to both the
[32] Contracting Parties at the time when the Treaty of *1846 was
signed, and the Government of the United States has never con-

tended for any such channel. Besides, Her Britannic Majesty's Government presumes that the true interpretation of the Treaty of 1846 is to be sought *rebus sic stantibus*, that is, upon the state of facts known to both parties at the time when the Treaty of 1846 was concluded.

On the above considerations of fact and of public law, Her Britannic Majesty's Government submits to His Imperial Majesty that the claim of Her Britannic Majesty's Government that the portion of the boundary line which, under the terms of the Treaty of 15th June, 1846, runs southerly through the middle of the Channel which separates the Continent from Vancouver Island, should be run through the Rosario Strait, is valid, and ought to be preferred to the claim of the Government of the United States, that it should be run through the Canal de Haro.

RECAPITULATION OF FACTS.

The considerations of fact may be briefly recapitulated:

1. That the Channel now designated as the Rosario Strait in British charts, which designation embraced the Channel to the north as well as the south of the 49th parallel of north latitude in Spanish charts, was the only Channel between the Continent and Vancouver Island generally known and commonly used by sea-going vessels at the time when the Treaty of 15th June, 1846, was made, and that the words "The Channel," in the signification which *common usage* affixed to them at that time, denoted those waters.

2. That the context of the first and second paragraphs of Article 1 of the Treaty of 15th June, 1846, requires that the boundary line should be continued through the middle of a Channel *so as to enter the head-waters of Fuca's Straits*, which is practicable, if the line should be run through the Rosario Strait, but is impracticable if it should be run through the Canal de Haro. Appendix No. 2.

[33] *3. That the proviso in the third paragraph of Article I, which secures to either Party the free navigation of *the whole of Fuca's Straits*, is intelligible, as a necessary precaution, if the boundary line is to be run through the Rosario Strait, but is unnecessary and unreasonable if the boundary line is to be run through the Canal de Haro.

4. That a boundary line run through the middle of the Channel now called the Rosario Strait satisfies the great aim which either party had in view prior to the conclusion of the Treaty 15th June, 1846; and as that Channel had no distinguishing name at the time when the Treaty was made, *it could not be otherwise described than as it is described in the Treaty*. On the other hand, the Canal de Haro had a distinguishing name, and there was no reason, if the Canal de Haro was contemplated by both the High Contracting Parties at the time when the Treaty was made, why it should not have been described by its distinguishing name to prevent all uncertainty.

5. That a line of boundary run through the middle of the Rosario Strait, in accordance with the knowledge which both the High Contracting Parties possessed at the time when the Treaty of 15th June, 1846, was made, would have been favourable to both Parties, whereas a line of boundary run through the Canal de Haro *would have deprived Her Britannic Majesty of a right of access to her own possessions* through the only then known navigable and safe channel.

6. That it is more in accordance with equity that His Imperial Majesty should pronounce in favour of the claim of Her Britannic Majesty's Government than in favour of the claim of the Government of the United

States, as a decision of His Imperial Majesty declaring the Rosario Strait to be the Channel through which the boundary line is to be run will continue to citizens of the United States the free use of the only Channel navigated by their vessels prior to the Treaty of 15th June, 1846; whilst a declaration of His Imperial Majesty in favour of the claim of the Government of the United States *will deprive British sub-*
[34] *jects of rights of navigation* **of which they have had the habitual enjoyment* from the time when the Rosario Strait was first explored and surveyed by Vancouver.

The evidence which Her Britannic Majesty's Government has thought it proper to offer to the consideration of His Imperial Majesty in support of the present case, has, for the convenience of His Imperial Majesty, been collected in an Appendix, which is annexed thereto.

*APPENDIX.

No. I.

Articles XXXIV to XLII of the Treaty between Great Britain and the United States of America, signed at Washington on the 8th May, 1871.

Article XXXIV.

Whereas it was stipulated by Article I of the Treaty concluded at Washington, on the 15th of June, 1846, between Her Britannic Majesty and the United States, that the line of boundary between the territories of the United States and those of Her Britannic Majesty, from the point on the 49th parallel of north latitude up to which it has already been ascertained, should be continued westward along the said parallel of north latitude "to the middle of the channel which separates the continent from Vancouver's Island, and thence southerly through the middle of the said channel and of Fuca Straits to the Pacific Ocean;" and whereas the Commissioners appointed by the two High Contracting Parties to determine that portion of the boundary which runs southerly through the middle of the channel aforesaid were unable to agree upon the same; and whereas the Government of Her Britannic Majesty claims that such boundary line should, under the terms of the Treaty above recited, be run through the Rosario Straits, and the Government of the United States claims that it should be run through the Canal de Haro, it is agreed that the respective claims of the Government of Her Britannic Majesty and of the Government of the United States shall be submitted to the arbitration and award of His Majesty the Emperor of Germany, who, having regard for the above-mentioned Article of the said Treaty, shall decide thereupon, finally and without appeal, which of those claims is most in accordance with the true interpretation of the Treaty of June 15, 1846.

Article XXXV.

The award of His Majesty the Emperor of Germany shall be considered as absolutely final and conclusive, and full effect shall be given to such award without any objection, evasion, or delay whatsoever. Such decision shall be given in writing and dated; it shall be in whatsoever form His Majesty may choose to adopt; it shall be delivered to the Representatives or other public Agents of Great Britain and of the United States respectively, who may be actually at Berlin, and shall be considered as operative from the day of the date of the delivery thereof.

Article XXXVI.

The written or printed case of each of the two parties, accompanied by the evidence offered in support of the same, shall be laid before His Majesty the Emperor of Germany within six months from the date of the exchange of the ratifications of this Treaty, and a copy of such case and evidence shall be communicated by each Party to the other through their respective Representatives at Berlin.

The High Contracting Parties may include in the evidence to be considered by the Arbitrator such documents, official correspondence, and other official or public statements bearing on the subject of the reference as they may consider necessary to the support of their respective cases.

After the written or printed case shall have been communicated by each Party to the other, each Party shall have the power of drawing up and laying before the Arbitrator a second and definitive statement, if it think fit to do so, in reply to the case of the other Party so communicated, which definitive statement shall be so laid before the Arbitrator, and also be mutually communicated in the same manner as aforesaid, by each party to the other, within six months from the date of laying the first statement of the case before the Arbitrator.

ARTICLE XXXVII.

If, in the case submitted to the Arbitrator, either Party shall specify or allude to any report or document in its own exclusive possession without annexing a copy, such Party shall be bound, if the other Party thinks proper to apply for it, to furnish that Party with a copy thereof, and either Party may call upon the other, through the Arbitrator, to produce the originals or certified copies of any papers adduced as evidence, giving in each instance such reasonable notice as the Arbitrator may require. And if the Arbitrator should desire further elucidation or evidence with regard to any point contained in the statements laid before him, he shall be at liberty to require it from either Party, and he shall be at liberty to hear one counsel or agent for each Party, in relation to any matter, and at such time and in such manner as he may think fit.

[38] *ARTICLE XXXVIII.

The Representatives or other public Agents of Great Britain and of the United States at Berlin, respectively, shall be considered as the Agents of their respective Governments to conduct their cases before the Arbitrator, who shall be requested to address all his communications and give all his notices to such Representatives or other public Agents, who shall represent their respective Governments generally in all matters connected with the arbitration.

ARTICLE XXXIX.

It shall be competent to the Arbitrator to proceed in the said arbitration, and all matters relating thereto, as and when he shall see fit, either in person, or by a person or persons named by him for that purpose, either in the presence or absence of either or both Agents, either orally or by written discussion, or otherwise.

ARTICLE XL.

The Arbitrator may, if he think fit, appoint a Secretary or Clerk, for the purposes of the proposed arbitration, at such rate of remuneration as he shall think proper. This, and all other expenses of and connected with the said arbitration, shall be provided for as hereinafter stipulated.

ARTICLE XLI.

The Arbitrator shall be requested to deliver, together with his award, an account of all the costs and expenses which he may have been put to in relation to this matter, which shall forthwith be repaid by the two Governments in equal moieties.

ARTICLE XLII.

The Arbitrator shall be requested to give his award in writing as early as convenient after the whole case on each side shall have been laid before him, and to deliver one copy thereof to each of the said Agents.

No. II.

Copy of Treaty between Great Britain and the United States of America, signed at Washington on the 15th June, 1846. [*Ratifications exchanged at London, July* 17, 1846.]

Her Majesty the Queen of the United Kingdom of Great Britain and Ireland, and the United States of America, deeming it to be desirable for the future welfare of both countries that the state of doubt and uncertainty which has hitherto prevailed respecting the Sovereignty and Government of the Territory on the North-west Coast of America, lying westward of the Rocky or Stony Mountains, should be finally terminated by an amicable compromise of the rights mutually asserted by the two Parties over the said Territory, have respectively named Plenipotentiaries to treat and agree concerning the terms of such settlement, that is to say:

Her Majesty the Queen of the United Kingdom of Great Britain and Ireland has, on Her part, appointed the Right Honourable Richard Pakenham, a Member of Her Majesty's Most Honourable Privy Council, and Her Majesty's Envoy Extraordinary and Minister Plenipotentiary to the United States; and the President of the United States of America has, on his part, furnished with full powers James Buchanan, Secretary of State of the United States; who, after having communicated to each other their respective full powers, found in good and due form, have agreed upon and concluded the following Articles:

ARTICLE I

From the point on the forty-ninth parallel of north latitude, where the boundary laid down in existing Treaties and Conventions between Great Britain and the United States terminates, the line of boundary between the territories of Her Britannic Majesty and those of the United States shall be continued westward along the said forty-ninth parallel of north latitude, to the middle of the channel which separates the continent from Vancouver's Island, and thence southerly, through the middle of the said channel, and of Fuca's Straits, to the Pacific Ocean; provided, however, that the navigation of the whole of the said channel and straits south of the forty-ninth parallel of north latitude remain free and open to both Parties.

ARTICLE II.

From the point at which the forty-ninth parallel of north latitude shall be found to intersect the great northern branch of the Columbia River, the navigation of the said branch shall be free and open to the Hudson's Bay Company, and to all British subjects trading with the same, to the point where the said branch meets the main stream of the Columbia, and thence down the said main stream to the ocean, with free access into and through the said river or rivers; it being understood that all the usual portages along the line thus described shall, in like manner, be free and open.

In navigating the said river or rivers, British subjects, with their goods and produce, shall be treated on the same footing as citizens of the United States; it being, however, always understood that nothing in this Article shall be construed as preventing, or intended to
[39] prevent, the Government of the *United States from making any
regulations respecting the navigation of the said river or rivers, not inconsistent with the present Treaty.

ARTICLE III.

In the future appropriation of the territory south of the forty-ninth parallel of north latitude, as provided in the First Article of this Treaty, the possessory rights of the Hudson's Bay Company, and of all British subjects who may be already in the occupation of land or other property lawfully acquired within the said territory, shall be respected.

ARTICLE IV.

The farms, lands, and other property of every description belonging to the Puget's Sound Agricultural Company, on the north side of the Columbia River, shall be confirmed to the said Company. In case, however, the situation of those farms and lands should be considered by the United States to be of public and political importance, and the United States Government should signify a desire to obtain possession of the whole, or of any part thereof, the property so required shall be transferred to the said Government at a proper valuation, to be agreed upon between the parties.

ARTICLE V.

The present Treaty shall be ratified by Her Britannic Majesty and by the President of the United States, by and with the advice and consent of the Senate thereof; and the ratifications shall be exchanged at London at the expiration of six months from the date hereof, or sooner, if possible.

In witness whereof the respective Plenipotentiaries have signed the same, and have affixed thereto the seals of their arms.

Done at Washington, the 15th day of June, in the year of our Lord 1846.

RICHARD PAKENHAM. [L. S.]
JAMES BUCHANAN. [L. S.]

No. III.

A Narrative of the Passage of His Britannic Majesty's ships Discovery and Chatham, under the Command of Captain Vancouver, through the Straits of Juan de Fuca, and through the channel known at the present day as the Rosario Strait, to Birch Bay, situated in the ancient Gulf of Georgia, S. 23 W. and N. 72 W. (Extracted from Vol. I of "Captain Vancouver's Voyages," published in 1798.)

On the 29th April, 1792, Captain Vancouver, in command of His Britannic Majesty's ships Discovery and Chatham, anchored, about eight miles within the entrance, on the southern shore of the supposed Straits of de Fuca. April 29, 1792, page 220.

On the following morning (30th) the expedition weighed anchor, with a favourable wind, and the same evening anchored off a low, sandy point, to which Captain Vancouver gave the name of New Dungeness. April 30, 1792.

On the 2nd May the expedition quitted New Dungeness, and subsequently anchored, in 34 fathoms water, about a quarter of a mile from the shore, in a harbour, to which was given the name of Port Discovery, after the vessel commanded by Captain Vancouver. May 2, 1792, page 227.

During the stay of the expedition at Port Discovery, namely, until the 18th May, boat expeditions were sent to explore the western shore of the Straits.

On the 18th May the ships quitted Port Discovery and entered Admiralty Inlet, and on the 19th they anchored off Restoration Point, the name given to an anchorage discovered therein. May 18, 1792, page 258.

During the period of the stay of the vessels at Restoration Point, several boating expeditions were dispatched to explore the shores in Puget Sound and Admiralty Inlet. May 19, 1792.

On the 30th May Captain Vancouver quitted Restoration Point and directed his course to the opening under examination by Mr. Broughton, who commanded the Chatham, the entrance to which lies from Restoration Point N. 20 E., 5 leagues distant, and there anchored for the night. May 30, 1792, page 279.

On the 31st May he again weighed anchor, and on the 2nd June Captain Vancouver anchored his vessels, in 50 fathoms water, in a branch of the Admiralty Inlet, which he called Possession Sound, distinguishing its western arm by the name of Port Gardner, and its smaller or eastern one by that of Port Susan. May 31, 1792, page 280. June 2, 1792, page 283.

On the 5th June the expedition quitted Possession Sound and anchored the same night about half a mile from the western shore of Admiralty Inlet. June 5, 1792, page 290.

On the 6th June the vessels worked out of the inlet, and reached its entrance at a point to which Captain Vancouver gave the name of Point Partridge, and, proceeding northward, after advancing a few miles along the eastern shore of the Gulf, the expedition was obliged to anchor in 20 fathoms water, finding no effect from the ebb or flood tides, and the wind being light from the northward. June 6, 1792, page 291.

"In this situation," Captain Vancouver stated, "New Dungeness bore by compass S. 54 W.; the east point of Protection Island, S. 15 W.; the west point of Admiralty Inlet, which, after my much esteemed friend, Captain George Wilson, of the navy, I distinguished by the name of Point Wilson, S. 35 E., situated in latitude 48° 10′, longitude 237° 31′; the

Description by Captain Vancouver of the passage through the channel, now called Rosario Strait, to Birch Bay, in His Majesty's ships Discovery and Chatham.

Page 291. June 7, 1792. nearest shore east, 2 leagues distant, a low, sandy island, forming at its west end a low cliff, above which some dwarf [40] trees are produced from N. 26 W. *to N. 40 W., and the proposed station for the vessels during the examination of the continental shore by the boats, which, from Mr. Broughton, who had visited it, obtained the name of Strawberry Bay, N. 11 W., at the distance of about 6 leagues, situated in a region apparently much broken and divided by water. Here we remained until 7 in the evening. We then weighed, butwith so little wind that, after having drifted to the southward of our former station, we were obliged again to anchor until 6 the next morning, when we made an attempt to proceed, but were soon again compelled to become stationary near our last situation."

June , 1792, page 293. "On the 7th June," Captain Vancouver continues, "about 6 in the evening, with a light breeze from the S. W., we weighed and stood to the northward; but after having advanced about eleven miles, the wind became light, and obliged us to anchor about 9 that evening, in 37 fathoms of water, hard bottom, in some places rocky; in this situation we were detained by calms until the afternoon of the following day. June 8, 1792. Our observed latitude here was 48° 29′, longitude 237° 29′; the country occupying the northern horizon in all directions appeared to be excessively broken and insular. Strawberry Bay bore by compass N. 10 W. about three leagues distant; the opening on the continental shore, the first object for the examination of the detached party, with some small rock islets before its entrance that appeared very narrow, bore, at the distance of about five miles, S. 37 E.; Point Partridge, S. 21 E.; the low sandy island, south; the south part of the westernmost shore, which is composed of islands and rocks, S. 37 W., about two miles distant; the nearest shore was within about a mile; a very dangerous sunken rock, visible only at low tide, lies off from a low rocky point on this shore, bearing N. 79 W.; and a very unsafe cluster of small rocks, some constantly, and others visible only near low water, bore N. 15 W. about two and a half miles distant.

"This country presented a very different aspect from that which we had been accustomed to behold further south. The shores now before us were composed of steep, rugged rocks, whose surface varied exceedingly in respect to height, and exhibited little more than the barren rock, which in some places produced a little herbage of a dull colour, with a few dwarf trees.

"With a tolerably good breeze from the north we weighed about 3 in the afternoon, and with a flood tide turned up into Strawberry Bay, where in about three hours we anchored in 16 fathoms, fine sandy bottom. This bay is situated on the west side of an island which, producing an abundance of upright cypress, obtained the name of Cypress Island. The bay is of small extent, and not very deep; its south point bore by compass S. 40 E.; a small islet, forming nearly the north point of the bay, round which is a clear good passage west; and the bottom of the bay east, at a distance of about three-quarters of a mile. This situation, though very commodious in respect to the shore, is greatly exposed to the winds and sea in a S.SE. direction."

June 11, 1792, page 296. In consequence of the anchorage being much exposed, Captain Vancouver resolved to proceed with his vessels up the gulf to the northwest in quest of a more commodious situation.

"With a light breeze from the SE., about 4 o'clock the next morning," (11th June,) Captain Vancouver states, "we quitted this station, and passed between the small island and the north point of the bay to the north westward, through a cluster of numerous islands, rocks, and rocky islets. On Mr. Broughton's first visit hither he found a quantity of very excellent strawberries, which gave it the name of Strawberry Bay; but, on our arrival, the fruit season was passed. The bay affords good and secure anchorage, though sometimes exposed; yet, in fair weather, wood and water may be easily procured. The island of Cypress is principally composed of high, rocky mountains, and steep perpendicular cliffs, which, in the centre of Strawberry Bay, fall a little back, and the space between the foot of the mountains and the sea-side is occupied by low, marshy land, through which are several runs of most excellent water, that find their way into the bay by oozing through the beach. It is situated in latitude 48° 36½′, longitude 237° 34′. The variation of the compass, by eighteen sets of azimuths, differing from 18° to 21°, taken on board and on shore, since our departure from Admiralty Inlet, gave the mean result of 19° 5′ eastwardly. The rise and fall of the tide was inconsiderable, though the stream was rapid. The ebb came from the east, and it was high water 2h. 37m. after the moon had passed the meridian.

"We proceeded first to the north-eastward, passing the branch of the gulph that had been partly examined, and then directed our course to the north-westward, along that which appeared a continuation of the continental shore, formed by low sandy cliffs, rising from a beach of sand and stones. The country, moderately elevated, stretched a considerable distance from the north-westward round to the south-eastward, before it ascended to join the range of rugged, snowy mountains. This connected barrier, from the base of Mount Baker, still continued very lofty, and appeared to extend in a direction leading to the westward of north. The soundings along the shore were regular, from 12 to 25 and 30 fathoms, as we approached or increased our distance from the land, which seldom exceeded two miles; the opposite of the gulph to the south-westward, composed of numerous islands, was at a distance of about two leagues. As the day advanced, the south-east wind gradually died away, and for some hours we remained nearly stationary.

"In the evening, a light breeze favouring the plan I had in contemplation, we steered for a bay that presented itself, where about 6 o'clock we anchored in 6 fathoms of water, sandy bottom, half a mile from the shore. The points of the bay bore by compass S. 32 W. and N. 72 W.; the westernmost part of that which we considered to be the main land west, about three leagues distant; to the south of this point appeared the principal direction of the gulph though a very considerable arm seemed to branch from it to the north-eastward. As soon as the ship was secured, I went in a boat to inspect the shores of the bay, and found, with little trouble, a very convenient situation for our several very necessary duties on shore; of which the business of the observatory was my chief object, as I much wished for a further trial of the rate of chronometers, now that it was probable that we should remain at rest a sufficient time to make the requisite observations for that purpose. Mr. Broughton received my directions to this effect, as also that the vessels should be removed, the next morning, about a mile further up the bay to the north-east, where they would be more conveniently stationed for our several operations on shore; and as soon as the busi ness of the observatory should acquire a degree of forward-
[41] *ness, Mr. Whidby, in the Discovery's cutter, attended by the Chatham's launch, was to proceed to the examination of that part of the coast unexplored to the south-eastward; whilst myself in the yawl, accompanied by Mr. Puget in the launch, directed our researches up the main inlet of the gulph."

No. IV.

A Narrative of the Voyages made by the Spanish Vessels Sutil and Mexicana, in the year 1792, *to explore the Strait of Fuca.* (*Extracted from the Account of the Voyage published at Madrid in* 1802.)

The two schooners Sutil and Mexicana quitted Nootka in the night between the 4th and 5th of June, 1792, and the following is an account of the progress of the expedition through the Strait of Juan de Fuca, translated from the Spanish narrative published at Madrid in 1802:

El viento cedió luego que salimos del canal que forma la entrada de Nutka, y siguió calmoso hasta las once de la manaña, que se entabló la virazon por el O.S.O. Fue refrescando en la tarde, y nosotros seguimos con toda vela, llegando á andar hasta siete millas por corredera, que es el mayor andar que advertimos en las goletas. De las cinco á las siete se fue quedando el viento, y al anochecer estabamos diez y seis millas al O. 10° N. de la entrada de Nitinat, y cinco millas de un islotillo que teniamos por nuestro traves.

The wind abated as soon as we left the channel which forms the inlet of Nootka, and it continued calm until 11 in the morning, when the sea-breeze set in from W.S.W. It freshened in the afternoon, and we proceeded with all sail, making as much as 7 miles by the log, which is the greatest way that we observed in the schooners. From 5 to 7 the wind continued, and at nightfall we were 16 miles W. 10° N. from the inlet of Nitinat, and 5 miles from a small islet which we had abreast of us.

Debiamos segun las circunstancias dirigirnos á adelantar el reconocimiento de la entrada de Juan de Fuca; por esta razon no nos detuvimos á examinar los puntos de la costa que teniamos á la vista, y solo corrimos bases para colocar algunos, y rectificar la carta que de ella habian levantado los oficiales y pilotos del departamento de San Blas, cuyo por menor hallamos bueno.

We were, according to circumstances, to employ ourselves in advancing the survey of the inlet of Juan de Fuca; for this reason we did not stop to examine the points of the coasts which we had in sight, and only ran bases to place some (of them) and to rectify the chart of it taken by the officers and pilots of the Department of San Blas, the detail of which we found good.

Seguimos navegando en la noche con toda vela al E. 5° S., con viento fresco por el O.S.O., en la confianza de que la claridad de la noche, que aumentó á las diez con la luz de la luna, nos proporcionaba toda seguridad; á las dos se quedó casi calma el viento, y amanecimos en estas circunstancias como media legua al S. E. de la punta E. de Nitinat, y á la vista de la boca del estrecho ó entrada de Juan de Fuca.

We continued our course in the night with all sail to E. 5° S., with a fresh wind from W.S.W., trusting that the clearness of the night, which was increased at 10 o'clock by the light of the moon, would afford us every security; at 2 o'clock the wind was almost calm, and thus day broke upon us about half a league S.E. of the east point of Nitinat, and in sight of the mouth of the strait or inlet of Juan de Fuca.

Hasta las once siguió la calma; les corrientes nos respaldáron para dentro del Estrecho como una legua. * * *

The calm continued until 11 o'clock; the currents carried us about a league within the Strait. * * * *

A las once se entabló el viento por el S.O., y nos dirigimos al E.S.E. para atravesar la boca del Estrecho.

* * * *

A las cuatro de la tarde avistamos el Puerto de Nuñez Gaona, y poco despues una corbeta en su fondeadero, que conjeturamos ser la nombrada "Princesa," perteneciente al Departamento de San Blas. Seguimos la derrota á costear la parte O. del puerto, y á poco llegó el Teniente de Navío Don Salvador Fidalgo, Comandante de dicha corbeta, y nos confirmó en la idea de que la costa O. del puerto era sucia, como lo indicaba el sargazo; la dejamos perdiendo barlovento, y á costa de algunos bordos conseguimos anclar á las seis y media de la tarde muy próximos á la "Princesa." * * *

Aunque el Alférez de Navío D. Manuel Quimper habia reconocido hasta el Puerto de Quadra, y el Teniente de Navío Don Francisco Eliza hasta el Canal de nuestra Señora del Rosario en los años anteriores, no habian examina-
[42] do las bocas de *Caamaño, de Flon, Seno de Gaston, Canal de Floridablanca, Bocas del Carmelo y de Mazarredo. Por las noticias que habian adquirido de los Indios, la de Caamaño internaba mucho, pero su fondo no permitia paso sino á las canoas; la de Flon era de muy poca consecüencia. Juzgaban, con alguna duda, cerrado el Seno de Gaston, y proponian como el reconocimiento mas interesante el de la Boca de Floridablanca, que segun se presentaba en la carta que habian trazado de estos canales, ofrecia dos entradas formadas por una isla colocada en su medianía, que despues de nuestro exámen se halló ser la Península de Cepeda y Lángara. El canal, segun habian comprehendido á los Indios, internaba mucho. * * *

Con tales noticias tratamos de internarnos para acabar de examinar el Seno de Gaston, y proceder al reconocimiento del Canal de Flori-

At 11 the wind set in from S.W., and we proceeded E.S.E. to cross the mouth of the Strait. * *

At 4 in the afternoon we sighted the port of Nuñez Gaona, and soon after a corvette in its anchorage, which we supposed to be that called Princess, belonging to the Department of San Blas. We shaped our course to coast along the west part of the port, and in a short time Lieutenant Don Salvador Fidalgo, Commander of the said corvette, came on board, and he confirmed us in our opinion that the west coast of the port was foul, as the kelp indicated; we dropped away from it, losing the favourable wind, and, after some tacks, succeeded in anchoring, at half past 6 p. m., very close to the Princess. * *

Although Sub-Lieutenant Don Manuel Quimper had surveyed as far as the port of Quadra, and Lieutenant Don Francisco Eliza as far as the Channel of Our Lady of the Rosary, in the preceding years, they had not examined the mouths of Caamaño, of Flon, Bay of Gaston, Channel of Floridablanca, mouths of Carmelo and of Mazarredo. From the information which they had obtained from the Indians, that of Caamaño went far inland, but its depth did not allow a passage except to canoes. That of Flon was of very little importance. They thought, though with some doubt, that the Bay of Gaston was closed; and they proposed, as the survey of most interest, that of the mouth of Floridablanca, which, as shown on the chart which they had drawn of those channels, presented two inlets formed by an island situated in its centre, which, after our examination, was found to be the peninsula of Cepeda and Lángara. The channel, as they had understood from the Indians, penetrated far. * * * *

With such information we thought of penetrating inwards to finish the examination of the Bay of Gaston, and to proceed to the survey of the

dablanca, dejando los de Caamaño y Flon como de menos entidad, y mas propios para ser reconocidos en el caso, que creiamos probable, de haber de retroceder. La direccion del Canal de Caamaño hácia el Sur, y la probabilidad de que fuese á salir á la boca de Ezeta próxîma á los 46° 14′ de latitud, fué otra de las consideraciones que tuvimos presentes al adoptar este plan.	Channel of Floridablanca, leaving those of Caamaño and Flon as of less importance, and more fitting to be surveyed in case of our having to fall back, which we thought probable. The direction of the Channel of Caamaño towards the south, and the probability of its issuing at the mouth of Ezeta, near 46° 14′ latitude, was another of the considerations which we had in mind when adopting this plan.
A las doce entró el viento flojo por el S. E.; el tiempo claro nos indicaba que en el canal reinaria el O. A las doce y media dimos la vela, y dirigimos á pasar por el pequeño canal que hay al E. de la isleta de la boca; lo que conseguimos con felicidad. Este canal es muy estrecho por las restingas que salen de las puntas que lo forman, y así solo debe seguirse cuando lo exîja la necesidad, ó se vea en ello una ventaja decidida. A nosotros nos pareció que adelantábamos la navegacion, pues pensábamos seguir la costa sur del Estrecho, por estar llena de excelentes fondeaderos. * * *	At 12 o'clock began a slack wind from S. E. The clear weather indicated that the W. would prevail in the channel. At half past 12 we made sail, and shaped our course to pass by the little channel which there is to the E. of the islet in the mouth. This channel is very narrow, on account of the reefs which issue from the points which form it, and, therefore, it ought only to be followed in a case of necessity, or if it appears decidedly advantageous. To us it appeared that we were advancing the navigation, for we thought of following the south coast of the strait, because it had plenty of excellent anchorages. *
Luego que salimos del canal, conocimos que la derrota que debia hacerse para internar en él era acercarse á la costa N., respecto de que en la que intentábamos seguir reinaba una perfecta calma. Cuando vimos el oleage que movia el viento fué preciso echar el bote al agua y armar los remos para salir á encontrarle. * * *	As soon as we got out of the channel, we found that the course to be taken to get inwards was to approach the N. coast, because on that which we were trying to follow a perfect calm prevailed. When we saw the waves which were moved by the wind, it was necessary to launch the boat and ship the oars to go to meet them. * * *
Luego que salimos al viento fuimos dirigiéndonos á la costa del N., navegando al N. N. E. y arribando para el E. al paso que nos íbamos acercando á ella: á las once de la noche nos pusimos á costearla á distancia de una legua escasa, y seguimos con el viento al O. N. O., fresco con un tiempo claro y hermoso.	As soon as we got out into the wind, we shaped our course to the N. coast, navigating to N. N. E. and bearing for E. as we were getting near to it. At 11 at night we began to coast along it at the distance of a short league, and we went on with the wind fresh from W. N. W., the weather calm and fine.
Amanecimos cerca de la Punta de Moreno de la Vega, y orzamos á pasar por entre ella y los islotes que tiene en su cercanía: derrota que indicaba Tetacus, y que recomendaban mucho los que habian	Day broke upon us near the Point of Moreno de la Vega, and we luffed to pass between it and the islands in its vicinity—a route pointed out by Tetacus, and much recommended by those who had

navegado en este Estrecho. Verificado este paso, abonanzó el viento, y seguimos con ventolinas del O. al S. toda la mañana. * * *

Nos dirigimos al puerto de Córdoba, donde Tetacus indicaba debia quedarse, y á que daba el nombre Chachimutupusas. Tetacus habia dormido con sosiego toda la noche, no desmintiendo jamas su franqueza y confianza; daba su trato continuas pruebas de su fácil comprehension; conocia en la carta la configuracion del estrecho é islas descubiertas, y nos dijo los nombres que él les daba. Doblada la Punta de Moreno de la Vega nos advirtió hiciésemos allí agua que era rica y abundante, porque pasado aquel sitio
[43] los manantiales *eran escasos
y el agua de mal sabor. Comia con aseo de cuanto le daban, imitando en todo nuestras acciones, que observaba siempre cuidadosamente. Se acordaba de los nombres de todos los capitanes Ingleses y Españoles que han visitado la costa de tierra-firme y archipiélagos de Claucuad y Nutka, y aun nos dió noticia de que habia dos embarcaciones grandes dentro del Estrecho.

Cuando nos hallábamos cerca de la rada de Eliza se acercáron á bordo de la "Mexicana" tres canoas con cuatro ó cinco Indios cada una, pero sin querer atracar al costado.

A las once de la mañana conseguimos tomar el puerto de Córdoba, y anclamos en seis brazas de agua, suelo arena, en la parte del S. del fondeadero. * * * Se despidió Tetacus de nosotros con la mayor cordialidad y se fué á tierra. * *

Por la tarde estuvimos en tierra visitando las rancherías de Tetacus, donde habia como cincuenta Indios. * * * Tetacus mostraba la mayor amistad á sus huespedes * * * y nos retiramos á bordo muy satisfechos. Por la noche hubo suma quietud en el puerto, y nosostros tuvimos la vigilancia que pedia el evitar una ocasion de desgracia. *

navigated in this strait. This passage having been made, the wind went down, and we proceeded with light breezes from W. to S. all the morning. * * *

We steered for the port of Cordova, where Tetacus said he was to stay, and to which he gave the name of Chachimutupusas. Tetacus had slept quietly all night, never belying his frankness and confidence; his behaviour gave continual proofs of his easy comprehension; he understood on the chart the configuration of the strait and the islands discovered, and he told us the names which he gave them. When the Point of Moreno de la Vega was doubled he advised us to take water there, as it was excellent and abundant, but after passing that place the springs were scanty, and the water of bad taste. He ate what was given to him with deeency, imitating our actions, which he always carefully observed in all things. He remembered the names of all the English and Spanish captains who had visited the coast of the mainland and the archipelagos of Claucuad and Nootka, and he also informed us that there were two large vessels within the strait.

When we were near the roadstead of Eliza, three canoes approached the Mexicana, with four of five Indians in each, but without wanting to come alongside. * * *

At 11 in the morning we succeeded in making the port of Cordova, and we anchored in six fathoms of water, sandy bottom, in the southern part of the anchorage * * * Tetacus took leave of us with the greatest cordiality, and went ashore. * *

In the afternoon we landed and visited the huts of Tetacus, where there were about fifty Indians. * * Tetacus was exceedingly friendly to his guests * * * and we returned on board very well satisfied. At night it was perfectly quiet in the port, and we exercised such vigilance as was necessary to prevent any chance of misadventure. *

El puerto de Córdoba es hermoso.

* * * * *

En este puerto fué donde la goleta "Saturnina" tuvo que cañonear las canoas de los habitantes para defender la lancha del paquebot San Cárlos, que venia en su conserva, y de la que obstinadamente querian apoderarse.

Como el tiempo nos habia favorecido para que determinasemos en el dia la latitud y longitud del puerto, nos levamos á las tres de la madrugada con la marea saliente. Desde las ocho de la mañana empezamos á gozar de la virazon, que entró bonancible por el S. S. O. Nos dirigimos á la medianía del canal para tener el viento en toda su fuerza y buscar las Islas de Bonilla, que son una buena marca para la derrota. Pasamos algunos escarceos muy fuertes de las corrientes, y avistadas las islas nos dirigimos á ellas, dejandolas por estribor. A las cinco de la tarde, que empezó á quedarse el viento, atracamos la punta S. E. de la Isla de San Juan para dar fondo á la parte E. de ella, lo que conseguimos á las nueve de la noche.

El objeto principal de tomar este ancladero era para observer en él una emersion del primer satelite de Jupiter. * * *

Al fondear estaba la marea parada; se examinó su fuerza, y nunca pasó de una milla y media por hora en direccion al S. S. E. hasta las tres y media, y á esta hora cambió para adentro. Subió el agua de ocho á nueve pies.

A las siete de la mañana se dejó sentir una ventolina por el S. S. E.; con ella dimos la vela para aprovechar lo restante de la marea favorable; el cielo estaba nublado, y el horizonte apenas era de una milla. Ceñimos el viento para atravesar á la costa del E., no solo para seguirla y no perder la boca del Canal de Güemes, que va por entre la isla de este nombre y la costa, sino tambien para montar los islotes que hay á la medianía del canal en que estábamos, y sobre los que nos respaldaba a corriente con rapidez. A propor-

The port of Cordova is beautiful.

* * * * *

It was in this port that the schooner Saturnina had to fire upon the canoes of the inhabitants to defend the launch of the packet-boat San Carlos, which came in her company, and of which they obstinately endeavoured to get possession.

As the weather had been so favourable as to enable us to determine the latitude and longitude of the port in the day time, we weighed at 3 in the morning with the tide going out. From 8 in the morning we began to enjoy the breeze which sprung up lightly from S. S.W. We steered for the middle of the channel to have the wind in all its force, and to seek the Islands of Bonilla, which are a good mark for the course. We passed some very strong races, and, having sighted the islands, we made for them and left them on the starboard hand. At 5 in the afternoon, when the wind began to fail, we neared the S. E. point of the Island of San Juan, in order to cast anchor at its eastern part, which we effected at 9 at night.

The principal object of taking this anchorage was to observe there an emersion of the chief satellite of Jupiter. * * *

On anchoring, the tide was at the slack; its force was examined, and it never exceeded a mile and a half an hour in the direction of S. S.E., until half past 3, when it changed for the direction inwards. The water rose from 8 to 9 feet.

At 7 in the morning a breeze was felt from S. S.E.; with it we set sail to avail ourselves of the remainder of the favourable tide; the sky was cloudy, and the horizon scarcely a mile. We hugged the wind to cross to the east coast, not only in order to follow it and not to lose the mouth of the channel of Güemes, which runs between the island of that name and the coast, but also to double the islets which are in the middle of the channel in which we were, and upon which the current was driving us with rapidity. In

cion que fuimos saliendo á la medianía fue tesando y alargándose la ventolina: arribamos al paso que nos acercábamos á la costa del E., y costeamos las dos Islas Morros con el auxîlio de la virazon que apuntó por el S. desde las ocho de la mañana, despejando el cielo. Llegamos á la punta S. O. del Canal de Güemes, y entramos en él, navegando al principio á medio
[44] *freo para libertarnos de la calma de la costa; pero ya dentro tomó el viento su direccion, y nos acercamos á la del Sur para libertarnos de la fuerza de la corriente contraria, que sempre contrarestamos con mucha ventaja, pues aunque el viento estaba flojo, andábamos tres millas y media por hora. La navegacion era muy agradable, por lo frondoso de la costas. En la del N., que á la entrada es de playa, vimos una rancheria próxîma á la punta N. O., que examinada con el anteojo se halló consistir en dos casas grandes; varios Indios corriéron á la playa, se embarcáron en una canoa, y se dirigiéron á las goletas, dándoles caza con tanto acierto como pudiera hacerlo el mas experto marino. * * * Entre tanto seguimos la costa del Sur del canal por cinco brazas de agua fondo arena hasta la punta S. E., y desde esta lo atravesamos dirigiéndonos á la punto tajada del N. E., de la que pasamos á muy corta distancia para seguir la costa de la Isla de Güemes, y por ella y las "Tres Hermanas" dirigirnos al Seno de Gaston.

proportion as we were getting into mid-channel the breeze freshened and veered aft; we bore away whilst we neared the eastern coast, and we coasted along the two Morros Islands with the aid of the breeze, which was direct S. from 8 in the morning, and cleared the sky. We reached the S.W. point of the channel of Güemes, and we entered it, navigating at first in mid-channel to avoid the calm of the coast; but when within, the wind took its direction, and we neared that of the S. to avoid the force of the contrary current, which we always resisted with great advantage, for although the wind was slack we went three miles and a half an hour. The navigation was very pleasant from the woodiness of the coasts. On that of the N., which at the entrance is a beach, we saw a station near the N.W. point, which, on being examined with a telescope, was seen to consist of two large houses; several Indians ran to the beach, embarked in a canoe, and made for the schooners, giving them chase with as much skill as the most expert seaman. * * * Meanwhile we followed the south coast of the channel in five fathoms of water, sandy bottom, to the S.E. point, and from that we crossed it towards the N.E. point, from which we passed at a very short distance to follow the coast of the Island of Güemes, and by that and the "Three Sisters" to make for the Bay of Gaston.

Luego que doblamos la punta N. E. quedamos en calma, y fué necesario acudir á los remos para verificar el paso, contrarestando algunas ventolinas escasas del O.S.O que se oponian; pero luego que pasamos las islas, llamó el viento al O. y ceñimos abiertos por babor para montar la Punta de Solano. El calor incomodaba mucho, pues aunque el termómetro á la sombra estaba en la graduacion templada, expuesto al sol subia hasta veinte y nueve grados y medio, y aun hu-

As soon as we doubled the N.E. point we were becalmed, and it was necessary to resort to the oars to make the passage, resisting some scanty breezes from W.S.W. which opposed us; but as soon as we passed the islands the wind veered to the W., and we hauled free to port to double the Point of Solano. The heat was very distressing, for, although the thermometer in the shade was at the temperate degree, when exposed to the sun it rose to 29½ degrees, and would even have

biera subido mas si no hubiéramos salida á encontrar la corriente del viento.

A las cinco entabló este por el S.; hicimos rumbo, y nos internamos en el Seno de Gaston, que aunque no estaba del todo reconocido, costeamos su parte E. para dirigirnos á su fondo, y ver si tenia en él algun canal. El viento fué refrescando, y favorecidos de él, estábamos al anochecer satisfechos de que, cuando mas, habria un rio pequeño en su parte interior. La costa que lo formaba era de tierra baja y anegadiza, que corria por entre dos lomas, y á alguna distancia aparentaban canal; el fondo era de seis á siete brazas, piedra, y pensábamos bordear para echarnos fuera, cuando caimos en cinco greda dura, por lo que se prefirió fondear contando, como hasta entonces habiamos visto, que el viento se quedaria en la noche. La situacion era buena para dejar caer el ancla, y poder reconocer mas prolijamente la parte interior de la ensenada en la mañana siguiente. Aferramos todo aparejo, avisó el timonel de la Sutil de cuatro brazas de fondo, y se dejó caer el ancla; pero despues de arriar treinta brazas de cable, se halló la goleta en dos y media de agua.

Inmediatamente mandó el Comandante sondar por la popa y las aletas; á dos cables de distancia si halláron dos brazas, y se conoció que el ancla habia caido en tres. Esta equivocacion del timonel nos puso en muy mala situacion. Se pasó la noche con cuidado, y durante toda ella vació el agua, de suerte que al amanecer estábamos en una braza y media. Habiamos visto claridades al S.E. de la montaña del Carmelo, y aun á veces algunas llamaradas, señales que no dejáron duda que hay volcanos con fuertes erupciones en aquellas cercanías. La Mejicana habia fondeado como dos cables mas al O., y en media braza menos de agua; el

risen higher if we had not gone out to meet the current of the wind.

At 5 o'clock the wind settled from the S.; we made our course, and we went into the Bay of Gaston. Although it was not at all surveyed, we coasted along its eastern part, in order to make for its extremity, and to see if there was any channel in it. The wind still freshened, and, favoured thereby, we were by nightfall satisfied that it could have, at most, but a small river in its inner part. The coast which formed it was of low, inundated land, which ran between two hillocks, and at some distance they appeared to be a channel. The depth was from 6 to 7 fathoms, stony, and we were about to tack to get out, when we fell into 5 fathoms hard chalk, wherefore it was thought best to anchor, reckoning, as we had found until then, that the wind would continue in the night. The situation was favourable for casting anchor and for examining more carefully the inner part of the inlet on the following morning. We made all fast, the steersman of the Sutil notified 4 fathoms depth, and the anchor was dropped, but, after paying out 30 fathoms of cable, the schooner was found to be in 2 and a half fathoms of water.

The commander immediately ordered soundings at the stern and the quarters; at two cables distance two fathoms were found, and it was ascertained that the anchor had fallen in three. This mistake of the steersman placed us in a very awkward situation. The night was passed with anxiety, and during the whole of it the water decreased, so that at daybreak we were in a fathom and a half. We had seen illuminations to the S.E. of the mountain of Carmelo, and even some flashes at times, indications which left no doubt that there are volcanoes with strong eruptions in those parts. The Mexicana had anchored about two cables more to

viento, que habia soplado en la noche bastante fresco por el S.S.E., habia levantado alguna marejada, con lo que empezó á tocar de popa. Dió una espía inmediatemente con su lancha, y sobre ella trató de dar la vela sin largar el cabo has-
[45] ta estar en viento. *Entre tanto la Sutil se llamó á pique del ancla, y se halló en dos brazas de agua; se estaba metiendo el bote para dar la vela quando avertimos que la Mejicana habia varado, por lo que se volvió á échar fuera, y se le envió para auxîliarla. Habia tenido aquella goleta la desgracia de venirsele el anclote, que habia dado con la espía, y se hallaba muy expuesta á dar un bandazo, siendo preciso á la gente hacer palanca con los remos para evitar este desastre. A la Sutil tambien se le vino el ancla en el instante de dar la vela, y por pronto que se acudió con el aparejo, varó en seis pies escasos de agua; pero tomadas las debidas providencias, al cabo de una hora saliéron las dos á flote.

the W., and in half a fathom less water; the wind, which had blown pretty freshly in the night from S.S.E., had raised a swell, with which it began to touch at the stern. She immediately gave out a warp with her launch, and upon that set about hoisting sail without loosing the rope until meeting the wind. Meanwhile the Sutil was shortening in her cable, and was found to be in two fathoms water; we were hoisting in the boat in order to set sail, when we noticed that the Mexicana had grounded; it was, therefore, got out again and sent to her assistance. That schooner had had the misfortune to drag home the stream anchor, which she had cast with the warp, and was in great danger of going over, so that it was necessary for the men to prop her with the oars to prevent such a disaster. The Sutil also dragged home her anchor at the moment of setting sail, and quickly as the tackle was resorted to she grounded in a scanty six feet of water; but, all due means having been applied, at the end of an hour both vessels were afloat.

Inmediatamente se procedió á disponer los buques para dar la vela y continuar la navegacion, y á las ocho y media de la mañana ya estaban bordeando con el viento fresco del S.S.E. para echarse fuera del Seno de Gaston, sin experimentar que hiciesen agua alguna, aunque habian dado muchos golpes en el fondo.

Preparations were immediately made for the vessels to set sail and continue the navigation, and at half past 8 in the morning they were tacking with a fresh S.S.E. wind to get out of the Bay of Gaston, and it was not found that they made any water, although they had frequently struck the bottom.

Despues de varios bordos montáron las puntas S. y O. del Seno de Gaston á las cuatro de la tarde, y entráron por el Canal de Pacheco; siguiéron por medio freo, cediendo algo el viento, y tomando la direccion del mismo canal, luego que entráron en él. Despues de salir del canal, en la Ensenada de Lara, vimos dos embarcaciones menores, la una con aparejo de místico, y la otra con vela redonda, que seguian la costa hácia el N. No dudamos que pertenecerian á los dos buques Ingleses que estaban en el Estrecho,

After various tacks they doubled the S. and W. points of the Bay of Gaston at 4 in the afternoon, and made for the Channel of Pacheco; they proceeded by mid-channel, the wind somewhat abating, and taking the direction of the channel itself as soon as they entered it. After leaving the channel, in the Creek of Lara, we saw two smaller boats, one with sliding sail-rigging, the other with square sail, which were following the coast toward the N. We had no doubt that they belonged to the two English vessels

segun las noticias de nuestro amigo Tetacus. Seguimos sin variar de rumbo, pensando navegar toda la noche con poca vela, y amanecer sobre la Punta de San Rafael para estar al principio del dia en la boca de Floridablanca, é internarnos en ella á verificar desde luego su reconocimiento que, como se ha dicho, teniamos motivo para creer fuese muy interesante. Atravesamos de diez á doce de la noche la Ensenada del Garzon, viendo luces dentro de ella, que nos indicáron que los buques á que pertenecian las embarcaciones menores estaban en aquel fondeadero.

which were in the Strait, according to the information of our friend Tetacus. We went on without changing course, thinking to navigate all night with little sail and to be off the Point of San Rafael at daybreak, so as to get to the mouth of Floridablanca early in the morning, to go within and to make the survey at once, which, as has been said, we had reason to believe would be very interesting. From 10 to 12 at night we crossed the Creek del Garzon, and saw lights within it which indicated that the vessels to which the smaller boats belonged were in that anchorage.

El viento, que veló fresco toda la noche, hizo cumplieramos la distancia hasta cerca de la Punta de San Rafael á la una de ella. Ceñimos con las gavias arraidas de la vuelta de fuera, y á las dos de la mañana viramos de la de dentro, sondando á poco tiempo en siete brazas de fondo; volvimos á tomar la vuelta de fuera, y continuó disminuyendo el fondo hasta cinco brazas arena. En esta situacion pareció oportuno dejar caer el ancla por no empeñarse de noche en buscar la salida, ni ser prudente el continuar hácia la boca sin tener de ella mas seguro conocimiento.

The wind, which kept fresh all night, enabled us to make the distance to near the Point of San Rafael by 1 o'clock. We stood outward with reefed topsails; and at 2 in the morning we veered inward, sounding soon in seven fathoms deep; we again stood outward, and the depth continued decreasing to five fathoms sand. In this situation it appeared fitting to cast anchor, so as not to run any risk in seeking the outlet at night, and as it was not prudent to continue near the mouth without having more certain knowledge of it.

Fondeamos, y con las primeras luces del dia vimos que estábamos á medio canal, en la enfilacion de Punta de San Rafael con la punta E. de la Península de Cepeda.

We anchored, and with the first light of day we saw that we were in mid-channel, in a line with the Point of San Rafael, and the East point of the Peninsula of Cepeda.

---

[46] **Relacion del Viage hecho por las Goletas Sutil y Mexicana en el Año de 1792, &c.*

A reference to the voyage of Sub-lieutenant Don Manuel Quimper, in 1790, to the Strait of Fuca, extracted from Chapter I of the Narrative of the Voyage of the Sutil and Mexicana, in 1792.

La noticia confusa del reconocimiento hecho en 1592 por el piloto Griego Juan de Fuca del canal de su nombre, era la única que teniamos hasta el año de 1789. Hallándose en Nutka el Alférez de Na-

The confused account of the examination made in 1592 by the Greek pilot John de Fuca, of the channel which bears his name, was the only one we had up to the year 1789. Sub-lieutenant (Alférez de

vío Don Estéban Martinez, despues de haber tomado posesion de este puerto en nombre de Su Magestad, recordó que en 1774, de vuelta de su expedicion al Norte, le habia parecido ver una entrada muy ancha por los 48° 20′ de latitud. Creyendo que pudiese ser la de Fuca, commisionó un segundo piloto mandando la goleta Gertrudis para que se cerciorase de si exîsta ó no dicha entrada; en efecto el piloto volvió diciendo la habia hallado de veinte y una milas de ancho, y cuya mediania estaba en 48° 30′ de latitud, y 19° 28′ al O. de San Blas.

Pasadas estas noticias á la superioridad, tuvo órden el Teniente de Navío Don Francisco Eliza en el año de 1790 para hacer practicar un reconocimiento prolixo de esta entrada. Destinó á esta fin al Alférez de la misma clase Don Manuel Quimper, mandando la balandra la Princesa Real. Este oficial se hizo á la vela del puerto de Nutka el 31 de Mayo, reconoció el puerto de Claucaud, se internó despues en el canal de Fuca, visitó algunos puertos y parte de la costa, levantó sus planos, y se retiró el 1 de Agosto, no habiéndole permitido los tiempos el continuar los trabajos.

Al año siguiente recibió Eliza órdenes del virey de Nueva España para llevar á su fin el reconocimiento ya empezado, y que causaba la curiosidad de los geógrafos. Dicho oficial salió de Nutka mandando el paquebot San Cárlos y goleta Horcasitas, con la intencion de elevarse á los 60° de latitud, y descender exâminando la costa hasta el canal de Fuca, é interiorizarse en él para reconocerlo completeamente; pero no permitiéndole los vientos en muchos dias el ganar al norte, resolvió empezar los reconocimientos por los 48°, y envocó el canal el dia 27 de Mayo. Permaneció en él hasta el 7 de Agosto, en que se vio precisado á retirarse por tener ya escorbútica parte de su tripulacion, y carecer

Navío) Don Esteban Martinez, being at Nootka, after having taken possession of that port in the name of Her Majesty, stated that, in 1774, in returning from his expedition to the north, he thought he saw a very wide entrance at 48° 20′ latitude. Believing that it might be that of Fuca, he directed a second mate (piloto) in command of the schooner Gertrudis to ascertain whether that entrance existed or not. The mate returned, saying that he had found it to be twenty-one miles wide, and its center in 48° 30′ latitude, 19° 28′ west of San Blas.

These accounts having been sent on to the authorities, Lieutenant Don Francisco Eliza received orders in the year 1790 to have a minute survey made of that entrance. He appointed Sub-lieutenant Don Manuel Quimper, who commanded the sloop Princesa Real, for that purpose. The said officer sailed from the port of Nootka on the 31st of May, examined the port of Claucaud, afterwards penetrated the channel of Fuca, surveyed some ports and part of the coast, drew plans of them, and retired on the 1st of August, the weather not having allowed him to continue his labors.

In the following year Eliza received orders from the viceroy of New Spain to complete the examination already begun, and which excited the curiosity of geographers. That officer left Nootka in command of the packet San Carlos and the schooner Horcasitas, intending to go up to 60° latitude, and to come down and examine the coast to the channel of Fuca, then to enter therein to examine it completely; but the wind not allowing him for many days to get to the north, he determined to begin his examinations at 48°, and entered the channel on the 27th of May. He remained in it till the 7th of August, when he found himself obliged to retire because part of his crew had the scurvy, and he had not

de dietas para suministrarle. En este tiempo hiza levantar planos de algunos puertos, y exâminar un trozo de la costa al piloto Don Joseph Narvaez, no pudiendo verificarlo por sí á causa de haber caido enfermo.

De vuelta á Nutka escribió al virey de Nueva España las resultas de su viage, y despues de otras reflexîones dice: "Asegurando á V. E. que el paso al océano que con tanto anhelo buscan sobre esta costa las naciones extrangeras, si es que lo hay, me parece no hallarse por otra parte que por este gran canal."

the necessary diet for them. During this time he caused plans to be made of some of the ports, and had part of the coast examined by the mate, Don Joseph Narvaez, being unable to do it himself because he had fallen sick.

On his return to Nootka he wrote the results of his voyage to the viceroy of New Spain, and, after other remarks, he said: "Assuring your excellency that the passage to the ocean which foreign nations seek for so eagerly on this coast, if there be one, will not be found, as it appears to me, elsewhere than by this great channel."

---

[47] *No. V.

Declarations of W. H. McNeill, W. Mitchell, Captain Swanson, Messrs. Anderson, H. G. Lewis, and Finlayson, master mariners, &c., who have commanded or are in command of vessels navigating the straits between Vancouver's Island and the continent of America.

To all to whom these presents shall come: I, Montague William Tyrwhitt Drake, of the city of Victoria, Province of British Columbia, Dominion of Canada, notary public, duly admitted and practicing in pursuance of an act of Parliament made and passed in the 6th year of the reign of His Majesty King William IV, intituled "An act to repeal an act of the present session of Parliament, intituled an act for the more effectual abolition of oaths and affirmations taken and made in various departments of the state, and to substitute declarations in lieu thereof, and for the more entire suppression of voluntary and extra-judicial oaths and affidavits, and to make other provisions for the abolition of unnecessary oaths," I do hereby certify that, on the day of the date hereof, personally came and appeared before me Henry Slye Mason, named and described in the declaration hereunto annexed, being a person well known and worthy of good credit, and, by solemn declaration which the said Henry Slye Mason then made before me, did solemnly and sincerely declare to be true the several matters and things mentioned and contained in the said annexed declaration.

In faith and testimony whereof I have set my hand and seal of office, and have caused the said declaration to be hereunto annexed.

Dated in Victoria, the 29th day of September, A. D. 1871.

M. W. TYRWHITT DRAKE,
Notary Public.

I hereby certify that Montague William Tyrwhitt Drake, whose signature is hereunto attached, is a notary public, duly admitted and practicing in the city of Victoria, Province of British Columbia, Dominion of Canada.

In testimony whereof I have hereunto set my hand and official seal, this 4th day of October, 1871.

CHARLES GOOD,
Colonial Secretary.

This is the paper writing marked Z, produced and shown to William Henry McNeill, William Mitchell, and John Swanson, and referred to in their several declarations, marked respectively A, B, and C, declared this 27th day of September, 1871.

Before me:

M. W. TYRWHITT DRAKE,
Notary Public.

Z.

I, Henry Slye Mason, of Victoria, in the Province of British Columbia, in the Dominion of Canada, clerk to the attorney-general, do solemnly and sincerely declare as follows:

That the following are the interrogatories submitted to Herbert G. Lewis, Alexander Caulfield Anderson, John Swanson, William H. McNeill, and William Mitchell; and on the perusal of which interrogatories they gave the answers respectively contained in the several accompanying statutory declarations, marked A, B, C, D, and E:

Interrogatories relative to the Northwest Water-Boundary Question submitted to Alexander Caulfield Anderson, Herbert G. Lewis, John Swanson, William H. McNeill, and William Mitchell.

1. About 1845–'46, had the Hudson's Bay Company any fort or settlement on the Fraser River?

2. How did trading-vessels or other craft communicate with that fort or settlement from foreign parts, and from other settlements on the Columbia River, or its neighborhood?

3. The date of the settlement of Fort Langley on Fraser River?

4. About the time of the negotiation of the Treaty of June, 1846, what was the common opinion of Great Britain insisting on the 49th parallel being deflected in a southerly direction through the Straits of Fuca to the Pacific, instead of cutting through Vancouver's Island?

5. If to secure access to the possessions to the northward of 49° parallel, state what possessions Great Britain held to the northward of 49°, and where.

6. If the free navigation of the straits and adjacent channel was not guaranteed to Great Britain, how could access be obtained to those possessions north of 49°?

7. When the Treaty was signed in June, 1846, and previous to that date, which channel was known and used by vessels amongst the islands forming the archipelagos between Vancouver's Island and the continent, to get access to our dominions north of 49°?

8. Forward proofs and affidavits, legally attested by captains of vessels, and others, who made use of the channel then known, and their reasons for making use of it.

9. Previous to the signing of the Treaty in 1846, and also at that time, how many channels were known to be navigable amongst the islands forming the archipelago between Vancouver's Island and the continent of America?

And I, Henry Slye Mason, above named, solemnly declare, that I make the above statements, conscientiously believing the same to be true; and by virtue of the provisions of an act made and passed in the 6th year of the reign of His Majesty King William IV, intituled "An act to repeal an act of the present session of Parliament, intituled
[48] an act for the more effectual abolition of oaths and *affirmations

taken and made in various departments of the state, and to substitute declarations in lieu thereof, and for the more entire suppression of voluntary and extra-judicial oaths and affidavits, and to make other provisions for the abolition of unnecessary oaths."

HENRY S. MASON.

Declared at Victoria, in the Province of British Columbia, Dominion of Canada, this 29th day of September, 1871.

Before me:

M. W. TYRWHITT DRAKE,
Notary Public.

To all to whom these presents shall come: I, Montague William Tyrwhitt Drake, of the city of Victoria, Province of British Columbia, Dominion of Canada, notary public, duly admitted and practicing in pursuance of an act of Parliament made and passed in the sixth year of the reign of His Majesty King William IV, intituled "An act to repeal an act for the more effectual abolition of oaths and affirmations taken and made in various departments of the state, and to substitute declarations in lieu thereof, and for the more entire suppression of voluntary and extra-judicial oaths and affidavits, and to make other provisions for the abolition of unnecessary oaths," do hereby certify that, on the day of the date hereof, personally came and appeared before me William Henry McNeill, named and described in the declaration hereunto annexed, being a person well known and worthy of good credit, and, by solemn declaration which the said William Henry McNeill then made before me, did solemnly and sincerely declare to be true the several matters and things mentioned and contained in the said annexed declaration.

In faith and testimony whereof I have set my hand and seal of office, and have caused the said declaration to be hereunto annexed.

Dated in Victoria the 29th day of September, A. D. 1871.

M. W. TYRWHITT DRAKE,
Notary Public.

I hereby certify that Montague William Tyrwhitt Drake, whose signature is hereunto attached, is a notary public, duly admitted and practicing in the city of Victoria, Province of British Columbia, Dominion of Canada.

In testimony whereof I have hereunto set my hand and official seal, this 4th day of October, A. D. 1871.

CHARLES GOOD,
Colonial Secretary.

This is the paper writing marked A, shown to Henry Slye Mason, at the time of making his declaration, and therein referred to on the 29th day of September, 1871.

Before me:

M. W. TYRWHITT DRAKE,
Notary Public.

A.

I, William Henry McNeill, of Gonzala Bay, Vancouver Island, in the Province of British Columbia, Dominion of Canada, now a settler, do solemnly and sincerely declare as follows:

I am sixty-eight years of age, and at twenty years of age I became a master mariner.

I have been on the Northwest Pacific coast since 1832, and have been employed as a master mariner during the greater part of that time till 1863 on the said coast.

From 1832 till 1837 I was employed by the Hudson's Bay Company, in the command of the ship Llama, which during that period plied between Columbia River and Fort Simpson, British Columbia, 54° north latitude.

On two occasions during that period, in going through the Straits of Fuca to Fraser River, and returning from Fraser to Columbia River, I passed through Rosario Straits. My reason for not passing through Haro Straits was that there was then no known or surveyed channel through Haro Straits; on the other occasions I went to the westward of Vancouver Island. During the whole of this period I never heard of a vessel passing through Haro Straits, and Rosario Straits was the only channel known and surveyed, and I was in constant communication during such period with sea-faring men who traversed the waters between Vancouver Island and the main-land. In 1837, and from thence till 1843, I commanded the steamer Beaver, belonging to the Hudson's Bay Company, and she was employed during that time in trading between Fort Simpson aforesaid, Fraser River, and Nisqually-Puget Sound. During all that time, between 1837 and 1843, I never heard of a vessel going through Haro Straits, and I was during that period, from 1837 till 1843, in constant communication with ship-masters trading on the said waters.

In 1843 I went to England, and continued absent from this Northwest Pacific coast for twelve months, and returning in 1844, I was still in the Hudson's Bay Company's service at Stekin, Fort Rupert, and Fort Simpson on the said Northwest Pacific coast, and from thence till 1846 I never heard of any vessel going through Haro Straits, with the exception of the steamer Beaver, in 1846. Till then she always went through Rosario Straits on her usual voyages in the Hudson's Bay Company's employ, the only then known channel.

During all this time till 1846, I never heard of Haro Straits being used by vessels, and I was in constant communication with ship-masters trading in the waters between Vancouver Island and the
[49] *main-land, and the Northwest Pacific coast. And since 1846
Rosario Straits has still been the most usual channel for sailing-vessels.

In navigating these waters between Vancouver Island and the main-land, I always used Vancouver's charts, and heard of no others till the chart made in pursuance of the survey of Captain Richards and his officers, with the exception of the old Spanish chart, which was of little value.

The first chart which I knew of as laying down a survey of Haro Straits, was Captain Richards' chart.

I further say that Vancouver Island was generally supposed to be united with what is now named Galiano Island on Richards' chart till after Captain Richards' survey.

In Rosario Straits the currents and tides are comparatively regular, but in Haro Straits, and round the islands adjacent to Vancouver Island, and in the waters about Vancouver Island itself, the tides and currents are always very irregular.

Referring to the questions submitted to me relative to the boundary line referred to in the treaty of Oregon, in answer to the first question I declare, as aforesaid:

1. That about 1845 and 1846 the Hudson's Bay Company had a settlement at Langley, on the Fraser River, and the said settlement existed since 1827 or 1828, to the best of my knowledge and belief.

2. In answer to the second question, I declare, as aforesaid, that trading-vessels or other craft communicated with the settlement of Langley from foreign parts, and from the settlements on the Columbia River or its neighborhood, by the Straits of Rosario and the Gulf of Georgia.

3. In answer to the third question, I declare, as aforesaid, that, to the best of my knowledge, information, or belief, Langley, on the Fraser River, was settled about the year 1827 or 1828.

4. In answer to the fourth question, I declare, as aforesaid, that, about the time of the negotiation of the Treaty of June, 1846, the common opinion as to the object of Great Britain insisting on the forty-ninth parallel being deflected in a southerly direction, and through the Straits of Fuca to the Pacific, instead of cutting through Vancouver Island, was that it was to secure access to her possessions to the northward of the forty-ninth parallel through the Straits of Fuca.

5. In answer to the fifth question, I declare, as aforesaid, that Great Britain then held British Columbia, up to the parallel of north latitude 54° 40′ and Vancouver Island.

6. In answer to the sixth question, I declare, as aforesaid, that, if the free navigation of the straits and adjacent channel was not guaranteed to Great Britain, access could only be secured and obtained to those possessions by ships going to the westward of Vancouver Island. And as regards those possessions on the coast of British Columbia between the fifty-first and forty-ninth parallel, access would have to be sought through a strait which is intricate and difficult of navigation, by reason of the strength of the tides, and almost impracticable for sailing-vessels.

7 and 8. In answer to the seventh and eighth questions, I declare, as aforesaid, that, when the treaty was signed in June, 1846, and previous to that date, the channel which was known and used by vessels amongst the islands forming the archipelago between Vancouver Island and the continent to get access to the dominions of Great Britain north of the forty-ninth parallel, was the Strait of Rosario, and that channel only, as it was then the only surveyed channel.

9. In answer to the ninth question, I declare, as aforesaid, that, previous to the signing of the Treaty in A. D. 1846, and also at that time, the only channel known to be navigable amongst the islands forming the archipelago between Vancouver Island and the continent, was the Strait of Rosario.

And I declare, as aforesaid, that, even since Haro Straits has been fully surveyed, I consider Rosario Strait as a much safer channel for a sailing-ship, in passing either from the Straits of Fuca to the Gulf of Georgia, or for a sailing-ship passing from the Gulf of Georgia to the Straits of Fuca, inasmuch as the Rosario Strait has good anchorage throughout its entire length, and has more regular tides than Haro Straits. The anchorage in Haro Strait is bad, on account of the great depth of its waters, and the irregularity and strength of its tides. The navigation of Haro Strait, moreover, is much impeded by numerous small islands and rocks.

During all the time between A. D. 1837 and the year A. D. 1843, I was in command, as aforesaid, of the Hudson's Bay Company's steamer Beaver, and I was in the habit of taking the said steamer once or twice every year during that period from Fort Simpson to Langley on the Fraser River, and from thence to Nisqually-Puget Sound; and from Nisqually back again to Langley and Fort Simpson, and on those occasions I always passed through Rosario Straits, as it was then the only surveyed channel between Fuca Strait and the Gulf of Georgia.

And I, William Henry McNeill, above named, solemnly declare that the questions hereinbefore referred to, are contained in the paper writing marked Z, produced and shown to me at the time of making this declaration, and that I make the above statements conscientiously, believing the same to be true; and by virtue of the provisions of an act made and passed in the sixth year of the reign of His Majesty King William IV, intituled "An act to repeal an act of the present session of Parliament, intituled an act for the more effectual abolition of oaths and affirmations taken and made in various departments of the state, and to substitute declarations in lieu thereof and for the more entire suppression of voluntary and extra-judicial oaths and affidavits, and to make other provisions for the abolition of unnecessary oaths."

WILLIAM H. McNEILL.

Declared at Victoria, in the Province of British Columbia, Dominion of Canada, this 27th day of September, 1871.

Before me:

M. W. TYRWHITT DRAKE,
Notary Public.

---

[50] *To all to whom these presents shall come: I, Montague William Tyrwhitt Drake, of the city of Victoria, Province of British Columbia, Dominion of Canada, notary public, duly admitted and practicing in pursuance of an act of Parliament made and passed in the sixth year of the reign of His Majesty King William the Fourth, intituled "An act to repeal an act of the present session of Parliament, intituled 'An act for the more effectual abolition of oaths and affirmations taken and made in various departments of the state, and to substitute declarations in lieu thereof, and for the more entire suppression of voluntary and extra-judicial oaths and affidavits, and to make other provisions for the abolition of unnecessary oaths,'" do hereby certify that, on the day of the date hereof, personally came and appeared before me William Mitchell, named and described in the declaration hereunto annexed, being a person well known and worthy of good credit, and, by solemn declaration which the said William Mitchell then made before me, did solemnly and sincerely declare to be true the several matters and things mentioned and contained in the said annexed declaration.

In faith and testimony whereof I have set my hand and seal of office, and have caused the said declaration to be hereunto annexed.

Dated in Victoria, the 27th day of September, A. D. 1871.

M. W. TYRWHITT DRAKE,
Notary Public.

I hereby certify that Montague William Tyrwhitt Drake, whose signature is hereunto attached, is a notary public, duly admitted and practicing in the city of Victoria, Province of British Columbia, Dominion of Canada.

In testimony whereof I have hereunto set my hand and official seal, this 4th day of October, A. D. 1871.

CHARLES GOOD,
Colonial Secretary.

This is the paper writing marked B, shown to Henry Slye Mason, at the time of making his declaration, and therein referred to on the 29th day of September, 1871.

Before me:

M. W. TYRWHITT DRAKE,
Notary Public.

B.

I, William Mitchell, of Victoria, Vancouver Island, in the Province of British Columbia, Dominion of Canada, master mariner, do solemnly and sincerely declare and state as follows:

I am sixty-eight years of age. I became a master mariner in 1851, and have been on the Northwest Pacific coast since 1837, and have been employed all the time in the Hudson's Bay Company's ships. From 1837 to 1846 I was constantly employed in passages from Victoria to Fraser River, and back again; from Columbia River to Fraser River, and back again; and from Nisqually-Puget Sound to Fraser River, and back again; and trading generally between those ports as well as sometimes to Honolulu and Sitka, and other between ports on the Northwest Pacific coast. And whenever the vessel I was in had occasion to go from the Straits of Fuca to the Gulf of Georgia, or back from the Gulf of Georgia to the Straits of Fuca, she always passed through Rosario Straits as the only then known navigable channel.

As late as the year 1855 I had occasion to pilot a vessel from Victoria to Nisqually, and from Nisqually to Nanaimo, and from Nanaimo to Victoria, and both in going to Nanaimo and returning therefrom made use of Rosario Strait as the best known channel.

Previous to 1846 there was only one channel known to be navigable, and that was the Rosario Straits.

In the year 1846, to the best of my knowledge, information, and belief, no chart of Haro Strait soundings existed.

The chart in use was that of Rosario Strait only, and from soundings made by Vancouver.

Referring to the questions submitted to me relative to the boundary line referred to in the Treaty of Oregon, in answer to the first question I declare, as aforesaid:

1. That about 1845 and 1846 the Hudson's Bay Company had a settlement at Langley, on the Fraser River, and the said settlement existed since 1827 or 1828.

2. In answer to the second question, I declare, as aforesaid, that trading-vessels or other craft communicated with the settlement of Langley from foreign parts, and from the settlements on the Columbia River, or its neighborhood, by the Straits of Rosario and the Gulf of Georgia.

3. In answer to the third question, I declare, as aforesaid, that, to the best of my knowledge, information, and belief, Langley, on the Fraser River, was settled about the year 1827 or 1828.

4. In answer to the fourth question, I declare, as aforesaid, that about the time of the negotiation of the Treaty of June, 1846, the common opinion as to the object of Great Britain insisting on the forty-ninth parallel being deflected in a southerly direction, and through the Straits of Fuca to the Pacific, instead of cutting through Vancouver Island, was, that it was to secure access to her possessions to the northward of the forty-ninth parallel through the Straits of Fuca.

5. In answer to the fifth question, I declare, as aforesaid, that Great

Britain then held British Columbia up to parallel of north latitude 55° 40′ and Vancouver Island.

6. In answer to the sixth question, I declare, as aforesaid, that if the free navigation of the straits and adjacent channel was not guaranteed to Great Britain, access could only be secured and obtained to those possessions by ships going to the westward of Vancouver Island; and as regards those possessions on the coast of British Columbia, between the fifty-first and forty-ninth parallel, access would have to be
[51] *sought through a strait which is intricate and difficult of navigation by reason of the strength of the tides.

7 and 8. In answer to the seventh and eighth questions, I declare, as aforesaid, that when the treaty was signed in June, 1846, and previous to that date, the channel which was known and used by vessels among the islands forming the Archipelago, between Vancouver's Island and the continent, to get access to the dominions of Great Britain north of the forty-ninth parallel, was the Strait of Rosario and that channel only, as it was then the only surveyed channel.

9. In answer to the ninth question, I declare, as aforesaid, that previous to the signing of the Treaty in 1846, and also at that time, the only channel known to be navigable among the islands forming the Archipelago between Vancouver Island and the continent was the Rosario Strait.

And I further say that, even since Haro Strait has been fully surveyed, I consider Rosario Strait a much safer channel for a sailing-ship in passing either from the Straits of Fuca to the Gulf of Georgia, or for a sailing-ship passing from the Gulf of Georgia to the Straits of Fuca, inasmuch as Rosario Strait has good anchorage throughout its entire length, and has more regular tides than Haro Straits. The anchorage in Haro Strait is bad on account of the great depth of its waters and the irregularity and strength of its tides. The navigation of Haro Strait, moreover, is much impeded by numerous small islands and rocks.

In the beginning of the year A. D. 1839, I recollect making a voyage, as first mate, from Columbia River to Fraser River, and thence back to the Columbia River in the bark Vancouver, and on these occasions she passed and repassed through Rosario Straits.

In A. D. 1840, I made two voyages in the schooner Cadboro, from Columbia River to Fraser River, and returned to the Columbia River in the Cadboro, and passed and repassed through Rosario Straits on these voyages.

In A. D. 1842, I made a voyage from Columbia River to Fraser River in the Cadboro, as first mate, and returned from Fraser River to the Columbia River, and on these occasions I passed and repassed through Rosario Strait. And between A. D. 1842 and 1846, I made several voyages in the schooner Cadboro, as first mate, from Columbia River and Victoria to Nisqually and Langley on the Fraser River, and thence returned to Victoria and Columbia River, and on such occasions I always passed and repassed through Rosario Strait, as it was the only then known channel.

And I, William Mitchell, above named, solemnly declare that the questions hereinbefore referred to are contained in the paper writing marked Z, produced and shown to me at the time of making this declaration; and that I make the above statements conscientiously, believing the same to be true; and by virtue of the provisions of an act made and passed in the sixth year of the reign of His Majesty King William the Fourth, intituled "An act to repeal an act of the present session of Parliament, intituled 'An act for the more effectual abolition of oaths and affirmations taken and made in various departments of the state, and to substitute declarations in lieu thereof, and for the more entire suppression of voluntary and extra-judicial oaths and affidavits, and to make other provisions for the abolition of unnecessary oaths.'"

WILLIAM MITCHELL.

Declared at Victoria, in the Province of British Columbia, Dominion of Canada, this 27th day of September, 1871.

Before me:

M. W. TYRWHITT DRAKE,
Notary Public.

To all to whom these presents shall come: I, Montague William Tyrwhitt Drake, of the city of Victoria, Province of British Columbia, Dominion of Canada, notary public, duly admitted and practicing in pursuance of an act of Parliament made and passed in the sixth year of the reign of His Majesty King William the Fourth, intituled "An act to repeal an act of the present session of Parliament, intituled 'An act for the more effectual abolition of oaths and affirmations taken and made in various departments of the state, and to substitute declarations in lieu thereof, and for the more entire suppression of voluntary and extra-judicial oaths and affidavits, and to make other provisions for the abolition of unnecessary oaths,'" do hereby certify that, on the day of the date hereof, personally came and appeared before me John Swanson, named and described in the declaration hereunto annexed, being a person well known and worthy of good credit, and, by solemn declaration which the said John Swanson then made before me, did solemnly and sincerely declare to be true the several matters and things mentioned and contained in the said annexed declaration.

In faith and testimony whereof I have set my hand and seal of office, and have caused the said declaration to be hereunto annexed.

Dated in Victoria the 27th day of September, A. D. 1871.

M. W. TYRWHITT DRAKE,
Notary Public.

I hereby certify that Montague William Tyrwhitt Drake, whose signature is hereunto attached, is a notary public, duly admitted and practicing in the city of Victoria, Province of British Columbia, Dominion of Canada.

In testimony whereof I have hereunto set my hand and seal of office this 4th day of October, A. D. 1871.

CHARLES GOOD,
Colonial Secretary.

[52] *This is the paper writing marked C, shown to Henry Slye Mason at the time of his making his declaration, and therein referred to, on the 29th day of September, 1871.

Before me:

M. W. TYRWHITT DRAKE,
Notary Public.

C.

I, John Swanson, of Victoria, Vancouver Island, in the Province of British Columbia, Dominion of Canada, master mariner, do solemnly and sincerely declare as follows:

I have been a master mariner since the year 1855, and have been in the employment of the Hudson's Bay Company on their ships trading on the Northwest Pacific coast, since the year 1842 to the present time, as a nautical man and mariner.

Referring to the questions submitted to me relative to the boundary line referred to in the Treaty of Oregon, in answer to the first question I declare, as aforesaid:

1. That, about 1845 and 1846, the Hudson's Bay Company had a settlement at Langley, on the Fraser River, and the said settlement existed since 1827 or 1828.

2. In answer to the second question, I declare, as aforesaid, that up to 1845 and 1846, Hudson's Bay Company's ships, bound from Honolulu, in the Sandwich Islands; from Fort Vancouver, on the Columbia River; and San Francisco and Sitka, to Langley, passed through Fuca Straits and Rosario Strait. Also vessels trading between Fort Nisqually and Langley used to pass through Rosario Strait. Also vessels trading between Victoria and Langley used to pass through Rosario Strait.

3. In answer to the third question, I declare, as aforesaid, that to the best of my knowledge, information, and belief, Langley, on the Fraser River, was settled about the year 1827 or 1828.

4. In answer to the fourth question, I declare, as aforesaid, that about the time of the negotiation of the Treaty of June, 1846, the common opinion as to the object of Great Britain insisting on the forty-ninth parallel being deflected in a southerly direction, and through the Straits of Fuca to the Pacific, instead of cutting through Vancouver Island, was, that it was to secure access to her possessions to the northward of the forty-ninth parallel, through the Straits of Fuca.

5. In answer to the fifth question, I declare, as aforesaid, that Great Britain then held British Columbia up to parallel of north latitude 54° 40′, and Vancouver Island.

6. In answer to the sixth question, I declare, as aforesaid, that if the free navigation of the straits and adjacent channel was not guaranteed to Great Britain, access could only be secured and obtained to those possessions by ships going to the westward of Vancouver Island; and, as regards those possessions on the coast of British Columbia between the fifty-first and forty-ninth parallel, access would have to be sought through a strait which is intricate and difficult of navigation by reason of the strength of the tides.

7 and 8. In answer to the seventh and eighth questions, I declare, as aforesaid, that when the treaty was signed in June, 1846, and previous to that date, the channel which was known and used by vessels amongst the islands forming the Archipelago between Vancouver Island and the continent, to get access to the dominions of Great Britain, north of the forty-ninth parallel, was the Strait of Rosario, and that channel only; and it was then the only surveyed channel.

9. In answer to the ninth question, I declare, as aforesaid, that previous to the signing of the treaty in 1846, and also at that time, the only channel known to be navigable amongst the islands forming the Archipelago between Vancouver's Island and the continent was the Strait of Rosario.

And I further declare, as aforesaid, that in the end of the year 1842 or beginning of 1843, I sailed from Vancouver, on the Columbia River, to Nisqually, on Puget Sound, and the vessel I was in was thence towed through Rosario Straits by the Hudson's Bay Company's steamer Beaver, and thence sailed through Gulf of Georgia and Johnston Strait to Sitka, and returned therefrom through Johnston Strait and Rosario Strait to Victoria.

During the years 1843 and 1844 I made several trips in the schooner Cadboro, from Victoria to Langley, through Rosario Strait, and back again from Langley to Victoria through Rosario Strait. I was occupied generally in making such voyages during those two years, and we always passed and repassed through Rosario Straits.

To the best of my recollection, in 1845 I made a voyage in the bark Vancouver, from the Columbia River to Fort Langley, through Rosario Strait, and back again to Victoria.

In the year 1846, to the best of my knowledge, information, and belief, no chart of Haro Strait soundings existed. The chart in use was that of Rosario Strait only, and from surveys made by Vancouver.

Previous to 1846, to the best of my knowledge, information, and belief, no sailing-vessel, except on the occasion of the Cadboro, went through Haro Strait under sail. If other sailing-vessels had, previous to 1846, passed through Haro Strait, I, as a sea-faring man on the northwest Pacific coast, should, in all probability, have heard of it.

The one occasion on which the Cadboro passed through Haro Strait was in 1843, and she then was carried by the tide in a calm, on her passage from Langley to Victoria, into Haro Straits, and we were then obliged to avail ourselves of the services of an Indian we met with as a pilot, as we had no chart by which to navigate.

And I, John Swanson above named, solemnly declare that the questions hereinbefore referred to are contained in the paper writing marked Z, shown to me at the time of making this declaration, and that I make the above statements conscientiously, believing the same to be true; and by virtue of the provisions of an act made and passed in the sixth year of the reign of His Majesty King William the Fourth, intituled "An act to repeal an act of the present session of Parliament, intituled 'An act for the more effectual abolition of oaths and affirmations
[53] taken and made in various departments of the *state, and to substitute declarations in lieu thereof, and for the more entire suppression of voluntary and extra-judicial oaths and affidavits, and to make other provisions for the abolition of unnecessary oaths.'"

JOHN SWANSON.

Declared at Victoria, in the Province of British Columbia, Dominion of Canada, this 27th day of September, 1871.

Before me:

M. W. TYRWHITT DRAKE,
Notary Public.

To all to whom these present shall come: I, Robert Edwin Jackson, of the city of Victoria, Province of British Columbia, in the Dominion of Canada, notary public, duly admitted and practicing, in pursuance of an act of Parliament made and passed in the sixth year of the reign of His Majesty King William IV, intituled "An act to repeal an act of the present session of Parliament, intituled an act for the more effectual abolition of oaths and affirmations taken and made in various departments of the state, and to substitute declarations in lieu thereof, and for the more entire suppression of voluntary and extra-judicial oaths and affidavits, and to make other provisions for the abolition of unnecessary oaths," do hereby certify that, on the day of the date hereof, personally came and appeared before me Alexander Caulfield Anderson, named and described in the declaration hereunto annexed, being a person well known and worthy of good credit, and, by solemn declaration which the said Alexander Caulfield Anderson then made before me, did solemnly and sincerely declare to be true the several matters and things mentioned and contained in the said annexed declaration.

In faith and testimony whereof I have hereunto set my hand and seal of office, and have caused the declaration to be hereunto annexed. Dated at Victoria aforesaid, the 15th day of September, in the year of our Lord 1871.

ROBT. E. JACKSON,
Notary Public.

I hereby certify that Robert Edwin Jackson, whose signature is hereunto attached, is a notary public, duly admitted and practicing in the city of Victoria, Province of British Columbia, Dominion of Canada.

In testimony whereof I have hereunto set my hand and official seal this 4th day of October, A. D. 1871.

CHARLES GOOD,
Colonial Secretary.

This is the paper writing marked D, shown to Henry Slye Mason at the time of his making his declaration, and therein referred to on the 29th day of September, 1871.

Before me:

M. W. TYRWHITT DRAKE,
Notary Public.

D.

I, Alexander Caulfield Anderson, now of Saanich, Vancouver Island, in the Province of British Columbia, Dominion of Canada, settler, do solemnly and sincerely declare as follows:

I am an ex-chief trader, of the Hudson's Bay Company, and late an agent of Lloyd's for the Columbia River and the adjacent coasts, and from 1833 and 1851 I was under the several appointments held by me as an officer of the Hudson's Bay Company, connected (with the exception of short intervals) directly or indirectly with the business of the said company on the Northwest Pacific coast, which business then required their vessels frequently to navigate the waters of the gulf, and the Archipelago, and Straits of Fuca, and during the greater portion of the said period, resided on, or was in constant communication with the Northwest Pacific coast.

1. In answer to the first question, I declare, as aforesaid, that about 1845 and 1846, the Hudson's Bay Company had a settlement at Langley on the Fraser River, and other settlements higher up the river.

2. In answer to the second question, I declare, as aforesaid, that trading-vessels or other craft communicated with the settlement of Langley from foreign parts, and from the settlements of the Columbia River or its neighborhood, by the Straits of Fuca, the Straits of Rosario, and the Gulf of Georgia.

3. In answer to the third question, I declare, as aforesaid, that, to the best of my knowledge, information, and belief, Langley, on the Fraser River, was settled about the year 1827 or 1828.

4. In answer to the fourth question, I declare, as aforesaid, that about the time of the negotiation of the Treaty of June, 1846, the common opinion as to the object of Great Britain insisting on the forty-ninth parallel being deflected in a southerly direction, through the Straits of

Fuca to the Pacific, instead of cutting through Vancouver Island, was to secure access to her possessions to the northward of the forty-ninth parallel.

5. In answer to the fifth question, I declare, as aforesaid, that Great Britain then held British Columbia up to parallel of north latitude 54° 40′, and Vancouver Island.

6. In answer to the sixth question, I declare, as aforesaid, that if the free navigation of the straits and adjacent channel was not guaranteed to Great Britain, access could only be obtained to those possessions by ships going to the westward of Vancouver Island; and as regards
[54] those possessions on *the coast of British Columbia, between the fifty-first and forty-ninth parallel, access would have to be sought through a strait which is intricate and difficult of navigation by reason of the strength of the tides.

7 and 8. In answer to the seventh and eighth questions, I declare, as aforesaid, that when the Treaty was signed in June, 1846, and previous to that date, the channel which was known and used by vessels amongst the islands forming the Archipelago between Vancouver Island and the continent, to get access to our dominions north of the forty-ninth parallel, was the Straits of Rosario, and that channel only, as it was then the only surveyed channel.

9. In answer to the ninth question, I declare, as aforesaid, that previous to the signing of the Treaty in 1846, and also at that time, the only channel known to be navigable amongst the islands forming the Archipelago between Vancouver Island and the continent of America was the Straits of Rosario.

I further declare, as aforesaid, the whole tenor of my experience during my said residence on or near the Northwest Pacific coast, was to the effect that the only recognized channel of approach to Fraser River, or to the northern parts by the inner passage through the Gulf of Georgia, was by the Straits of Rosario.

I further declare, as aforesaid, that in the winter of 1834, while on my way from Fort Simpson to the Columbia River, on board the Hudson's Bay Company's brig Dryad, Captain Kipling, we had orders to touch at Fort Langley on Fraser River. The track indicated to me upon Vancouver's chart by the master, and which we purposed to follow, was by the Rosario Strait, the usual and only known channel at that time. Stress of weather and the failure of provisions compelled us to bear up for the Columbia, after endeavoring to enter the Straits of Fuca without having fulfilled our object of proceeding to Langley.

In 1841, while I was in charge of the Hudson's Bay Company's establishment at Fort Nisqually, on Puget Sound, the United States Exploring Expedition, under Commodore Wilkes, arrived there. Commodore Wilkes was desirous of detaching a surveying-vessel (the Porpoise, Commander Ringgold) towards Fraser River, and on his application for a pilot, one of the crew of the Hudson Bay Company's steamer Beaver was sent on board. This pilot (whose name I think was Wade) was acquainted only with the Rosario Channel.

In June, or early in July, 1848, having conducted for the first time the brigade with the returns from the interior to Fort Langley on Fraser River, I traveled by canoe from that station to Victoria on Vancouver Island. Crossing the Gulf of Georgia, we passed through what has since been known as Plumper, or Active Pass, and then by the Strait of Haro. This was at that time known as the canoe-route, as distinguished from the established ship-route by the Rosario Strait.

In July, 1850, the schooner Cadboro, Captain Scarborough, arrived at

Langley during my visit there from the interior, bringing supplies for the trade. The following year another vessel belonging to the company (the Recovery, I think) came to the mouth of Fraser River to receive our furs. In neither case did I hear any mention of the Haro Channel, or that any deviation from the old established track had occurred.

That as late as 1851, I may distinctly state my conviction, from personal knowledge of facts, that the Rosario Strait was the only authorized channel of communication followed by the vessels of the Hudson's Bay Company. I have heard, indeed, that an experimental trip through the Haro Strait had, on one occasion, been made with the steamer Beaver, under Captain Brotchie, at that time master, but I understood likewise that the master was reprimanded on this occasion for his temerity. Whatever the partial explorations that had been made at an earlier period by the Spaniards, and afterwards by Commander Ringgold, of the United States Navy, the passage was incompletely known; and it was only after the survey performed under the direction of the present hydrographer of the Admiralty, Admiral Richards, in Her Majesty's ship Plumper, that the capacity of the Haro Strait as a channel of communication, superseding to some extent the original route by the Rosario Strait, was publicly recognized.

In conclusion, I distinctly state that, up to the winter of 1852–'53, when we were surprised by the adverse position then suddenly advanced, no doubt was entertained by me, or any one that I know of in this quarter, acquainted with the facts, as to that interpretation of the Treaty which refers the water-line to the only ship-channel then known, the Rosario Strait.

And I, the above-named Alexander Caulfield Anderson, solemnly declare that I make the above statements conscientiously, believing the same to be true, and by virtue of the provisions of an act made and passed in the sixth year of the reign of His Majesty King William IV, intituled "An act to repeal an act of the present session of Parliament, intituled an act for the more effectual abolition of oaths and affirmations taken and made in various departments of the state, and to substitute declarations in lieu thereof, and for the more entire suppression of voluntary and extra-judicial oaths and affidavits, and to make other provisions for the abolition of unnecessary oaths."

ALEXR. C. ANDERSON.

Declared at Victoria, Province of British Columbia, Dominion of Canada, this 16th day of September, 1871.

ROBT. E. JACKSON,
Notary Public, Victoria, British Columbia.

I hereby certify that Robert Edwin Jackson, whose signature is attached to this document, is a notary public by royal authority, duly authorized, admitted, and sworn, and that he is resident and practicing in Victoria, Province of British Columbia, Dominion of Canada.

CHARLES GOOD,
Colonial Secretary.

SEPTEMBER 21, 1871.

---

[55] *To all to whom these presents shall come: I, Montague William Tyrwhitt Drake, notary public by royal authority, duly authorized, admitted, and sworn, residing and practicing in Victoria, Province of British Columbia, Dominion of Canada, in pursuance of act of Par

liament, made and passed in the sixth year of the reign of His Majesty King William IV, intituled "An act to repeal an act of the present session of Parliament, intituled an act for the more effectual abolition of oaths and affirmations taken and made in various departments of the state, and to substitute declarations in lieu thereof, and for the more entire suppression of voluntary and extra-judicial oaths and affidavits, and to make other provisions for the abolition of unnecessary oaths," do hereby certify that, on the day of the date hereof, personally came and appeared before me Herbert G. Lewis, named and described in the declaration hereunto annexed, being a person well known and worthy of good credit, and, by solemn declaration which the said Herbert G. Lewis then made before me, did solemnly and sincerely declare to be true the several matters and things mentioned and contained in the said annexed declaration.

In faith and testimony whereof I have hereunto set my hand and seal of office, and have caused the declaration to be hereunto annexed. Dated at Victoria, the 14th day of September, in the year of our Lord 1871.

M. W. TYRWHITT DRAKE,
Notary Public.

I hereby certify that Montague William Tyrwhitt Drake, whose signature is hereunto attached, is a notary public, duly admitted and practicing in the city of Victoria, Province of British Columbia, Dominion of Canada.

In testimony whereof I have hereunto set my hand and official seal, this 4th day of October, A. D. 1871.

CHARLES GOOD,
Colonial Secretary.

This is the paper writing marked E, shown to Henry Slye Mason at the time of his making his declaration, and therein referred to on the 29th day of September, 1871.

Before me:

M. W. TYRWHITT DRAKE,
Notary Public.

E.

HERBERT G. LEWIS.

My name is Herbert G. Lewis, master mariner. I have been a master mariner since 1859. I came to this coast in 1847. I have been in the Hudson Bay Company's service from that time till now, and during the greater part of that time I have been trading on the North Pacific coast, in charge of that company's vessels.

2. In answer to question 2, I say: To the best of my knowledge, information, and belief, the only channel used by sailing-vessels going to Fort Langley on the Fraser River, through the Straits of Fuca, was the Rosario Straits, in the year 1848–'49.

4. In answer to question 4, I say: In the latter part of 1847 and in 1848 it was considered that the object was to give free access to British territory on the Northwest Pacific coast, up to the fifty-second parallel of latitude.

5. In answer to question 5, I say: She held Vancouver Island and she held British Columbia up to 54° 40′ north latitude.

6. In answer to question 6, I say: Only by going to the westward of Vancouver Island.

7. In answer to question 7, I say: I can only speak to the period after 1847, and to the best of my knowledge, information, and belief, from thence to 1848 and 1849 the Haro Straits were not used by sailing-vessels; if they had been so used, I, as a sea-faring man on the Northwest Pacific coast, should have heard of it.

8. In answer to question 8, I say: The reason for Haro Straits not being used by sailing-ships in 1847, 1848, and 1849, was that it was then unsurveyed.

9. In answer to question 9, I say: As I before said, in 1847, 1848, and 1849, Rosario Strait was used as a surveyed channel, and Haro Straits had not been surveyed, and was not so used by ships.

Vancouver's charts were used for these waters in 1847, and till 1854. I never knew the Spanish chart used, or any American chart used, about that time. To the best of my knowledge I never heard of a vessel going through Haro Straits, but only through Rosario Straits in 1847, 1848, and 1849.

The map A, especially as regards Haro Straits, is a most inaccurate representation of what was nautically known in 1847, 1848, and 1849; Haro Straits being then unknown, and Rosario Straits generally used by ships.

From 1847 till 1852 I was employed on board ships of the said company, trading between Honolulu and Victoria for the Hudson's Bay Company, and Haro Straits have been from time to time navigated since 1852 by me.

Tides are very irregular on the east coast of Vancouver Island. This irregularity could hardly exist if Haro Strait was the channel through which the main volume of water ebbed and flowed.

Off East Point and Patos Island a current with the ebb and flood tide sets so strong as to render that part of Haro Straits unsafe for sailing-vessels.

And I, Herbert G. Lewis, above named, solemnly declare that I make the above statements conscientiously, believing the same to be true, and by virtue of the provisions of an act made and passed in the sixth year of the reign of His Majesty King William IV, intituled "An act to repeal an act of the present session of Parliament, intituled an
[56] act for the more effectual abolition of oaths *and affirmations,
taken and made in the various departments of the state, and to substitute declarations in lieu thereof, and for the more entire suppression of voluntary and extra-judicial oaths and affidavits, and to make other provisions for the abolition of unnecessary oaths."

HERBERT G. LEWIS.

Declared at Victoria, Province of British Columbia, this 14th day of September, 1871.

M. W. TYRWHITT DRAKE,
Notary Public.

I hereby certify that M. W. Tyrwhitt Drake, whose signature is attached to this document, is a notary public by royal authority, duly authorized, admitted, and sworn; and that he is resident and practicing in Victoria, Province of British Columbia, Dominion of Canada.

CHARLES GOOD,
Colonial Secretary.

SEPTEMBER 21, 1871.

To all to whom these presents shall come: I, Robert Edwin Jackson, of the city of Victoria, Province of British Columbia, Dominion of Canada, notary public, duly admitted and practicing, in pursuance of the act of Parliament made and passed in the sixth year of the reign of His Majesty King William IV, intituled "An act to repeal an act of the present session of Parliament intituled 'An act for the more effectual abolition of oaths and affirmations taken and made in various departments of the state, and to substitute declarations in lieu thereof, and for the more entire suppression of voluntary and extra-judicial oaths and affidavits, and to make other provisions for the abolition of unnecessary oaths,'" do hereby declare that, on the day of the date hereof, personally came and appeared before me Roderick Finlayson, named and described in the declaration hereunto annexed, being a person well known and worthy of good credit, and, by solemn declaration which the said Roderick Finlayson then made before me, did solemnly and sincerely declare to be true the several matters and things mentioned and contained in the said annexed declaration.

In faith and testimony whereof I have hereunto set my hand and seal of office, and have caused the said declaration to be hereunto annexed. Dated the 30th day of September, A. D. 1871.

ROBT. E. JACKSON,
Notary Public.

I hereby certify that Robert Edwin Jackson, whose signature is hereunto attached, is a notary public, duly admitted and practicing in the city of Victoria, Province of British Columbia, Dominion of Canada.

In testimony whereof I have hereunto set my hand and official seal, this 4th day of October, A. D. 1871.

CHARLES GOOD,
Colonial Secretary.

This is the exhibit marked F, referred to in the annexed declaration of Roderick Finlayson, declared the 13th day of September, 1871.

Before me:

ROBT. E. JACKSON,
Notary Public.

F.

Interrogatories relative to the northwest water-boundary question submitted to Roderick Finlayson.

1. About 1845–'46, had the Hudson's Bay Company any fort or settlement on the Fraser River?

2. How did trading-vessels or other craft communicate with that fort or settlement from foreign parts, and from other settlements on the Columbia River or its neighborhood?

3. The date of the settlement of Fort Langley on Fraser River?

4. About the time of the negotiation of the Treaty of June, 1846, what was the common opinion of Great Britain insisting on the forty-ninth parallel being deflected in a southerly direction, through the Straits of Fuca to the Pacific, instead of cutting through Vancouver Island?

5. If to secure access to the possessions to the northward of the 49° parallel, state what possession Great Britain held to the northward of 49° and where?

6. If the free navigation of the straits and adjacent channel was not

guaranteed to Great Britain, how could access be obtained to those possessions north of 49°?

7. When the Treaty was signed in June, 1846, and previous to that date, which channel was known and used by vessels amongst the islands forming the Archipelagos between Vancouver's Island and the continent, to get access to our dominions north of 49°?

8. Forward proofs and affidavits, legally attested, by captains of vessels and others who made use of the channel then known, and their reasons for making use of it.

9. Previous to the signing of the treaty in 1846, and also at that time, how many channels were known to be navigable amongst the islands forming the Archipelago between Vancouver Island and the continent of America?

I, Roderick Finlayson, of Victoria, Vancouver Island, in the Province of British Columbia, Dominion of Canada, Chief Factor in the Hudson's Bay Company, do solemnly and sincerely declare as follows:

[57] *I have been on the Northwest Pacific coast since A. D. 1840, and during all that time have been in the Hudson's Bay Company's employ. I have been a Chief Factor since 1859, and a Lloyd's Agent since 1856, and from A. D. 1844 to 1847 I was the Chief Agent of the Hudson's Bay Company at Victoria.

Referring to the interrogatories relative to the northwest water-boundary question hereunto annexed, marked F, shown to me at the time of making this declaration, in answer to the first interrogatory I declare, as aforesaid:

1. That about A. D. 1845 and 1846, the Hudson's Bay Company had a settlement at Langley, on the Fraser River, and the said settlement existed since 1827 or 1828.

2. In answer to the second interrogatory, I declare, as aforesaid, that up to A. D. 1845 and 1846, Hudson's Bay Company's ships, bound from Honolulu, in the Sandwich Islands, from Fort Vancouver, on the Columbia River, and San Francisco and Sitka, to Langley, passed through Fuca's Straits and Rosario Straits; also vessels trading between Fort Nisqually and Langley used to pass through Rosario Strait.

3. In answer to the third interrogatory, I declare, as aforesaid, to the best of my knowledge, information, and belief, Langley, on the Fraser River, was settled about the year 1827 or 1828.

4. In answer to the fourth interrogatory, I declare, as aforesaid, that about the time of the negotiation of the Treaty of June, 1846, the common opinion as to the object of Great Britain in insisting on the forty-ninth parallel being deflected in a southerly direction, and through the Straits of Fuca to the Pacific, instead of cutting through Vancouver Island, was that it was to secure access to her possessions to the northward of the forty-ninth parallel through the Straits of Fuca.

5. In answer to the fifth interrogatory, I declare, as aforesaid, that Great Britain then held British Columbia up to parallel of north latitude 54° 40′, and Vancouver Island.

6. In answer to the sixth interrogatory, I declare, as aforesaid, that if the free navigation of the straits and adjacent channel was not guaranteed by Great Britain, access could only be secured and obtained to those possessions by ships going to the westward of Vancouver Island; and as regards those possessions on the coast of British Columbia, between the fifty-first and forty-ninth parallel, access would have to be sought through a strait which is intricate and difficult of navigation by reason of the strength of the tides.

7 and 8. In answer to the seventh and eighth questions, I declare, as

aforesaid, that when the Treaty was signed in June, 1846, and previous to that date, the channel which was known and used by vessels among the islands forming the Archipelago between Vancouver Island and the continent, to get access to the dominions of Great Britain north of the forty-ninth parallel, was the Strait of Rosario, and that channel only; and it was the only surveyed channel.

9. In answer to the ninth interrogatory, I declare, as aforesaid, that previous to the signing of the Treaty in 1846, and also at that time, the only channel known to be navigable among the islands forming the Archipelago between Vancouver Island and the continent was the Strait of Rosario.

And I further declare, as aforesaid, that in A. D. 1840, I went from the Hudson's Bay Company's Station at Nisqually, Puget Sound, in the steamer Beaver, to Sitka, through Rosario Strait and Johnson Strait; and, in A. D. 1843, I returned from Sitka and other stations through Johnson Strait and Rosario Strait to Vancouver Island in the Beaver.

Previous to A. D. 1846, Rosario Strait was the channel for vessels coming to Victoria from Fraser River and the Northwest Pacific coast, or going from Victoria thereto.

And I, Roderick Finlayson, above named, solemnly declare that I make the above statements conscientiously, believing the same to be true, and by virtue of the provisions of an act made and passed in the sixth year of the reign of His Majesty King William IV, intituled "An act to repeal an act of the present session of Parliament, intituled 'An act for the more effectual abolition of oaths and affirmations taken and made in various departments of the state, and to substitute declarations in lieu thereof, and for the more entire suppression of voluntary and extra-judicial oaths and affidavits, and to make other provisions for the abolition of unnecessary oaths.' "

RODK. FINLAYSON.

Declared at Victoria, in the Province of British Columbia, Dominion of Canada, this 30th day of September, 1871.

Before me:

ROBT. E. JACKSON,
Notary Public.

[58]

*No. VI.

ATTESTED COPY OF THE LOG OF HER MAJESTY'S STEAMSHIP CORMORANT, IN THE MONTHS OF SEPTEMBER AND OCTOBER, 1846.

Nineteenth day of September, 1846.—*At Fisgard Harbor.*

Initials of the officer of the watch.	Hours.	Knots.	Tenths.	Standard compass courses.	Leeway points.	Wind.		Weather.	Deviation of standard compass.	Height of—		Temperature of the sea.	Remarks.
						Direction.	Force.			Barometer.	Thermometer.		
	1					S. W.	1	o. g. c.					A. M. 5.—Lighted fire under after boilers. 6.20.—Steam up, unmoored ship; hove into twelve fathoms on B. B. 6.30.—Weighed and proceeded out of harbor working expansively, cutting off at 1/5 stroke. 8.—Trial Island West, 1¼ m. Employed clearing deck and ship below. Noon.—Saddle Island, N. W. by N. 2 m. Expended—Coals: Tons 2, Cwt. 19 Wood: Tons 3, Cwt. 16
	2												
	3												
	4			At anchor in Fisgard Harbor									
	5												
	6					Calm	0	o. c. m.					
	7			Proceeding to the eastward, north of Smith's Island, for passage east of Saddle Island and Rocks for west point of Strawberry Bay.									
	8					East	1	c. m.					
	9					E. N. E.							
	10						2	g. c. m.					
	11						3						
	Noon.						2						
	1			Proceeding to the northward, west of Strawberry Island, for Birch Bay and Point Roberts.									P. M. 5.—Sounded off Point Roberts, 50 fathoms. 5.30.—Eased, stopped and came to with B. B. in 11 fathoms. Veered to 48 fathoms. Banked up fires. Point Roberts, S. 55° E. South Point Fraser's River, N. 48° W.
	2					E. N. E.	1	b. c. m.					
	3					Calm	0						
	4							c. m.					
	5							g. c. m.					
	6					N. E.	1	o. c. d.					
	7			At anchor under Point Roberts			2						
	8					N. N. E.	3						
	9						2	o. c.					
	10						1	c. r.					
	11												
	Midn't.							c. r.					

Fifth day of October, 1846.—*From Sangster's Harbor to Birch Bay.*

Initials of the officer of the watch.	Hours.	Knots.	Tenths.	Standard compass courses.	Leeway points.	Wind. Direction.	Wind. Force.	Weather.	Deviation of standard compass.	Height of— Barometer.	Height of— Thermometer.	Temperature of the sea.	Remarks.
	1					East	1	b. c.					A. M. Fires banked. 4.30.—Drew fires forward. 4.45.—Steam up. 5.—Weighed and proceeded out to the eastward, working two after boilers expansively, cutting off at 1/6 of stroke. 6.30.—East Point, Sangster Island, S. S. E. 9.—Exercised at general quarters. 10.45.—Sounded 50 fathoms. Noon.—Point Gray, N. 45° E. Point Roberts, S. 83° E. Lat. obs. 49° 8′ N. Expended—Coals: Tons 8, Cwt. 2 Wood: Tons 6, Cwt. 0
	2	....	....	At anchor in Sangster's Harbor									
	3					E. N. E	2						
	4												
	5												
	6	....	....	Proceeding out		....	....	c.					
	7	....	....	E. S. E. towards Point Roberts									
	8					Easterly							
	9												
	10	....	....	....		E. S. E.							
	11												
	Noon	....	....	....		S. E. by E.	....	b. c.					
	1					E. S. E	3	b. c.					P. M. 0.45.—Entered discolored water off Fraser's River. 4.—Point Roberts, N. N. W. 3 m. 3.30.—Eased, stopped, came to with B. B. in Birch Bay in 7 fathoms., and veered to 32 fathoms. Banked up fires. Point Roberts, S. 83° W. Called the north point of bay, bearing N. 47° W., Point Lacy after the third lieutenant; south point of bay, a white bluff S. 41° E., Point Nutt after the surgeon of the ship. Midnight.—Fires banked under after boilers.
	2	....	....	Proceeding eastward, towards Point Roberts and Birch Bay.									
	3					East.							
	4												
	5												
	6	....	....	....		....	2						
	7												
	8	....	....	At anchor in Birch Bay		S. E.							
	9												
	10												
	11												
	Midn't	....	....	....		South	1	c.					

[59]

Sixth day of October, 1846.

Hours			Courses		Winds	Force	Weather					Remarks
1 2 3 4	...	...	At anchor in Birch Bay.	...	....	2	o. c.					A. M. 4.30.—Drew the fires forward. 4.45.—Steam up. 4.50.—Weighed and proceeded out to the southward working expansively, cutting off at 1/5 of stroke. 7.25.—Passed eastward of Quinlan's Rocks, named after the second lieutenant of this ship. 7.45.—Off the north end of Cyprus Island, called the new point, Scarborough Bluff, after the master of the Cadboro. 8.—Saddle Island 5½ E. 8.20.—Passed the S. W. point of Cyprus Island; called it Finlaison Point, after the officer in charge of Fort Victoria. 9.—Exercised at general quarters. 10.—Loosed sails to dry. Noon.—Point Gonzalo, N. 39° W. Clover Point, N. 89° W.
5 6 7 8	...	...	Proceeding out westward of Cyprus Island towards Saddle Island, towards Smith's and Trial Island.	...	South. S. S. W.... Vble......	... 1	c.					
9 10 11 Noon	...	...	....	...	Calm	0	b. c.					Expended—Coal: 9 Tons, 4 Cwt.; Wood: 1 Tons, 8 Cwt.
1 2 3	...	...	Proceeding for Port Victoria........	...	E. N. E ...	2	b. c.					P. M. Opened tea, 13.44; beef, 136.3; pork, 30.80. 1.—Eased, stopped, and came to with B. B. in 9 fathoms. Veered to 40 fathoms, banked up fires. Points of entrance, S. 74° E., and S. 74° W. Rocky point, S. 25° W. Employed cutting wood for fuel. 2.—Furled sails, unbent maintopsail. Ship's draught—forward....14 feet. aft........15 feet. Remaining water, 29 tons.
4 5 6 7 8	...	...	At anchor in Port Victoria.	...	N. E.							
9 10 11 Midn't..	...	...	....	...	North	1						

The within copy of the log-book of Her Majesty's ship Cormorant, for the days above specified, has been examined and compared with the original in this Department.

A. SCOTT.

ADMIRALTY, SOMERSET HOUSE, *November* 16, 1871.

III.

REPLY OF THE UNITED STATES

TO

THE CASE OF THE GOVERNMENT OF HER BRITANNIC MAJESTY,

PRESENTED TO

HIS MAJESTY THE EMPEROR OF GERMANY,

AS ARBITRATOR,

UNDER THE PROVISIONS OF THE TREATY OF WASHINGTON, JUNE 12, 1872.

REPLY.

The United States on the 12th of December last presented their Memorial, on the Canal de Haro as the boundary line of the United States of America, to the Imperial Arbitrator, and to the representative of Her Britannic Majesty's Government at Berlin. To the Case of the Government of Her Britannic Majesty, likewise submitted at that time, they now offer their reply. A formal answer to every statement in the British Case to which they take exception, would require a wearisome analysis of almost every one of its pages. They hold it sufficient, to point out a few of the allegations which they regard as erroneous; to throw light upon the argument on which the British principally rest their Case; to establish the consistency of the American Government by tracing the controversy through all its changes to its present form; and, lastly, to apply to the interpretation of the Treaty some of the principles which Her Britannic Majesty's Government itself has invoked.

I.—THE BRITISH CASE.

The argument of Her Britannic Majesty's Government has kept in the background the clear words of the Treaty describing the bound-
[4] ary, and has made no attempt to bring *them into harmony with the British claim. On the contrary, in the statement of the question submitted for arbitration, it assumes that the Treaty of 1871 speaks "as if there were more than one channel between the continent and Vancouver Island through which the boundary may be run." The United States are of the opinion that the Treaty of 1846 designates the Haro Channel precisely as the only channel of the boundary. The words are: "The channel that separates the continent from Vancouver Island;" and there is but one such channel. The so-called Straits of Rosario touch neither the continent nor Vancouver Island.

British Case, p. 3.

The name of the continent of South America, as used by geographers, includes the group of islands south of the Straits of Magellan. The continent of Asia includes Ceylon and Sumatra; the continent of Europe includes Great Britain and Ireland, and the Hebrides. Asia Minor includes Lesbos, and Scio, and Samos, and Rhodes, and Tenedos; and so the continent of North America includes all adjacent islands, to the great Pacific.

Were the question to be asked, "What channel separates the continent of Europe from Candia?" the answer would not draw the line north of the greater part of the Ægean Archipelago, but, like all European diplomacy, would point to the channel south of Santorin. In like manner, when the Treaty speaks of "that channel which separates the continent from Vancouver Island," nothing is excepted but Vancouver Island itself.

The United States assented, in 1871, to no more than that Great Britain might lay her pretensions before an impartial tribunal, all the while believing and avowing, that the simple statement which has just been made is absolutely conclusive on the point submitted for arbitration.

British Case, p. 33.

The British Case seeks to draw an inference unfavorable to the American demand from the proviso in the Treaty of 1846 which secures to either party the free navigation of the whole
[5] *of Fuca's Straits. It is quite true that the right was safe, and was known to be safe "under the public law;" yet it appears from documents printed at the time, that, as the recent assertion by the Russian Government of a claim to the exclusive navigation of a part of the Northern Pacific Ocean was recollected, it was thought best to insert the superfluous clause, recognizing the straits of Fuca as an arm of the sea.

Senate Documents, vol. ix, Doc. 489, p. 44. Appendix to Memorial, p. 47.

British Case, pp. 10, 32.

The British argument seems suited to mislead by its manner of using the name "straits of Rosario." The first channel from the straits of Fuca to the north, that was discovered and partly examined in 1790, was the Canal de Haro. The expedition under Lieutenant Eliza explored that channel in June, 1791, with the greatest industry and care, and discovered the broad water which is its continuation to the north. That water, lying altogether to the north of the northern termination of Haro Channel, was named by the expedition, El Gran Canal de Neustra Señora del Rosario la Marinera. Thus the Canal de Haro and the true Spanish Channel of Rosario form at once the oldest historical continuous channel, as it is the one continuous boundary-channel of the Treaty of 1846.

Appendix No. 62, p. 100, l. 37, 38.

Map K.
Map C.

The passage which the British authorities now call the Straits of Rosario, appears as early as 1791 on the map of Eliza as the Channel of Fidalgo. Vancouver, coming after Eliza, transferred the name of Rosario to the strait east of the island of Texada. The British Admiralty, soon after receiving the surveys made under its orders in 1847 by Captain Kellett, suddenly removed the name of the straits of Rosario from the narrow water between the continent and the island of Texada, where it had remained on British maps for fifty years, to the passage which the Spaniards called the channel of Fidalgo. And yet the Government of Her Britannic Majesty advances the assertion, that "how the name has come to be" so "applied in modern days does not appear." For this act of the British Admiralty in February, 1849, there exists no historical justification whatever.

Admiralty Map of Vancouver Island and the Gulf of Georgia. From the surveys of Captain G. Vancouver, R. N., 1793, Captains D. Galiano and C. Valdes 1792, Captain H. Kellett, R. N., 1847. Published Feb. 28, 1849.

British Case, p. 10.

[6] *The United States have obtained from the Hydrographical Bureau in Madrid a certified copy of two reports, made in 1791, of the explorations of de Eliza, and a fac-simile of a map which accompanied them. On this authentic map, of which a lithographic copy is laid before the Imperial Arbitrator, the position of the canal de Haro, of the Spanish canal de Rosario, and of the channel of Fidalgo may be seen at a glance, as they were determined by the expedition of Eliza in the year 1791.

Map K.

The British Case exaggerates the importance of the voyage of Captain Vancouver. So far were American fur-traders from following his guidance, they were his forerunners and teachers. Their early voyages are among the most marvelous events in the history of commerce. So soon as the Independence of the United States was acknowledged by Great Britain, the strict enforcement of the old, unrepealed navigation laws cut them off from their former haunts of commerce, and it became a question from what ports American ships could bring home coffee, and sugar, and spices, and tea. All British colonies were barred against them as much as were those of Spain. So American ships sailed into eastern oceans, where trade with the natives was free. The great Asi-

atic commerce poured wealth into the lap of the new republic, and Americans, observing the fondness of the Chinese for furs, sailed fearlessly from the Chinese seas or round Cape Horn to the northwest coast of America in quest of peltry to exchange for the costly fabrics and products of China. They were in the waters of northwest America long before the Hudson's Bay Company. We know, alike from British and from Spanish authorities, that an American sloop, fitted out at Boston in New England, and commanded by Captain Kendrick, passed through the straits of Fuca just at the time when the American Constitution went into operation—two years before Vancouver, and even before Quimper and de Haro. Americans did not confine themselves to one pas-
[7] sage in preference to others, but entered every *channel, and
inlet, and harbor, where there was a chance of trafficking with a red Indian for skins; and they handed down from one to another the results of their discoveries.

Meare's Voyage. lvi, 235. Vancouver's Voyages, vol. i, xx. [Quimper Ms. Journal. Documento existento en el archivo de Indias en Sevilla.' Appendix No. 62, p. 101.

The instruction from the British Admiralty to Captain Vancouver was prompted by an account, which they had seen, of the voyage of Kendrick, and the belief, derived from that account, that the waters of the Pacific might reach far into the American continent. Vancouver was therefore instructed to search for channels and rivers leading into the interior of the continent, the farther to the south the better, in the hope that water communication might be found even with the Lake of the Woods. In conformity to these instructions, founded on the voyage of Americans, he entered the straits of Fuca, and keeping always as near as he could to the eastern shore, he vainly searched the coast to the southern limit of Puget Sound. Turning to the north, he passed through the channel of Fidalgo, or the spurious Rosario, because his instructions required him to keep near the shore of the continent.

Appendix No. 63, pp. 101, 102.

The inference of Her Britannic Majesty's Government, that the so-called Rosario Strait is the channel of the Treaty because Vancouver sailed through it, is a fallacy. He never committed such a mistake as to represent the so-called Rosario, which he apparently did not even think worthy of a name, as being comparable to the channel of Haro.

The argument of Her Britannic Majesty's Government misstates the character and exaggerates the value of the chart of Vancouver by assuming that he prepared directions to mariners for navigation. But the chart which is produced is only one map among many, never published apart from a work, too voluminous, expensive, and rare to find a place on board the small vessels of fur-traders. The line on his map is nothing more nor less than the track of his own course while engaged in explorations under controlling instructions, and is a track which no ship has followed or is likely to follow.

[8] *The British argument frequently refers to the soundings taken
by Vancouver in the Fidalgo-Rosario Channel. Only two such soundings appear on his map, while there are five or six on an arm of the Canal de Haro, and one on its edge, showing that its waters were found to be more than two hundred feet deep. The chart of these waters for mariners, published by the Spaniards in 1795, exhibits many soundings to facilitate the use of the Canal de Haro. If this excellent chart contains no soundings in the great center of the channel of Haro, it is for a reason to which Vancouver repeatedly refers, that the usual sounding-lines of those days were not long enough to touch bottom in the deep waters where walls of igneous rock go perpendicularly down hundreds of feet, close even to the shore. "Even nearest the islands,"

British Case, pp. 11, 18, 19, 28, 31.

Map L.

Appendix No. 64, p. 102.

writes De Eliza, "we could not find bottom with a line of forty fathoms." "Proximo á las islas, no se encuentra fondo con 40 brazas."

The British Case assigns in like manner an undue prominence to the

British Case, pp. 11, 32.

trade in the Vancouver waters prior to the treaty of 1846. As to general commerce, there was none. As to settlements, properly so called, there could be none; for under the British treaty with Spain, and the treaty of non-occupation between the United States and Great Britain, impliedly at least, there could be no grants or holdings of territory by individuals or companies of either party. The American voyages on the northwest coast were entirely broken up by the maritime orders and acts of England which preceded the war of 1812; and the American fur-trade never recovered from the effects of that war. The trade became a monopoly of the Hudson's Bay Company,

Appendix No. 67, pp. 104, 105.

and that company boasted officially that "they compelled the Americans one by one to withdraw from the contest." The United States acknowledge that the boast was true. At rare intervals of years, Americans may have entered Fuca's Straits, but a careful search fails to discover proof that even one single United States vessel sailed into those waters between the year 1810 and the [9] * arrival of the American Exploring Expedition under Wilkes in 1841. A monopoly of the trade was maintained by the Hudson's Bay Company, not against Americans only, but against all ships but their own. What then becomes of the British argument, that trading-vessels of other nations were in all that time not known to pass through the Canal de Haro?

The Hudson's Bay Company was once a company of commercial importance, as well as of political influence, But the hunting-ground over which it ranged was enormously wide, stretching from Labrador to California and to the Russian settlements in northwestern America. They could spare very little of their limited resources for the waters around San Juan Island. Their leading settlement in the West, until 1843, was at Fort Vancouver on Columbia River. Of shipping in their employ, nothing is heard for many years, except of one small steamer,

Appendix No. 53, p. 66, l. 15.

the Beaver, and of one small schooner, the Cadboro. Wilkes in 1841 met only the Beaver. These vessels were accustomed twice a year to make the trip from Fort Vancouver to the various posts,

Appendix, p. 66, l. 18-21; No. 56, pp. 69, 70, p. 72, l. 20-40, p. 73, l. 1-27; No. 59, p. 76.

to distribute supplies and to collect furs. If in these trips they chose to pass through the Fidalgo-Rosario channel, rather than the Canal de Haro, the British Case has omitted to state the reason of the choice. In the semi-annual trip from Fort Vancouver to the trading posts, the first one that was visited

British Case, p. 51, p. 48.

was Nisqually, at the head of Puget Sound. A vessel sailing from that part of the United States to Fraser's River would naturally pass through the Fidalgo-Rosario channel. To have

Map N.

taken any other would have been circuitous. A geographical sketch is annexed, from which the reason will appear why the vessels on these trips passed through the so-called Rosario Straits; not because it was the great channel from the Straits of Juan de Fuca to the north, but because it was the shortest passage between Nisqually in Puget Sound and Fort Langley on Fraser's River. The return voyage, when there was no need of touching at Nisqually, was sometimes made by the Channel of Haro.

Appendix No. 53, p. 66.

[10] * "There were no vessels engaged in those waters, writes Rear-Admiral Wilkes of his visit to them in 1841, "except the small and very inefficient steamer, called the Beaver, commanded by Captain McNeill, who spoke of it [the Strait of Haro]

to me as the best passage, although he was obliged to pass through the Rosario passage."

Again, in narrating the survey of the Haro channel by the United States exploring expedition, in 1841, the British Case shapes the narrative so as to give the impression that the American British Case, p. 19. expedition regarded the so-called straits of Rosario as superior to the Haro, while the opposite is the truth. Commodore Wilkes, who commanded the expedition, detached a subordinate officer in the Vincennes to survey the channels among the islands of the archipelago; he reserved for himself the more important but less difficult office of surveying the channel of Haro.

On the 26th page of the British Case it is asserted that the late Mr. Daniel Webster stated in the Senate of the United States that the great aim of the United States in 1846 was to es- British Case, p. 26. tablish the forty-ninth parallel of north latitude as the line of boundary on the western side of the Rocky Mountains, "not to be departed from for any line further south on the continent."

The inference drawn from this is, that Mr. Webster demanded the line of the parallel of 49° for "the continent" only, and was indifferent as to "the islands."

Mr. Webster was not at that time a member of the Government of the United States, but the leader of the political minority in the Senate, which opposed the administration of that day. The United States, therefore, may, without questioning the great authority of his name, deny that he is to be received as an interpreter of the views of the cabinet which negotiated the treaty of 1846. It may, however, surprise the Imperial Arbitrator to learn that Mr. Webster not only did not entertain the opinions attributed to him, but expressed himself in a sense exactly the reverse.

[11] *Some members of the Senate insisted on the parallel of 54° 40′ as the American boundary; Mr. Webster declared himself content with the parallel of 49°. But his words were absolute. The British Case puts words into his mouth which he never uttered. What Mr. Webster said was, that the line of 49° was "not to be departed from for any line further south." The words "on the continent" are an interpolation made by the British Case. In the same debate and on the same day Mr. Webster, to guard against misrepresentation, observed with great solemnity: "The Senate will do me the justice to allow, that I said as plainly as I could speak, or put down Appendix No. 65, words in writing, that England must not expect anything pp. 102, 103. south of forty-nine degrees."

The Government of Her Britannic Majesty includes in the charts annexed to its Case a map of Oregon and Upper California British Case. drawn by one Preuss, and yet in its printed Case there is not Map No. 5. one single word explaining why the map has been produced. The United States know only that on a former occasion Captain, now Admiral Prevost, the British Boundary Commissioner, wrote of it, Appendix No. 70, in his official character, to the American Boundary Commis- p. 109, l. 1-4. sioner: "I beg you to understand that I do not bring this map forward as any authority for the line of boundary."

Forty years ago the mountain ranges and upland plains from which the water flows to the Gulf of California, or is lost in inland seas, still remained as little known as the head springs of the Congo and of the Nile. Frémont had thrice penetrated those regions, once or more with Preuss in his service as draughtsman. On the return of Frémont from his third expedition, the Senate of the United States, although he was

not then in the public service, instead of leaving him to seek a publisher, on the 5th and 15th of June, 1848, at the instance of Mr. Benton, voted to print his geographical memoir on Upper California,
[12] and the map of Oregon and *California, "according to the projection to be furnished by the said J. C. Frémont."

In representative governments, each branch of the legislature may order printed what it will; but the order gives no sanction to what is printed. Last winter, for example, the German Diet printed at the public cost, that the German constitution is not worth the paper it is written on. Neither Frémont nor Preuss had ever been within many hundred miles of the straits of Fuca, and Frémont himself says, "The part of the map which exhibits Oregon is chiefly copied from the works of others." The Senate never saw the map as delivered to the lithographer. The work was printed, not under the revision of officers of the Senate, but solely "subject to the revision of its author." Except for the regions which he had himself explored, Frémont abandoned the drawing of the map to Preuss, who followed "other authorities." While Mr. Preuss was compiling his map, Mr. Bancroft, the representative of his country in London, with full authority from the President and Secretary of State of the United States, delivered to the British Government in the clearest words the declaration of his own Government that the boundary line passes through the middle of the Haro channel. Any error of Mr. Preuss was therefore perfectly harmless.

Senate Miscellaneous Documents No. 148, 30th Congress, 1st session.

Appendix No. 51, p. 62, l, 5, 6, p. 63, l. 9, 10.

And under any circumstances what authority could attach to a draught by Mr. Preuss? He was one of the many adventurers who throng to the United States, a mechanic, possessing no scientific culture, and holding his talent as a draughtsman at the command of any who would employ him.

The United States are unable to inform the Imperial Arbitrator what authority served as a guide to Mr. Preuss when he drew the Oregon boundary to suit British pretensions. Not Mr. Benton; his opinion was well known. Not the Senate, which is the only permanent body under our Constitution, and which, in the twenty-five years since the treaty was made, has inflexibly maintained the right of the United
[13] States to the *Haro boundary. Not Mr. Buchanan, the Secretary of State, whose instructions on the Haro as the boundary, sanctioned by the President and his cabinet, date from the year in which the treaty was made. Neither could Preuss have copied the line from printed materials. No such printed materials existed at that time. A wish expressed by the British minister at Washington slumbered in the Department of State, and was known only to the President and his cabinet.

Mr. Preuss is no longer living to explain by whom he was misled. Mr. Frémont remembers that Mr. Preuss had among his materials a copy of a manuscript map of the northwest territory by the Hudson's Bay Company, received from one of its officers. Be this as it may, it is enough for the United States to have shown that the map never had the sanction of any branch of their Government.

Analogous mistakes have been made in Great Britain, and under weightier authority. Pending the discussion between the two countries, Messrs. Malby & Co. of London, "manufacturers and publishers to the Society for the Diffusion of Useful Knowledge," sent out a large and splendid globe, on which they assigned to the United States by line and color the whole northwestern territory up to the latitude of 54° 40′.

To treat mistakes like these as important is unsuited to negotiations

between great powers. The United States do not complain that the map of Preuss is produced by Her Majesty's Government, for the production of it is a confession of the feebleness of the British Case. They might complain that Her Britannic Majesty's Government did not state what it hoped to prove by the map. They might complain that it produced the map without an acknowledgment of its well-known worthlessness as an exposition of American opinion. And above all they might complain of the British Government for submitting the map to the Imperial Arbitrator without avowing that its own archives contain a con-
[14] temporaneous, explicit, and authoritative *declaration from the American Government, that the straits of Haro are the boundary channel of the treaty of 1846.

II.—REPLY TO THE ARGUMENTS OF THE BRITISH CASE.

Having thus drawn attention to the character of the paper which the Government of Her Britannic Majesty has presented as its Case, its allegations in support of its pretensions are next to be examined. The Government of Her Britannic Majesty presents but one argument, and that argument has two branches. The British Government admits, and even insists, that the channel of the treaty must be a continuous channel from the forty-ninth parallel to the straits of Fuca; and it argues, first, that the strait which is now called Rosario, but which, at the time of making the treaty of 1846, had "no distinguishing name," must have been the channel contemplated by the treaty, because the British, at that time, "had no assurance" that the canal de Haro "was even navigable;" "had a firm belief that it was a dangerous strait;" and, secondly, that Fuca Straits extend from Cape Flattery to Whidbey Island. In discussing these two points their order will be reversed.

First, then, do the straits of Fuca, as now pretended by Great Britain, reach to Whidbey Island? The answer depends in part on the definition of the word "strait." Her Majesty's Government forget that the word applies only to a narrow "passage connecting one part of a sea with another." Such is a lesson taught by all geographers, whether British, or French, or American, or German. As soon as the southeast cape of Vancouver Island is passed, the volume of water spreads into a broad expanse, filled with numerous islands, and becomes a gulf or bay, but is no longer a strait.

Neither can it be pretended that any exception takes place in the geographical usage of the name "straits of Fuca," as employed
[15] in all the scientific explorations and maps pre*vious to June, 1846. On the contrary, the pretension is hazarded in the face of them all.

The first map of the strait is by the pilot Lopez de Haro; on that the mouth of the so-called strait of Rosario is named Boca de Fidalgo, and the water to the south of it bears the name of the gulf of Santa Rosa. Map J

The map of Eliza, in 1791, confines the name of the straits of Juan de Fuca to the straits that separate Vancouver Island on the south from the continent; and that officer in his report repeats the name of the gulf of Santa Rosa as the name of the interior waters. Map K

The explorers in the Sutil and Mexicana, alike in the Spanish chart of 1795, and in the map annexed to the publication of their voyage in 1802, call the straits "Entrada," a Spanish word that can extend to no more than an entrance. Map L

Next came Vancouver, and the great authority of the British navigator overthrows the British argument beyond room for cavil; for he not only, like all his predecessors, confines the name of Straits of Juan de Fuca to the passage between Vancouver Island on the south and the continent, but, alike in his narrative and on his map, expressly distinguishes those straits from "the interior sea," which he, with great solemnity, named the gulf of Georgia.

Map C.

The map of Duflot de Mofras, of 1844, and that of Wilkes, in 1845, confine the name of the straits of Fuca strictly to the waters that really form a strait between the continent and the southern line of Vancouver Island.

Map E.
Map F.

The government of Her Britannic Majesty cannot produce one single map older than 1846 in defense of its views.

The common use of language among the British in Vancouver still corresponds with the undivided testimony of the maps. Pemberton, surveyor-general of Vancouver Island, in a work published in 1860, writes thus of a "stranger steaming, for
[16] the first time, eastward into the straits of Juan de Fuca:" *"On his right hand is Washington Territory; on his left is Vancouver Island; straight before him is the gulf of Georgia."

Appendix No. 66, pp. 103, 104.

The statement of Commander Mayne is, if possible, still more precise. Of the Strait of Juan de Fuca, he writes in these words: "At the Race Islands the strait may be said to terminate, as it there opens out into a large expanse of water." Now the Race Islands, or Race Rocks, alike on the British and American maps, lie to the southwest of the channel of Haro. On the point in question there could be no better authority than Commander Mayne, as he is a man of science, and was employed on the surveys during the period in which Captain, now Admiral, Prevost and Captain Richards acted as the British Boundary Commissioners.

Appendix No. 66, p. 103.

But to refute the British assumption, we need not go outside of the British Case itself. On page 27 it claims the chart of Vancouver as the chart according to which Her Majesty's Government framed the first article of the treaty, and then most correctly says: "The name of the gulf of Georgia is assigned on that chart to the whole of the interior sea."

British Case, p 27.

Thus this branch of the argument offered by the British Government is in flat contradiction to the proper use of language, to nature, to the concurrent testimony of every competent witness, and is given up before the end of the very paper in which it is presented.

We now come to the other branch of the British argument: that prior to 1846 there was no assurance that the canal de Haro was even navigable. That channel is now universally acknowledged to be the best and most convenient for the British. It forms the only line of communication regularly used by them. The mail steamers take only that route. It is the broadest, it is the deepest, it is the shortest passage; and so it is the only one used by the government, the traders, the immigrants, and inhabitants of British Columbia. It became
[17] the exclusive channel as soon as gold-hunting *lured adventurers to that region, and the navigation of those waters was no longer confined to the vessels coasting from one to another of the trading-posts of the Hudson's Bay Company. Its superiority appears alike from the chart of the British Admiralty and of the American Coast Survey. A map is annexed exhibiting in several cross-sections the relative depths of its channel.

Appendix Nos. 53, 54, 55, 57, 58, 61.

Map M.

The plea of ignorance on the part of the British up to 1846 is irrelevant. The treaty does not designate the channel which was or was not most in use, but the channel which separates the continent from Vancouver.

In negotiating the treaty neither side had in view the tracks of the few former fur-traders whose course was run; but the great channels provided by nature for future commerce. American statesmen officially foretold at the time to the British negotiators that, under American auspices, flourishing commonwealths, such as we now see in California and Oregon, would rise up on the Pacific.

The plea of Lord Aberdeen's ignorance of the Haro waters rests not on anything real and tangible which can be investigated, but on something purely ideal; on an unspoken, unwritten opinion attributed to him. It was not set up till after the death of Sir Robert Peel, who professed to understand "the local conformation of that country," and explained it to the House of Commons; nor till after Lord Aberdeen in 1855 had finally retired into private life. It is not pretended by any one that the opinion was well founded; and as it is erroneous in itself, and never obtained the sanction either of Sir Robert Peel or of Lord Aberdeen, it must be classed among the dreams that come from the realm of shades through the ivory gate.

Moreover, the attention of Lord Aberdeen, two days before he sent out the treaty to Mr. Pakenham, was specially called to the islands of the Haro Archipelago. On the 15th of May, 1846, he definitively assented, as Mr. MacLane understood him, to the Haro channel as the boundary. On the 16th, Sir John Pelly, then governor of the
[18] Hudson's Bay Com*pany, the same who boasted that that company had "compelled" the Americans to withdraw from the fur-trade, waited upon Lord Aberdeen with map in hand, pointed out to him the group of islands, wholly on the south of the parallel of 49°, and described in distinct and unequivocal language, as well "as colored red," "the water demarkation line" which would secure every one of the Haro islands. Lord Aberdeen, after having his mind thus closely and exactly drawn to the position of those islands, like "the straightforward man" of honor the United States took him for, rejected the "explicit" advice which would, indeed, have prevented the consummation of the treaty; and, in his instructions and in his draught of the treaty, stipulated only for the channel, "leaving the whole of Vancouver's Island in the possession of Great Britain."

Appendix No. 67, p. 106.

Further, this plea of ignorance in 1846 that the channel of Haro was navigable, is in itself absurd. For what is a channel? canal? Fahrwasser? Seegat? A channel means the depest part of a river, or bay, where the main current flows. The word is never used except of water that is navigable. Geographies are full of the names of channels, and the maps of Europe and Asia are studded with them; and who ever before thought of denying any one of them to be navigable? The present British suggestion is without precedent. To say that the canal de Haro was not known to be navigable is to say that the canal de Haro was not known to be the "canal de Haro."

It is very unlucky for the Government of Her Britannic Majesty that its plea of ignorance relates to the waters inside of Fuca straits. The emoluments of the fur-trade; the Spanish jealousy of Russian encroachments down the Pacific coast; the lingering hope of discovering a northwest passage; the British desire of finding water communication from the Pacific to the great lakes; the French passion for knowledge; the policy of Americans to investigate their outlying possessions; all
[19] conspired to cause more frequent and more thorough examina*tions

of these waters, even before 1846, than of any similarly situated waters in any part of the globe.

Before that epoch, the waters east and south of Vancouver Island had been visited by at least six scientific expeditions, from four several nations: three from Spain, one from Great Britain, one from France, and one from the United States; and the discoveries of all the four nations had been laid before the world.

De Haro, of the Spanish exploring party of 1789, discovered, and partly sounded and surveyed, the one broad and inviting channel which then seemed, not merely the best, but the only avenue by water to the north; and he left upon it his name.

Appendix No. 62.

The official reports of the expedition of Lieutenant de Eliza in 1791, and the large and excellent map which accompanied his narrative, prove that on the 31st day of May, 1791, an armed boat was ordered to enter and survey the canal of Lopez de Haro; but the survey was interrupted by the hostile appearance of six Indian canoes, filled by more than a hundred warriors. On the 14th day of June, the exploration of the canal de Haro was resumed, and was continued till the whole line of the canal de Haro was traced from Fuca's straits to its continuation in the great upper channel.

Map I.

But the Imperial Arbitrator may ask if these discoveries were published to the world; and the United States answer that they were published before the end of the century, both in Spain and in England. In 1792 the Spanish vessels Sutil and Mexicana, commanded by Captains Galiano and Valdes, taking with them the map of Lieutenant de Eliza, verified and completed the exploration of the interior waters. The results of the three Spanish expeditions were published officially by Spain in 1795, in an elaborately prepared chart for mariners, of which a lithographed copy accompanies this reply.

[20]

Appendix to Memorial No. 12, pp. 13, 14.

The map of Eliza was also communicated to Vancouver in 1792, at the time when he met Galiano and Valdes, in the *waters east of Vancouver Island. Thus Captain Vancouver became equally well aware of the superiority of the channel of Haro. That he put trust in the communications made to him by the Spaniards, is proved beyond a doubt, for he incorporated them into his map. The discoveries of the Spaniards, enriched by additional surveys of Vancouver himself, were published in Great Britain in 1798, in connection with his voyage. Before the end of the eighteenth century, therefore, the relative importance of the channels in the waters east of Vancouver Island was known to every one who cared to inquire about it, and who could gain access either to the chart published in Cadiz, or to the account of Vancouver's voyage which was issued in London. Her Majesty's Government seems certainly to have been in possession of the surveys of Captains D. Galiano and C. Valdes, for in the first chart drawn by the British Admiralty of Vancouver Island and the Gulf of Georgia, and published in February, 1849, they are cited as equal in authority to the chart of Vancouver, and as equally well known.

Appendix to Memorial No. 48, p. 55.

As to the result of the French explorations, Duflot de Mofras, in his work published in 1844, reports:

Dans l'espace qui s'étend de la terre ferme jusqu'à la partie Est de la grande île de Quadra, il existe une foule de petites îles qui, malgré les abris sûrs qu'elles offrent aux navires, présentent à la navigation de grandes difficultés. Le passage le plus facile est par le canal de Haro, entre l'île de Quadra et Vancouver et celle de San Juan.

In the space between the continent and the eastern part of the large island of Quadra, there is a multitude of small islands, which, in spite of the safe shelters that they offer to ships, present great difficulties to navigation. The most easy passage is through the canal de Haro, between the island of Quadra and Vancouver and that of San Juan.

The testimony of Duflot de Mofras is clear and unequivocal. It is impartial, and it is authoritative, as it occurs in a formal report to his sovereign.

[21] * Commodore Wilkes himself, in 1841, made all the surveys and soundings that were necessary for the safe navigation of the Haro channel, and, in 1845, published officially, both in London and America, that he had done so.

The American adventurers who collected furs in those waters for the trade with China knew the relative value of the two channels. At Boston, in 1845, Mr. Sturgis, the great representative of that class, describes the Haro channel correctly as the northernmost navigable channel, and draws the boundary line through the center of its waters. And his pamphlet and his map were known and approved by Lord Aberdeen before the treaty was framed.

Thus in Cadiz, in Paris, in Philadelphia, in Boston, and in London, the character of the Haro channel had been publicly made known before the end of 1845.

The British claim that the Hudson's Bay Company navigated those waters from 1827 or 1828 to 1846. Is it credible that for nineteen years they should have sailed a distance of six German miles, and, at the end of that time, be able to affirm that they were ignorant of the most obvious, broadest, shortest, nearest, and best channel to Fraser's River? Unless they took the channel of Haro, they must have passed it twice on every voyage, and a sailor, from the mast-head of a vessel, or even from the deck, could have seen it in all or nearly all its extent.

Governor Douglas, one of the most enterprising and inquisitive of men, famous for his "intimate acquaintance with every crevice on the coast," came in 1842, with the knowledge and approval of Lord Aberdeen, to select the station for the Hudson's Bay Company near the southeast of Vancouver. From the hill that bears his name, his eye could have commanded the whole of the canal de Haro, and his experience of the sea would have revealed to him at a glance the great depth of its waters. Moreover, in a good boat, with a favoring wind and tide, he could have passed through the whole

Appendix, No. 66, p. 104, l. 12-14.

[22] channel * in less than three hours. To say that he was not thoroughly well aware of its merits is, to those who know the character of the man, beyond the bounds of credibility.

The British Government has not produced one particle of evidence of an older date than 1846, that any one questioned the navigability of the Haro channel, while all the evidence which the American Government has thus far produced to establish it, is older than the treaty, is supported by the testimony of four different nations, and proves beyond all possibility of doubt, that before the treaty of 1846 the superiority of the canal de Haro was known by all who cared to know anything on the subject.

The testimony which Her Britannic Majesty's government of to-day brings forward to prove the ignorance of its predecessors is found to be the more groundless the more it is examined. It would be difficult to state too strongly the objections which any British court of law would make to it. The declarations are taken by the one party without notice to the other. The distinguished officers of the Hudson's Bay Company, men like Governor Douglas, are passed by; for they could not be expected to stultify themselves by pleading ignorance of the merits of

Haro channel. Obscure men bear positive testimony to that about which they knew nothing. A set of written questions is presented to them, and in different places, and on different days, they answer in large part in the same words, implying that answers, as well as questions, were prepared beforehand. The testimony thus picked up is of the less value, as the witnesses were not cross-examined; and yet, without being confronted or cross-examined, they involve themselves in contradictions if not in falsehoods.

The questions are framed so as to seem to be to the point, and yet most of them are of no significance.

William H. McNeill pretends to have used Vancouver's charts, not knowing that Vancouver made no charts except as an illustration of his own voyage. Then he affirms that

British Case, pp. 48, 49.

[23] *in coming south from Fraser's River he went through Rosario straits; while the Rosario straits on Vancouver's map lie far to the north of Fraser's River. Again, he says that the navigation of Haro straits is much impeded by numerous small islands and rocks; whereas it may be seen by the charts of the British Admiralty, as well as those of the United States Coast Survey, that the channel is broad and singularly deep, and where the bottom is marked rocky, the soundings show a depth of three hundred, six hundred, and even a thousand feet. The same man puts his name to the statement that what he calls the strait of Rosario was the only surveyed channel; whereas the canal de Haro had been surveyed both by Spanish and American expeditions.

William Mitchell testifies twice over that the so-called Rosario strait was the only known channel; while the channel of Haro appears on the Spanish chart, on the French, on the American, and is given by Vancouver himself. The same William Mitchell testifies, like McNeill, and equally falsely, that in June, 1846, the straits of Rosario, so called, were the only surveyed channel.

British Case, p. 51.

But Alexander C. Anderson exceeds others in alacrity. He testifies that as late as 1851 the passage through the Haro strait was incompletely known. Now the large charts prepared by Wilkes and his officers had been for several years exposed for sale to anybody that chose to buy them, and it is absolutely certain that they were presented by the American minister at London to Lord Palmerston, British Secretary of State for Foreign Affairs, and by him thankfully acknowledged, in the year 1848; so that the Government of Her Britannic Majesty happily possesses the means of correcting the rash declarations of the last-named witness.

British Case, p. 54.

Appendix No. 51.

The American Government cannot offer the rebutting testimony of American mariners, for their fur-trade on the northwest coast had been broken up by the British before 1810, and when at a later day
[24] they attempted to renew it, they *had been forcibly compelled by the officers and servants of the Hudson's Bay Company to give up the field. The American sailors, therefore, who were familiar with those regions have long since gone to slumber with their fathers.

But the British Case enables the American Government to cite the log-books of the Hudson's Bay Company. It nowhere ventures to say that the log-books of the vessels of the Hudson's Bay Company prove that they never went through the Haro channel, but only that they used the so-called Rosario straits as the "leading channel." This is a confession that the log-books of those vessels show that sometimes one channel was used by them, sometimes the other.

British Case, p. 11.

It is admitted by the British Case that in 1843 the Cadboro sailed through Haro straits, and that once, at least, the

British Case, pp. 52, 48.

Hudson's Bay Company's steamer Beaver chose the same route. Commander Mayne admits that when the Hudson's Bay Company established their headquarters at Victoria, the canal de Haro became used. In corroboration of this use of the channel of Haro, especially from the year 1842 to 1846, some affidavits and statements are offered, correcting the testimony contained in the British Case, and confirming facts which the British Case itself admits. From the want of time, no notice could be given to the other party; but among the witnesses will be found some of the highest officers in the Army and Navy of the United State, as well as men known by their works to the scientific world.

Mayne's Four Years in British Columbia, p. 39.

Appendix Nos. 53, 54, 55, 57, 58, 59. 60, 61.

It is a remarkable characteristic of the British Case, that while it seems to make assertions in language of the most energetic affirmation, it qualifies them so as to make them really insignificant. It might almost be said that the British Case gives up its own theory of the ignorance of Lord Aberdeen as to the character of the Haro channel; for it affirms, not that he was ignorant about its navigability, but that he "had no assurance that it was even navigable in its upper waters."

British Case, p. 30.

"No assurance" is a very vague expression; so is
[25] *the phrase "upper waters;" and with them both nothing is asserted, while the form of the statement is an ample confession that Lord Aberdeen was at least perfectly well acquainted with the existence of the strait. When, using the same words with which they introduced their total misapprehension of Mr. Webster's opinion, they write of the Haro channel, "It is not too much to say that Her Majesty's Government had a firm belief that it was a dangerous strait," it is enough to reply that not one word has been presented to show that Lord Aberdeen believed it a dangerous strait; and without his positive testimony, which has not been produced, this is an idle and groundless assertion.

Strange as it is for a great nation to come before a tribunal like that of the German Emperor, and complain that the treaty which they themselves draughted contains an ambiguity due, not to bad faith, but to ignorance, the United States have avowed themselves ready to abrogate that part of the treaty on the ground alleged by the British Government, that it might have been made under a mutual misunderstanding; and to re-arrange the boundary which was in dispute before the treaty was concluded. When put to the test, the British are compelled practically to acknowledge the candor and forbearance of the Americans in the formation of the treaty, and that, if the work were to be done over again, they have no hope of a settlement so much to their advantage. The treaty, as it is understood by the United States, made very large concessions to Great Britain; and the British Government insists upon preserving it.

Proctocols 36 and 37 of Conference between the High Commissioners, at Washington.

Then, since Her Majesty's Government will not consent to cancel the treaty, it must be accepted according to its plain meaning; and if its meaning is not plain, the party which draughted it must suffer the consequences of the ambiguity.

[26] *III.—PROCEEDINGS UNDER THE TREATY OF 1846.

The United States have always held the treaty to be free from ambiguity, and have maintained their understanding of it with unvarying consistency. If between a channel that had a name, and one that had none, the British Government intended to take the channel without a name, it should have described it with distinctness and care; instead of which, the words of their description

British Case, pp. 28, 33.

exclude the channel without a name, and apply exactly and alone to the Haro Channel.

In January, 1848, the British minister at Washington, treating the "islets" of the San Juan archipelago as of "little or no value," expressed a "wish" to the United States that the passage used by Vancouver in passing from Admiralty Inlet to the north, might be mutually considered as the channel of the treaty. No claim whatever was preferred, and the wish was excused, "because otherwise much time might be wasted in surveying the various intricate channels formed by the numerous islets which lie between Vancouver's Island and the main-land, and some difficulty might arise in deciding which of those channels ought to be adopted for the dividing boundary." The letter of Lord Palmerston, under which the British minister at Washington expressed this wish of Her Majesty's Government, has never been communicated to the Government of the United States.

Appendix No. 68, p. 107.

To Mr. Bancroft, who, immediately after the ratification of the treaty, was selected as the United States minister at London, and who on all occasions spoke and wrote of the canal de Haro as the boundary channel, Lord Palmerston, then Secretary of State for Foreign Affairs, never presented any counter claim; and the American minister was persuaded that danger to the immediate peaceful execution of the treaty arose, not from within the ministry, but from the
[27] parlia*mentary influence of the Hudson's Bay Company, whose desires the ministry seemed reluctant to adopt.

Appendix No. 51, pp. 60, 61.

Mr. Bancroft did not suffer the authoritative interpretation of the treaty on the part of his Government to rest on the uncertainty of conversations which time might obliterate, or memory pervert.

On the last day of July, 1848, Lord Palmerston observed that he had no good chart of the Oregon waters; and having asked to see a traced copy of Wilkes' chart, Mr. Bancroft immediately sent it to him with this remark:

* * Unluckily this copy does not extend quite so far north as the parallel of 49°, though it contains the wide entrance into the straits of Haro, the channel through the middle of which the boundary is to be continued. The upper part of the straits of Haro is laid down, though not on a large scale, in Wilkes' map of the Oregon Territory.

Obtaining from Washington an early copy of Wilkes' surveys, Mr. Bancroft delivered it to Lord Palmerston with the following official note:

NOVEMBER 3, 1848.

MY LORD: I did not forget your lordship's desire to see the United States surveys of the waters of Puget's Sound, and those dividing Vancouver's Island from our territory.

These surveys have been reduced, and have just been published in three parts, and I transmit for your lordship's acceptance the first copy which I have received.

The surveys extend to the line of 49°, and by combining two of the charts your lordship will readily trace the whole course of the channel of Haro, through the
[28] middle of which our boundary line passes. I think you will esteem *the work done in a manner very creditable to the young Navy officers concerned in it.

I have the honor, &c.,

GEORGE BANCROFT.

Viscount PALMERSTON, *&c.*, *&c.*

To this formal and authorized announcement of the Haro as the boundary, the answer of Lord Palmerston, written after four days, was in like manner official, and ran as follows:

FOREIGN OFFICE, *November* 7, 1848.

SIR: I beg leave to return you my best thanks for the surveys of Puget's Sound and of the Gulf of Georgia, which accompanied your letter of the 3d instant.

The information as to soundings contained in these charts will no doubt be of great service to the commissioners who are to be appointed under the treaty of the 15th of June, 1846, by assisting them in determining where the line of boundary described in the first article of the treaty ought to run.

I have the honor, &c.,

PALMERSTON.

GEORGE BANCROFT, Esq., *&c.*, *&c.*

Here is no pretense of an ignorance of the channel of Haro as affecting the interpretation of the treaty—that theory was not started until after the death of Sir Robert Peel—but a calm, wise, assent to the use of the large charts of Wilkes in running the boundary. And this assent was virtually a concession that the American interpretation was just and true. Lord Palmerston declined all controversy about the
channel. He received a formal, authoritative statement of the
[29] line as understood by the United States, and in his *reply made
no complaint and proposed no other interpretation. This note is the first and the last and the only word that the United States possess from Lord Palmerston under his own hand on the subject of the boundary. The correspondence relating to it is inserted in full in
the Appendix. The American minister of that day had Appendix No. 51.
very good opportunity to know what was going forward, and every motive to give the most correct information to his Government.

In December, 1852, Lord Aberdeen came to the head of affairs. The last official word of the Americans to Great Britain on the boundary had been that it passes through the center of the channel of Haro. At the beginning of his ministry, in the winter of 1852–'53, the territorial legislature of Oregon included the whole of the archipelago of Haro in one of its counties. Had Lord Aberdeen been dissatisfied with the state of the question, he, who made the treaty and now had returned to power, was bound to have taken this subject earnestly in hand; but he remained silent, made no excuses that he had draughted the treaty in ignorance, and entered no counter pretension to the American view.

The administration which, in February, 1855, succeeded that of Lord Aberdeen, was one over which the Hudson's Bay Company exercised great influence. The progress of colonization demanded a settlement of the question of jurisdiction—the more so, as the British Government had made a grant of the island of Vancouver to that company. Accordingly, in 1856 the two Governments agreed to send out commissioners to mark the line of boundary.

The United States, in perfect good faith, gave their commissioner full powers, and communicated his instructions unreservedly to the British Government. The British Government gave its commissioner ostensible instructions, which were readily communicated to the United States, but fettered him by additional ones, which were kept secret, and of
which the United States repeatedly but vainly solicited a copy,
[30] *until, some years later, Lord Malmesbury, in the ministry of
Lord Derby, became once more Secretary of State for Foreign Affairs.

Could the Hudson's Bay Company obtain possession of the island of San Juan, they would have exclusive possession of the best channel, and of the only safe one in time of war. No British authority in Great Britain or in Vancouver expressed any desire for the so-called Rosario channel, on which the British Case now affects to lay so much stress. The members of Her Britannic Majesty's Government did not pretend among themselves to a right to it "as the channel indicated by the words of the treaty," but, yielding to the importunity of the influential government of Vancouver, they were willing to hazard an experimental attempt to gain the island of San Juan. To accomplish this end, the British commissioner received the following secret instruction:

Appendix No. 69, p. 108.

If the commissioner of the United States will not adopt the line along Rosario Strait, and if, on a detailed and accurate survey, and on weighing the evidence on both sides of the question, you should be of opinion that the claims of Her Majesty's Government to consider Rosario Strait as the channel indicated by the words of the treaty cannot be substantiated, you would be at liberty to adopt any othor intermediate channel which you may discover, on which the United States commissioner and yourself may agree as substantially in accordance with the description of the treaty.

According to his commission, and according to his ostensible instructions, Captain Prevost was a commissioner, and no more than a commissioner, to mark the boundary line according to the treaty of 1846; but by his secret instructions, which he resolutely refused to communicate, he was in fact a plenipotentiary appointed to negotiate for a channel which should take the island of San Juan from the United States.

[31] *It must be borne in mind that Captain Prevost had authority to offer a compromise only on the condition that, after personal examination and the weighing of evidence on both sides of the question, he "should be of opinion that the claims of Her Majesty's Government to consider Rosario Strait as the channel indicated by the words of the treaty cannot be substantiated." After having been five months within the straits of Fuca, and after having verified and approved the accuracy of the United States Coast Survey chart of the channels and islands between Vancouver Island and the continent, and after consenting to adopt it for the purpose of determining the boundary line, he proposed such a compromise as would have left to the United States the so-called Rosario Straits and every island in the archipelago except San Juan.

Appendix No. 70, p. 109, l. 5-15.

The commissioner of the United States, Mr. Archibald Campbell, divined the character of the secret instructions under which Captain Prevost was acting, adhered with intelligence and uprightness to his duty as commissioner, and "declined to accede to any compromise."

Appendix No. 72, p. 110, l. 5,6.

Captain Prevost, the British commissioner, who, by his offer of compromise, had conceded that the British claim to the so-called Rosario straits "cannot be substantiated," struggled hard to recover the position of a zealous champion of the right of Great Britain to that channel. But for this he had drifted too far, and he was too honest to succeed. As an interpreter of the treaty Captain Prevost writes very correctly: "The channel mentioned should possess three characteristics: 1. It should separate the continent from Vancouver's Island; 2. It should admit of the boundary line being carried through the middle of it in a southerly direction; 3. It should be a navigable channel." He adds: "It is readily admitted that the Canal de Arro is a navigable channel, and therefore answers to one characteristic of the channel of the treaty."

Appendix No. 70.

[32] *This admission, written from on board a ship anchored within sight of the Haro channel, is conclusive as to the first point. As to his second characteristic, a glance at the map will show the Imperial Arbitrator that the line which is drawn due south from the middle of the channel on the parallel of 49°, strikes the channel of Haro, and leaves the so-called Rosario far to the east.

Map O.

As to Captain Prevost's remaining characteristic, the United States again cite his testimony, for he writes: "The canal de Haro is the channel separating Vancouver's Island from the con-

Appendix No. 70, p. 108, l. 21-25.

tinent." To be sure he adds, it "cannot be the channel which separates the continent from Vancouver Island." But in that ground no anchor can hold. It is as if one were to own, that in latitude 53° 10′, St. George's channel separates Ireland from England, and yet insist that England is separated from Ireland by the strait of Menai.

In January, 1848, during the administration of which Lord John Russell, now Earl Russell, was the chief, the British minister at Washington, timidly and by way of experiment, expressed a wish that the channel through which Vancouver sailed might be agreed upon by the two Governments as the boundary.

Appendix No. 68.

In August, 1859, when the internal commotions, which appeared to threaten the disruption of the United States, were already spreading their baleful influences, Lord John Russell, then British Secretary of State for Foreign Affairs, first ventured upon a distinct avowal of the purpose of Her Britannic Majesty's Government to obtain the island of San Juan. In pursuing this object, he sought, in an interview with the Earl of Aberdeen, to obtain the support of that minister.

Appendix No. 73, pp. 111, 112.

The chief interest in this narrative, as far as persons are concerned, centers in Lord Aberdeen. So far as the United States know, he never consented to set his hand to any paper which they would have a right to regard as disingenuous. The United States have shown in
[33] their memo*rial that Mr. MacLane, after an interview with Lord Aberdeen on the 15th of May, 1846, reported to his Government that the treaty line would pass through the canal de Haro.

Appendix to Memorial, No. 42 p. 47, l. 8-11.

The present agent of the United States in this arbitration resided as minister in England during the three years following the treaty, became well acquainted with Lord Aberdeen, conversed with him on its interpretation, and never heard from him one word that conflicted with the report of Mr. MacLane. Nor did he ever hear a different interpretation of the treaty from Sir Robert Peel. Nor during his whole residence in England did he ever hear such difference of interpretation attributed by any one to either of the two.

And, in 1859, Lord Aberdeen is appealed to by Lord John Russell for the aid of his testimony. Unhappily there exists no written answer of his own to the questions put to him; but only a very short report of the interview by Lord John Russell. According to that report, Lord Aberdeen did not deny that he used the name of the canal de Haro with Mr. MacLane, though he had no recollection of having done so. Now, nothing is more likely than that the words uttered in conversation thirteen years before, might have dropped from his memory; and against this failure of memory is to be weighed the dispatch of Mr. MacLane, written at the moment of the conversation. But, as to the channel which Lord Aberdeen had in view, he is represented as declaring that he knew none other than that "described in the treaty itself." Now, the channel described in the treaty, and in Lord Aberdeen's instructions to Mr. Pakenham, is, as we have seen, no other than the canal de Haro.

Appendix No. 73, pp. 111, 112.

Left without support by Lord Aberdeen, the British Foreign Office brought forward, as its witness, Sir Richard Pakenham, who, with Mr. Buchanan, signed the boundary treaty of June, 1846.

[34] In that same year, while everything was still fresh in *memory, Mr. Buchanan had recorded his interpretation of the treaty in an instruction to Mr. Bancroft, the American minister at London, who, as his colleague in Washington, had taken part in its negotiation, and

knew every step of its progress. An instruction written under such circumstances is the portraiture of the inmost mind of its author. "It is not probable," wrote Mr. Buchanan, "that any claim will be seriously preferred on the part of Her Britannic Majesty's Government to any island lying to the eastward of the Canal of Arro, as marked in Captain Wilkes's 'map of the Oregon Territory.'"

Appendix No. 51, p. 60, l. 3-7.

Of the testimony, given more than twelve years later by Sir Richard Pakenham, every word, as far as communicated to the United States, is presented in the Appendix. It has no date, but was communicated to the United States in the year 1859. Captain Prevost, in his final letter to Mr. Campbell, the American commissioner, of November 24, 1857, had written: "I will at once frankly state how far I am willing to concede, but beyond what I now offer I can no further go. * * * I am willing to regard the space above described [that is, the space between the continent and Vancouver Island, south of 49°] as one channel, having so many different passages through it, and I will agree to a boundary line being run through the 'middle' of it, in so far as islands will permit." This is the lead which Sir Richard Pakenham followed. He who signed the treaty on the British side declared positively, as his interpretation of it, that the so-called straits of Rosario are not the channel intended by the treaty; and we must hold the British Government to this confession, as it received its official approbation.

Appendix No. 73, pp. 112-114.

Appendix No. 70, p. 109.

It is true he also denied the straits of Haro to be the channel of the treaty, using these words:

> The Earl of Aberdeen, in his final instructions, dated 18th May, 1846, says nothing whatever about the Canal de Haro, but, on the contrary, desires that the line
> [35] might be drawn "in a southerly *direction through the center of King George's Sound and the Straits of Fuca to the Pacific Ocean."

Now why was Sir Richard Pakenham introduced to give testimony as to the instruction which he received from Lord Aberdeen? The instruction itself was in the Foreign Office, and was the best authority on the subject, and would have given the whole truth. Sir Richard Pakenham in his testimony leaves out the most important words of his final instructions. Lord Aberdeen, it is true, did not name in them the channel of Haro by name, but so far from writing anything to "the contrary," he defined it exactly, when, in those same "final instructions," he describes the channel of the treaty as the channel "leaving the whole of Vancouver Island, with its ports and harbors, in the possession of Great Britain."

Appendix to Memorial No. 43, p. 50, l. 5, 7.

The final interpretation of the treaty by Sir Richard Pakenham runs as follows:

> The conditions of the treaty, according to their liberal tenor, would require the line to be traced along the middle of the channel, meaning, I presume, the whole intervening space which separates the continent from Vancouver Island.

Thus Mr. Pakenham, the British signer of the treaty, adopting the theory first communicated to the United States by Captain Prevost eleven years after the treaty was ratified, rejects entirely the channel of the so-called Rosario as the channel of the treaty. The question now is not between the so-called Rosario and some channel intermediate between it and that of Haro. It is whether the claims of the United States to the Haro, or those of Great Britain to the so-called Rosario, are more in accordance with the true interpretation of the treaty. The instructions to Captain Prevost show that the British Government had no confidence in the so-called Rosario as being the treaty channel; the

testimony of Sir Richard Pakenham is that the British government at the time of negotiating the treaty did not intend the so-called
[36] Rosario *as the channel, while the words which he suppressed from Lord Aberdeen's final instructions prove the channel of the treaty to be the canal de Haro. Adopting the theory of Captain Prevost and Sir Richard Pakenham, Lord John Russell somewhat peremptorily demanded of the United States the acceptance of that theory, and in an instruction which the British minister at Washington was directed to communicate to the United States, he wrote:

The adoption of the central channel would give to Great Britain the island of San Juan, which is believed to be of little or no value to the United States, while much importance is attached by British colonial authorities, and by Her Majesty's government, to its retention as a dependency of the colony of Vancouver's Island. Appendix No. 73, p. 112.

Her Majesty's Government must, therefore, under any circumstances, maintain the right of the British Crown to the island of San Juan. The interests at stake in connection with the retention of that island are too important to admit of compromise, and your lordship will consequently bear in mind that whatever arrangement as to the boundary line is finally arrived at, no settlement of the question will be accepted by Her Majesty's government which does not provide for the island of San Juan being reserved for the British Crown.

To this naked and even menacing demand the American Government made the only fitting reply; and certainly the Imperial Arbitrator will not give an award to Great Britain, because the Vancouver colonial authorities and Her Majesty's Government covet the possession of San Juan.

When the attention of the British Secretary of State was called to the absoluteness and to the motives of this communication, he answered: Appendix No. 75 p. 117, l. 17-22.

Her Majesty's Government were by implication abandoning a large part of the territory they had claimed, and were merely insisting on the retention of an island
[37] which, from the peculiarity of *its situation, it was impossible for Her Majesty's Government to cede, without compromising interests of the gravest importance.

Lord John Russell acknowledged the necessity of supporting his pretensions by bringing them into agreement with the words of the treaty; and therefore, giving up the channel of the so-called Rosario, he entered into an argument in favor of the channel called on the United States Coast Survey "the San Juan Channel," on the British Admiralty chart "Douglas Channel," as the channel of the treaty. Appendix No 75, p. 118, l. 4-22.

In other words, he interpreted the treaty simply as giving the island of San Juan to the British, by which they would gain the exclusive possession of the Haro channel.

A conclusion is thus made very easy. Captain Prevost, Sir Richard Pakenham, and Lord John Russell unite in renouncing any treaty right to the so-called Rosario channel, and unite in the opinion that the Douglas Channel has a better right to be regarded as the channel of the treaty than the so-called Rosario. There is no escape from this cumulated evidence thus furnished by the British Government: first, in the instructions of Lord Aberdeen to Mr. Pakenham; second, in Mr. Pakenham's declaration of the meaning of the British Government at the time the treaty was negotiated; third, in the instructions to Captain Prevost; and fourth, in the statements of Lord John Russell, that the so-called Rosario strait was not the channel through which, in the interpretation of the British Government, the boundary line was to be run. It further shows that up to the date of the instructions to Captain Prevost in 1856, the British Government had never suggested any other than the Haro and the so-called Rosario channel. Their own evidence, excluding the Rosario straits from their contemplation at the date of the treaty, leaves the Haro as the only possible channel within the contemplation of either party, and the only one in accordance with the true interpretation of the treaty.

[38] *One more effort was made for the settlement of the question by the two Governments. On the 15th day of March, 1871, the commissioners on the part of the United States and the commissioners on the part of Great Britain, in a conference at Washington took up the northwestern boundary question, and when no agreement could be arrived at respecting the proper interpretation of the treaty of June, 1846, the American commissioners expressed their readiness to abrogate the whole of that part of the treaty of 1846, and re-arrange the boundary line which was in dispute before that treaty was concluded. At the conference on the 20th of March, 1871, the British commissioners declined the proposal.

XXXVI. Protocol of conference between the high commissioners, at Washington.

On the 19th of April the British commissioners, willing to renounce all claim to the so-called Rosario, renewed the offer of the line which had before been pressed by Captain Prevost, and maintained as the line of the treaty by Sir Richard Pakenham and by Lord John Russell. The American commissioners on the instant declined to entertain the proposal, and the British commissioners could not consent to regard the channel of Haro as the boundary, "except after a fair decision by an impartial arbitrator."

IV.—INTERPRETATION OF THE TREATY OF 1846.

The United States have already asked Your Majesty's attention to rules of international law applicable to the interpretation of the treaty submitted for arbitration.

They agree with the British Government, that "the words of a treaty are to be taken to be used in the sense in which they were commonly used at the time when the treaty was entered into," and ask Your Majesty to interpret the words "Fuca's straits" according to the usage established by all the maps and reports prior to 1846.

British Case, p. 14.

[39] *They further agree that "treaties are to be interpreted in a favorable rather than an odious sense;" but they did not in their Memorial invoke this rule, though it so decisively confirms their rights, because they had no fear that the German Emperor could give to the convention an odious interpretation. Since, however, this rule of interpretation has been brought forward by the government of Her Britannic Majesty, the United States must explain the immeasurably odious nature of the interpretation which the British government desires Your Majesty to adopt.

British Case, p. 29.

The United States, in signing the treaty of 1846, had in view permanent relations of amity with Great Britain, and therefore dealt with it generously in the treaty, that there might remain to that power no motive for discontent or cupidity. When they consented that Great Britain should hold the southern cape of Vancouver Island, they knew that the harbor of that cape was the very best on the Pacific, from San Francisco to the far north. The United States took also into consideration that Great Britain needed to share, and had a right to expect to share in the best line of communication with its possessions to the north.

A ship using the so-called Rosario strait may be exposed to cannon-shot, not only as it enters that strait, but nearly all the way as it sails through it. One British Ministry after another has shown that it set no value upon it whatever, and has represented that it was not contemplated by treaty as a boundary, and has used the claim to it only as a means of driving the United States into a surrender of the island of San Juan.

A ship, as both parties agree, can enter the channel of Haro and not be under any necessity of passing within territorial waters on either side of the central line.

This passage by the Haro channel to the British possessions
[40] north of 49°, is the shortest, the most convenient, *the best, and the only perfectly safe one, alike in peace and in war. Of this channel, the United States by the treaty of 1846 concede the joint possession to the British, but they concede it with circumstances of peculiar generosity, or rather magnanimity. In passing from the lower part of the Haro channel to the upper interior waters, they allow to Great Britain equal rights with themselves to pass through the Haro channel to the true Rosario of the Spaniards, the British gulf of Georgia. Thus far the United States reserve to themselves no advantage over the English. They go farther. There are two other channels connecting the straits of Haro with the upper waters; one of them a little above 49°, at the Portier pass; the other Map O. below 49°, through Swanson channel and Active pass. As to both of these, the United States leave to the British the exclusive possession of the islands on each side. This is a great concession, far outweighing in value any advantage the Americans may gain in the so-called Rosario straits. The regular track of the British steamers between south Vancouver and Fraser's river is through the channel of Swanson and Active pass, a wide, sheltered channel, to them the shortest and most convenient, never freezing in winter, with water nowhere less than ninety feet deep, as easy of navigation as any part of the broadest and most magnificent river in Europe.

To keep all these advantages and to acquire exclusive possession of the channel of Haro became the uncontrollable desire, first of the Hudson's Bay Company, then of the politicians of Vancouver Island. The conduct of the United States merited a better requital.

The demand of the government of Her Britannic Majesty is as contrary to every principle of convenience, equity, and comity, as it is to the intention and the language of the treaty of 1846. To ask the United States to give up their equal right in the canal de Haro is to ask them to shut themselves out of their own house. They own the
[41] continent *east of these waters to the lake of the Woods, a distance of 28° of longitude. Is it within the bounds of belief that they should have given up to Great Britain the exclusive possession of the best channel, and the only safe channel, by which they could approach their own vast dominions on the north? Grant the English demand, draw the line of boundary through the so-called Rosario channel, and the Americans would have access to their own immense territory from the Pacific, only by the good will of the English. Such an interpretation of the treaty is so unequal, so partial to Great Britain, so opposite to the natural rights of the United States, so inconsistent with the words of the treaty, that the American Government holds itself deeply aggrieved by the British persistence in demanding an interpretation in so "odious a sense."

The United States, it may once more be said, had not the intention to present the subject in this light to the Imperial Arbitrator, for they confide entirely in his justice. But since Her Majesty's government apparently assumes that an award in favor of the American Government would be "odious," the United States must not neglect to invite attention to the true aspect of the case.

The American Government is the more surprised at this manner of presenting the subject by the government of Her Britannic Majesty, inasmuch as Captain Prevost, after months employed in exploring the waters, conceded that the British claim to the so-called Rosario Strait "could not be substantiated," and this opinion was formally adopted by Sir Richard Pakenham and by Lord John Russell; the latter of whom himself declares that he abandoned by implication all but the island of San Juan.

Another reason why an award in favor of the so-called Rosario as the channel would be odious, is, that it would transfer to the foreign allegiance of Great Britain, islands east of San Juan which have long
[42] been and are now in the undisputed posses*sion of the United States. The United States have likewise been virtually in possession of the island of San Juan; though each party maintains in it a small garrison. The civil population on that island is thoroughly American.

Appendix No. 76.

Out of ninety-six resident males of twenty-one years of age and upward, the number of American citizens is fifty-six; the number of those born in Great Britain and Ireland is but twenty-six. Of both sexes and all ages, there are one hundred and seventy-nine Americans and but fifty-two of British nationality on the island of San Juan. In the whole archipelago, the American population numbers three hundred and fourteen, the British but ninety. How unsuitable it would be, then, to assign to Great Britain islands which have never been out of the possession of the United States, and which are occupied almost exclusively by their citizens!

Appendix to Memorial No. 10 and No. 19, p. 22, l. 2-6.

The United States do not understand how a controversy could have arisen on the meaning of the boundary treaty of June 15, 1846. It will be remembered that it was they who, in the administration of Sir Robert Peel, recalled the intimation of Mr. Huskisson in 1826, and suggested that the disputed boundary might be arranged by just so much deflection from the forty-ninth parallel, as would leave the whole of Vancouver island to Great Britain. For more than two years, through two successive envoys, they continued to propose this settlement. At length Lord Aberdeen consented to it. The language of the treaty for carrying out the arrangement came from him. The United States accepted it in the sense in which they had suggested it; and by all rules for the equitable construction of contracts, Great Britain ought not now o attach to it a sense different from that in which Lord Aberdeen must have known that the United States accepted it. Moreover, before the treaty of June, 1846, was signed, Lord Aberdeen, well knowing by the experience of more than two years that the United States had proposed as their ultimatissimum, not to divide Vancouver island, instructed the British minister at Washington, that
[43] what England *was to obtain was the channel "leaving the whole of Vancouver's island in the possession of Great Britain." Thus both parties had the same object in view; both parties intended the same thing and expressed in writing their intentions before the treaty was signed. The Government of the United States of that day assented to the treaty of 1846, with the understanding, communicated in advance to the British Government, that the boundary line was to deflect from the forty-ninth parallel for the sole purpose of giving the south of Vancouver Island to Great Britain, so that it was necessarily to

pass through the canal de Haro. The American Senate accepted it in that sense, and only in that sense. After it had been accepted, and before the ratifications were exchanged, Sir Robert Peel in the House of Commons announced in memorable words, that Her Majesty's government had made the contract in the same sense. Not long afterwards the present agent of the United States in this arbitration, then the plenipotentiary of the United States near the Court of St. James, officially called the official attention of Lord Palmerston to this construction; and from Lord Palmerston, then the British Secretary of Foreign Affairs, who, on the 29th of June, 1846, had, as a member of the House of Commons, listened to Sir Robert Peel's interpretation of the treaty, and, with the knowledge of this interpretation, had on the same evening welcomed it as honorable to both countries, the note of the American plenipotentiary received the acquiescence of silence.

Appendix to Memorial No. 46.

The broad and deep channel of Haro, in its ceaseless ebb and flow, is the ever faithful and unimpeachable interpreter of the treaty. Time out of mind, it formed the pathway for the canoe fleets of the Red Men. It is the first channel discovered by Anglo-Americans or Europeans within the strait of Fuca; it is the first that was explored and surveyed from side to side; it is the first through which Europeans sailed
[44] from the Fuca Strait to the waters above the parallel *of 49.
And now, in the increase of emigration and trade, it approves itself as "the channel" of commerce by the unanimous choice of the ships of all nations.

Everything favors a peaceful adjudication. The influential and active Hudson's Bay Company has ceased to exist. The United States have paid them, and all other British companies or citizens, for their possessory rights large indemnities, which they themselves and the British government acknowledge to be most ample. The generation of Britons who reluctantly assumed the unwelcome task of keeping the fruitful region of Northwest America in a wilderness condition, has passed away. Under the genial influence of the United States, cities rise on the stations of fur-traders, and agriculture supersedes hunting and trapping. This condition of the country facilitates the final recognition of the rights of the United States, and encourages the belief that an award favorable to them will be accepted without an emotion of surprise or discontent.

APPENDIX TO THE REPLY.

No. 51.

CORRESPONDENCE BETWEEN MR. BANCROFT, MR. BUCHANAN, AND LORD PALMERSTON.

Mr. Bancroft to Mr. Buchanan.

LONDON, *November* 3, 1846.

SIR: * * * * * * *

While in the Navy Department I caused a traced copy of Wilkes's chart of the Straits of Haro to be made. If not needed in the Navy Department I request that the President will direct it to be sent to this Legation. It is intimated to me that questions may arise with regard to the islands east of that strait. I ask your authority to meet any such claim at the threshold by the assertion of the central channel of the Straits of Haro as the main channel intended by the recent treaty of Washington. Some of the islands, I am well informed, are of value.

The straits of Haro the treaty boundary.

Very respectfully, &c.,

GEORGE BANCROFT.

Hon. JAMES BUCHANAN,
Secretary of State.

Mr. Buchanan to Mr. Bancroft.

DEPARTMENT OF STATE,
Washington, December 28, 1846.

SIR: I have obtained from the Navy Department, and now transmit to you, in accordance with the request contained in your dispatch No. 1, [November 3,] the traced copy of Wilkes's chart of the Straits of Haro. This will enable
[60] you to act understandingly *upon any question which may hereafter arise between the two governments in respect to the sovereignty of the islands situate between the continent and Vancouver's Island. It is not probable, however, that any claim of this character will be seriously preferred on the part of Her Britannic Majesty's government to any island lying to the eastward of the Canal of Arro, as marked in Captain Wilkes's "Map of the Oregon Territory." This, I have no doubt, is the channel which Lord Aberdeen had in view, when, in a conversation with Mr. MacLane, about the middle of May last, on the subject of the resumption of the negotiation for an amicable settlement of the Oregon question, his lordship explained the character of the proposition he intended to submit through Mr. Pakenham. As understood by Mr. MacLane, and by him communicated to this department in

Mr. Buchanan instructs Mr. Bancroft that Haro is the boundary channel.

his dispatch of the 18th of the same month, it was, "First, to divide the territory by the extension of the line on the parallel of 49° to the sea; that is to say, to the arm of the sea called Birch's Bay; thence by the Canal de Haro and Straits of Fuca to the ocean," &c.

I am, sir, respectfully, your obedient servant,

JAMES BUCHANAN.

GEORGE BANCROFT, Esq., *&c., &c., &c.*

[Inclosure: Chart of the Straits of Juan de Fuca, Puget Sound, &c. By the U. S. Ex. Ex., 1841.]

Mr. Bancroft to Mr. Buchanan.

LEGATION OF THE UNITED STATES,
London, March 29, 1847.

SIR: * * * * * * *

Mr. Bancroft warns Mr. Buchanan of the designs of the Hudson's Bay Company.

While on this point I ought to add that my attention has again been called to the probable wishes of the Hudson's Bay Company to get some of the islands on our side of the line in the Straits of Fuca. I speak only from my own judgment and inductions from what I observe and hear; but it would not surprise me if a formal proposition should soon be made on the part of the British Government to run the line between the two countries at the west from the point where it first meets the water through the straits to the Pacific Ocean.

Such a proposition is in itself very proper, if there be no ulterior
[61] motive to raise unnecessary doubts and to claim islands *that are properly ours. The ministry, I believe, has no such design. Some of its members would be the first to frown on it. But I am not so well assured that the Hudson's Bay Company is equally reasonable, or that on the British side a boundary commissioner might not be appointed favoring the encroaching propensities of that company. * *

I am, &c.,

GEORGE BANCROFT.

JAMES BUCHANAN, Esq., *&c., &c., &c.,*
Washington City.

Mr. Bancroft to Mr. Buchanan.

UNITED STATES LEGATION,
London, August 4, 1848.

SIR: * * * * * * *

Mr. Bancroft's interview with Lord Palmerston.

The Hudson's Bay Company have been trying to get a grant of Vancouver's Island. I inquired, from mere curiosity, about it. Lord Palmerston replied that it was an affair that belonged exclusively to the Colonial Office, and he did not know the intentions of Lord Grey. He then told me, what I had not known before, that he had made a proposition at Washington for marking the boundaries in the northwest by setting up a landmark on the point of land where the forty-ninth parallel touches the sea, and for ascertaining the division line in the channel by noting the bearings of certain objects. I observed that on the main-land a few simple astronomical observations were all that were requisite; that the water in the channel of Haro did not require to be divided, since the navigation was free to both parties; though, of course, the islands east of the center of the channel of Haro were ours. He had no good chart of the Oregon waters, and asked me to let him see the traced copy of Wilkes's chart. He spoke of the propriety of settling definitively the ownership of the several islands, in order that settlements might not be begun by one party on what properly belongs to the other. On returning home I sent him my traced copy of Wilkes's chart, with a note, of which I inclose a copy.

I am, &c.,

GEORGE BANCROFT.

JAMES BUCHANAN, Esq.,
Secretary of State, Washington. D. C.

62] **Mr. Bancroft to Lord Palmerston.*

90 EATON SQUARE, *July* 31, 1848.

MY DEAR LORD: As your lordship desired, I send for your inspection the traced copy made for me at the Navy Department of Wilkes's chart of the Straits of Juan de Fuca, Puget's Sound, &c. Unluckily this copy does not extend quite so far north as the parallel of 49°, though it contains the wide entrance into the Straits of Haro, the channel through the middle of which the boundary is to be continued. The upper part of the Straits of Haro is laid down, though not on a large scale, in Wilkes's map of the Oregon Territory, of which, I am sorry to say, I have not a copy, but which may be found in the atlas to the narrative of the United States Exploring Expedition.

Mr. Bancroft writes to Lord Palmerston that Haro is the boundary.

I remain, my dear lord, very faithfully, yours,

GEORGE BANCROFT.

Viscount PALMERSTON, *&c., &c.*

Mr. Bancroft to Mr. Buchanan.

UNITED STATES LEGATION,
London, October 19, 1848.

SIR: I send you a map of Vancouver's Island, recently published by James Wyld, geographer to the Queen. It purports to mark, by a dotted line, the boundary between the United States and Great Britain. You will see that this map suggests an encroachment on our rights by adopting a line far to the east of the Straits of Haro. You may remember that Mr. Boyd, more than two years ago, suggested to you that a design of preferring some such claims existed. I inferred, from what I could learn at that time, that this design grew up with the Hudson's Bay Company, and I had no reason to suppose it favored by the Colonial Secretary. * * *

Mr. Bancroft continues the suggestion that unjust claims may be made.

I am, &c.,

GEORGE BANCROFT.

JAMES BUCHANAN, Esq.,
Secretary of State, Washington, D. C.

[63] **Mr. Bancroft to Lord Palmerston.*

108 EATON SQUARE, *November* 3, 1848.

MY LORD: I did not forget your lordship's desire to see the United States surveys of the waters of Puget's Sound and those dividing Vancouver's Island from our territory.

Mr. Bancroft officially informs Lord Palmerston that the boundary runs through the middle of the channel of Haro.

These surveys have been reduced, and have just been published in three parts, and I transmit for your lordship's acceptance the first copy which I have received.

The surveys extend to the line of 49°, and by combining two of the charts your lordship will readily trace the whole course of the channel of Haro, through the middle of which our boundary line passes. I think you will esteem the work done in a manner very creditable to the young navy officers concerned in it.

I have the honor, &c.,

GEORGE BANCROFT.

Viscount PALMERSTON, *&c.*, *&c.*

Lord Palmerston to Mr. Bancroft.

FOREIGN OFFICE, *November* 7, 1848.

SIR: I beg leave to return you my best thanks for the surveys of Puget's Sound and of the Gulf of Georgia, which accompanied your letter of the 3d instant.

Lord Palmerston gives the acquiescence of silence to the Haro channel as the boundary.

The information as to soundings contained in these charts will no doubt be of great service to the commissioners who are to be appointed under the treaty of the 15th of June, 1846, by assisting them in determining where the line of boundary described in the first article of that treaty ought to run.

I have the honor to be, with high consideration, sir, &c.,

PALMERSTON.

GEORGE BANCROFT, Esq., *&c.*, *&c.*, *&c.*

---

[64] *No. 52.

Mr. Bancroft to Mr. Campbell.

NEW YORK, *June* 15, 1858.

SIR: Your letter of May 27 has but just reached me, in consequence of my absence from home on a long journey.

Mr. Bancroft refers Mr. Campbell to his correspondence with Lord Palmerston.

I was in the administration of Mr. Polk at the time when Mr. Buchanan perfected the treaty for settling the boundary of Oregon. The basis of the settlement was the parallel of 49°, with the concession to Britain of that part of Vancouver's Island which lies south of 49°. The United States held that both parties had a right to the free navigation of the waters round Vancouver's Island, and therefore consented that the British boundary should extend to the center of the Channel of Haro. Such was the understanding of everybody at the time of consummating the treaty in England and at Washington. The Hudson's Bay Company may naturally enough covet the group of islands east of that channel, but the desire, which never can amount to a claim, should not be listened to for a moment.

While I was in England no minister was preposterous enough to lend the authority of the British government to the cupidity of the Hudson's Bay Company in this particular. I think you must find in the Department of State a copy of a very short letter of mine to Lord Palmerston, inclosing him a chart of those waters as drawn by our own Coast Survey. I think in that letter I mentioned the center of the Straits of Haro as the boundary. That chart would show by the depths of the soundings that the Straits of Haro are the channel intended in the treaty, even if there had not been a distinct understanding on the part of the British government as well as the American at the time of the signing of the treaty. Lord Palmerston, in his reply acknowledging the receipt of the chart, made no pretense of adopting the wishes of the Hudson's Bay Company, and he never did so, even in conversation. I never had occasion in England to make any peremptory statement on the subject, because nothing was ever said or hinted there which required it; but whenever conversation turned upon the subject, whether with Lord Palmerston or with the Under Secretary of the Colonial
[65] Office, *I always spoke of the Strait of Haro as undeniably the channel of the the treaty, and no member of the British government ever took issue with me. In running the line through the center of the Straits of Haro there may be one or two small islands about which a question might be raised, but as to the important group that the Hudson's Bay Company covet, the demand, if made, should be met at the outset as one too preposterous to be entertained as a question.

Yours, sincerely,

GEORGE BANCROFT.

ARCHIBALD CAMPBELL, Esq.,
Commissioner, &c.

No. 53.

Declaration of Rear-Admiral Wilkes.

WASHINGTON CITY, *February* 16, 1872.

Rear-Admiral Wilkes on the Channel of Haro.

In answer to the memorandum on the Haro question, I have to state that I have a full knowledge of the Islands and waters lying between the Straits of Fuca and the Gulf of Georgia, having surveyed the whole whilst I was in command of the United States exploring expedition, and I state of my own knowledge that the Canal de Haro is the best and shortest route between the same. The depth of water is very great and all obstructions to the navigation of the Canal de Haro are visible. Indeed it may be said to be an arm of the sea passing from the Straits of Fuca to the Gulf of Georgia and separating the Island of Vancouver from the main or continent of America, comprising now the Territory of Washington, and it is the natural communication between the Gulf of Georgia and Fuca Straits, leading or trending north and south, and has now become the great highway of commerce, between Victoria, on the Island of Vancouver, and the Fraser's river, a few miles north of the forty-ninth parallel, the boundary of the United States and the Northwest British America. The strait of Haro may be navigated at all times, day or night, with perfect

safety, and nature has conferred upon it all that could be desired to be a well-defined national highway, between the island of Vancouver and the smaller and intricate passages through the small archipelago lying on its eastern side, which all are more or less intricate, narrow in places to a few hundred yards, and with very rapid tides. One of these
[66] passages *lying on the east of this small archipelago was named by me as Ringgold Channel, but at times called the Rosario Strait; its width does not entitle it to the name of a strait, and with its many and dangerous islets, rocks, and shoals, it is a very unsafe and difficult channel to navigate even in the day time, and impossible with any assurance of safety in the night time. It cannot be compared with the Strait of Haro in any point of view, and can only be used by small vessels seeking anchorage in the event of disaster, and bad or boisterous weather. While the Strait of Haro affords like facilities for anchorage under the islands on the east side, it may be safely navigated, and affords ample protection in its sea-room for the largest class of vessels.

The Strait of Haro, though known at the time of my survey in 1841, it was not visited, as there were no vessels engaged in those waters, except the small and very inefficient steamer called the Beaver, commanded by Captain McNeil, who spoke of it to me as the best passage, although he was obliged to pass through the Rosario passage on account of the necessity of seeking the small coves at night in passing along the east shore towards Fraser's river to supply the Post of the Hudson's Bay Company, and this was only achieved twice a year.

All the vessels now engaged in the trade from Victoria to Fraser's river and the Gulf of Georgia, invariably pass through the Haro Straits, which verifies my opinion when I first surveyed it that it would become the great and only highway between the Straits of Fuca and the Gulf of Georgia, and such it has now become. I consider that in the treaty between the British government and the United States there is no other passage that could be considered as adapted to the terms of the treaty, and both parties to that instrument must have been of like views in relation to it. All the charts used as information show the same broad channel and superiority of the Gulf of Haro over any other line to the sea, and there can scarcely be a doubt that it was so understood by the Commissioners of both sides.

CHARLES WILKES,
Rear-Admiral of the United States Navy.

---

[67] *No. 54.

Commodore Case to the Secretary of the Navy.

BUREAU OF ORDNANCE, NAVY DEPARTMENT,
February 13, 1872.

SIR: * * * * * * *

Statement of Commodore Case on the canal de Haro.

I was a Lieutenant on board of the sloop-of-war "Vincennes," attached to the United States expedition commanded by Lieutenant Charles Wilkes, and one of the surveying party in July, 1841, which surveyed the canal de Haro, the main ship-channel for vessels bound from the sea northward inside of Vancouver's Island, for the Strait of Georgia, Fraser's River, &c.

The canal is deep, clear, and navigable for vessels of all sizes or draught.

While we were engaged in the survey of the Straits of Juan de Fuca and its adjacent waters, the only vessel then navigating them was the Hudson Bay Company's steamer Beaver, which was employed by it supplying stores to, and collecting peltry from, its trading-ports on the coast, and which, I am of the opinion, used either the canal de Haro, or Straits of Rosario channels according as to where she was coming from and bound to.

When coming from the sea and bound north for the straits of Georgia, Fraser's river, or any place inside of and adjacent to Vancouver's Island, the main ship-channel is the Canal de Haro, it being the nearest and most direct. But when coasting along the main-land and bound north, from any of the ports in Puget's sound, Hood's canal, &c., for the strait of Georgia, Fraser's River, &c., the straits of Rosario would be the nearest and most direct. * * * * * * *

H. LUDLOW CASE, *U. S. N.*,
Commodore and Chief of Bureau.

No. 55.

Mr. Gibbs to the Secretary of State.

77 WALL STREET, NEW HAVEN,
February 20, 1872.

SIR: * * * * * * *

Statement of Mr. George Gibbs on the canal de Haro.

The superior depth and width of the Canal de Haro are fully exhibited not only on Wilkes's Charts, but on those of our own Coast Survey, and I presume on those
[68] of the British Commission *on the boundary. It would be therefore useless to add any merely verbal statement as to that fact. The reason for Vancouver's not surveying it was, that his object being to find a passage to the eastward, he hugged the main shore on returning from the examination of Admiralty Inlet and Puget's Sound, and thus went northward through what is now called Rosario Strait; but that it was known to him from the charts of Quadra is evident from his having laid it down on his chart by the name of the canal de "Arro," and his delineation of the whole group of the disputed islands. The reason that Governor Simpson, in his voyage from Nisqually to Sitka, (Overland Journey Round the World, during the years 1841 and 1842, by Sir George Simpson,) took the same passage, was doubtless because, however roundabout from the Strait of Fuca, it is the most direct from Admiralty Inlet. The pretense that the Hudson Bay Company was unaware of the existence of the Canal de Haro is as absurd as it would be, were the inhabitants of Brooklyn to ignore the passage between Long and Staten Islands, and claim the Kill von Kull as the outlet of the Sound and Hudson River to the sea. * * *

It appears from Mr. R. M. Martin's work on "The Hudson's Bay Territories and Vancouver Island, London, 1849," page 35, that "the Chief Factor" [since Governor Sir James Douglas] "surveyed the south coast of Vancouver's Island in 1842, and, after a careful survey, fixed on the port of Camosack" [now Victoria] "as the most eligible site for the Hudson's Bay Company's factory within the Straits of de "Fuca;" and further, Mr. Douglas, after investigating the south coast of the Island, says, "Camosack is a pleasant and convenient site for the establishment, within fifty yards of the anchorage, on the border of a large tract of clear land, which extends eastward to Point Gonzalez at the southeast end of the island," &c. No man who knows Governor Douglas will charge him with stupidity, negligence, or want of knowledge of his own interests, and it is drawing too much on human credulity to suppose that his examinations did not lead to a knowledge of the strait, if he was not aware of it before. At any rate the Indians who frequented the new trading-post, coming not only from the Gulf of Georgia, Johnston's Straits, and the northern end of Vancouver Island, but from Queen Charlotte's Islands and the whole northwest coast as far as the Russian possessions, knew and pursued the passage of the Canal de Haro and that only, and do so still.

[69] *With regard to the channel actually in use at present, I can positively state that the Rosario Strait is not followed at present at all, by vessels of the Hudson's Bay Company; nor is the Strait of Haro in its entire length. Vessels bound northward from Victoria follow the latter as far as Stuart Island, and thence take the channel between Salt Spring Island on the east and the Saturna group on the west, going out into the Gulf of Georgia by Active Passage, between that group and Galiano Island, thus cutting off the detour round Java Head, and taking an almost straight line from the southern entrance of the Canal de Haro to the middle of the Gulf of Georgia on the forty-ninth parallel, and to the mouth of Fraser river. This interior passage is perfectly navigable for large vessels, as in fact it is beyond the forty-ninth parallel, Captain Prevost himself having gone through Virago passage in Her Britannic Majesty's ship of that name long before the Boundary Commission was organized.

There seems to exist a general misapprehension of the amount of trade carried on by the Hudson's Bay Company's or other British vessels on these waters. Prior to the treaty of 1846, Fort Vancouver, on the Columbia river, was the great depot for the receipt and distribution of goods for the northwest coast, as well as the interior, and the annual ship from London delivered its cargo there. All furs were likewise received and packed there for transportation. Fort Langley, on Fraser River, was the nearest post of any magnitude. Fort Nisqually, on Puget's Sound, belonged to the Puget's Sound Agricultural Company, and according to the testimony in the case of the Hudson's Bay and Puget's Sound Agricultural Companies' Claims, the goods received there were purchased of and accounted for to the Hudson's Bay Company. It never was a distributing post of the latter. * * * * *

GEORGE GIBBS,

Late United States Geologist, Northwestern Boundary Survey.

No. 56.

Extract from letter of Messrs. Campbell and Parke to the Secretary of State.

WASHINGTON, *February* 3, 1872.

SIR: * * * * * * *

Why the vessels of the Hudson's Bay Company used the so-called Rosario straits.

A map should be examined showing the relative position of the Hudson Bay Company's establishment at
[70] Victoria on Van*couver's Island, Nisqually on Puget Sound, and Fort Langley on Fraser River, and the

position of the Canal de Haro and Rosario Straits as avenues of communication between the three points. It would be well also to consider the relative importance of these three establishments in those waters.

* * * * * * * * *

It is not at all probable that any vessel from foreign parts or from the Columbia River ever did communicate directly with Fort Langley (on Fraser River) without touching at the other posts on the lower waters, Victoria and Nisqually. It is well known, on the contrary, that these trips of the Hudson's Bay Company's vessels were made periodically for the purpose of distributing the regular supplies of food and merchandise for trading purposes, and receiving in return the furs collected at the several posts. Now, by referring to the map, it will be seen that a vessel leaving the Columbia River for the foregoing purpose would first touch at Victoria, then at Nisqually, and then at Fort Langley on Fraser River. In making this trip no navigator would dream of taking the Canal de Haro in sailing from Nisqually to Fort Langley, when the more direct and much shorter route lay through Rosario Straits. * * Although Rosario Strait was generally used, (and good reasons have been given herein for this general use,) the Canal de Haro was not only known by these very Hudson Bay Company's employés to be navigable, but by their own affidavits it is shown that two of their own vessels made successful passages through this channel prior to the date of the treaty. * * * * * *

ARCHIBALD CAMPBELL,
Late United States Boundary Commissioner.
JNO. G. PARKE,
Major of Engineers, Brevet Major-General.

No. 57.

Mr. Campbell to the Secretary of State.

WASHINGTON, *January* 19, 1872.

SIR: * * * * * * *

I can say from my own knowledge that after the discovery of gold on Fraser River in 1858, the canal de Haro was the
[71] *ordinary channel of communication between Victoria and British Columbia, and doubtless now is, and ever will be.

The Haro channel the usual channel.

ARCHIBALD CAMPBELL,
Late United States Boundary Commissioner.

No. 58.

The Attorney-General to the Secretary of State.

DEPARTMENT OF JUSTICE,
Washington, April 6, 1872.

SIR: I have the honor to inclose for your consideration and use * * a statement prepared and addressed to me by Henry R. Crosby, esq., for whose reliability I am willing to vouch. * * *

GEO. H. WILLIAMS,
Attorney-General.

Hon. HAMILTON FISH,
Secretary of State.

Mr. Crosby to the Attorney-General.

WASHINGTON, D. C., *April* 2, 1872.

SIR: In compliance with your request that I would furnish you with any information which I may possess with regard to the navigation of Rosario Straits by British and other vessels previous to 1846, and whether this or the canal de Haro was the channel most frequently used up to that period and since, these being the channels now in dispute as to which is the true boundary line on the northwest coast between the United States and Great Britain, I have the honor to make the following statement, prefacing it with a brief account of my opportunities for acquiring this information, and the sources from which it was derived.

I was a resident of Washington Territory from 1853 to 1860. I was for several terms a member of the territorial legislature and
[72] *in the discharge of my official duties had occasion to thoroughly investigate the subject of the claims of the Hudson Bay Company, and its branch organization, the Puget Sound Agricultural Company, which foreign corporations at that time, and for several years afterward, retained their trading-posts and establishments in different portions of the territory. This was a source of much complaint, as they claimed large tracts of unoccupied land, and thus materially interfered with the settlement of the country.

The searching for the foundation of these extensive claims necessarily involved the history of all the region west of the Rocky Mountains and north of the Columbia River to the forty-ninth parallel.

My information, other than the facts of which I was personally cognizant during my seven years' residence, was derived from statements made me by persons who had been in the country many years. Among these were the earlier missionaries, both Protestant and Catholic, the first settlers, old trappers, and, in many instances, the chief factors and traders of the Hudson Bay Company. One of the topics of frequent conversation was the early navigation of Puget Sound and the adjacent waters. I gleaned from corroborating evidence the following facts. At the time of the treaty of 1846, the vessels employed between Victoria, the trading-post at Nisqually, near the head of the Sound, Fort Langley on Fraser River, and the other posts on the northern coast, were the Hudson Bay Company steamer Beaver and the schooner Cadboro. The company owned two or three small brigs, which were principally used in the trade with California and the Sandwich Islands. Each year two ships were dispatched from England, bringing out trading goods and other supplies and returning with the furs collected at the depots of Victoria and Fort Vancouver, on the Columbia River, from the various trading-posts on the coast and in the interior, west of the Rocky Mountains. On the arrival of these ships all of the posts, both of the interior and the coast, were fitted out with what was estimated as a supply sufficient to answer for trading purposes and the support of the employés for a year ahead.

The usual course for the two vessels especially assigned to this duty on the sound and northern coast was in the spring of each year—which was the time of the arrival and distribution—to take supplies up to Nisqually for that post and the station at Cowlitz Plains, some
[73] fifty miles south. The extensive farm at this *latter place was started for the purpose of raising grain, potatoes, and other vegetables, for the supply both of the northern posts and the Russian possessions at Sitka and the Aleutian Islands. For their breadstuffs the Russian-Americans were entirely dependent upon this farm, and the

Puget Sound Agricultural Company had therefore with them a large and lucrative trade. At Nisqually were large herds of cattle, which were slaughtered as required and salted down. These provisions were taken on board the Beaver and Cadboro, and, with the other supplies, delivered at the posts on Fraser River and up the coast.

Coming down from Nisqually, the masters of the vessels naturally, in their trips to Fraser River, turned into Rosario Straits. From up the sound it was the first channel which led off to the north.

Why the so-called Rosario Strait was used.

I have mentioned this customary manner of delivering the annual supplies, because it is the principal reason why the Rosario Straits at that time was generally used by the fur company's vessels. Another cause may be found in the fact that the canal de Haro is a broad, deep arm of the sea, being, in fact, but a continuation of the straits of Fuca, sweeping in with a rushing tide, and meeting the waters of the Gulf of Georgia at its northern end. Its extreme depth made it difficult to find good anchorage.

Rosario Straits is a very much narrower channel. It is not comparatively deep, is well sheltered, and affords everywhere secure anchorage. Of late years it has been found to be dangerous for large ships on account of sunken rocks, but the vessels then navigating it were small, and therefore of light draught, and ran little or no risk on that account.

The canal de Haro used by the vessels of the Hudson Bay Company before 1846.

The statement that the canal de Haro is a channel but recently known is absurd. The steamer Beaver went through it years before the treaty, and that the schooner Cadboro did so is established by the fact that one of the passages leading into the canal de Haro is known by the name of the Cadboro Pass. All the northern Indians who came to Victoria to trade passed through the canal de Haro, as did also the Indians from Fraser River and the company's factors and traders at the posts on that river who frequently visited Victoria between the trips of the supply-vessels. In 1853 Admiral (then Lieutenant) Alden passed through the canal de Haro in the United States Coast-Survey steamer Active. Governor Douglas, of Vancouver's Island, gave him much valuable information concern-
[74] ing it, and evinced a thorough and complete *knowledge of its tides and depth of water. Douglas was the governor by virtue of being the senior chief factor of the Hudson Bay Company. He had selected the site and established the post at Victoria in 1842. A man of great energy, he made himself acquainted with everything relating to the interests of the company he represented, and this involved not only a knowledge of the fur-trade and the character of the Indians, but also that of the surrounding country and its adjacent waters.

Canal de Haro the passage to the north.

In the spring of 1854, on a visit to Victoria, I was a witness to the fact that Canal de Haro was the channel used by the English vessels. At that time quite a considerable trade had sprung up with Nanaimo, in consequence of the working of the extensive coal-mines at that place, which is on the eastern side of Vancouver's Island, near the fiftieth parallel. I was standing, with several other persons, watching a large bark, which had just left the harbor, and under full sail was heading up the passage, when one of the party, an old Hudson Bay Company ship-master, remarked, "If the breeze holds she will go through Haro straits flying; but if it fails, she will drift a long way before finding anchorage. The channel is so broad and the straits so deep that it is like being out at sea."

From 1854 to 1860, I was frequently at Vancouver's Island, and know personally that Canal de Haro was the usual route to Fraser river, the Nanaimo coal-mines, and the saw-mills at Burrard's Inlet.

In 1857, the British steam corvette "Satellite" and the surveying steamer Plumper arrived at Vancouver's Island. Captains Prevost and Richards, commanding these vessels, were the British commissioners to settle the boundary line. When they went to Nanaimo for coal, they passed through Canal de Haro.

In 1858 occurred what is known as the Fraser river excitement, consequent upon the discovery of gold in that river and its tributaries. During that year I made frequent visits to Victoria, and was also up Fraser river. Victoria was the disembarking point for the ocean steamers from San Francisco. Steamers to be used between Victoria and Fraser river were brought up from California; others were hastily built on the sound for that purpose; some of these smaller steamers also plied between the American towns and the river. In the great rush of gold-miners, the steamers, though crowded to their utmost capacity,
[75] could not convey all seeking *passage. Every other means there-
fore of water conveyance was in addition brought into service—schooners, sloops, boats, and canoes. The route at first adopted was entirely through the canal de Haro, but the steamers eventually went by a still nearer passage. After going part of the way up the canal de Haro, they turned into the channel on the western side of Saturna island, passing into the Gulf of Georgia by what is known as the "Active pass."

In 1859, I was for several months on San Juan island, and frequently saw the steamers and other vessels passing between Victoria and Fraser river. The canal de Haro and the nearer route inside of Saturna island were the only routes used; nor did I ever see or hear of any steamer or sailing-vessel during the gold excitement going from Victoria to Fraser river by the way of Rosario straits. In the hurry of those stirring times, the master of any vessel who took such a roundabout route to reach his destination would have been not only severely ridiculed, but in all probability would have lost his carrying trade, both of passengers and of goods.

Worthlessness of the middle channel.

The "middle channel" which was proposed by Captain Prevost as a compromise, at its entrance, between the islands of San Juan and Lopez, is so narrow that it cannot be seen until you are quite near. A vessel approaching it has to run in by the landmarks. It is but a few hundred yards across, and is only used by vessels going into San Juan harbor, which is on the inner side of the island, a short distance from the entrance. The avowed object of this proposal was, to obtain San Juan Island, the most valuable of the islands in the Archipelago. The channel designated passes into the canal de Haro, near its northern end, and would present the anomaly of the canal de Haro being adopted as the boundary for a portion of its course in its direct passage to the ocean, and then diverged from, thus conflicting with the clause in the Treaty which expressly stipulates the course of the water-line shall be through a continuous channel.

The assertion that San Juan is essential for the protection of Vancouver's Island is as absurd as the pretended ignorance of the navigability of the canal de Haro. The nearest portion of San Juan is eighteen miles from the entrance to Victoria harbor, and owing to the immense width of the channel, there is no point at which fortifications could be established which could interfere with the passage of vessels to the settlements of British Columbia.

Difference between Haro and Rosario straits.

[76] *The canal de Haro is the only one of the channels which is over a cannon-shot across. The difference in width and depth of water between it and Rosario Straits is so great that it appears like contrasting an inland sea with a river.

With the growing commerce of that section Rosario straits has completely fallen into disuse, and the canal de Haro is now, and has been for many years, the route exclusively used between Victoria and British Columbia.

Very respectfully, your obedient servant,

HENRY R. CROSBY.

Hon. GEO. H. WILLIAMS,
Attorney-General.

No. 59.

Brigadier-General Canby to the Assistant Adjutant-General at San Francisco.

[Extract.]

HEADQUARTERS DEPARTMENT OF THE COLUMBIA,
Portland, Oregon, April 2, 1872.

SIR: * * * * * * *

Why the so-called Rosario strait was used.

I am informed that the vessels of the Hudson Bay Company, on their upward-bound trips, usually passed through Rosario Straits, because their business required them to touch at the in-shore stations of the company, but almost invariably through the canal de Haro in returning to Vancouver.

ED. R. S. CANBY,
Brigadier-General Commanding.

No. 60.

Report of Captain G. H. Richards, October 23, 1858, *in papers relating to British Columbia, presented to both Houses of Parliament, by command of Her Majesty, August* 12, 1859.—*Part II, p.* 14.

Description of Haro channel by Capt. Richards, British Boundary Commissioner.

"The Haro Strait lies between Vancouver Island and the principal islands composing the archipelago. * * In the Haro Strait, Cordova Bay on the western or Vancouver shore offers good anchorage. On Stewart Island, which helps to form the eastern side of the strait, there are snug and land-
locked harbors, easily accessible to steamers; and among the
[77] Saturna group—the western *boundary of the strait where it
enters the Gulf of Georgia—there is good shelter for a fleet, accessible either to sailing-vessels or steamers."

No. 61.

AFFIDAVITS CONCERNING THE NAVIGATION OF THE CAÑAL DE HARO.

Statements of Remington F. Pickett, made before the United States consul at Victoria, Vancouver Island, on this twelfth day of March, A. D. 1872, *touching the navigation of the Canal de Haro and Rosario Straits.*

Affidavits on the canal de Haro.

On this twelfth day of March, A. D. one thousand eight hundred and seventy-two, personally appeared before me, David Eckstein, Consul of the United States of America for the Province of

British Columbia, Dominion of Canada, residing at Victoria, Vancouver Island, Remington F. Pickett, who, being first duly sworn, states as follows:

My age is thirty-seven years. My occupation that of merchant and shipping agent. My place of residence is Victoria, Vancouver Island, and have resided here most of the time since eighteen hundred and fifty-nine.

For the last ten years I have been agent for a line of sail-vessels running between San Francisco and ports in British Columbia.

During all the time since eighteen hundred and fifty-nine, vessels, both sail and steam, in making trips from Victoria to the Gulf of Georgia and Fraser River, have invariably used the canal de Haro as a passage.

I have also heard masters of steamers and sail-vessels invariably speak of the canal de Haro as the channel used by them, and of its superiority, for purposes of navigation, over any other channel between the continent and Vancouver Island.

All English steamers have used the canal de Haro as a passage in making trips from Victoria to Fraser River, since my residence at this place, and continue to do so at this time. American steamers have done the same and do now. In fact the canal de Haro is the only channel used by steam and sail vessels, at the present time, and has been the only one used for years.

REMINGTON F. PICKETT.

[78] *CONSULATE OF THE UNITED STATES OF AMERICA,
Victoria, Vancouver Island, British Columbia:

Affidavits on the canal de Haro.

I, David Eckstein, Consul of the United States of America, residing at Victoria, Vancouver Island, do hereby certify that Remington F. Pickett personally appeared before me and made oath and subscribed to the truth of the foregoing statements, on this the twelfth day of March, A. D. one thousand eight hundred and seventy-two; I further certify that the said Remington F. Pickett is personally known to me, that he is a respectable and credible person, to whose representations full faith and credit can be given.

In witness whereof I have hereunto subscribed my name and affixed the seal of my office, this twelfth day of March, A. D. one thousand eight hundred and seventy-two.

[SEAL.]

DAVID ECKSTEIN,
United States Consul.

Statements of George Thomas Seymour, made before the United States Consul, residing at Victoria, Vancouver Island, March 13th, A. D. 1872, touching upon the navigation of the Canal de Haro and Rosario Straits.

On this thirteenth day of March, A. D. one thousand eight hundred and seventy-two, personally appeared before me, David Eckstein, Consul of the United States of America for the Province of British Columbia, Dominion of Canada, residing at the port of Victoria, Vancouver Island, George Thomas Seymour, who, being first duly sworn, states as follows: My age is forty-nine years; and I have resided at Victoria, Vancouver Island, since eighteen hundred and fifty-eight. My occupation is that of merchant. I have been acquainted with the routes of travel by water between Victoria and points on the Gulf of Georgia and Fraser River, since the year eighteen hundred and fifty-eight. The canal de Haro has been the channel used by steamers and sail-vessels, British and others, since eighteen hundred and fifty-eight, and is the one now generally, if not exclusively, used in making trips to and from the above-named points, both night and day. It is in fact the main channel, and the only one regarded as really safe by masters of steamers and sail-vessels, who are acquainted with the waters between the continent and Vancouver Island.

[79] *Ever since my residence at Victoria, in eighteen hundred and fifty-eight, the canal de Haro has been the channel invariably used by navigators in going from Victoria to points on the Gulf of Georgia and Fraser river. No navigator would ever think of using any other channel, unless he had some special reason for it.

Affidavits on the canal de Haro.

GEORGE THOMAS SEYMOUR.

CONSULATE OF THE UNITED STATES OF AMERICA,
Victoria, Vancouver Island, British Columbia:

I, David Eckstein, Consul of the United States of America, residing at Victoria, Vancouver Island, do hereby certify that on this thirteenth day of March, A. D. one thousand eight hundred and seventy-two, personally appeared before me George Thomas Seymour, and made oath and subscribed to the truth of the foregoing statements. I further certify that the said George Thomas Seymour is personally known to me, and that he is a respectable and credible person, to whose representation full faith and credit can be given.

In witness whereof I have hereunto set my hand and affixed the seal of my office this thirteenth day of March, A. D. one thousand eight hundred and seventy-two.

[L. S.] DAVID ECKSTEIN,
United States Consul.

Statements of Albert Henry Guild, made before the United States Consul, residing at the Port of Victoria, Vancouver Island, March 16, 1872, touching the navigation of the Canal de Haro and Rosario Straits.

On this sixteenth day of March, A. D. one thousand eight hundred and seventy-two, before me, David Eckstein, Consul of the United States of America, for the Province of British Columbia, Dominion of Canada, residing at the Port of Victoria, Vancouver Island, personally appeared Albert Henry Guild, who, being first duly sworn, states as follows:

My age is fifty-eight years; my residence, Victoria, Vancouver Island, and have resided here since the year eighteen hundred and fifty-eight; my occupation is that of merchant.

[80] *I am familiar with the route of travel by water, by steamers and sail-vessels, British and American, from Victoria to points on the Gulf of Georgia and Fraser river.

Affidavits on the canal de Haro.

The canal de Haro is the channel now exclusively used by all classes of vessels, British and others, carrying pilot or no pilot, in making trips between the above-named points, and has been so used, to the best of my knowledge, since eighteen hundred and fifty-eight.

During my residence at Victoria I have frequently passed through the canal de Haro as passenger in Hudson Bay Company's steamers; and, in fact, I never knew them to use any other channel in making trips to and from the above-named points.

Vessels coming into the Straits of Juan de Fuca from the ocean, bound for ports or places on the Gulf of Georgia or Fraser River, invariably pass through the canal de Haro, whether touching at Victoria or not, and have done so since my residence here in eighteen hundred and fifty-eight.

ALBERT HENRY GUILD.

CONSULATE OF THE UNITED STATES OF AMERICA,
Victoria, Vancouver Island, British Columbia:

I, David Eckstein, Consul of the United States of America, residing at Victoria, Vancouver Island, do hereby certify that on this sixteenth day of March, A. D. one thousand eight hundred and seventy-two, personally appeared before me Albert Henry Guild, and made oath and subscribed to the truth of the foregoing statements. I further certify that the said Albert Henry Guild is personally known to me, and that he is a respectable and credible person, to whose representation full faith and credit can be given.

In witness whereof I have hereunto subscribed my name and affixed the seal of my office the day and year first above written.

[SEAL.] DAVID ECKSTEIN,
United States Consul.

Extracts from the Affidavit of William J. Waitt.

UNITED STATES OF AMERICA,
Territory of Washington, ss:

I, William J. Waitt, of the City of Olympia, County of Thurston, and Territory aforesaid, do solemnly declare upon oath that I am
[81] *a master mariner, of the age of thirty-two years; that I came to Victoria, Vancouver's Island, in the spring of 1868, and for the next four years was engaged in steamboating between said City of Victoria and Fraser's River, in British Columbia; fifteen months of that period I was master, the remainder pilot and mate. In 1862 I commenced running between Victoria and Olympia, with occasional trips from Victoria to New Westminster. During all this time the canal de Haro has been the only channel used in going from Victoria or the Straits of Fuca, northward into the Gulf of Georgia and places on the Northern Coast. I know both Haro Canal and Rosario Straits. The first is the only one ever used in the large trade between Puget Sound and the British Columbia Mines; between Victoria and the said mines; between San Francisco and the main land of British Columbia. It is the only one by which the heavy coal trade of Nanaimo Mines is carried on. It is straighter, shorter, deeper, fewer rocks, less currents, and is much the safest route, particularly going through at night or in a fog.

Affidavits on the canal of Haro.

I am intimately acquainted with Capts. McNeil, Swanson, Ella, and Lewis. I knew Capt. Morrat in his life-time. They are old Captains who were in the service of the Hudson's Bay Company as early as 1840. I have talked with each and all of them on these matters, as it was my business to learn. * * * * * * *

All their statements to me justify my declaration upon oath, that since Fort Victoria was established on Vancouver Island, this channel was exclusively used in all trips of their steamers, between said Fort Victoria and their trading-posts North on the Gulf of Georgia, and on the upper Fraser's River. No other channel but this was talked about by either of them. None other had ever been used in their regular trade, since Fort Victoria was established, which I believe on information was in 1842. Capt. McNeil told me he had been through here in his own vessel, which he brought from Boston, before he was bought out by the Hudson's Bay Company, and employed in the Company's service. He also spoke of going through in the steamer Beaver, of which he was Master, when Captain Wilkes was here. * * * * * *

Haro channel used exclusively for northern trade since establishment of Fort Victoria in 1842.

The Northern Indians always came and went by the same channel in their trips to Victoria, and over to Washington Territory, since I have been here; and from information, and knowledge of Indian customs, I state the opinion they always did use such Canal de Haro in
[82] their trips to and from Victoria and their Northern *residences.
They always used the same channel when coming to the American side of the straits of Fuca, and the settlements on Puget sound.

Affidavits on the canal de Haro.

CAPT. W. J. WAITT.

TERRITORY OF WASHINGTON,
County of Thurston, ss:

Before me, Joseph H. Houghton, Clerk of the Supreme Court of said Territory, came William J. Waitt, who being first duly sworn, did depose and say that he had carefully read the foregoing statement, and knew the contents thereof; that the same had been dictated by him. And that so much thereof as was stated from his own knowledge was true, and so much thereof as was stated on information he verily believes to be true.

In testimony whereof I have hereunto set my hand and affixed the seal of said Court, this sixteenth day of March, A. D. 1872.

[SEAL.] JOSEPH H. HOUGHTON,
Clerk Sup. Ct. W. T.

Extracts from the Affidavit of Francis Tarbell.

UNITED STATES OF AMERICA,
Territory of Washington, ss:

I, Francis Tarbell, of the City of Olympia, County of Thurston, and Territory aforesaid, do solemnly declare upon oath, that I am a native-born Citizen of the United States, aged forty-one years. I went to Victoria, Vancouver's Island, on the 14th July, 1858, and continued to reside there, doing business as a wholesale merchant, up to 1866. In 1862 I became a Director in the Victoria and British Columbia Steamboat Company, and from my connection with said Company, and my business, I became thoroughly acquainted with the Vessels, Steamboats, Route, &c., used by the Steam and other vessels, to and from said City of Victoria. From that knowledge I declare positively and without reserve, that the Canal de Haro was the only channel used by Vessels going to the Gulf of Georgia from Victoria, or from sea-voyages via Straits of Juan de Fuca. In the last fourteen years I have probably been five hundred times to New Westminster at the mouth of Fraser's

River, in British Columbia. In these trips or voyages, no other channel but the Haro Canal was ever used. * * * *

[83] *I am well and intimately acquainted with Capt. McNeil, Capt. Swanston, Capt. Lewis, and Capt. Ella. I was well acquainted with Capt. Wm. A. Morrat in his life-time. These were all old Captains formerly in the employ of the Hudson's Bay Company. From their statements to me, and from other sources, several of them were here, if not all, before 1840. In my eight years' residence in Victoria, I was in company with these men a great deal, conversing very freely on the subject of Steamboats, Routes up the Coast, Trade of the Coast, &c. It was in the direct line of my business to learn these matters. I freely inquired as to their knowledge, and they freely communicated with me. I have been told frequently by all those gentlemen that the channel now used to reach the Gulf of Georgia in going from Victoria to Nanaimo, Fraser's River, or to the Northern Coast, or in returning from the same to Victoria, has been invariably used by the Vessels of the Hudson's Bay Company since Fort Victoria was established. * * *

Affidavits on the canal de Haro.

Haro channel used by Hudson's Bay Company since establishment of Fort Victoria.

I am also positive that Captain McNeil has told me on several occasions that he used the same channel when sailing a Vessel for the Hudson Bay Company long prior to 1846; and I have heard him make the same statement in regard to the vessel he brought out from Boston before he went into the Company's service. I am also positive that he has told me that after going into the Company's employ, long anterior to 1846, he passed through this channel in the steamer Beaver, of which he was Captain, about the time Capt. Wilkes made his survey of these waters. * * * *

Hudson's Bay Company used Haro channel before 1846.

FRANCIS TARBELL.

TERRITORY OF WASHINGTON,
County of Thurston, ss:

Before me, Joseph H. Houghton, Clerk of the Supreme Court of said Territory, came Francis Tarbell, who, being first duly sworn, did depose and say that he had carefully read the foregoing statement, and knew the contents thereof; that the same had been dictated by him; and that so much thereof as was stated from his own knowledge was true, and so much thereof as was stated on information he verily believes to be true.

Witness my hand and the seal of the said Court this 16th day of March, A. D. 1872.

[SEAL OF THE SUP. COURT.] JOSEPH H. HOUGHTON,
Clerk Sup. Ct., W. T.

---

[84] **Extracts from the Affidavit of Charles Willoughby.*

Affidavits on the canal de Haro.

UNITED STATES OF AMERICA,
Territory of Washington, ss:

I, Charles Willoughby, of the City of Port Townsend, County of Jefferson, in said Territory, do solemnly swear that I am a native-born American Citizen, aged 41 years, a Master Mariner, and have, since December, 1850, been Master of a Vessel. * * * *

In 1861 I made another voyage in Bark Naramisse to Nanaimo for Coal. Took a pilot at Victoria, who was recommended to me by the Harbor Master as an old and experienced Hudson Bay Co. pilot; his name I have forgotten. We were again piloted, as before, through Haro Canal. In the latter voyage we encountered a gale from S. E., veering to south, which struck the ship at 6 A. M., and lasted eight hours; ship under close-reef main top-sails, and blowing very heavy all the time. The position of the ship at the time we took the gale was off Chatham Island, with ebb tide. The pilot, as well as myself, entertained no fears for the safety of the ship, as the shores were bold, the water deep, currents so regular, and plenty of sea-room; and we had no fears of the result. I would not like to be caught in Rosario Straits in the same manner. When the gale broke, we were up by Sidney Island—nearly up to the Active Pass. From my experience then and knowledge now, I pronounce the Haro Channel the best Channel or passage between any of the Islands, or between the Main-land and Islands North of the Straits of Fuca. * * * * * * *

CHAS. WILLOUGHBY.

TERRITORY OF WASHINGTON,
County of Thurston, ss:

Before me, Joseph H. Houghton, Clerk of the Supreme Court of said Territory, came Charles Willoughby, who, being first duly sworn, did depose and say that he had carefully read the foregoing statement, and knew the contents thereof; that the same had been dictated by him; and that so much thereof as was stated from his own knowledge was true, and so much thereof as was stated on information he verily believes to be true.

In testimony whereof I have hereunto set my hand and affixed the Seal of the Court this 16th day of March, A. D. 1872.

[SEAL OF THE SUP. COURT.] JOSEPH H. HOUGHTON,
Clerk Sup. Ct., W. T.

---

[85] **Extracts from the Affidavit of James S. Lawson.*

UNITED STATES OF AMERICA,
Territory of Washington, ss:

Affidavits on the canal de Haro.

I, James S. Lawson, Assistant United States Coast Survey, and at present a resident of Olympia, County of Thurston, and Territory of Washington, do solemnly declare upon oath, that I am a native-born citizen of the United States, aged forty-four years; that I came to the Western coast of the United States in June, 1850, in the coast survey, and have been engaged in the same from that time to the present, in all capacities from aid to assistant in charge of a party. From 1852 to 1859, both inclusive, I spent each working season in the surveys of straits of Juan de Fuca, Canal de Haro, Rosario Straits, Gulf of Georgia to forty-ninth parallel of North latitude, and Admiralty Inlet, and since 1866 I have been permanently located in this section, with a residence at Olympia.

* * * * * * *

From several years of such experience and service, I assert the great superiority of the Canal de Haro over the Rosario Strait as a Ship-Channel or Channel of any character, depth of water, width, directness, and freedom from obstructions, rocks, &c. The currents are strong in both, but as a ship-channel the Haro Canal is decidedly superior.

While working in the Gulf of Georgia in 1858 and 1859, vessels bound from Victoria to Fraser's River, Nanaimo, or farther north, invariably made use of Canal de Haro; in fact I have never heard of a single instance of a vessel sailing from Victoria since 1852, when I came to this section, and bound for any of the above-mentioned places, making use of Rosario Strait. My experience has shown that the Indians of the Northwest Coast always made use of the Canal de Haro, on their visits to Victoria and returning.

* * * * * * *

JAS. S. LAWSON.

TERRITORY OF WASHINGTON,
County of Thurston, ss:

Before me, Joseph H. Houghton, Clerk of the Supreme Court of said Territory, came James S. Lawson, who, being first duly sworn, did depose and say, that he had carefully read the foregoing statement, and knew the contents thereof; that the same had been dictated by
[86] him; and that so much thereof as was stated from *his own knowledge was true, and so much thereof as was stated on information he verily believes to be true.

Affidavits on the canal de Haro.

In testimony whereof I have hereunto set my hand and affixed the Seal of said Court this 16th day of March, A. D. 1872.

[SEAL OF THE SUP. COURT.] JOSEPH H. HOUGHTON,
Clerk Supreme Court, Washington Territory.

Affidavit of Thomas McManus.

UNITED STATES OF AMERICA,
Territory of Washington, ss:

I, Thomas McManus, of the City of Townsend, County of Jefferson, and Territory of Washington, do solemnly declare that I am a citizen of the United States, of the age of fifty-one years.

On the 2d day of May, 1841, I was serving as an ordinary seaman, on board the United States ship Vincennes, in the United States exploring expedition, Charles Wilkes, United States Navy, Commanding Expedition, and we entered these waters about the above date. I was in the Boat Expedition, surveying both Canal de Haro and Rosario Straits. I served during the whole cruise of the expedition.

Wilkes surveys canal de Haro in 1841.

In 1858 I returned to Washington Territory, and since that time I have been constantly sailing in these waters. I know both channels well, and have been frequently in them, but never in Rosario Straits in a Ship. From my knowledge of said Rosario Straits, I do not think it a safe passage for sailing-vessels. From uncertainty of winds during summer months, and adversity of currents, the passage is unsafe without the use of towing; and in my knowledge it is not, nor has it ever been used by vessels going to or coming from the Gulf of Georgia. The Canal de Haro is the natural route for vessels from Victoria to the Gulf of Georgia and the Northern Coast. It is a safe and good ship-channel, broad, deep, and plenty of sea-room, and less danger from hidden rocks than in Rosario Straits. For heavy-draught Vessels it is the only Channel which can be used.

Since I have been here (1858) the Canal de Haro is the Channel invariably used by vessels, American and English, Steam and other vessels going into the Gulf of Georgia from Victoria or the Straits of Fuca.

THOMAS McMANUS.

[87] *TERRITORY OF WASHINGTON,
County of Thurston, ss:

Before me, Joseph H. Houghton, Clerk of the Supreme Court of said Territory, came Thomas McManus, who being first duly sworn, did depose and say that he had carefully read the foregoing statement, and knew the contents thereof; that the same had been dictated by him; and that so much thereof as was stated from his own knowledge was true, and so much thereof as was stated on information he verily believes to be true.

Affidavits on the canal de Haro.

Witness my hand and the Seal of said Court this 20th day of March, A. D. 1872.

[SEAL.] JOSEPH H. HOUGHTON,
Clerk Supreme Court, Washington Territory.

Affidavit of Adam Benson.

UNITED STATES OF AMERICA,
Territory of Washington, ss:

I, Adam Benson, of Pierce County, Washington Territory, do solemnly declare upon oath that I am a citizen of the United States, of the age of fifty-six years, and a native of the North of Scotland. I came to this Territory, then Oregon, in the service of the Hudson Bay Company in 1836, and stopped at Fort Nisqually, in what is now Pierce County. I was a shepherd and herder of the Company's sheep, after Fort Victoria was established in 1842. I made a trip in charge of the company's sheep from Fort Nisqually to Fort Victoria, in the spring of 1845, just before potato planting. From thence the Steamer Beaver towed the ship Columbia to the mouth of Fraser's River. We went through the Channel between Vancouver's Island and San Juan Island. Captain Dodd was the master of the Steamer Beaver. I fix the year 1845, because it was the year that Colonel Simmons came and settled at New Market. I remember that Fort Victoria had only been established two or three years, and all the buildings were not up when I was there.

The steamer Beaver towed the ship Columbia through Haro channel in 1845.

ADAM BENSON.

TERRITORY OF WASHINGTON,
County of Thurston, ss:

Before me, Joseph H. Houghton, Clerk of the Supreme Court of said Territory, came Adam Benson, who, being first duly sworn, did
[88] depose and say that he had carefully read the foregoing state*ment, and knew the contents thereof; that the same had been dictated by him and was true.

Affidavits on the canal de Haro.

In testimony whereof I have hereunto set my hand, and affixed the seal of said Court this twenty-seventh day of March, A. D. 1872.

[SEAL.] JOSEPH H. HOUGHTON,
Clerk Supreme Court, Washington Territory.

Affidavit of William N. Horton.

UNITED STATES OF AMERICA,
Territory of Washington, ss:

I, William N. Horton, now of the City of Olympia, County of Thurston, and Territory aforesaid, do solemnly declare upon oath, that I am a native-born citizen of the United States, of the age of forty-two years, and am a Steamboat Engineer by profession. I came to Portland, Oregon, in June, 1850. I came to Puget Sound in May or June, 1854, since which time Olympia has been my residence when upon shore. Early after coming to the Sound, I made a trip in the Sloop Sarah Stone, Captain Thomas Slaten, to all of the Sound Ports, extending our voyage to Fort Victoria, and Nanaimo, upon Vancouver's Island. We went and returned through the Canal de Haro; at that time it was the only channel used by all Coal Vessels going to and from Nanaimo, by the Hudson's Bay Company's Steamers Beaver and Otter in their trips North from Fort Victoria to the trading-posts on the Northern Coast. Indeed it is the only channel which can be profitably or safely used in going from the Straits of Fuca into the Gulf of Georgia, and the inland waters to the North. It was then used by those Steamers, for on that trip, or shortly after, I have seen both of those Steamers, either going from or returning to the then Fort Victoria, now the City of Victoria, on Vancouver's Island.

From the spring of 1855 up to 1858, I was running a Steamer on the Sound, and made numerous trips to Victoria, and saw Steam and other vessels in the Canal de Haro. I never saw or heard of any vessel ever using the Rosario Straits to get into the Gulf of Georgia. In 1858 I was employed on various Steamers running to Fraser's River, and
continued in that business until 1861. The whole trade between
[89] Victoria and Fraser's River,*in all classes of vessels, was entirely
and exclusively done in the Canal de Haro.

Affidavits on the canal de Haro.

I know both channels, having run in both as pilot and Engineer. Haro Channel for all vessels is infinitely superior to Rosario Straits. It is broader, deeper, more direct, less sunken rocks, and the Canal de Haro is perfectly safe at night or in a fog, which I cannot say of Rosario Straits. The currents are strong in both, but in the Canal de Haro much the more regular.

I have very frequently seen the Northern Indians coming and going through Haro Channel, and from my information I believe that such Channel has always been used by them in their trading trips from the North to Fort Victoria. Indians follow customs tenaciously, and do not change their routes; and as this was their custom in 1854, I am positive it was previous thereto.

W. N. HORTON.

TERRITORY OF WASHINGTON,
County of Thurston, ss:

Before me, Joseph H. Houghton, Clerk of the Supreme Court of said Territory, came William N. Horton, who, being first duly sworn, did depose and say, that he had carefully read the foregoing statement, and knew the contents thereof; that the same had been dictated by him; and that so much thereof as was stated from his own knowledge was true, and so much thereof as was stated upon information he verily believes to be true.

In testimony whereof, I have hereunto set my hand and affixed the Seal of said Court this 30th day of March, A. D. 1872.

[SEAL.] JOSEPH H. HOUGHTON,
Clerk Supreme Court, Washington Territory.

Affidavit of John McLeod.

UNITED STATES OF AMERICA,
Territory of Washington, ss:

I, John McLeod, of Pierce County, Washington Territory, do solemnly declare upon oath that I am a naturalized citizen of the United States, of the age of fifty-six years, and was born in Lewes Island, North of Scotland. I arrived in this Territory, then Oregon, in the service
[90] of the Hudson's Bay Company, in the Fall *of 1838, at Fort Nisqually on Puget Sound, and immediately was put on board of the Company's Steamer Beaver; Captain McNeil was then master. While I was on board, she was also commanded by Captain Brotchie and Captain Duncan. My duty was that of Stoker. Up to 1842, when Fort Victoria was established on Vancouver's Island, she made two trips up North from Fort Nisqually annually, in collecting furs. I continued on board until the spring of 1844, (April, I think,) since which time I have lived in Pierce County, near Fort Nisqually. I know San Juan Island, and the channel between it and Vancouver's Island. I made in the Steamer Beaver, after 1842, and till I was discharged, at least two trips to the North each year, that is to say in 1842 and 1843. While building the Fort at Victoria till the buildings were well up, we staid in the harbor as a Guard against the Indians, and while thus delayed the Beaver towed the Schooner Cadboro, two or three times to the mouth of Fraser's River. In all her trips North from Fort Victoria to Fort Simpson, and back, and in towing the Cadboro to Fraser's River, we always went through the channel between Vancouver's Island and San Juan Island. After 1842 the Steamer Beaver only came to Fort Nisqually on particular business. Her regular trips twice a year were made between Fort Victoria, on the Island of Vancouver, and the trading-posts north of the Gulf of Georgia. I can remember at least eight or nine trips through the channel between Vancouver's Island and San Juan Island, while I was engaged as Stoker on the Steamer Beaver.

Canal de Haro regularly navigated by vessels of Hudson's Bay Company since 1842.

His
JOHN + McLEOD.
Mark.

TERRITORY OF WASHINGTON,
County of Thurston, ss:

Before me, Joseph H. Houghton, Clerk of the Supreme Court of said Territory, personally came John McLeod, who, being by me first duly sworn, did declare and say that he knew the contents of the foregoing affidavit; that the same had been dictated by him and carefully read to him, and that the same was true.

In testimony whereof, I have hereunto set my hand and the seal of said Court, this third day of April, A. D. 1872.

[SEAL.] JOSEPH H. HOUGHTON,
Clerk Supreme Court, Washington Territory.

---

[91] **Affidavit of W. H. Gray.*

ASTORIA, *April* 8, 1872.

The undersigned was in Fort Vancouver, on the Columbia River, Oregon, in the month of January, 1837. During my stay at that port of the Hudson's Bay Company, news came that

Affidavits on the canal de Haro.

one of the Company's vessels, I think it was the Steamer Beaver, had passed Haro Straits, and found it a shorter, deeper, and better channel from the Gulf of Georgia to Victoria than that nearer the main land.

I was informed, by the Masters of the Hudson's Bay Company's vessels, several of whom I have been well acquainted with since the winter of 1837, that the Haro Channel was the safest and the one they preferred to any other.

From 1858, and onward, I have frequently and invariably passed through the Haro Channel in American and the Company's steamers, and been assured by all the masters that it was preferable to any other.

As to the question of the Company or British ignorance of the Haro Channel, I verily believe it wholly fictitious, and that it was well known to them as early as 1837, and that the Steamer Beaver had passed and repassed it from Victoria, on Vancouver's Island, to Fort Langley, on Fraser's River.

I, W. H. Gray, do solemnly swear that the foregoing statements are true to the best of my knowledge and belief. So help me God.

W. H. GRAY.

Subscribed and sworn to before me, this 8th day of April, 1872.

[L. S.] A. VAN DUSEN,

Notary Public for Clatsop County, State of Oregon.

Affidavit of J. A. Gardiner.

The undersigned was one of the seamen on the Exploring Squadron of Captain Wilkes, of the United States, on the American Coast in 1840
–'41, and knows that the Channel de Haro, or Belview Channel,
[92] was explored during the continuance of the surveying *expedition upon the Coast, in 1841, and knows that it has been for the last thirteen years universally used by both British and Americans, and is the preferable Channel to any other.

Affidavits on the canal de Haro.

J. A. GARDINER,

First Officer S. S. California.

STATE OF OREGON, *County of Clatsop, ss:*

On this 16th day of April, A. D. 1872, personally appeared before me the above-named J. A. Gardiner, and to me personally known, who subscribed his name in my presence and swore, according to law, to the truth of the above statement.

[NOTARIAL SEAL.] A. VAN DUSEN,

Notary Public.

Statements of William H. Oliver made before the Consul of the United States of America, residing at Victoria, Vancouver Island, March 13, A. D. 1872, touching upon the navigation of the Canal de Haro and Rosario Straits.

On this thirteenth day of March, A. D. one thousand eight hundred and seventy-two, personally appeared before me, David Eckstein, Consul of the United States of America for the Province of British Columbia, Dominion of Canada, residing at the port of Victoria, Vancouver

Island, William H. Oliver, who, being first duly sworn, states as follows:

My age is forty-eight years; my residence is Victoria, Vancouver Island. I have resided here most of the time since eighteen hundred and fifty-eight. I am a retired merchant. I am acquainted with the route of travel by water, by steamers and sail-vessels, British and American, in making trips from Victoria to the Gulf of Georgia and Fraser River, since the year eighteen hundred and fifty-eight. So far as my knowledge extends, the Canal de Haro has been and now is universally used by all classes of vessels.

Affidavits on the canal de Haro.

In eighteen hundred and fifty-eight, in December, or in January, eighteen hundred and fifty-nine, I went, as a passen-
[93] ger, on the *Hudson Bay Company's steamer Beaver, from Victoria to "Derby" or "Old Langley," as it was called, on Fraser River, and passed through the Canal de Haro, in going and returning. At that time and since, the Canal de Haro is the channel generally, and I think exclusively used by British Steamers and others in going to and returning from Fraser River and Gulf of Georgia to Victoria. Masters of vessels, and navigators generally, have expressed the opinion to me repeatedly, that the Canal de Haro was not only a superior channel to any other between the Continent and Vancouver Island, but was the only one used by mariners in passing from Victoria to the Gulf of Georgia and the Fraser River.

I have been acquainted with William H. McNeil, formerly Chief Factor in the Hudson Bay Company, personally since 1864, and by reputation since 1858. Since the sixth of the present month I have had a conversation with William H. McNeil, in which I asked him to state at what time the Hudson Bay Company commenced using the Canal de Haro, by steamers and other vessels employed in carrying their fur trade, and the reasons why they had not used it at an earlier day. He stated to me that the Hudson Bay Company commenced using the Canal de Haro, for the above purpose, soon after they established their Trading-post on Vancouver Island, which was, as he said, in eighteen hundred forty-two, or eighteen hundred and forty-three; and that the Company continued to use it, more or less, from that time on.

And, further, that the Hudson Bay Company ascertained the value of the Canal de Haro for purposes of navigation, at the time of their commencing to use it as above stated. He further stated that the reason why the Hudson Bay Company had not used the Canal de Haro previous to establishing their Trading-post on Vancouver Island, was their want of knowledge of its real value for purposes of navigation.

Canal de Haro regularly navigated by vessels of Hudson's Bay Company since 1842.

On pressing my inquiries further upon the subject, the said William H. McNeil stated to me distinctly and positively that the Hudson Bay Company navigated the Canal de Haro with their Steamers as early as one thousand eight hundred and forty-two and continued to navigate the said Canal de Haro thereafter exclusively, in carrying on their trade between Victoria and points on the Gulf of Georgia and Fraser River. William H. McNeil has been in the Hudson Bay Company service since 1837.

W. H. OLIVER.

[94] *CONSULATE OF THE UNITED STATES OF AMERICA,
Victoria, Vancouver Island, British Columbia.

Affidavits on the canal de Haro.

I, David Eckstein, Consul of the United States of America, residing at Victoria, Vancouver Island, do hereby certify, that on this thirteenth day of March, A. D. one thousand eight hundred and seventy-two, personally appeared before me William H. Oliver and made oath and subscribed to the truth of the foregoing statements; I further certify that the said William H. Oliver is personally known to me, and that he is a respectable and credible person, to whose representations full faith and credit can be given.

In witness whereof I have hereunto set my name and affixed the seal of my Office, this thirteenth day of March, A. D. one thousand eight hundred and seventy-two.

[L. S.] DAVID ECKSTEIN,
United States Consul.

Affidavit of Charles M. Bradshaw.

UNITED STATES OF AMERICA,
Territory of Washington, ss:

I, Charles M. Bradshaw, of the City of Port Townsend, County of Jefferson, in said Territory, do solemnly declare upon oath that I am a native-born citizen of the United States, aged forty years; that I came to Washington Territory, then included in the Territory of Oregon, in November, 1852. In March, 1853, I went to Dungeness, on the South side of the Straits of Fuca, in Clallam County, Washington Territory—and took up a Donation Claim—fronting upon the Harbor which is but an indentation in said Straits of Juan de Fuca, where I continued to reside until some time in 1867.

From my house, without the weather was very hazy or foggy, I had an unobstructed view to the entrance of Victoria Harbor, the shore of Vancouver Island, the entrance to Canal de Haro, the shore of San Juan Island, and the entrance of Rosario Straits. Between 1853 and 1855 there were no steamers in those localities, except those belonging to the Hudson Bay Company, at Victoria, Vancouver Island, or British vessels of war, and the sight of a vessel propelled by steam was a novelty, and always attracted my attention. It was not an unfrequent occurrence to see a steamer leaving Victoria Harbor, passing around Trial
[95] Island, and disappear up de Haro *Straits, on its way to the Gulf of Georgia, and the trading-posts to the North. The Steamers referred to by me were without any doubt the Hudson's Bay Company's Steamers Beaver and Otter, and I have no hesitancy in declaring at this time to have been one or the other or both of those vessels. I have yet to see the first Steamer or Sailing vessel come out of Victoria Harbor and go into Rosario Straits. After 1855, at times there were American Steamers making trips between Olympia, Washington Territory, and Victoria.

Affidavits on the canal de Haro.

In the spring and summer of 1858 I made a number of trips to Fraser's River from Victoria, and returned from there to Victoria, each time going through Haro Channel and returning the same way. On two of those trips to Fraser's River, I was accompanied by from forty to fifty small boats and canoes, many of which boats piloted by Indians, and old Hudson Bay Company bargemen, and discharged servants. In every one of those trips no other route was proposed than through Haro Straits. At that time, and ever since, the Haro Channel was the recognized route of travel from Victoria to the Gulf of Georgia, and to the main-land of British Columbia at and above the mouth of the Fraser's River. All the Steamers to and from Victoria used that Channel, and none other was spoken of or used either for sailing Vessels or Steamers.

Since 1858, I speak from positive knowledge, the Canal de Haro has been exclusively used in the navigation and commerce between Victoria on Vancouver's Island, and British Columbia, and the Northern Coast.

CHARLES M. BRADSHAW.

TERRITORY OF WASHINGTON,
County of Thurston, ss:

Before me, Joseph N. Houghton, Clerk of the Supreme Court of said Territory, came Charles M. Bradshaw, who, being first duly sworn, did depose and say that he had carefully read the foregoing statement, and knew the contents thereof; that the same had been dictated by him; and that so much thereof as was stated from his own knowledge was true, and so much thereof as was stated on information he verily believes to be true.

Witness my hand and the seal of said Court this 16th day of March, A. D. 1872.

[SEAL.] JOSEPH N. HOUGHTON,
Clerk Supreme Court, Washington Territory.

---

[96] **Extract from the statement of Uriah Nelson, made before the United States Consul, residing at the Port of Victoria, Vancouver Island, March 18, 1872, touching the navigation of the Canal de Haro and Rosario Straits.* Affidavits on the canal de Haro.

On this 18th day of March, A. D. 1872, personally appeared before me, David Eckstein, Consul of the United States of America for the Province of British Columbia, Dominion of Canada, residing at the Port of Victoria, Vancouver Island, Uriah Nelson, who, being first duly sworn, states as follows:

My age is forty-five years, my residence Victoria, Vancouver Island. Since 1859 I have resided here part of the time, and the rest of the time at Yale and Clinton, on the main-land of British Columbia. My occupation is that of Merchant and Forwarding Agent. I am acquainted, since the year 1859, with the course pursued by all classes of vessels, British and American, plying between Victoria and ports or places on the Gulf of Georgia and Fraser River. The Canal de Haro has been since 1859, and is now, universally used as the Channel by all Steamers and Sail-Vessels, British and others, in making trips between the above-named points.

Since the year 1859 I have made about one hundred trips between Victoria and New Westminster on the Fraser River, as passenger, in Hudson Bay Company Steamers and others, and every time passed through the Canal de Haro, in going and returning.

The Canal de Haro is in fact the main Channel, and the only one regarded as safe by Masters of Steamers and Sail-Vessels, who are acquainted with the waters between the Continent and Vancouver Island.

URIAH NELSON.

CONSULATE OF THE UNITED STATES OF AMERICA,
Victoria, Vancouver Island, British Columbia:

I, David Eckstein, Consul of the United States of America, residing at the Port of Victoria, Vancouver Island, do hereby certify that on this 18th day of March, A. D. 1872, personally ap- Affidavits on the canal de Haro.

[97] peared before me *Uriah Nelson, and made oath and subscribed to the truth of the foregoing statements; I further certify that the said Uriah Nelson is personally known to me, and that he is a respectable and credible person, to whose representations full faith and credit can be given.

In witness whereof I have hereunto set my hand and affixed the seal of my Office, the day and year first above written.

[SEAL.] DAVID ECKSTEIN,
United States Consul.

No. 62.

Extracts of the report of the Voyage of de Eliza, forwarded December 29, 1791, *from San Blas, by Juan Pantoja y Arriaga. From a certified copy of the original Report in the Hydrographical Bureau at Madrid.*

Snrvey of the canal de Haro by the Spaniards in 1791.

El 31 del mismo, como à las cinco de la mañana, salió la lancha armada en guerra, à las órdenes del segundo piloto D^{n} José Verdia con el fin de explorar la boca é interiores del Canal de Lopez de Aro y à las 10½ regresé con toda diligencia y dió parte al Comand^{te} de que no podia continuar la Commision al que lo habia destinado por haberse visto sorprendido desde que entró por el Canal por muchas Canoas de Indios, á quienes se vió precisado á hacer fuego y que de haber seguido consideraba se exponia á perderse con la gente y lancha, pues ademas de la mucha Indiada que habia concurrido, veia concurrir mucha mas en tierra, echando canoas al aqua y al mismo tiempo oyeron en ella estruendo como de tambor, y en las Canoas andaba uno muy solícito, animando y repartiendo zurrones de flechas, con cuya noticia y atrevimiento nos hemos asegurado ser cierto lo que sus mismos paisanos nos han significado, y en la retirada echaron à pique una canoa grande, y mataron algunos Naturales de los que mas se empeñaban en atracar la lancha por todas partes con gruesas lanzas, y los puntos de hierro arponadas. En vista de lo acaceido determinó el Comand^{te} esperar la Goleta para seguir el expresado reconocimiento, la que fondeo próxima à nosotros el 11 de Junio, y su capitan comunicó al Comandante ser la entrada ó boca de Carrasco un grande archipiélago de islas
[98] *pequeñas que tiene de E^{te} à O^{te} C leguas, y de N. á S. 4 leguas, y tienne en lo interior de la tierra dos brazos de mar de media legua de ancho que se internan mucho, demorando el uno en el 1er cuadrante y el otro en el 4° los cuales no pudo explorar mas que tres leguas por haberselo impedido los fuertes temporales con copiosa lluvia que tuvo por espacio de doce dias, y que hallándoce sin víveres se vió precisado à dejar la commision sin concluir y durante el dicho tiempo lo insultaron los Indios por tres ocasiones à quienes rechazó con la artilleria, tirando varios canoñazos al viento para separarlos de la Goleta, lo que en breve conseguia pues de haberlos dejado que se empeñasen en la accion mariba la destruccion tan grande que haria en ellos con la metralla de los cañones por venir numerosa Indiada en Muchas Canoas juntas, demostrando ser muy guerreros y atrevidos y en lo que anduvo vio cuatro grandes rancherias y todas visten lo mismo que los de Noca, con alguno diferencia en el idioma.

El 14 de dho. Junio mandò el Comandante armar la lancha eu guerra proveer la Goleta de 29 tiros para el cañon y pedreros que lleva monta-

dos que son seis y tripuló una y otra con treinta hombres de mar y ocho soldados hábiles y de espíritu de los voluntarios de Cataluña, y me entregó el mando de la Comision, con el objeto de examinar prolijamente cuanto comprenda el canal de Lopez de Aro, y castigar à los Indios siempre que vuelvan ó quieran insultarnos como lo hicieron con D^{n} José Verdia, y à las nueve de la mañana nos largamos con toda fuerza de vela y con viento fresco de So. con el cual navegamos la vuelta del 1er cuadrante haciendo los rumbos convenientes para entrar por el canal de Lopez de Aro, lo que conseguimos á las $10\frac{1}{2}$ por entre varias tiletas y algunas piedras que tienne próximas á la costa, y en toda encontramos muy recia corriente la que hacia remolinos tan grandes que parecia navegabamos por un Rio muy caudaloso, y hallándonos á las 11 rebasados enteramente, seguimos en vuelta del cuarto cuadrante por ser la direccion que lleva este canal, por el cual navegamos con viento fresco del tercer cuadrante hasta las $12\frac{1}{4}$ que refrescó algo mas, por cuya razon no me era posible seguir à la vela por lo mucho que me sotaventeaba de la Goleta (que se habia mandado tender la base) y por lo mismo los aferré, y echando abajo los palos seguí al remo en su demanda, haciendo mucha agua que me entraba por la borda por estar la mar picada. La Goleta, notándome que nada podia grangear se
[99] puso à la Capa, y habiendo à la $1\frac{1}{2}$ llegado à su bordo, *mandé arbolar los palos, y largando las velas seguí por la popa de remolque de cuya conformidad seguimos hasta las 8 de la tarde que viendo se estaba poniendo el sol y no teniamos ya mas que ventolinas y que por este motivo no podiamos llegar à un fronton de tierra que habiamos demarcado en donde nos parecia se concluia este brazo del 4° cuadrante me largué al remo en la demanda, y habiendo reconocido eran dos bocas que sus direcciones iban la una al 1er cuadrante y la otra al 3ro, retrocedí llegué á la Goleta á las $10\frac{1}{2}$ la cual estaba fondeada proxima à tiera en 20 brazas de agua fondó lama, donde paramos la noche, sin haber visto en todo el dia mas que un Indio y varias humaredas en el grande bosque que hay à orillas de la playa de todo el pedazo de Costa, en donde hicieron sus naturales retroceder al piloto D^{n} José Verdia.

Nota—que el haber determinado el Comandante saliese con la lancha en conserva con la Goleta ha sido con el fin de que tomasemos con las dos embarcaciones las dos costas de este canal, por habor concebido todos seria mucho mas angosto que el Estrecho, y siendolo pudieramos con mas prontitud concluir su reconocimiento, y por este concepto me dió cuatro dias de término, pero ha sucedido todo muy al contrario, pues nos hallamos en un imponderable archipiélago de islas, con rocas y bocanas, por cuya razon hemos determinado no sepeararnos, tanto por que no serian capaces de encontranos en muchos dias, cuanto por que la lancha no es appropósito para semejante comision en brazos tan anchos por ser muy pequeña y no tener buque para acomodar los necesarios correspondientes al efecto, y asi hemos dispuesto siga la lancha por la popa de la Goleta al remolque y que se ayude con sus velas cuando haya viento y cuando este se calme pase à proa de la Goleta à darle remolque, y erto despesto me pasé à la Goleta a ayudar à mis compañeros, à hacer las muchas marcaciones, enfilaciones y rectificaciones que hay que hacer, y en la tarde hemos dejado por la parte del O^{te} varias bocanas y brazos formados al parecer de muchas islas que sus direcciones prometen alguna estension por ser tierras quebradas y rasas y sin verse por detras serrania alguna, los canales no hemos seguido por haber comprendido con bastante fundamento ser necessaros imuchos dias, y traer nosotros muy pocos dias de término, y tambien por que en la navegacion que

hemós hecho esta tarde avistamos por la banda del E^{te} un brazo de mucha mas estension que las bocas que hemos rebasado, y promediando à primera vista ser mucho mas útil seguir este porsu esten-
[100] *sion, lo hemos acordado asi para que luego que principie el crepúsculo del dia seguir su demanda.

El 15 del dicho amaneció el tiempo claro y el terralito bonancible del Levante, por lo que à las tres de la mañana nos levamos y seguimos con el remolque á la lancha y los ocho remos á la Goleta de la vuelta del E^{te} con el fin de irnos aproximando al brazo expresado en cuya distancia hemos reconocido varios promontorios de tierra, segun sus estremos demuestran ser grandes islas. A las 6 nos vimos precisados à dar fondo por haber refrescado el terral del E^{te} y lo ejecutamos en 11 brazos de agua fondo canajo, proximo à una punta que parecia tener una pequeña entrada, y habiendome largado con la lancha, reconoci un buen puerto aunque pequeño pues lo mas largo de él tiene una y media millas, y lo mas ancho una, pero resguardada de todo viento y su fondo es de 13 hasta 2 brazos arena fina y se halla situado en lo mas sur de la isla de Sayas, y le puse puerto de San Antonio. A las 9½ calmó el terral, y habiendo llegado à la Goleta como à las diez de la mañana, nos levamos y seguimos con los remos de ella y el remolque de la lancha la vuelta del 1er cuadrante hasta el medio dia que atravesando por la boca de una profunda ensenada, dimos fondo en ella en 18 brazos de agua cascagillo, y luego sali con la lancha á reconocerla, la cual tiene de largo de No. SE. 7 millas (y en su fondo dos bocas en el 1° y 4° cuadrante, siendo esta del 4° la que ayer tarde reconocé giraba para el 1°) y de ancho 2½, y habiendo à las 3 de la tarde concluido el mismo exámen que en tan corto tiempo sepodia hacer nos levamos y luego que la montamos, se nos quedó el viento calma y seguimos con el remolque de la lancha y los remos de la Goleta à atracar una punta saliente que nos demoraba en el primer cuadrante, lo que conseguimos à las siete y luego que la rebasamos vimos por el cuarto cuadrante un muy grande y dilatado canal, pues segun lo claro del horizonte se alcanzaba á ver mucha distancia, y en el medio de él se distinguia como à perder de vista un pequeño cerro, à modo de Pan de Azucar, siendo advertencia que los estremos ó puntas de tierra que forman este canal es serrania muy elevada, cubierta de nieve, al cual le puse, en honor de nuestra Patrona, por ser el punto de mas consideracion que hasta lo presente hemos descubierto El Gran Canal de N^{tra} S^{ra} del Rosario, la marinera. * * *

Discovery of the broad upper channel of Rosario.

El 12 de Julio entró en este puerto y pasó por nuestro castillo con las mechas encendidas y gente armada, el Capitan Juan Ken-
[101] *drique Bostones, con bandera de su nacion, en la Balandra Wasinton aparejada de bergantin, y se fué à fondear al invernadero que llaman de Malbinas que se halla tres leguas al N^{te} de esta entrada, y grande puerto de Noca; siendo este individuo el que encontró D^{n} Esteban Martinez el ano de 89 en este mismo invernadero, mandando la espresada Balandra y la Fragata Columbia, que ya tiene remitida desde Macao al N^{te} de América, à Provincias Unidas. Al pasar por el Castillo se le preguntó con la bocina, quien era y de donde venia, y respondió no entender, por cuya razon, y sin pérdida de tiempo le pasé oficio el Comandante interno de este Establicimiento D^{n} Ramon Saavedra, que hasta la presente pertenecia esta tierra al dominio de N^{tro} Soberano y que por lo mismo no podia entrar, ni comerciar sin el debido permiso, y que dijese de donde venia y la causa de entrar en este puerto, à que respondió: de Macao con destino de comerciar de toda la costa en pieles de Nútrias, y que luego que con-

Voyage of Kendrick in 1789.

cluyese su comision pensaba largarse, lo que verificó el dia 2°, saliendo à la mar sin pasar por el Castillo pues lo ejecutó por el brazo de agua salada que va por dentro de este puerto à la Bahia de Buena Esperanza, que se halla 10 leg. al N[te] de esta entrada de Noca, que tiene su entrada ó boca al mar sobre la misma costa, siendo toda ella una gran isla, como en el adjunto plano se manifiesta, del mismo modo que todo lo que se ha descubierto, pues para ello el espresado plano va en Carta Esférica y comprende solo desde la punta de Bosse hasta lo mas Sur del Estrecho, con todos los interiores de la costa que se han reconocido.

No. 63.

Extract from the Instructions to Commander George Vancouver, by the Commissioners for executing the office of Lord High Admiral of Great Britain and Ireland, &c.

[*Vancouver's Voyage, I. Introduction, page XXII.*]

Vancouver followed the lead of Americans. His instructions.

The particular course of the survey must depend on the different circumstances which may arise in the execution of a service of this nature; it is, however, proper that you should, and you are therefore hereby required and directed to pay a particular attention to the examination of the supposed Straits of Juan de Fuca, said to be situated between 48° and 49° north latitude,
[102] and *to lead an opening through which the sloop Washington is reported to have passed in 1789, and to have come out again to the northward of Nootka. The discovery of a near communication between any such sea or strait, and any river running into or from the lake of the Woods, would be particularly useful.

If you should fail of discovering any such inlet, as is above mentioned, to the southward of Cook's river, there is the greatest probability that it will be found that the said river rises in some of the lakes already known to the Canadian traders, and to the servants of the Hudson's bay company; which point it would, in that case, be material to ascertain; and you are, therefore, to endeavor to ascertain accordingly, with as much precision as the circumstances existing at the time may allow; but the discovery of any similar communication more to the southward (should any such exist) would be much more advantageous for the purposes of commerce, and should, therefore, be preferably attended to, and you are, therefore, to give it a preferable attention accordingly.

No. 64.

Extract of Voyage of Captain Vancouver.

No soundings appear on Vancouver's map where the water is of great depth.

Soundings in some places only could be gained close to the shore; and in the middle no bottom had anywhere been found with 100 fathoms of line, although the shores were in general low, and not half a league asunder.—(Vol. 1, p. 240.)

As we stood to the westward, our depth soon increased to fifteen fathoms, after which we gained no bottom until we reached the western shore of the gulf.—(Vol. 1, p. 299.)

No. 65.

Extracts from the remarks of Mr. Daniel Webster in the Senate of the United States, March 30, 1846.

The Government of the United States has never offered any line south of forty-nine, (with the navigation of the Columbia,) and it never will. It behooves all concerned to regard this as a settled point.
[103] As to the navigation of the Columbia, permanently or for a *term of years, that is all matter for just, reasonable, and friendly negotiation. But the forty-ninth parallel must be regarded as the general line of boundary, and not to be departed from for any line further south. As to all straits, and sounds, and islands in the neighboring sea, all these are fair subjects for treaty stipulation. If the general basis be agreed to, all the rest, it may be presumed, may be accomplished by the exercise of a spirit of fairness and amity. * * What I meant, and what I said, was, that if 49° should be agreed on as a general basis, I was satisfied to negotiate about all the rest. But the gentleman from Ohio and the Senate will do me the justice to allow that I said, as plainly as I could speak or put down words in writing, that England must not expect anything south of 49°. I said so in so many words.

No. 66.

Four Years in British Columbia and Vancouver Island. By Commander R. C. Mayne, R. N., F. R. G. S. London, 1862.

The breadth of the Strait of Juan de Fuca, at its entrance between Cape Flattery, its southern point upon American territory, and Bonilla point in Vancouver Island, is thirteen miles. It narrows soon, however, to eleven miles, carrying this breadth in an east and northeast direction some fifty miles to the Race Islands.—(P. 20.)

Where Fuca's strait ends.

At the Race Islands the Strait may be said to terminate, as it there opens out into a large expanse of water, which forms a playground for the tides and currents, hitherto pent up among the islands in the comparatively narrow limits of the Gulf of Georgia, to frolic in.—(Pages 21, 22.)

Facts and Figures relating to Vancouver Island and British Columbia. By J. Despard Pemberton, Surveyor-General of Vancouver Island. London, 1860.

Limited extent of Fuca's straits.

Steaming for the first time eastward into the Straits of Juan de Fuca, the scene which presents itself to a stranger is exceedingly novel
[104] and interesting. On his right hand is Washington *Territory, with its snowy mountain range stretching parallel to his course for sixty miles, flanked with Mount Ranier and culminating in the center with Mount Olympus. Of these mountains the base is in some places at the coast, in others many miles from it. This range is occasionally intersected with deep and gloomy valleys, of which the Valley of Angels is the gloomiest and most remarkable; and every suc-

cession of cloud and sunshine changes the panorama. On his left is Vancouver Island, in contrast looking low, although even there as late as June some specks of snow may be detected on distant mountain tops. Straight before him is the Gulf of Georgia, studded with innumerable islands.—(P. 8.)

Victoria was selected by Governor Douglas, whose intimate acquaintance with every crevice in the coast ought to carry considerable weight, as "the site" in 1842, when he expressed his confidence "that there was no sea-port north of the Columbia, where so many advantages could be combined;" an opinion which was confirmed by Sir George Simpson in his dispatch of June 21, 1844, in which he states, "The situation of Victoria is peculiarly eligible, the country and climate remarkably fine, and the harbor excellent." And again: "June, 1846.—Fort Victoria promises to become a very important place."—(P. 50.)

No. 67.

Extract from a letter of Sir J. Pelly, Governor of the Hudson's Bay Company, to the Lords of the Committee of Privy Council for Trade.

HUDSON'S BAY HOUSE, *February* 7, 1838.

The Hudson's Bay Company expel Americans from the fur-trade.

MY LORDS: For many years previous to the grant of exclusive trade to the Hudson's Bay Company, the trade of that coast was engrossed by the subjects of the United States of America and Russia, the only establishment occupied by British traders being "Astoria," afterward named "Fort George," at the mouth of the Columbia River, while no attempt was made, through the means of shipping, to obtain any part of the trade of the coast; and so unprofitable was it in the years 1818, 1819, 1820, 1821, and 1822, and so difficult of management, that several of the leading and most intelligent
[105] persons *in the country strongly recommended that the Company
should abandon it altogether. The Company, however, felt that the honor of the concern would, in a certain degree, be compromised were they to adopt that recommendation; holding as they did under Government the License in question, and with a degree of energy and enterprise which I feel assured your Lordships will admit reflects much credit on themselves and on their officers and servants in the country, they directed their efforts so vigorously to that branch of the business, that they compelled the American adventurers, one by one, to withdraw from the contest.

The outlay and expense attending this competition in trade are so heavy that the profits are yet but in perspective, none worthy of notice having been realized, the result showing some years a trifling loss, and in others a small gain, fluctuating according to the degree of activity with which the contest is maintained.

Affidavit of W. H. Gray.

In a conversation had with Dr. John McLaughlin, while he was in charge of the affairs of the Hudson Bay Company, (time I cannot state, except I am confident it was before the news of the treaty of 1846 reached us,) Dr. McLaughlin said to me in relation to Captain N. Wyeth, who left this country in 1836, "That if he (Captain Wyeth) had not accepted his proposition for the purchase of his goods and Forts, the Company would have insisted on other means to get rid of his (Captain Wyeth's) competition in the fur trade." I have always understood this intimation to mean that the Company would insist upon letting loose their Indian or Aboriginal allies upon Captain Wyeth or any other American fur-trader that might presume to compete with them in the fur trade, the same as I am fully satisfied they did in the case of a Mr. G. Smith, the partner of Sublit & Jackson, in 1828. The Indians were informed that in case they robbed or killed the Americans, the Company would not punish them or take any notice of it. Smith's party were, eleven of them, killed, his furs received by the company, who paid a nominal price for them, as per testimony of G. L. Meak, Hudson's Bay Company, V. S. U. S.

[106] I solemnly swear that the first part of the foregoing state*ment is true, and that I believe the latter part to be true. So help me God.

W. H. GRAY.

Subscribed and sworn to before me this 8th day of April, 1872.

[L. S.] A. VAN DUSEN,

Notary Public for Clatsop County, State of Oregon.

Extract from a letter of Sir J. Pelly, Governor of the Hudson's Bay Company, to the Earl of Aberdeen. [Precise date not stated, but from internal evidence certainly later than May 16, 1846.]

The Hudson's Bay Company suggest to Lord Aberdeen to draw the boundary line through the channel used by Vancouver.

I have been considering the subject on which I had the honor of conversing with your lordship on Saturday last, [May 16, 1846,] and feeling that, in the multiplicity of business which comes before your lordship, some parts may have been overlooked, or that I may not have been sufficiently explicit, I have thought it advisable to trouble you with a few lines.

In the first place, I assume that the forty-ninth degree of latitude, from its present terminus, will be continued across the continent to the waters known as the Gulf of Georgia, and be the line of demarkation of the continent between Great Britain and the United States.

The next question on which the government of the two countries will have to decide will be as to the islands abutting on and in the Gulf of Georgia, viz, one, Vancouver Island, intersected by the parallel of 49°, and others which are wholly on the south of that parallel. With respect to the former, I think upon the principle of mutual convenience, (and which I think should form the foundation of the treaty,) Great Britain is entitled to the harbor on its southeast end, being the *only* good one, those in Puget Sound being given up to the United States; that with respect to the other islands, the water demarkation line should be from the center of the water in the Gulf of Georgia in the forty-ninth degree along the line colored red, as navigable in the chart made by Vancouver, till it reaches a line drawn through the center of the Straits of Juan de Fuca.

[107] *No. 68.

Mr. Crampton to Mr. Buchanan.

[Extract.]

WASHINGTON, *January* 13, 1848.

But in regard to this portion of the boundary line a preliminary question arises, which turns upon the interpretation of the treaty, rather than upon the result of local observation and survey.

The British government wishes the American to agree on the channel used by Vancouver as the boundary.

The convention of the 15th June, 1846, declares that the line shall be drawn through the middle of the "channel" which separates the continent from Vancouver's Island. And upon this it may be asked what the word "channel" was intended to mean.

Generally speaking, the word "channel," when employed in treaties, means a deep and navigable channel. In the present case it is believed that only one channel—that, namely, which was laid down by Vancouver in his chart—has in this part of the gulf been hitherto surveyed and used; and it seems natural to suppose that the negotiators of the Oregon convention, in employing the word "channel," had that particular channel in view.

If this construction be mutually adopted, no preliminary difficulty will exist, and the commissioners will only have to ascertain the course of the line along the middle of that channel, and along the middle of the Straits of Fuca down to the sea.

It is, indeed, on all accounts, to be wished that this arrangement should be agreed upon by the two governments, because otherwise much time might be wasted in surveying the various intricate channels formed by the numerous islets which lie between Vancouver's Island and the main-land, and some difficulty might arise in deciding which of those channels ought to be adopted for the dividing boundary.

The main channel marked in Vancouver's chart is, indeed, somewhat nearer to the continent than to Vancouver's Island, and its adoption would leave on the British side of the line rather more of those small islets with which that part of the gulf is studded, than would remain on the American side. But these islets are of little or no value.

JOHN F. CRAMPTON.

Hon. JAMES BUCHANAN.

---

[108] *No. 69.

Extract from Additional Instructions to Captain Prevost.

FOREIGN OFFICE, *December* 20, 1856.

If, however, the commissioner of the United States will not adopt the line along Rosario Strait, and *if*, on a detailed and accurate survey, and on weighing the evidence on both sides of the question, *you should be of opinion that the claims of Her Majesty's government to consider Rosario Strait as the channel indicated by the words of the treaty cannot be substantiated*, you would be at liberty to adopt any other intermediate channel which you may discover, on which the United States commissioner and yourself may agree as substantially in accordance with the description of the treaty.

The British government in 1866 does not claim the so-called Rosario as the boundary.

Captain PREVOST.

No. 70.

Captain Prevost to Mr. Campbell.

[Extracts.]

HER BRITANNIC MAJESTY'S SHIP SATELLITE,
Simiahmoo Bay, Gulf of Georgia, October 28, 1857.

Admiral Prevost on the channel of the treaty.

4. By a careful consideration of the wording of the treaty, it would seem distinctly to provide that the channel mentioned should possess three characteristics: 1st. It should separate the *continent* from Vancouver's Island. 2d. It should admit of the boundary line being carried through the middle of it in a southerly direction. 3d. It should be a navigable channel. To these three peculiar conditions the channel known as the Rosario Strait most entirely answers.

5. It is readily admitted that the Canal de Arro is also a navigable channel, and therefore answers to one characteristic of the channel of the treaty.

NOVEMBER 9, 1857.

The Canal de Haro, or Arro, is undoubtedly the navigable channel which, at its position, separates *Vancouver's Island* from the *continent*, and therefore, while other channels exist more adjacent to the continent, cannot be the channel which "separates the *continent* from *Vancouver's Island.*"

[109] *NOVEMBER 24, 1857.

7. With reference to your remarks upon the map drawn by "Charles Preuss," * * I beg you to understand me that I do not bring this map forward as any *authority* for the line of boundary. * * I will at once frankly state how far I am willing to concede, but *beyond what I now offer I can no further go.* In contemplating your view that all the channels between the continent and Vancouver's Island, from the termination of the Gulf of Georgia to the eastern termination of the Straits of Fuca, are but a continuation of the channel of the Gulf of Georgia, I see a way by which I can in part meet your views without any gross violation of the terms of the treaty. I am willing to regard the space above described *as one channel*, having so many different passages through it, and I will agree to a boundary line being run *through the "middle" of it*, in so far as islands will permit.

No. 71.

Mr. Edward Everett to Mr. Campbell.

[Extract.]

BOSTON, *May* 29, 1858.

Mr. Everett on the channel of the treaty.

As the radical principle of the boundary is the forty-ninth degree of latitude, and the only reason for departing from it was to give the whole of Vancouver's Island to the party acquiring the largest part of it, the deflection from the forty-ninth degree southward should be limited to that object, and the nearest channel adopted which fulfills the above conditions.

EDWARD EVERETT.

ARCHIBALD CAMPBELL, Esq.

No. 72.

Mr. Campbell to Mr. Cass.

[Extracts.]

WASHINGTON CITY, *February* 10, 1858.

Lucid statement of Mr. Campbell on the channel of the treaty.

Captain Prevost finally proposed such a compromise as would throw within the territory of the United States all the islands
[110] but *San Juan, the largest and most valuable of the group. Being fully satisfied, from my own observation, that the Canal de Haro is the main channel, and consequently "the channel" intended by the treaty, and being supported in this opinion by indisputable contemporaneous evidence of the highest official character, I declined to accede to any compromise.

U. S. NORTHWEST BOUNDARY COMMISSION CAMP,
Simiahmoo, Forty-ninth Parallel, September 25, 1858.

Practically it can make no difference whether the main channel be adopted as "*the* channel" intended by the treaty upon the "generally admitted principle" recognized by Mr. Crampton, and assented to by Her Majesty's government in 1848, or whether the Canal de Haro be adopted on the proof of contemporaneous evidence that it was proposed by the British government, and in good faith accepted by the United States as the boundary channel. In either case the Canal de Haro would be the boundary channel. In advocating it with Captain Prevost, I did not confine myself singly to either of these sufficient grounds, but maintained both, with others equally forcible and tenable.

Under the mere letter of the treaty, without any knowledge of, or reference to, the motives which induced the adoption of the water boundary, "the channel which separates the continent from Vancouver's Island" may fairly be construed as follows:

1. As "*the* channel," that is, the *main channel*, if there be more than one. And this is the view taken by nautical men generally, including officers of our navy whom I have consulted in reference to the language of the treaty.

2. The channel nearest to *Vancouver's* Island, without regard to its size, so that it is navigable; the proviso to the first article requiring that the *navigation* of said channel shall be free and open to both parties. If it had been intended to mean any other channel than that nearest Vancouver's Island, that island need not to have been mentioned at all, or, if referred to, "the channel which separates the continent from the archipelago east of Vancouver's Island," or "the channel nearest the continent," would have been the proper description of the channel now claimed by the British commissioner under "the peculiarly precise and clear" language of the treaty.

3. Upon the international ground that islands are natural appendages to the continent, and that, unless otherwise agreed, *all*
[111] *the islands between the continent and Vancouver's Island east of the nearest navigable channel to Vancouver's Island pertain to the continent.

The Canal de Haro would be the channel under either of the above legitimate readings of the treaty.

But leaving the mere letter of the treaty, and referring to the history of the negotiation to ascertain the cause which prevented the United States and the British government from agreeing upon the prolongation of the forty-ninth parallel to the ocean, it will be found that the southern end of Vancouver's Island was alone the stumbling-block. The British government refused to concede it to the United States, four-fifths of the island being north of the forty-ninth parallel; and the southern end, with its harbors, being the most valuable portion. The United States, considering the disadvantages of a divided jurisdiction of the island, and the probabilities of difficulties arising therefrom, reluctantly yielded it. This was the sole object in deviating from the forty-ninth parallel, and reduces the water boundary to a very simple question. It was a second compromise line. Divested of all quibbles, the meaning of the treaty is that the forty-ninth parallel shall be the dividing line between the territories of the United States and the British possessions until it reaches "the middle" of the nearest natural boundary to *Vancouver's* Island; and thence the line shall be run to the ocean by the nearest natural boundary, in such a direction as will give the whole of Vancouver's Island to that power upon whose side the greatest portion would fall by the prolongation of the parallel to the ocean.

ARCHIBALD CAMPBELL,
Commissioner Northwestern Boundary Survey.

Hon. LEWIS CASS,
Secretary of State.

No. 73.

Lord John Russell to Lord Lyons.

[Extracts.]

FOREIGN OFFICE, *August* 24, 1859.

The Earl of Aberdeen, to whom I have referred, informs me that he distinctly remembers the general tenor of his conversation with
[112] Mr. MacLane on the subject of the Oregon boundary, and it * is certain that it was the intention of the treaty to adopt the *mid-channel of the straits* as the line of demarkation, without any reference to islands, the position, and, indeed, the very existence, of which had hardly, at that time, been accurately ascertained; and he has no recollection of any mention having been made during the discussion of the Canal de Haro, or, indeed, any other channel than those described in the treaty itself.

The British government announces its intention of obtaining the island o San Juan.

I also inclose a memorandum drawn up by Sir Richard Pakenham, the negotiator of the treaty of 1846. * * *

The adoption of the central channel would give to Great Britain the island of San Juan, which is believed to be of little or no value to the United States, while much importance is attached by British colonial authorities, and by Her Majesty's government, to its retention as a dependency of the colony of Vancouver's Island.

Her Majesty's government must, therefore, under any circumstances, maintain the right of the British Crown to the island of San Juan. The interests at stake in connection with the retention of that island are too important to admit of compromise, and your lordship will consequently bear in mind that whatever arrangement as to the boundary line is finally arrived at, no settlement of the question will be accepted by Her Majesty's government which does not provide for the island of San Juan being reserved to the British Crown.

J. RUSSELL.

LORD LYONS, &c., &c., &c.

Sir Richard Pakenham on the Water Boundary under the Oregon treaty of 1846.

Sir R. Pakenham in 1859 denies the Rosario to be the channel of the treaty.

I have examined the papers put into my hands, by Mr. Hammond, relating to the line of boundary to be established between the British and the United States possessions on the north-west coast of America, and I have endeavored to call to mind any circumstance which might have occurred at the time when the Oregon treaty was concluded (15th June, 1846) of a nature either to strengthen or invalidate the pretension now put forward by the United States Commissioner, to the effect that the boundary contemplated by the treaty would be a line passing down the middle of the channel
[113] called Canal de Haro, and not, as suggested on the part *of
Great Britain, along the middle of the channel called Vancouver's or Rosario Strait, neither of which two lines could, as I conceive, exactly fulfill the conditions of the treaty, which, according to their literal tenor, would require the line to be traced along the middle of the channel (meaning, I presume, the whole intervening space) which separates the continent from Vancouver's Island. And I think I can safely assert that the treaty of 15th June, 1846, was signed and ratified without any intimation to us whatever, on the part of the United States Government, as to the particular direction to be given to the line of boundary contemplated by article I of that treaty.

All that we knew about it was that it was to run "through the middle of the channel which separates the continent from Vancouver's Island, and thence southerly through the middle of the said channel and of Fuca's Straits to the Pacific Ocean."

It is true that in a dispatch from Mr. MacLane, then United States minister in London, to the Secretary of State, Mr. Buchanan, dated 18th May, 1846, which dispatch, however, was not made public until after the ratification of the treaty by the Senate, Mr. MacLane informs his government that the line of boundary about to be proposed by Her Majesty's government would "probably be substantially to divide the territory by the extension of the line in the parallel of 49° to the sea, that is to say, to the arm of the sea called Birch's Bay, thence by the Canal de Haro and straits of Fuca to the ocean."

It is also true that Mr. Senator Benton, one of the ablest and most zealous advocates for the ratification of the treaty, (relying, no doubt, on the statement furnished by Mr. MacLane,) did, in his speech on the subject, describe the intended line of boundary to be one passing along the middle of the Haro channel.

Sir R. Pakenham misstates Lord Aberdeen's instruction by suppressing his description of the channel of the treaty.

But, on the other hand, the Earl of Aberdeen, in his final instructions, dated 18th May, 1846, says nothing whatever about the Canal de Haro, but, on the contrary, desires that the line might be drawn "in a southerly direction through the center of King George's Sound and the Straits of Fuca to the Pacific Ocean."

It is my belief that neither Lord Aberdeen, nor Mr. MacLane, nor Mr. Buchanan possessed at that time a sufficiently accurate knowledge of the geography or hydrography of the region in question to enable them to define more accurately what was the intended line of boundary
[114] than is expressed in the words of the *treaty, and it is certain
that Mr. Buchanan signed the treaty with Mr. MacLane's dispatch before him, and yet that he made no mention whatever of the "Canal de Haro" as that "through which the line of boundary would run, as understood by the United States government."

My own dispatch of that period contains no observation whatever of a tendency contrary to what I thus state from memory, and they, therefore, so far, plead in favor of the accuracy of my recollection.

No. 74.

Mr. Cass to Mr. Dallas.

DEPARTMENT OF STATE,
Washington, October 20, 1859.

SIR: * * * * * * *

Mr Cass on the channel of the treaty.

The words of the treaty are "through the middle of said channel and of Fuca's Straits to the Pacific Ocean." Ordinarily, and in the absence of any other controlling circumstances, the way which would be selected from one given point to another would be the shortest and the best way. In the present case this is the Canal de Haro, which is, undoubtedly, the broadest, the deepest, and the shortest route by which the Straits of Fuca can be reached from the point of deflection. This pre-eminence was given to it by De Mofras as long ago as 1841, and it has been fully confirmed by subsequent surveys. The Canal de Haro may, therefore, be fairly regarded, from its own intrinsic merits merely, as the main channel down the middle of which the treaty boundary is to pass to the Straits of Fuca.

It is the only channel, moreover, which is consistent with the purpose of those who negotiated the treaty, for it is the only channel which separates Vancouver's Island from the continent without leaving something more to Great Britain south of the forty-ninth parallel than the southern cape of that island. The Rosario Channel, claimed by Captain Prevost, would surrender to Great Britain not only Vancouver's Island, but the whole archipelago between that island and itself; while
[115] the middle channel, which is *proposed as a compromise by Lord John Russell, would, in like manner, concede the important island of San Juan.

These considerations seem to be almost conclusive in favor of the Haro Channel. But they are abundantly confirmed by evidence contemporaneous with the negotiation of the treaty. The description given by Mr. MacLane, immediately after he had an interview on the subject with Lord Aberdeen, of what the British proposal would be, has already been mentioned, and carries the line in so many words down the Canal de Haro. Equally clear is the statement of Senator Benton as to what the proposition was. Colonel Benton was one of the most earnest members of the Senate in his support of the treaty; and he was better acquainted, perhaps, than any other member with the geography of the region in dispute. His construction, therefore, of the treaty, at the very time it was before the Senate for ratification, is entitled to no inconsiderable weight. On that occasion he said: "The first article is in the very words which I myself would have used, * * * and that article constitutes the treaty. With me it is the treaty. * * * The great question was that of boundary. * * * * When the line reaches the channel which separates Vancouver's Island from the continent * * * it proceeds to the middle of the channel, and thence turning south through the channel de Haro (wrongly written

Arro in the maps) to the Straits of Fuca." Mr. Buchanan, who signed the treaty, was equally explicit in his understanding of this part of it.

On the 28th December, 1846, Mr. Bancroft having written to him on the subject from London, he inclosed to him a traced copy of Wilkes's Chart of the Straits of Arro, and added in his letter: "It is not probable, however, that any claim of this character will be seriously preferred by Her Britannic Majesty's government to any island lying to the eastward of the Canal de Arro, as marked in Captain Wilkes's map of the Oregon Territory." Mr. Bancroft, who was a member of President Polk's Cabinet when the treaty was concluded, wrote repeatedly to Lord Palmerston after receiving this chart, and uniformly described the Straits of Arro "as the channel through the middle of which the boundary is to be continued." * * * The Canal de Haro, then, as being the best channel leading from the point of deflection to the Straits of Fuca; as answering completely the purpose for which the deflection was made; as being the only channel between the island
[116] and the main-land *which does answer this purpose, and as being
supported, also, by a large amount of personal testimony contemporaneous with the treaty, must fairly be regarded, in my judgment, as the treaty channel.

Nor are there any important difficulties which seem to me to be necessarily in conflict with this conclusion. Lord John Russell, indeed, says that it is beyond dispute that the intentions of the British government were that the line of boundary should be drawn through Vancouver's Channel. But this assumption is wholly inconsistent, not only with the treaty itself, but with the statements both of the Earl of Aberdeen and of Sir Richard Pakenham. Lord Aberdeen declares that it was the intention of the treaty to adopt the *mid-channel of the straits* at the time of demarkation, without reference to islands, the position of which, and indeed the very existence of which, had hardly at that time been accurately ascertained; "and he has no recollection of any mention having been made during the discussion of any other channel than those described in the treaty itself." Sir Richard Pakenham is still more explicit. "Neither the Canal de Haro nor the channel of Vancouver," he says, "could, as I conceive, exactly fulfill the conditions of the treaty which, according to their literal tenor, would require the line to be traced along the middle of the channel, meaning, I presume, the whole intervening space which separates the continent from Vancouver's Island." He adds further, that he has no recollection whatever that any other channel was designated in the discussions than that described in the language of the treaty. Surely there is nothing in this testimony which supports the statement of Lord John Russell that the channel of Vancouver was the channel intended by the treaty; but on the contrary another and entirely different channel is suggested as that which the convention requires. After these statements of Lord Aberdeen and Sir Richard Pakenham, the Rosario Channel can no longer, it seems to me, be placed in competition with the Canal de Haro. Whether the latter is the true channel or not, in the opinion of the British negotiation, it is quite certain, by the concurrent testimony of both the American and British negotiators, that the former channel is not. In respect, moreover, to the Canal de Haro, the other considerations to which I have referred appear to me to quite outweigh the mere want of recollection of Lord Aberdeen and Sir Richard Pakenham, or their general impression at this time as to what is required by the literal language of the treaty.

[117] *There is one allusion in Sir Richard Pakenham's memorandum
to which I think it right to call your special attention. It is the

reference which he makes to his final instructions from Lord Aberdeen, dated May 18, 1846, and describing the boundary line which he was authorized to propose to Mr. Buchanan. These instructions were shown by Lord Napier to Mr. Campbell, and according to his clear recollection, the description quoted by Sir Richard Pakenham was followed in dispatch by these words: "Thus giving to Great Britain the whole of Vancouver's Island and its harbors." This places beyond controversy the object which was intended by deflecting the treaty boundary south of the parallel of 49°, and ought to have great weight, undoubtedly, in determining the true channel from the point of deflection to the Straits of Fuca. * * *

LEWIS CASS.

GEORGE M. DALLAS, Esq.

No. 75.

Lord John Russell to Lord Lyons.

[Extracts.]

FOREIGN OFFICE, *December* 16, 1859.

The British government in 1859 does not claim the so-called Rosario as the boundary.

MY LORD: In pointing out, therefore, to your Lordship that in whatever manner the question was ultimately settled, Her Majesty's government could not yield the island of San Juan, Her Majesty's government were, by implication, abandoning a large part of the territory they had claimed, and were merely insisting on the retention of an island, which, from the peculiarity of its situation, it was impossible for Her Majesty's government to cede without compromising interests of the gravest importance.

* * * The fact is, that, by the instructions with which Captain Prevost was furnished, he was authorized, in case he should be of opinion that the claims of Her Majesty's government, to consider the Rosario Strait as the channel of the treaty, could not be sustained, to adopt any other intermediate channel on which he and the United States commissioner might agree.

[118] * * * *Sir R. Pakenham seems to think that the conditions of the treaty would obtain their most exact fulfillment if the line were carried through the Douglas Channel.

* * * Or, again, if it would be inconvenient to both nations to have five or six islands partially divided between them, would it not be fair and expedient to look for a channel which shall be the nearest approximation to that line, midway between the continent and the island of Vancouver, which is designated by the treaty? And if Douglas's Channel fulfills this condition, is it not the line most in accordance with the treaty, as well as with general policy and convenience?

Lord J. Russell does injustice to the moderation of his own administration in 1848. Lord Palmerston gave the acquiescence of silence.

* * * If I notice General Cass's allusion to the letters which he says Mr. Bancroft repeatedly wrote to Lord Palmerston in 1848, it is only for the purpose of placing on record what, no doubt, Mr. Bancroft duly reported to his government at the time, viz, that Lord Palmerston gave Mr. Bancroft distinctly to understand that the British government did not acquiesce in the pretensions of the United States that the boundary line should be run down the Haro Channel. * * *

J. RUSSELL.

LORD LYONS.

No. 76.

UNITED STATES OF AMERICA,
Department of State.

To all to whom these presents shall come, Greeting:

I certify that the paper hereto annexed is a correct copy of the Statement furnished by the Acting Superintendent of the Census, of the returns of the Ninth Census, from the "disputed" Islands in the County of Whatcom, Territory of Washington. In testimony whereof, I, Hamilton Fish, Secretary of State of the United States, have hereunto subscribed my name and caused the seal of the Department of State to be affixed. Done at the City of Washington, this twenty-ninth day of March, A. D. 1872, and of the Independence of the United States of America the ninety-sixth.

HAMILTON FISH.

[119] *Abstract of the returns at the Ninth Census, from the "disputed" islands in the County of Whatcom, Territory of Washington.*

The population of the Haro archipelago more than two-thirds American.

Names of islands.	Aggregate number of males, 21 years of age and upwards.	Males 21 years of age and upwards, born in the United States.	Males 21 years of age and upwards, born in foreign countries, but claiming to be citizens of the United States.	Males 21 years of age and upwards, born in Great Britain and Ireland, not claiming to be citizens of the United States.	Males 21 years of age and upwards, born in foreign countries other than Great Britain and Ireland, not claiming to be citizens of the United States.
Blakeley	1	1			
Decatur	4	2	2		
Henry	1	1			
Lopez	23	5	12	4	2
Orcas	52	26	9	16	1
San Juan, excluding the English and American garrisons.	(*b*)96	21	35	26	(*b*)14
Shaw's	(*a*)1	(*a*)1			
Speidan	1			1	
Stewart's	(*a*)1	(*a*)1			
Waldron	4	4			
Total	184	62	58	47	17

(*a*) Indian. (*b*) Including 2 Chinese.

[120] *CHARTS AND MAPS TO MEMORIAL AND REPLY.

A. Photograph of Map of de Haro. 1790. (*See page* 17.)
B. Photograph of Map of Eliza. 1791. (*See page* 17.)
C. Photograph of Map of Vancouver. 1798. (*See page* 15.)
D. Photograph of Map of Galiano and Valdes. 1802. (*See page* 17.)
E. Photograph of Map of Duflot de Mofras. 1844. (*See page* 15.)
F. Photograph of Map of Wilkes. 1845. (*See page* 11.)
G. Photograph of Map of W. Sturgis. 1845. (*See page* 9.)

H. Lithograph of U. S. Coast Survey Map of Washington Sound and Approaches. (*See end of the volume.*)

J. Lithograph of Map of de Haro. 1790. (*See end of the volume.*)

K. Lithograph of Map of Eliza. 1791. (*See end of the volume.*)

L. Lithograph of Spanish Chart published in 1795. (*See end of the volume.*)

M. Cross Sections of Haro and Rosario Channels. (*See page* 130.)

N. Sketch to illustrate the route of the vessels of the Hudson's Bay Company. (*See page* 126.)

O. Copy of Map *H*, with a blue line drawn southerly from the center of the Gulf of Georgia in latitude 49°; with red lines to show the channels through Haro northward; and a yellow line to show the so-called Rosario Channel. (*See end of the volume.*)

IV.

NORTHWEST AMERICAN WATER BOUNDARY.

SECOND AND DEFINITIVE STATEMENT

ON BEHALF OF THE

GOVERNMENT OF HER BRITANNIC MAJESTY,

SUBMITTED TO

HIS MAJESTY THE EMPEROR OF GERMANY,

UNDER THE

TREATY OF WASHINGTON OF MAY 8, 1871.

CONTENTS.

NORTHWEST AMERICAN WATER BOUNDARY.

SECOND AND DEFINITIVE STATEMENT ON BEHALF OF THE GOVERNMENT OF HER BRITANNIC MAJESTY.

1. The Government of Her Britannic Majesty, in pursuance of Article XXXVI of the Treaty of Washington of 1871, have drawn up and now lay before His Majesty the Emperor of Germany, as Arbitrator, this their second and definitive Statement, in reply to the Memorial or Case presented in the name of the United States Government by Mr. Bancroft.

2. The matter of Mr. Bancroft's Memorial (as far as it is of an argumentative character) may, for the purposes of the examination to which Her Majesty's Government propose here to subject it, be ranged in the following divisions:

I. Mr. Bancroft assumes that at the date of the Treaty of 1846 the United States had a clear tide to the whole Oregon district, up to the forty-ninth parallel of latitude at least; represents the arrangement embodied in the Treaty as a pure concession on the part of the United States; and contends that the concession should consequently be confined within the narrowest limits.

II. He maintains that the object of the arrangement embodied in the Treaty was to secure to Her Majesty the whole of Vancouver's Island, and no more.

III. He adduces what he considers evidence to show that the construction now contended for by the United States was the admitted construction at the time of the making of the Treaty.

IV. He represents the Treaty as specially the work of Her Majesty's Government, and seems to suggest that they are consequently precluded from maintaining any construction of the Treaty not admitted by the other side.

V. He maintains that the language of the Treaty admits no interpretation but the American, and that it points to the Canal de Haro, and to that channel alone.

[2] *3. An examination of the arguments on these points, to be intelligible, must be accompanied by an historical explanation of the circumstances attendant on the Treaty. For that purpose many documents must be set out at length. It is, therefore, more convenient to present the explanation in the form of a separate paper. It is accordingly subjoined to this Statement as an Historical Note; and Her Majesty's Government beg that the Note, with the other papers appended to this Statement, may be taken as part thereof.

4. The Note shows the relative positions of the principal actors in the matter of the Treaty; in London, the Earl of Aberdeen, Her Majesty's Principal Secretary of State for Foreign Affairs, and Mr. MacLane, the United States Minister Plenipotentiary; at Washington, Mr. Pakenham, Her Majesty's Minister Plenipotentiary, and Mr. Buchanan, the

United States Secretary of State.[1] It is designed to bring out the facts which will be seen in the course of this Statement to be of cardinal importance, namely, that the Treaty was formally negotiated at Washington between Mr. Pakenham and Mr. Buchanan; that it was on two distinct occasions discussed and approved by the Senate of the United States, in their capacity, under the Constitution, of a co-ordinate branch of the treaty-making power; that the project or draught of the Treaty was prepared in London by Lord Aberdeen, and sent to Mr. Pakenham, as embodying the proposal which Mr. Pakenham was instructed to make to the Government of the United States; that this project was, as regards the words now in discussion, identical with the Treaty as signed and ratified; and that, although Mr. MacLane was not formally empowered to conduct negotiations in the matter on behalf of his Government, yet Lord Aberdeen discussed with him the nature of the proposal which Her Majesty's Government contemplated making to the United States, and even showed him the project of the Treaty before it was sent to Mr. Pakenham.[2]

I.

5. Mr. Bancroft's assumption that the United States were clearly entitled to the whole Oregon district up to the forty-ninth parallel is not warranted by the facts of the case. Territorial rights in the whole district were claimed by both parties with equal persistency, and their respective contentions were supported by arguments drawn from like sources, such as the history of discovery and the terms of international engagements. In the official documents on both sides the alternative of war was shadowed forth. In the end there was a compromise; each party yielded a portion of what it had contended in argument was its right.

6. When, on one occasion in the course of this long controversy between the two Governments, Mr. Cass, the United States Secretary of State, had put forward an assumption like this of Mr. Bancroft, Lord John Russell, then Her Majesty's Principal Secretary of State for Foreign Affairs, said:[3]

> Undoubtedly, the title by which Great Britain now holds British Columbia and Vancouver's Island is the same as that by which the United States possess the
> [3] Oregon State and Washington *Territory, namely, the Treaty of 1846; but when General Cass asserts, that previously to that Treaty the title of the United States to the whole of the territory between the parallels 42° and 54° 40′ had been clear and unquestionable, Her Majesty's Government can only reply that, in their opinion, it was the title of Great Britain to that territory which was clear and indisputable.

It is plain that when this was written, Her Majesty's Government had not adopted the notion that in 1846 the concession had been all on the side of the United States; nor have they ever changed their position.

---

[1] For the convenience of the Arbitrator, there are appended to the Historical Note, (1) a Chronological List, showing the names and dates of appointment of the various Principal Secretaries of State for Foreign Affairs in Great Britain and British Ministers at Washington, and of the various Presidents and Secretaries of State of the United States and United States Ministers at London, from 1818 to 1872; and (2) a Memorandum relative to the origin and privileges of the Hudson's Bay Company, a corporation frequently named in this discussion.

[2] Historical Note, p. xx.

[3] Lord John Russell to Lord Lyons, December 16, 1859; read, and copy given, to United States Secretary of State.

7. Mr. Bancroft further assumes that the United States had, before the Treaty, the forty-ninth parallel as an admitted boundary line on the Continent. Such an admission had never been made by Her Majesty's Government. That boundary would not (it is plain) have been conceded on the Continent without a concurrent arrangement satisfactory to Her Majesty's Government respecting Vancouver's Island and the navigation of the adjacent waters.

8. The passage in Mr. Bancroft's Memorial in which his assumptions under this head are most strongly put is the following, (page 30:)

> Again, "where a right admits of different degrees, it is only the smallest degree which may be taken for granted." (Ist ein Recht verschiedener Abstufungen fähig, so darf zunächst nur die geringste Stufe als zugestanden angenommen werden.") This rule of Heffter fits the present case so aptly, that it seems made for it. There being degrees in the departure from the parallel of 49°, it must be taken that only the smallest degree was conceded.

The rule cited from Dr. Heffter's work does not touch the present case. This is not the case of a party making a concession in derogation of a clear and admitted right. It is the case of one concession set off against another; of a give-and-take arrangement.[1]

9. The preamble of the Treaty is express on this point. The two Powers (it says:)

> Deeming it desirable for the future welfare of both countries that the state of doubt and uncertainty which has hitherto prevailed respecting the sovereignty and government of the territory on the Northwest coast of America, lying westward of the Rocky or Stony Mountains, should be finally terminated by an amicable compromise of the rights mutually asserted by the two parties over the said territory, have respectively named Plenipotentiaries to treat and agree concerning the terms of such settlement.

II.

10. Closely connected in character with the arguments of Mr. Bancroft under the first head, and equally inconclusive, as Her Majesty's Government submit, are his arguments under the second.

11. Mr. Bancroft alleges in effect that the intention of the Contracting Parties was only to avoid cutting off the end of Vancouver's Island, and he infers that the line is to be strictly so drawn as to effect this object, and no more. Her Majesty's Government dispute both the allegation and the inference.

12. There is no evidence that the prevention of the severance of Vancouver's Island was the sole object of the arrangement. There
[4] is nothing to support the allegation, *either in the preamble of
the Treaty, or in the Article describing the boundary; nor can it be sustained on the ground of anything contained in any of the contemporaneous documents exchanged between the Contracting Parties. It is true that the severance of Vancouver's Island by a boundary line drawn continuously on the forty-ninth parallel was the salient objection raised on the part of Her Majesty's Government to the United States proposal for continuing the boundary on that parallel from the Rocky Mountains to the Pacific. That proposal disregarded the physical conditions of the tract through which the line would run. It is true also that a deflection of the line so as not to sever Vancouver's Island was made in effect a condition *sine qua non* on the part of Her Majesty. It may even be admitted that the prevention of this severance was the motive for Article I of the Treaty. The nature of the motive is not necessarily a measure of the scope of the stipulation.

13. It is plain on the face of the Article that the Contracting Parties

[1] Historical Note, p. viii.

had further and other aims. If the sole object of the stipulation had been to keep Vancouver's Island one, a very simple provision would have sufficed. It would have been enough to say the whole of Vancouver's Island shall belong to Her Britannic Majesty. The Article in effect says this, but it says more in two respects. First, it in effect vests in Her Majesty, as against the United States, the whole territorial sovereignty and property over and in all land and sea adjacent to the island on its eastern and southern sides, lying within the mid-channel line, (wherever drawn,) although lying beyond the ordinary territorial three-mile limit. Secondly, it secures to Her Majesty's subjects freedom of navigation throughout the whole extent of the boundary-channel and of the Straits of Fuca. These two provisions in combination effect what was plainly one of Lord Aberdeen's main objects in the arrangement, namely, the preservation to Her Majesty's subjects of unquestionable and abundant facilities of access to the British coasts and harbors north of the 49th parallel. Had the boundary line been continued on the 49th parallel to the ocean, the navigation of the Gulf of Georgia from the southward would have been sealed to British subjects.

14. The Article speaks for itself. The preservation of the unity of Vancouver's Island was of the essence of the arrangement, but there were collateral arrangements. The difference now referred to arbitration presupposes the existence of such arrangements; the controversy is as to their extent.

15. Lord Aberdeen's instructions to Mr. Pakenham cannot be read so as to cut down the effect of the Treaty. They must be interpreted so as to correspond in scope with the project of the Treaty prepared and sent contemporaneously by Lord Aberdeen. The words quoted by Mr. Bancroft (page 19) from Lord Aberdeen's instructions are:

> Leaving the *whole of Vancouver's Island, with its ports and harbors, in the possession of Great Britain.*[1]

The form of expression requires little explanation. Lord Aberdeen naturally dwelt on the most prominent part of the arrangement which Mr. Pakenham was to propose, namely, the securing the possession to this country of the whole of Vancouver's Island. He referred only to the broad geographical features, the mention of which was supposed to be sufficient for the matter under discussion. There is nothing in his words to exclude any additional advantage which the terms of the project of the Treaty would give to this country, and more (it is plain) the project did give.

[5] *16. Mr. Bancroft further cites (page 20) a passage from a report of a speech of Sir Robert Peel in the House of Commons:

> Those who remember the local conformation of that country will understand that that which we proposed is the continuation of the forty-ninth parallel of latitude till it strikes the Straits of Fuca; that that parallel should not be continued as a boundary across Vancouver's Island, thus depriving us of a part of Vancouver's Island, but that the middle of the channel shall be the future boundary, thus *leaving us in possession of the whole of Vancouver's Island,* with equal right to the navigation of the Straits.

It can scarcely be seriously contended that, because Sir Robert Peel, describing in a popular way the effect of the Treaty, spoke of it as leaving us in possession of the whole of Vancouver's Island, this

---

[1] In this passage the words in italics are, in Mr. Bancroft's Memorial, printed with widened spaces between the letters, the mode of printing used in German to show emphasis, corresponding to the use of italics in the printing of English. The like observation applies to other passages cited in this Statement from Mr. Bancroft's Memorial.

amounts to a declaration by him that the effect of the Treaty is to exclude us from any possession other than Vancouver's Island, although lying within the future boundary, which he in the same breath specifies accurately as the middle of the channel.

17. In connection with the reference to Sir Robert Peel's speech, Mr. Bancroft (page 20) says:

> Sir Robert Peel quoted from a dispatch which proved that he was aware of the three days' debate in the American Senate on the Treaty before its approval.

Here, as in some other parts of Mr. Bancroft's Memorial, it is difficult to discover the object of statements made by him, but not put into an argumentative form. The object of this statement would seem, from the context, to be to suggest that Sir Robert Peel was at this time cognizant of the particulars of a speech of Mr. Benton, a Senator of the United States, made in the Senate (referred to just before by Mr. Bancroft and to be particularly considered hereafter in this Statement.) If this is the suggestion meant, there are three answers to it:

(i.) The deliberation of the Senate, reported in Mr. Pakenham's dispatch, read in part by Sir Robert Peel, was not the debate in which Mr. Benton's speech was made. The dispatch relates to the deliberation consequent on the preliminary Message of the President, asking the advice of the Senate, not to the debate on the ratification. It was the latter debate in the course of which Mr. Benton's speech was made.

(ii.) Even if Mr. Benton's speech had been spoken before Mr. Pakenham's dispatch, and the fact had been mentioned therein, there would still be no force in Mr. Bancroft's suggestion, inasmuch as the debates in the Senate were secret, and the injunction of secrecy was not removed until after the date of the exchange of ratifications in London.[1]

(iii.) The dispatch of Mr. Pakenham (of which the part relating to this matter is printed by Mr. Bancroft in the extract from Sir Robert Peel's speech in Appendix No. 46 to the Memorial) gives no information as to the name of any speaker, or the particulars of any speech, in the Senate. It simply says:[2]

> After a few hours' deliberation on each of the three days, Wednesday, Thursday, and Friday, the Senate, by a majority of 38 votes to 12, adopted yesterday evening a resolution advising the President to accept the terms proposed by Her Majesty's Government.

[6] *It is clear, therefore, that Sir Robert Peel had not at the time of speaking (if he ever had) any knowledge of what was said by Mr. Benton in the Senate. If this is not the point of Mr. Bancroft's reference to the debate in the Senate, Her Majesty's Government do not know why the reference is made.

III.

18. The third division of Mr. Bancroft's arguments comprises his endeavors to shew that there is evidence, contemporaneous with the making of the Treaty, in support of the contention of the United States. Mr. Bancroft says (page 18:)

---

[1] Ratifications exchanged July 17. Resolution of Senate removing injunction of secrecy, August 6. Earliest publication of Mr. Benton's speech known to Her Majesty's Government, August 29, (in Niles's National Register, a weekly newspaper published at Baltimore.)

[2] Historical note, p. xix.

With this knowledge of Mr. MacLane's character, and of the confidence reposed in him by Lord Aberdeen, I request the Imperial Arbitrator to take in hand the map of the Oregon Territory by Wilkes, which had been published in England as well as in America in 1845, and which was the latest, most authentic, and best map of the territory, as well as the only one recognized by the American Senate, and, with this map in hand, to read the following extract from Mr. MacLane's official report of the interview, made on the 18th of May, 1846:

"I have now to state that instructions will be transmitted to Mr. Pakenham by the steamer of to-morrow to submit a new and further proposition on the part of this Government, for a partition of the territory in dispute.

"The proposition, most probably, will offer substantially:

"First, to divide the territory by the extension of the line on the parallel of forty-nine to the sea, that is to say, to the arm of the sea called Birch's Bay, thence *by the Canal de Arro and Straits of Fuca to the ocean.*" * * * * * * *

Here follow other clauses, conceding to the Hudson's Bay Company a temporary use of the Oregon River for navigation, with other advantages, and protection to British subjects who would suddenly come under the jurisdiction of the United States. To these clauses the phrase "most probably" applies, for they were not precisely ascertained; but not to the boundary: on that point the further statement of Mr. MacLane in the same dispatch leaves no room for a doubt. His words are: "During the preceding Administration of our Government, the extension of the line on the forty-ninth parallel to the Straits of Fuca, *as now proposed by Lord Aberdeen, was actually suggested by my immediate predecessor (Mr. Everett)* as one he thought his Government might accept."

Now what the proposal of Mr. Everett had been we know from the citations which I have made from his dispatches; and I have actually referred to the fact that he had drawn the line of demarkation on the map, and specially directed the attention of Lord Aberdeen to it.

19. In this passage Mr. Bancroft puts forward prominently Mr. MacLane's letter, but he nowhere deduces distinctly the inference he wishes the Arbitrator to draw from it. In whatever light, however, the letter is regarded, it will appear that, when all the circumstances are candidly considered, the letter furnishes no ground for any inference favorable to the United States in the present discussion.

(i.) Mr. MacLane does not profess in his letter to report the words of the contemplated Treaty. He had seen the words, and knew that the Canal de Haro was not specified. He must then (it would seem) have considered the words he saw as amounting substantially (according to his own expression) to the proposal of a line by the Canal de Haro. He applied (whether accurately or not is not the question) his geographical information to the words shown to him, and inferred in his own mind that a line such as he saw described would run through the Canal de Haro. Under this impression he wrote to his Government. If this is the true explanation of the facts, (and no other explanation is apparent,) his statement is of no weight on the question, what is the channel of the Treaty. That question, which is the question now under arbitration, remains unaffected by his letter.

[7] *(ii.) One circumstance in Mr. MacLane's letter tends to support this explanation, that is, his mention of Birch Bay, (incorrectly called by him Birch's Bay,) which he treats as being on the forty-ninth parallel. This geographical error (which is peculiar in this controversy to Mr. MacLane) has been accounted for thus by Mr. Archibald Campbell:[1]

Mr. MacLane, in tracing on the map the forty-ninth parallel "to the sea, that is to say, *the arm of the sea* called Birch's Bay," evidently supposed that the space between

[1] Mr. Archibald Campbell was Commissioner on behalf of the United States, when Commissioners were appointed (as mentioned in the preamble of Article XXXIV of the Treaty of Washington of 1871) on behalf of the two Governments in 1856, to determine the water boundary under the Treaty of 1846. The document of Mr. Campbell's quoted or referred to here and elsewhere in this Statement, is a report made by him to Mr. Cass, the United States Secretary of State, dated 20th January, 1859.

the Continent and Vancouver's Island at the forty-ninth parallel was designated as Birch Bay. And from the conspicuous position given to the name of Birch Bay on Wilkes's map, and even on Vancouver's chart, such an error might very naturally occur. In reality, however, Birch Bay is only the small indentation on the main-land at the extreme right of the name, and is a few miles south of the forty-ninth parallel. The name of the *Gulf of Georgia* is intended by Wilkes to extend from the parallel of 50° as far south as the northern extremity of the Canal de Haro, including the space supposed by Mr. MacLane to be Birch Bay.

This explanation is simple and reasonable, and it strongly confirms the suggestion of Her Majesty's Government that Mr. MacLane was merely interpreting, according to his own lights, the words of the project which Lord Aberdeen had shown him, and was not reporting to his Government Lord Aberdeen's interpretation, or an agreed interpretation. There is no suggestion, and no ground for a suggestion, that Lord Aberdeen ever spoke of Birch Bay. If, then, it is probable that Mr. MacLane did not derive from Lord Aberdeen his mention of Birch Bay, in just the same degree is it probable that he did not derive from Lord Aberdeen his mention of the Canal de Haro.[1]

(iii.) The use by Mr. MacLane of Wilkes's map (which is thus made almost certain) goes far to account for his mention of the Canal de Haro, (or Arro, as it is written on Wilkes's map, and by Mr. MacLane,) for that passage is so conspicuously marked on Wilkes's map as to seem to be the only direct channel between the Continent and Vancouver's Island leading into the Straits of Fuca. But, however it is to be accounted for, there is no ground whatever for the suggestion that Mr. MacLane's mention of the Canal de Haro was authorized by anything said to him by Lord Aberdeen.

(iv.) In 1859 Lord Aberdeen, on being referred to by Lord John Russell, then Her Majesty's Principal Secretary of State for Foreign Affairs, informed Lord John Russell that he (Lord Aberdeen) distinctly remembered the general tenor of his conversations with Mr. MacLane on the subject of the Oregon boundary, and he had no recollection of any mention having been made during the discussion of the Canal de Haro, or, indeed, any other channel than those described in the Treaty itself.[2]

(v.) Mr. MacLane was not negotiating with Lord Aberdeen. His connection with the question was (as he himself says) "in a great degree informal."[3] The negotiations were being carried on at Washington by Mr. Pakenham (acting immediately under Lord Aberdeen's instructions) on the one hand, and Mr. Buchanan on the other hand.[4]
[8] *Lord Aberdeen was at liberty to inform Mr. MacLane of his views and intentions; he was at liberty to refrain from doing so. Anything that passed between Lord Aberdeen and Mr. MacLane was not negotiation in a proper sense, and no binding compact can be extracted from it, taken alone.

(vi.) Mr. MacLane perfectly understood this position. Lord Aberdeen's project of Treaty was so far from being the result of a bargain made between him and Mr. MacLane, that Mr. MacLane in reporting it to his

---

[1] There is nothing in the explanation here given of Mr. MacLane's words inconsistent with the character of him drawn by Mr. Bancroft, (page 18:) "Mr. MacLane was a calm and experienced statesman, trained in business, exact in his use of words, careful especially in reporting what was said by others."

[2] Lord John Russell to Lord Lyons, 24th August; 1859, read, and copy given, to nited States Secretary of State. Extract, Appendix No. 1.

[3] Appendix No. 32 to Mr. Bancroft's Memorial.

[4] Mr. Bancroft correctly says (page 14) with reference to the time just before the Treaty: "Meantime the negotiation on the Oregon question had been transferred to the new British Minister at Washington." And again, (page 16:) "Lord Aberdeen confessed that it now fell to him to propose a peaceful solution of the long controversy."

Government disapproved of it, and (it would appear) tried to induce his Government to reject it.[1] He says, (among other things:)[2]

It is scarcely necessary for me to state that the proposition as now submitted has not received my countenance. Although it has been no easy task, under all the circumstances, to lead to a re-opening of the negotiations by any proposition from this Government, and to induce it to adopt the parallel of 49 as the basis of a boundary, nevertheless I hoped it would have been in my power to give the present proposition a less objectionable shape, and I most deeply lament my inability to accomplish it. I have, therefore, felt it my duty to discourage any expectation that it would be accepted by the President; or, if submitted to that body, approved by the Senate.

(vii.) If Mr. MacLane had been in a position to enter into a contract with Lord Aberdeen it is plain he never would have used the qualification "most probably." Mr. Bancroft, seeing the force of this consideration, endeavors to get over the difficulty by alleging that the phrase "most probably" applies, not to the boundary, but to the other parts of Lord Aberdeen's proposal; for, he says, those other parts "were not precisely ascertained." Mr. MacLane's letter (as far as it relates to the Oregon question) is printed in the Historical Note, and is open to the judgment of the Arbitrator. It appears to Her Majesty's Government to afford no ground to justify this limited application of the phrase "most probably." This phrase is in immediate connection, grammatically, and in the arrangement of the matter, with the passage relating to the boundary. The three subjects, (1,) boundary; (2,) possessory rights of British subjects; (3,) navigation of the Columbia, are discussed throughout the letter on the same footing. The proposal on any one subject is treated in the letter as being quite as much settled and definitive as the proposal on any other. Moreover, in point of fact, the exact proposal was as much ascertained on any one point as on any other, and this must have been so in Mr. MacLane's apprehension, as Lord Aberdeen had shown him the project of the Treaty.

(viii.) The boundary, however, it is argued by Mr. Bancroft, was precisely ascertained, because Mr. MacLane states that the line as proposed by Lord Aberdeen had been suggested by Mr. Everett, and what the proposal of Mr. Everett was (he says) is known from the citations in the Memorial from his (Mr. Everett's) dispatches. The passage in Mr. Bancroft's Memorial, relating to Mr. Everett's suggestion, is as follows, (page 11:)

On the 29th of November, 1843, soon after Mr. Everett's full powers had arrived, he and Lord Aberdeen had a very long and important conversation on the Oregon question; and the concessions of Lord Aberdeen appearing to invite an expression of the extremest modification which the United States could admit to their former proposal, Mr. Everett reports that he said: "I thought the President might be induced so far to depart from the forty-ninth parallel as to leave the whole of Quadra and Vancouver's Island to England, whereas that line of latitude would give us the southern extremity of that island, and consequently the command of the Straits of Fuca on both sides. I then *pointed out on a map the extent of this concession;* and Lord Aberdeen said he would take it into consideration."

The next day Mr. Everett more formally referred to the subject in a note to the British Secretary:

[9] *"46 GROSVENOR PLACE, *November* 30, 1843.

"MY DEAR LORD ABERDEEN: * * * It appears from Mr. Gallatin's correspondence that * * * Mr. Huskisson had especially objected to the extension of the forty-ninth degree to the Pacific, on the ground that it would cut off the southern extremity of Quadra and Vancouver's Island. My suggestion yesterday would obviate this objection. * * * *A glance at the map shows its importance* as a modification of the forty-ninth degree. * * *

"EDWARD EVERETT."

---

[1] The character of the letter in this respect is brought out by Mr. Pakenham's comments in his dispatch of the 29th July, 1846, Historical Note, p. xx.

[2] Historical Note, p. xiv.

On the 2d of February, and on the 1st of April, 1844, Mr. Everett reports that he continuously insisted with Lord Aberdeen that the only modification which the United States could, in his opinion, be brought to agree to, was that they should waive their claim to the southern extremity of Vancouver's Island, and that Lord Aberdeen uniformly answered, "he did not think there would be much difficulty in settling the question."

During the following months Mr. Everett and Lord Aberdeen, both wishing sincerely to settle the controversy, had further frequent conversations, and, as the result of them all, Mr. Everett reported that England would not accept the naked parallel of 49° to the ocean, but would consent to the line of the forty-ninth degree, provided it could be so modified as to leave to Great Britain the southern extremity of Vancouver Island. "I have spared no pains," wrote Mr. Everett on the 28th of February, 1845, "to impress upon Lord Aberdeen's mind the persuasion that the utmost which the United States can concede is the forty-ninth parallel with the modification suggested, taking always care to add that I had no authority for saying that even that modification would be agreed to."

To one fact I particularly invoke the attention of the Imperial Arbitrator: not the least room for doubt was left by Mr. Everett with regard to the extent of the modification proposed. *He had pointed it out to Lord Aberdeen on the map*, and had so often and so carefully directed his attention to it, that there could be no misapprehension on the limit of the proposed concession.

It is difficult to see the force of this reference from the letter of Mr. MacLane to the writings and acts of Mr. Everett. It seems to Her Majesty's Government to be a process of ascertaining a thing uncertain in itself by means of something still more uncertain. It does not appear that Mr. Everett pointed out on a map, or referred in any manner to, the Canal de Haro; yet this is the whole question. The fair inference from Mr. Everett's statements is that he did not speak of the water boundary at all, but only pointed out on a map how much of Vancouver's Island would be cut off by the forty-ninth parallel. Mr. Bancroft appears to overstrain Mr. Everett's words. Mr. Everett says he "pointed out on a map the extent of the concession," as regards the southern extremity of Vancouver's Island; Mr. Bancroft says (page 19) Mr. Everett "had drawn the line of demarkation upon the map," which seems to be a very different thing. If this had been stated by Mr. Everett, and if it also appeared that the line of demarkation drawn by him on the map passed down the Canal de Haro, then Mr. Bancroft's inference that Lord Aberdeen was proposing a line through the Canal de Haro, from the fact that Mr. MacLane says that the line proposed by Lord Aberdeen had been suggested by Mr. Everett, would not be so remote or so weak as it is.

(ix.) The statements of Mr. MacLane to his own Government can in no way bind Her Majesty's Government. Mr. MacLane does not say that he did, and there is no evidence that he did, ever specify any channel in his conversations with Lord Aberdeen. There is no evidence that he ever told Lord Aberdeen what he was going to report to his Government. The presumption to be drawn from Lord Aberdeen's dispatch of 29th June, 1846, to Mr. Pakenham, is to the contrary.[1] Mr. MacLane's letter was not published, even in the United States, until after the exchange of ratifications in London.[1] It could not, therefore, have reached Lord Aberdeen's knowledge before the transaction was closed.

(x.) Nor is there anything to affect Her Majesty's Government through Mr. Pakenham. There is no suggestion that Mr. Buchanan com-
[10] municated to Mr. Pakenham *Mr. MacLane's letter. On the contrary, it is evident from Mr. Pakenham's dispatch of the 29th July, 1846, that the letter was unknown to him till its unauthorized publication, as mentioned in that dispatch.[1] Nor did Mr. Buchanan in any

[1] Historical Note, p. xx.

manner inform Mr. Pakenham of Mr. MacLane's view. In a Memorandum,[1] written in 1858, Sir Richard (formerly Mr.) Pakenham states that Mr. Buchanan on the occasion of the Treaty "made no mention whatever of the Canal de Haro as that through which the line of boundary should run as understood by the United States Government." If, indeed, Mr. Buchanan had done so, that mere fact would be of no importance as against Her Majesty's Government. Mr. Pakenham was acting under strict instructions. If Mr. Buchanan had indicated the Canal de Haro as the boundary channel, Mr. Pakenham could only have answered as he did on the question of the effect of Article II, namely, the Article speaks for itself.[2] He had no power to modify the project of Treaty in substance, and no power to bind his Government by assenting to or acquiescing in an interpretation which would have been equivalent to a serious modification.

20. It appears to Her Majesty's Government that this examination of Mr. MacLane's letter justifies them in submitting to the Arbitrator that the letter affords no support to the contention of the United States.

21. In addition to Mr. MacLane's letter, Mr. Bancroft refers to the speech of Mr. Benton in the Senate before mentioned. The passage in Mr. Bancroft's Memorial is as follows, (page 19:)

> A suspicion of ambiguity could not lurk in the mind of any one. Mr. Benton found the language so clear that he adopted it as his own. In his Speech in the Senate on the day of the ratification of the Treaty, he said:
>
> "The first Article of the Treaty is *in the very words* which I myself would have used if the two Governments had left it to me to draw the boundary line between them
>
> * * * * * * *
>
> "The line established by the first Article follows the parallel of 49° to the sea, with a slight deflection through the Straits of Fuca *to avoid cutting off the south end of Vancouver's Island* * * * . When the line reaches the channel which separates Vancouver's Island from the Continent, it proceeds to the middle of the channel, and thence turning south *through the Channel de Haro* (wrongly written Arro on the maps) to the Straits of Fuca, and then west through the middle of that Strait to the sea. This gives us * * * * the *cluster of islands* between *de Haro's Channel and the Continent.*"

22. Her Majesty's Government submit that the speech of Mr. Benton is even of less value, as evidence in support of the contention of the United States, than is Mr. MacLane's letter.

(i.) It seems probable that Mr. Benton founded his exposition of the draught Treaty on Mr. MacLane's letter,[3] extracts from which had been communicated by the President of the United States to the Senate. If so, Mr. Benton's interpretation is only a reflection of Mr. MacLane's.

(ii.) Mr. Benton may indeed have formed his opinion not directly on Mr. MacLane's letter, but on the same sort of ground on which it would appear Mr. MacLane's statement was made, namely, a knowledge (whether complete or accurate, or not) of the local conditions.[4] In that case his statement would amount to no more than a declaration
[11] of *his opinion that, on the true construction of the words of the
Treaty, the line described would run down the Canal de Haro. But Mr. Benton's opinion on this question of construction is not alleged to be of any special value, and its authority in the present discussion is

---

[1] Inclosed in Lord John Russell's dispatch to Lord Lyons, 24th August, 1859; read, and copy given, to United States Secretary of State. Appendix No. 1.

[2] Historical Note, p. xx.

[3] This was Sir Richard Pakenham's view, as expressed in his Memorandum, Appendix No. 1.

[4] Mr. Cass describes Mr. Benton as being "better acquainted, perhaps, than any other member [of the Senate] with the geography of the region in dispute."—To Mr. Dallas, 20th October, 1859; read, and copy given, to Her Majesty's Secretary of State for Foreign Affairs.

not admitted. The question whether or not the line runs down the Canal de Haro, according to the construction of the Treaty, is the question before the Arbitrator.

(iii.) But whatever was the foundation of Mr. Benton's observations, and whatever title they have to consideration, Her Majesty's Government cannot be affected either through Mr. Pakenham or through Lord Aberdeen by anything that was said on this occasion in the Senate. The debates in the Senate were in Secret Session. No publication of them was permitted or made until after the time when the ratifications had been exchanged in London.[1]

23. Mr. Bancroft adduces no further evidence whatever on this point, yet he goes so far as to say, (page 20:)

> The language of the Treaty seemed perfectly clear to the Senate, to the President, to his Secretary of State, and to every one of his constitutional advisers, as departing from the line of the parallel of 49° only so far as to yield the southern extremity of Vancouver's Island, and no more.

With respect to the view of the language of the Treaty formed at the time by the Senate (as a body) or by the President, or by any one of the President's constitutional advisers other than his Secretary of State, Mr. Buchanan, Her Majesty's Government have no information, either from Mr. Bancroft's Memorial or otherwise. The exception of Mr. Buchanan is here made, not on account of anything in Mr. Bancroft's Memorial, but because, in the course of the controversy between the two Governments, a statement respecting Mr. Buchanan's opinion has been made on behalf of the United States. It has been said[2] that, in a letter to Mr. MacLane, dated 6th June, 1846, the day on which the draught Treaty was presented to Mr. Buchanan by Mr. Pakenham, Mr. Buchanan mentions the Canal de Haro as the channel intended by the Treaty. This letter has not been seen by Her Majesty's Government. It may be supposed that it is simply (so to speak) an echo of Mr. MacLane's conjectures as to what would be found to be the substantial effect of Lord Aberdeen's proposal, when it came to be worked out. But whether that is so or not, statements passing between Mr. Buchanan and Mr. MacLane, not communicated to Mr. Pakenham or to Lord Aberdeen, are not admissible as against Her Majesty's Government. Sir Richard Pakenham, in his Memorandum before cited, says:

> It is certain that Mr. Buchanan signed the Treaty with Mr. MacLane's dispatch before him, and yet that he made no mention whatever of the Canal de Haro as that through which the line of boundary should run, as understood by the United States Government.

And this, after Mr. Buchanan had had read to him, by Mr. Pakenham, such an extract from Lord Aberdeen's instructions as comprised the paragraph containing the description of the line of demarkation to be proposed, and had himself read over the extract again in Mr. Pakenham's presence;[3] which two readings must have shown Mr. Buchanan the erroneousness of any expectation that the Canal de Haro would be specified.

24. The examination has now been completed of everything that can reasonably be regarded as contemporaneous evidence in favor of
[12] the United States of the intention * of their Government in concluding the Treaty. Her Majesty's Government submit to the

[1] Page 199, above, and note [1] there.
[2] Mr. Cass to Mr. Dallas, 20th October, 1859; read, and copy given, to Her Majesty's e cretary of State for Foreign Affairs.
[3] Historical Note, p. xvii.

Arbitrator that it is of little, if any, weight. All that it amounts to is this, that some of the persons concerned on the part of the United States, on the occasion of the Treaty, anticipated that the Treaty, couched in the words proposed on one side and adopted on the other, would have a certain effect. These anticipations were not communicated at the time to Her Majesty's Government, or to any representative of that Government, and are, therefore, in no degree binding on them to their detriment.

25. But before parting from this branch of the subject, Her Majesty's Government will advert to two other pieces of evidence which have been in the course of the controversy adduced as "personal testimony contemporaneous with the Treaty,"[1] and which it is possible may be brought up again as such in the present discussion.

(1.) It is stated[1] that, on 28th December, 1846, Mr. Bancroft (who was then the United States Minister at London) having written to Mr. Buchanan on the subject from London, Mr. Buchanan inclosed, in a letter to Mr. Bancroft, a traced copy of Wilkes's chart of the Straits of Arro, (that is, the Canal de Haro,) and added:

> It is not probable, however, that any claim of this character will be seriously preferred by Her Majesty's Government to any island lying to the eastward of the Canal de Arro, as marked in Captain Wilkes's map of the Oregon Territory.

The correspondence at this time between Mr. Bancroft and Mr. Buchanan, as far as the same is known to Her Majesty's Government, is set forth in the Appendix to this Statement.[2] Her Majesty's Government submit to the Arbitrator that if this correspondence is proposed to be used on the present occasion as evidence on behalf of the United States, it ought to be rejected. First, it was from its nature entirely unknown at its dates to Her Majesty's Government; secondly, any declarations it contains were made *post litem motam*. Even if admitted, it would be of little value, as it cannot carry the case further than it is carried by Mr. MacLane's letter, on which Mr. Buchanan's statements in this correspondence explicitly rest. Mr. Buchanan does not use a word that can fairly be considered as conveying his personal testimony as to the intention of himself or his Government at the time of the making of the Treaty. Finally, if this correspondence is admitted as evidence, then Her Majesty's Government would ask that there be taken into consideration along with it the report of Mr. Buchanan's views in 1848, made by Mr. Crampton, Her Majesty's Minister at Washington, and the subsequent communication thereon made to the United States Government.[3]

(2.) The other piece of evidence referred to by Her Majesty's Government as having been adduced on behalf of the United States is the following:[4]

> Mr. Bancroft, who was a member of President Polk's Cabinet when the Treaty was concluded, wrote repeatedly to Lord Palmerston after receiving this chart, [the traced copy of Wilkes's chart above mentioned,] and uniformly described the Straits of Arro "as the channel through the middle of which the boundary is to be continued."

The communications between Mr. Bancroft and Viscount Palmerston here referred to were in July and November, 1848. The letters
[13] are set forth in the Appendix,[5] together * with the published

[1] Mr. Cass to Mr. Dallas, 20th October, 1859; read, and copy given, to Her Majesty's Secretary of State for Foreign Affairs.

[2] Appendix No. 2.

[3] Appendix No. 3.

[4] Mr. Cass to Mr. Dallas, 20th October, 1859; read, and copy given, to Her Majesty's Secretary for Foreign Affairs.

[5] Appendix No. 4.

extract of a letter from Mr. Bancroft to Mr. Buchanan, describing a conversation which he (Mr. Bancroft) had had with Lord Palmerston. No statement of Mr. Bancroft made more than two years after the exchange of ratifications can be reasonably regarded as "personal testimony contemporaneous with the Treaty," in which category it is placed in the paper of Mr. Cass adducing it. The only use to which these documents could now be fairly applied would be to show that Lord Palmerston had then made to Mr. Bancroft admissions now binding on Her Majesty's Government. But the documents afford no ground for such a suggestion.[1] The course taken by Lord Palmerston on Mr. Bancroft's second letter (in which he for the second time intimated his view that the boundary was to pass through the Canal de Haro) is conclusive as to Lord Palmerston's view of the position. It is plain, on the face of Lord Palmerston's answer to that letter, that the answer was deliberately framed so as not to amount to an admission of the claim put forward by Mr. Bancroft. If there could be any doubt of this, on the words of the letter, the doubt would be put an end to by a reference to the minutes on Mr. Bancroft's letter which preceded the preparation of the draught of Lord Palmerston's answer. On Mr. Bancroft's letter the Under-Secretary of State made the following minute for Lord Palmerston:

Shall this letter be acknowledged and Mr. Bancroft be thanked for it? And if so, shall the underlined assumption of Mr. Bancroft be passed over without observation?

The underlined words were, "through the middle of which our boundary line passes." Lord Palmerston's minute in answer was as follows

Thank him, and say that the information contained in these charts as to soundings will no doubt be of great service to the Commissioners to be appointed, by assisting them in determining where the line of boundary described by the Treaty ought to run.[2]

IV.

26. The next class of Mr. Bancroft's arguments is to be found in those passages in which he contends, in effect, that Her Majesty's Government are precluded from disputing the interpretation put on the Treaty by the United States, on the ground that the framing of the Treaty was (as he represents) the work of Her Majesty's Government.

27. He says, (page 22:)

The draught of the Treaty was made entirely, even to the minutest word, by the British Ministry, and was signed by both parties without change. The British Government cannot, therefore, take advantage of an ambiguity of their own, otherwise the draught of the Treaty would have been a snare. Such is the principle of natural right, such the established law of nations. Hugo Grotius lays down the rule that the interpretation must be made against the party which draughted the conditions: "Ut contra eum fiat interpretatio, qui conditiones elocutus est." But no one has expressed this more clearly than Vattel, who writes: * * *

[14] *28. Her Majesty's Government submit that the fact that the project of the Treaty emanated from them can be in no way used to their disadvantage. The Treaty, as it comes before the Arbitrator,

[1] "If I notice General Cass's allusion to the letters which he says Mr. Bancroft repeatedly wrote to Lord Palmerston in 1848, it is only for the purpose of placing on record what, no doubt, Mr. Bancroft duly reported to his Government at the time, namely, that Lord Palmerston gave Mr. Bancroft distinctly to understand that the British Government did not acquiesce in the pretensions of the United States that the boundary line should be run down the Haro Channel."—Lord John Russell to Lord Lyons, 16th December, 1859; read, and copy given, to United States Secretary of State.

[2] These observations may not be thought too minute when it is stated that Lord Palmerston's letter has been treated by Mr. Archibald Campbell as a virtual admission of the Canal de Haro as the Treaty channel.

must be regarded as the work of both parties. It was in the power of the President or of the Senate of the United States to insist on any alteration of the terms. They had abundant opportunity for considering the terms. The project was delivered by Mr. Pakenham to Mr. Buchanan, and considered by them in conference, on the 6th of June. It was sent by the President to the Senate on the 10th of June. It was considered by the Senate on the 10th, 11th, and 12th of June. The Treaty was signed on the 15th of June. It was sent to the Senate for ratification on the 16th of June. The Treaty, with various incidental motions, was before the Senate on the 16th, 17th, and 18th of June. Mr. Buchanan intimated to Mr. Pakenham that the President's message sending the project to the Senate might, and probably would, suggest some modifications in it. An entire counter-proposal was made and divided on in the Senate; in the preliminary deliberation a formal motion was divided on for adding a proviso to Article II; and Mr. Buchanan made representations to Mr. Pakenham respecting the effect of that Article.[1] Some of the reasons that prevailed with the Senate to induce them to adopt the project as it stood may be gathered from Mr. Benton's speech. He objected to any alteration (first) on the ground of the delay that would be caused, which would be injurious to the interests, particularly the commercial interests, of the United States; and (secondly) because of the importance to the United States of closing the question, as they were then engaged in war with the Republic of Mexico. In all these circumstances, the words of the Treaty must be taken to be, as they in fact are, the words, not of Lord Aberdeen and Mr. Pakenham only, but the words also of Mr. Buchanan and of the President and Senate of the United States.

29. The words cited by Mr. Bancroft from Grotius's book are not applicable to the present case. The passage from which they are extracted relates to the case of dictation of conditions of peace. The whole chapter to which they belong is on that and cognate subjects. The sentence from which Mr. Bancroft's citation is taken reads in a more complete form thus:

> In dubio autem sensu magis est ut contra eum fiat interpretatio, qui conditiones elocutus est, quod esse solet potentioris: est ejus qui dat non qui petit conditiones pacis dare [dicere,] ait Annibal.

The passage produced by Mr. Bancroft from Vattel's work appears to Her Majesty's Government to be as capable of an application favorable to them as of one unfavorable to them.

30. In another place (page 30) Mr. Bancroft says:

> A party offering the draught of a Treaty is bound by the interpretation which it knew at the time that the other party gave it. Lord Aberdeen cannot have doubted how the Treaty was understood by Mr. MacLane, by Mr. Buchanan, and by the Senate of the United States. "Where the terms of promise," writes Paley, whose work was long a text-book at Oxford, "admit of more senses than one, the promise is to be performed in the sense in which the promiser apprehended at the time that the promisee received it. This will not differ from the actual intention of the promiser, where the promise is given without collusion or reserve; but we put the rule in the above form to exclude evasion, wherever the promiser attempts to make his escape through some ambiguity in the expressions which he used."

[15] *Her Majesty's Government are not here concerned to dispute the general proposition that a party offering to another the draught of a Treaty is bound by the interpretation which it (the party offering) knew at the time the other party gave to the draught. But they do dispute, and submit they have disproved, Mr. Bancroft's particular prop-

[1] Appendix No. 5, and Historical Note, p. xix.

osition. Lord Aberdeen (he says) cannot have doubted how the Treaty was understood by Mr. MacLane, by Mr. Buchanan, and by the Senate of the United States. Her Majesty's Government have proved that Lord Aberdeen did not know until after the exchange of ratifications (if personally he ever knew) of Mr. MacLane's letter to Mr. Buchanan, of Mr. Buchanan's letter to Mr. MacLane,[1] or of Mr. Benton's speech (the views expressed in which Mr. Bancroft seems to ascribe to the Sen ate as a body.)

31. The doctrine contained in the passage cited by Mr. Bancroft from Dr. Paley's treatise on Moral and Political Philosophy appears to Her Majesty's Government generally true,[2] but here irrelevant. That doctrine applies to a promise in the ordinary sense, a unilateral promise, or an engagement taken by one party wholly or mainly. It is not appropriate to the case of a contract, which the same treatise defines as a mutual promise. A few pages further in that treatise, the following is stated as "a rule which governs the construction of all contracts:"

> Whatever is expected by one side, and known to be so expected by the other, is to be deemed a part or condition of the contract.

This rule Her Majesty's Government submit to be judged by. Even if it were admitted (as it is not) that Mr. Bancroft has shown what amounts (in the phraseology of Dr. Paley) to an expectation on the side of the United States, he has entirely failed to show on the other side (that of Her Majesty's Government) a knowledge of the existence of that expectation. On the contrary, Her Majesty's Government have demonstrated their necessary ignorance on the point.

32. Sir Richard Pakenham (in his Memorandum before cited) says, (he is writing some twelve years after the Treaty, and he speaks therefore in guarded phrase, but his testimony is clear:)

> I think I can safely assert that the Treaty of 15th June, 1846, was signed and ratified without any intimation to us whatever on the part of the United States Government as to the particular direction to be given to the line of boundary contemplated by Article I of that Treaty.

V.

33. It remains to examine the arguments by which Mr. Bancroft endeavors to show that the language of the Treaty points to the Canal de Haro and to that channel alone.

(i.) Mr. Bancroft refers (page 24) to the concise form of expression by which, he says, in both countries the line was described as the line of the "forty-ninth parallel and Fuca's Straits." Two observations occur: (1) Many persons, including Mr. Greenhow, used the name Fuca's Straits to embrace the waters, or at least the southern waters, of the Gulf of Georgia. (2) If, in this phrase, the name is not so understood, then the use of this expression (the forty-ninth parallel and Fuca's Straits) is of no weight in favor of Mr. Bancroft's argument; for the whole ques-
[16] tion is where the line is to run, which is required to form *a connecting link between the forty-ninth parallel and Fuca's Straits, (that name being used in the modern sense.)

(ii.) Mr. Bancroft says, (page 25:)

> When the Treaty speaks of "the channel," for that part south and west of Birch's Bay, it must mean the Channel of Haro, for no other "channel" was known to the negotiators.

---

[1] Above, paragraph 23.

[2] It is, however, not altogether unimpeachable, as will appear from the criticisms of another English author, Austin, Lectures on Jurisprudence, vol. ii, p. 122.

And he proceeds to instance maps on which the Canal de Haro and no other channel is named. This argument assumes that the reference in the Treaty is necessarily to some named channel. Her Majesty's Government, on the contrary, have submitted that the absence of any name in the Treaty is strong evidence in favor of their contention. The fact that the Rosario Straits had no name specially fits that passage to be the nameless channel of the Treaty. The Canal de Haro was conspicuously named on Vancouver's chart and Wilkes's map. If it had been intended to be the channel of the Treaty, it would have been obvious and easy to name it. Mr. Bancroft can scarcely mean to contend that the Rosario Straits are not a channel, because they do not bear a name of which the word "channel" is part.

(iii.) Mr. Bancroft proceeds, (page 26:)

> Again, the word "channel" when employed in Treaties, means a deep and navigable channel, and when there are two navigable channels, by the rule of international law, preference is to be given to the largest column of water.

That the word "channel" means a navigable channel in Treaties generally, and in the Treaty under consideration in particular, is maintained also by Her Majesty's Government. But they do not admit the existence of such a rule as is here alleged. If navigability is of the essence of a channel, then, as between two channels, preference should be given to the one which is the better fitted for navigation. Now, at the time when the Treaty was made, at which time it must be read as speaking, the Canal de Haro was almost unknown to and unused by practical navigators. It can scarcely, in the true sense of language, regarded as used at that day, be called a navigable channel. Even at the present day, when thoroughly explored and surveyed, it is found to be of difficult and dangerous navigation, especially for sailing-vessels, and only one steamer had penetrated into those waters at the date of the Treaty.[1]

(iv.) Then Mr. Bancroft says, (page 26:)

> Now, compared with any other channel through which a ship could pass from the sea at the forty-ninth parallel, to the Straits of Fuca, the Channel of Haro is the broadest and the deepest, the shortest and the best. * * * * With regard to depth, the contrast is still more striking. * * * *

But, although depth of channel may be an advantage in river navigation, and may therefore well weigh in the choice of one channel as a boundary in preference to one or another less deep, yet depth beyond a certain limit—a limit, perhaps, never reached in river navigation—becomes a disadvantage in navigation of every kind, as it lessens the facilities for anchoring, and thus increases the dangers of navigation. The Canal de Haro is an instance. Its depth is so great that there are but few anchorages in it, and there are none in the main channel; and with this defect, and its rapid and variable currents, it becomes an unsafe passage for sailing-vessels. The Rosario Straits, on the other hand, while they are deep enough for vessels of the very largest class, have many anchorages, conveniently and securely situated; and at the same time the regularity of the currents in them makes them comparatively easy of navigation.

[17] *(v.) Mr. Bancroft further says (page 26) that the Canal de Haro is "the shortest and most direct way between the parallel of 49° and Fuca Straits." But there is nothing in the Treaty to show that the line between the forty-ninth parallel and the Straits of Fuca is to be run by what may now be held to be the shortest and most direct

[1] On these points Her Majesty's Government refer to the evidence in the Appendix to their Case, presented to the Arbitrator in December, 1871.

way. The line is to be drawn by the channel of the day, the ordinary and frequented navigable channel.

(vi.) Mr. Bancroft, in favor of the Canal de Haro, says, (page 26,) "Duflot de Mofras describes it as notoriously the best." From this and other references in the Memorial to this writer, it might be supposed that he was entitled to high respect as an authority on the hydrography and navigation of the region. The fact is he was attached to a European Legation in Mexico in 1840–'42, and was sent thence to report on the Oregon district and neighboring countries. In his account he says, with regard to the difficulty of navigation of these waters, that the Canal de Haro is "le passage le plus facile." He was not a naval officer, and appears to have been employed solely in a civil capacity. Mr. Archibald Campbell, after quoting the passage in which the observation referred to by Mr. Bancroft is made, says:

> And this opinion he [Duflot de Mofras] must have derived from the general report of those engaged in the navigation of these waters, as his own explorations are considered very superficial.

It is plain that he has no personal authority on a question of navigation.

(vii.) Mr. Bancroft contends (pages 27 and 29) that the Canal de Haro is the only channel which separates the Continent from Vancouver's Island; that there are other passages which divide islands from islands, but none other separates the Continent from Vancouver's Island; and that the Rosario Straits touch neither the Continent nor Vancouver's Island. But Her Majesty's Government submit that, even if the present state of knowledge is to be taken into account, the distinctions here attempted are not tenable, as the map attached to Mr. Bancroft's Memorial shows. The Rosario Straits are, by the evidence of that map in the respects here mentioned, as much entitled as the Canal de Haro to be regarded as the dividing channel between the Continent and the Island. But the question must be referred back to the time of the Treaty, and then the Rosario Straits will be the dividing channel, as being the ordinary track of vessels passing up and down on the waters lying between the island and the main-land.

(viii.) Mr. Bancroft (page 27) founds an argument on the word "southerly;" but, as to this expression, there seems little room for discussion. It is evidently used in a large and loose sense, as contrasted with a line carried westward to the Pacific, or deflected northward up the Gulf of Georgia. This is the more evident when it is observed that, on a strict construction, the word is applied to the continuation of the line through the Straits of Fuca, where its direction would in fact be westerly, or even in part northwesterly.

(ix.) Mr. Bancroft further says, (page 28:)

> The Treaty contemplates a continuous channel to the Pacific; the channel of Haro and Fuca's Straits form such a continuous channel, and a glance at the map will show that no other channel can pretend to do so.

Mr. Bancroft's map speaks for itself; it is difficult to see on it a higher degree of continuity in the Canal de Haro than in Rosario Straits. In fact the waters passing southerly through the Rosario Straits are derived from the Gulf of Georgia alone and uninterruptedly, while the Canal de Haro is in the southerly direction supplied only partly and indirectly by the waters from the southern termination of the Gulf of Georgia, and partly and more directly from the waters flowing through the passages between Vancouver's Island and the archipelago off its eastern coast. This is obvious on the map, and is

confirmed by observation. The flow of an interrupted body of water from the Gulf of Georgia through the Rosario Straits causes a
[18] marked regularity of current in *that passage, while in the
Canal de Haro, on the contrary, the currents are irregular, the waters flowing into it being broken and dispersed by the islands in and near its northern entrance.

(x.) Mr. Bancroft labors the point (page 28) that the name Rosario Straits was not given till of late to the channel through which Vancouver sailed. Her Majesty's Government are not concerned to dispute this. But they have not invented the name of Rosario Straits (as Mr. Bancroft seems to think) for the purposes of the present discussion. Mr. Archibald Campbell gives a history of the names borne at different times by the channel, ending thus: "It is now [1859] universally called Rosario Straits." It is, in fact, called so over and over again in United States official documents, and it had been named Rosario Strait on the map of the United States Coast Survey (by Lieutenant Alden, United States Navy,) published in 1854.

(xi.) Lastly, Mr. Bancroft says, (page 29:)

> Now, the so-called straits of Rosario lead only to a Sound, which Spanish voyagers called the bay of Santa Rosa; they do not connect with Fuca's straits, which cease at the southeastern promontory of Vancouver island.

Her Majesty's Government submit that it is plain that Fuca's Straits, even in the more modern and restricted sense of that name, extend to the western coast of Whidbey Island. Formerly, they used to be considered, at least by many persons, including Mr. Greenhow, as sweeping round to the north and northwest through the archipelago which lies between the Canal de Haro and Rosario Straits, and as including in their waters both those passages. On Quimper's map, indeed, the easternmost part of the Straits is marked Seno de Santa Rosa. But that map (the earliest extant) is a very imperfect representation of the land and water of the district, and the name of the Bay of Santa Rosa never appears again on any map known to Her Majesty's Government.

34. In connection with this branch of the subject Her Majesty's Government desire to guard against an error that might be caused by the map attached to Mr. Bancroft's Memorial, (which may be taken as a sample of the most modern maps.) This map represents a state of geographical and hydrographical knowledge very different from that which existed at the date of the Treaty. In one respect this consideration is of great importance. The islands shown on this map, forming a chain along the eastern coast of Vancouver's Island, named Galiano Island, Mayne Island, Samuel Island, and Saturna Island, were at the date of the Treaty supposed by both Contracting Parties to be parts of Vancouver's Island. A comparison of maps of the date of the Treaty with maps of the present day will show this conclusively. Her Majesty's Government adopt the words of Mr. Archibald Campbell:

> None of the maps extant at that day [the date of the Treaty] present a perfectly correct idea of the space between the continent and Vancouver's Island, at, and immediately south of, the forty-ninth parallel. The Straits of Fuca and the Archipelago east of the Canal de Haro are fairly enough represented; but between the Haro Archipelago and the forty-ninth parallel the space is inaccurately represented as free from islands, and, consequently, with but a single channel between the continent and Vancouver's Island. The surveys made subsequently to the conclusion of the Treaty show that what was laid down by the early Spanish navigators, by Vancouver and by Wilkes, as the eastern coast of Vancouver's Island, is, in fact, the coast of an extensive archipelago skirting the shore of the main island between latitude 48° 47′ and 49° 10′.

Now, Her Majesty's Government submit it to the Arbitrator as a clear proposition that the Treaty is to be interpreted according to the com-

[19] mon knowledge and under*standing of the Contracting Parties at the time.[1] Therefore, in prolonging the forty-ninth parallel to the middle of the channel between the Continent and Vancouver's Island, and in drawing the mid-channel line southerly therefrom to Fuca's Straits, the Arbitrator will have to consider the channel, at and immediately to the southward of the forty-ninth parallel, as bounded on the west, not by the eastern coast of Vancouver's Island, as now ascertained, but by the broken line of coast, which is, in fact, formed by the eastern shores of Galiano Island and the other islands of that chain.

35. With reference to maps, another distinction requires notice. The map spoken of as Wilkes's map of the Oregon Territory (an extract of which is Mr. Bancroft's map F) is merely a map, in the ordinary sense, and is not a chart with soundings marked or otherwise adapted for purposes of navigation.[2]

36. Mr. Bancroft speaks (page 28) of the place of a particular name "*on every map used by the negotiators.*" Who are meant by the negotiators does not appear. In the ordinary sense, the negotiators were Mr. Pakenham and Mr. Buchanan. There is no evidence known to Her Majesty's Government of any particular map, or of any map, having been used for the purposes of the negotiations which issued immediately in the Treaty. There was a map before Mr. Everett and Lord Aberdeen in one of their conversations,[3] but what map does not appear. Mr. MacLane, it would seem, used Wilkes's map,[4] but there is no evidence that he and Lord Aberdeen together referred to that or any other map. As regards Lord Aberdeen himself, he probably used Vancouver's chart, but it would rather seem that he did not give much attention to a map in the matter. In his instructions to Mr. Pakenham,[5] he makes a slip in using the name of King George's Sound, an obsolete name for Nootka Sound, instead of the Gulf of Georgia;[6] and, in his statement to Lord John Russell in 1859,[7] he says it was the intention of the Treaty to adopt the mid-channel of the straits as the line of demarkation without any reference to islands, the position, and, indeed, the very existence of which (he adds) had hardly at that time been accurately ascertained.

---

[1] Mr. Bancroft says, (page 5:) "Since the intention of the negotiators must rest on the knowledge in their possession at the time when the Treaty was made, I shall use the charts and explorations which have advanced, or profess to have advanced, our knowledge of the country in question, and which are anterior to that date."

[2] There was no chart issued with the Narrative of the United States Exploring Expedition, under Lieutenant Wilkes, as part of the atlas connected with it, or otherwise. Indeed, no chart, showing the surveys of that Expedition in the Oregon region, appears to have been published up to the time of the correspondence between Mr. Bancroft and Lord Palmerston in July to November, 1848, Appendix No. 4.

[3] Above, paragraph 19, (viii.)

[4] Above, paragraph 19, (ii.)

[5] Historical Note, p. xii.

[6] Mr. Archibald Campbell remarks on this point: "Lord Aberdeen, in tracing the boundary line, follows the forty-ninth parallel to the sea-coast and deflects 'thence in a southerly direction through the center of *King George's Sound* and the Straits of Fuca to the ocean.' On either of the accompanying tracings, and indeed upon any map of the northwest coast, we may look in vain for 'King George's Sound' between the Continent and Vancouver's Island. This mistake is not so readily accounted for as Mr. MacLane's in regard to Birch Bay, as the name is nowhere to be found on Vancouver's chart, which is said to have been used by the British Government in reference to the water boundary. 'King George's Sound' is the name that was given in 1778, by Captain Cook, to Nootka Sound, on the western coast of Vancouver's Island, between latitude 49° and 50°. The name was never much in vogue, except to distinguish a mercantile association formed soon after the discovery of Nootka, called the 'King George's Sound Company.' There is, however, no need of conjecture as to Lord Aberdeen's actual meaning. He simply miscalled the Gulf of Georgia."

[7] Appendix No. 1.

37. Finally, it should be noted that the fact that the Canal de Haro has long borne a proper name on the maps is no evidence of the
[20] superiority of that passage for purposes *of navigation. It would
seem to have been accidentally distinguished by a name, before and at the date of the treaty, from the circumstance that it obtained a name (Canal de Lopez de Haro) on the Spanish map of Quimper's observations of the Straits of Fuca in 1790.[1] But it was little known, except by name, at the date of the Treaty, and for some time after.

38. Her Majesty's Government have now finished their examination of Mr. Bancroft's Memorial. They do not trouble the Arbitrator with any remarks on such parts of it as refer to the Lecture or Pamphlet of Mr. Sturgis, the observations of Mr. Bates, the articles in the Quarterly Review and the Examiner, and other matters which seem to them to have little (if any) bearing on the question to be decided. The interpretation of the Treaty cannot be affected by the public discussions which preceded it, nor can any amount of unofficial declarations as to what ought to be done be evidence of what the Governments of the two countries intended by the Treaty to do.

39. Nor have Her Majesty's Government thought it necessary to examine in detail the passage in the Memorial (page 23) which is headed "Plea for the integrity of Sir Robert Peel's Ministry," or the corresponding passage (page 31) which forms the concluding paragraph of the Memorial. Her Majesty's Government see no necessity for any such plea, and no ground for the suggestions in the passage last referred to. The characters of Sir Robert Peel and Lord Aberdeen place them beyond suspicion of having acted with insincerity or duplicity in any part of this transaction. Moreover, the frankness with which Lord Aberdeen communicated to Mr. MacLane the project of Treaty, in which no mention is made of the Canal de Haro as the channel through which the boundary should run, sufficiently shows that Mr. MacLane had no sure ground for his surmise that the Canal de Haro was contemplated by Lord Aberdeen as the boundary channel, or, at all events, was so at the time when Lord Aberdeen framed the project of Treaty.

40. The Arbitrator will not fail to observe that the explanation given in this Statement of the mention by Mr. MacLane and Mr. Benton of the Canal de Haro, far from involving any dishonoring imputation, is entirely consistent with the view, which Her Majesty's Government sincerely entertain, that Mr. MacLane, and all those who in any degree represented the United States on the occasion of the Treaty, acted with perfect good faith. Mr. MacLane, it seems almost certain, misled himself by a misapplication of Wilkes's map, and Mr. Benton was misled either by Mr. MacLane's letter, or by a misapplication of his own geographical knowledge, or by both.

41. Her Majesty's Government then submit to His Majesty the Arbitrator, on the whole case, that, whether he looks at the general position of the two nations with reference to their claims to the Oregon
[21] district, or at the circumstances attending the *particular transac-
tion which issued in the Treaty, or at the language of the Treaty, he will be led to adopt the conclusions of Her Majesty's Government.

---

[1] A copy of this map was not in the possession of Her Majesty's Government at the time of the preparation of their Case presented to the Arbitrator in December, 1871. The map, which seems to be the result of mere eye-sketches, is of small value in itself. It describes itself as made by Quimper's "primer piloto," (first mate, or master,) Don Gonzalo Lopez de Haro. This fact may account for the prominence given to the channel bearing the name of Haro. But little more than the southern mouth of the channel is shown. The southern entrance of Rosario Straits is indistinctly shown as Boca de Fidalgo.

42. His Majesty the Arbitrator has been pleased to take on himself to ascertain the channel of the Treaty, on the failure of the Commissioners appointed by the two Governments to agree. In the execution of this task, he has to look at the state of things as they existed at the time of the Treaty. He has to determine through which of the two channels, the Rosario Straits or the Canal de Haro, the line ought to have been drawn by Commissioners appointed for the purpose the day after the exchange of the ratifications.

43. The considerations, connected with the hydrography of the region and with the history and existing conditions of the navigation of its waters, on which, as Her Majesty's Government submit, this determination cannot fail to be in accordance with their conclusions, are fully set forth in the Case presented by them to the Arbitrator in December, 1871. The channel of the Treaty is that one of the two channels in question which was the main navigable channel, as known and used at the date of the Treaty. That channel is the Rosario Straits.

HISTORICAL NOTE.—1818 TO 1846.[1]

1818.

In 1818 an agreement was come to between the Government of His Britannic Majesty and that of the United States respecting the boundary line between the British and United States territories in Northwestern America.

It was agreed in substance that for the space extending from the Lake of the Woods westward to the Rocky (then called the Stony) Mountains, the boundary line should be the forty-ninth parallel of north latitude.

With respect to any country that might be claimed by either party on the northwest coast, westward of the Rocky Mountains, it was agreed that for ten years the same, with its harbors and the navigation of its rivers, should be free and open to the vessels, citizens, and subjects of the two Powers; with a proviso that the agreement was not to prejudice any claim which either party might have to any part of that country.

This agreement was embodied in a Treaty made at London, 20th October, 1818.

The district between the Rocky Mountains and the Pacific, or part of it, came to be known as Oregon or the Oregon Territory or district, the name being taken from the Oregon River, now usually called the Columbia.

The northern boundary of this district, as it was in question between the two Governments, was the parallel of 54° 40′ north latitude, being the southern boundary of the Russian territory, as recognized by Treaty. The southern boundary was the parallel of 42° north latitude, being the northern boundary of the Spanish territory, as recognized by Treaty.

The British Plenipotentiaries who negotiated the Treaty of 1818 acceded to the arrangement relating to the country west of the Rocky Mountains in the hope that by thus leaving that country open to the trade of both nations, they substantially secured every present advantage, while removing all prospect of immediate collision, without precluding any further discussion for a definite settlement. In their judgment the American Plenipotentiaries were not authorized to admit any territorial claim of Great Britain in that quarter to the southward of the Straits of Fuca, although they would have consented to leave those straits and the waters connected with them in the possession of Great Britain.

1824.

In 1824 negotiations were resumed for the settlement of questions between the two nations, including the question of the boundary west of the Rocky Mountains.

The British Plenipotentiaries contended for the right of British subjects to make settlements in the disputed territory, a right which they

[1] Referred to in the Statement, page 2, par. 3.

maintained was derived not only from discovery, but also from use,
[ii] occupancy, and settlement. They proposed that Article III *of
the Treaty of London of 1818 should cease to have effect, and that the boundary line west of the Rocky Mountains should be drawn due west to the point where the forty-ninth parallel strikes the great north-easternmost branch of the Oregon or Columbia River, marked on the maps as McGillivray's River, thence down along the middle of that river, and down along the middle of the Oregon or Columbia to its junction with the Pacific Ocean.

The proposal of the United States Plenipotentiaries was to the effect that the term of ten years limited in Article III of the Treaty of 1818 should be extended to ten years from the date of a new Treaty, but that the rights of settlement and other rights should be restricted during the new term, so that the citizens of the United States should form no settlements to the north of the forty-ninth parallel, and that British subjects should form no settlements to the south of that parallel, or to the north of the fifty-fourth.

Terms were not agreed on, and the Conference came to an end in July, 1824.

1826, 1827.

In November, 1826, negotiations were again resumed.

The United States proposal was, that if the forty-ninth parallel should be found to intersect the Oregon or McGillivray's River at a navigable point, the whole course of that river thence to the ocean should be made perpetually free to British vessels and subjects.

The British Plenipotentiaries were authorized to offer that if the United States would consent to the Columbia being the southern British frontier, the United States should have the harbor in De Fuca Strait, called by Vancouver Port Discovery, with land five miles in breadth encircling it.

Should this offer not fully satisfy the United States, the British Plenipotentiaries were then authorized to extend the proposition, so as to include the cession by Great Britain to the United States of the whole peninsula comprised within lines described by the Pacific to the west, De Fuca's Inlet to the north, Hood's Canal (so called in Vancouver's charts) to the east, and a line drawn from the southern point of Hood's Canal to a point ten miles south of Gray's Harbor to the south, by which arrangement the United States would possess that peninsula in exclusive sovereignty, and would divide the possession of Admiralty Inlet with Great Britain, the entrance being free to both parties.

The negotiations ended in a Convention dated 6th August, 1827. This Convention continued Article III of the Treaty of 1818 indefinitely, but with power to either party to put an end to it on twelve months' notice, (after 20th October, 1828.)

The Convention also contained a saving for the claims of either party to any part of the country west of the Rocky Mountains.

1827–1842.

Negotiations on the Oregon question remained in abeyance until the special mission of Lord Ashburton to the United States in 1842, when he received the following instructions on this subject:

Your lordship may, therefore, propose to the Government of the United States, as a fair and equitable adjustment of their[the two Governments] respective claims, a line

> of boundary commencing at the mouth of the Columbia River; thence by a line drawn along the middle of that river to its point of confluence with the Great Snake River; thence by a line carried due east of the Rocky or Stony Mountains; and thence by a line drawn in a northerly direction along the said mountains until it strikes the forty-ninth parallel of north latitude. The southern bank of the Columbia River would
> [iii] thus be *left to the Americans and the northern bank to the English, the naviga-
> tion of the river being free to both, it being understood that neither party should form any new settlement within the limits assigned to each on the north or south side of the river respectively.
>
> Should your lordship find it impracticable to obtain the line of boundary above described, Her Majesty's Government would not refuse their assent to a line of boundary commencing at the Rocky or Stony Mountains at the point where the forty-ninth parallel of north latitude strikes those mountains; thence along that parallel to the point where it strikes the great northeasternmost branch of the Columbia River, marked in the map as McGillivray's River; thence down the middle of that river and down the middle of the Columbia River to its junction with the ocean. But your lordship will reject the proposal formerly made by the American Government, in case it should be repeated, of following the forty-ninth parallel of latitude from the Rocky Mountains to the Ocean, as the boundary of the territory of the two States.
>
> If the Government of the United States should refuse the proposed compromise, and should nevertheless determine to annul the Convention of 1827, the rights of the British Government to the whole of the territory in dispute must be considered as unimpaired.

This mission resulted in the Treaty of Washington of 9th August, 1842, which contained no arrangement respecting Oregon. The main reason that induced Lord Ashburton to abstain from proposing to carry on the discussion on this subject was the apprehension that thereby the settlement of the far more important matter of the Northeastern boundary might be impeded or exposed to the hazard of failure.

1843.

In August, 1843, Mr. Fox, Her Majesty's Minister at Washington, was asked whether the United States Government were taking any steps in furtherance of the Oregon Boundary negotiation, and to state that Her Majesty's Government were willing to transfer the negotiation to Washington should the United States Government object to London.

In October instructions were sent to Mr. Everett, the United States Minister in London, to treat with Her Majesty's Government for the adjustment of the Boundary. In the mean time Mr. Pakenham had been appointed Her Majesty's Minister to the United States in succession to Mr. Fox. Before his appointment had been gazetted, Mr. Everett informed Lord Aberdeen orally that he had received powers to negotiate the Oregon question in London. Lord Aberdeen, however, stated to him that a new Minister had already been appointed by Her Majesty to negotiate at Washington.

In consequence of this arrangement the negotiations were removed to Washington, and Mr. Everett stated in a dispatch to his Government[1] that he would use his best efforts to produce such an impression on Lord Aberdeen's mind as to the prominent points of the question as might have a favorable influence in the preparation of the instructions to be given to Mr. Pakenham.

In an interview with Lord Aberdeen, Mr. Everett urged that the boundary should be carried along the forty-ninth parallel to the sea. Lord Aberdeen said that this proposal had been made in 1824 and 1826, and rejected, and that there was no reason for believing that this country, more than the United States, would then agree to terms which had been previcusly declined, and that consequently there must be conces-

[1] Appendix No. 19 to Mr. Bancroft's Memorial.

sion on both sides, on which principle Lord Aberdeen expressed himself willing to act.

In December Mr. Pakenham was authorized to re-open negotiations at Washington on the Oregon question. He was directed to make substantially the same proposals for the settlement of the boundary as had been made by Great Britain in 1826.

He was authorized to add, should that proposition be found to
[iv] be unacceptable, that *Her Majesty's Government would be willing
to convert into a free port any harbor, either on the main-land or on Vancouver's Island, south of the forty-ninth parallel, which the United States Government might desire.

Further, if he should think that the extension of the privilege would lead to the final adjustment of the question, he was authorized to declare that Her Majesty's Government would be willing to make all the ports within De Fuca's Inlct, and south of the forty-ninth parallel, free ports.

Should these proposals be rejected, he was then to propose that the whole question should be referred to the arbitration of a friendly Sovereign State.

In the event of the United States Government refusing to agree to arbitration, he was then to propose that the Treaty of 1818–27 should be renewed for a further period of ten years.

In the event of negotiations being broken off, he was then to declare to the United States Government that Her Majesty's Government still asserted and would maintain an equal right with the United States to the occupation of the whole of the territory in dispute, and that as Her Majesty's Government would carefully and scrupulously abstain and cause Her Majesty's subjects to abstain from any act which might be justly considered as an encroachment on the rights of the United States, so they expected that the Government of the United States would exhibit and enforce on their part an equal forbearance with respect to the rights of Great Britain, which rights, believing them to be just, Great Britain would be prepared to defend.

1844.

In February, 1844, Mr. Pakenham addressed a note to the United States Secretary of State proposing a renewal of the negotiations, which proposal was favorably received by him.

On 22nd August, Mr. Pakenham received a notification from Mr. Calhoun, then the Secretary of State, that he was prepared to proceed with the negotiation.

At a conference on the 26th, Mr. Pakenham laid before Mr. Calhoun the proposal authorized by his instructions relative to a free port either on the main-land or on Vancouver's Island south of the forty-ninth parallel.

This proposal was declined by Mr. Calhoun. He afterwards presented a paper (dated September 3) stating his reasons. The paper began thus:

> The Undersigned American Plenipotentiary declines the proposal of the British Plenipotentiary, on the ground that it would have the effect of restricting the possessions of the United States to limits far more circumscribed than their claims clearly entitle them to. It proposes to limit their northern boundary by a line drawn from the Rocky Mountains along the forty-ninth parallel of latitude to the northeasternmost branch of the Columbia River, and thence down the middle of that river to the sea, giving to Great Britain all the country north, and to the United States all south of that line, except a detached territory extending on the Pacific and the Straits of

Fuca, from Bullfinch's Harbor to Hood's Canal. To which it is proposed in addition to make free to the United States any port which the United States Government might desire, either on the main-land or on Vancouver's Island south of latitude 49°.

By turning to the map hereto annexed, and on which the proposed boundary is marked in pencil, it will be seen that it assigns to Great Britain almost the entire region on its north side drained by the Columbia River, and lying on its northern bank. It is not deemed necessary to state at large the claims of the United States to this territory, and the grounds on which they rest, in order to make good the assertion that it restricts the possessions of the United States within narrower bounds than they are clearly entitled to. It will be sufficient for this purpose to show that they are fairly entitled to the entire region drained by the river; and to the establishment of this point, the Undersigned proposes accordingly to limit his remarks at present.

The paper proceeded with arguments, and ended thus:

[v] *Such are our claims to that portion of the territory, and the grounds on which they rest. The Undersigned believes them to be well founded, and trusts that the British Plenipotentiary will see in them sufficient reasons why he should decline his proposal.

The Undersigned Plenipotentiary abstains, for the present, from presenting the claims which the United States may have to other portions of the territory.

The Undersigned, &c.

In answer to this statement, Mr. Pakenham delivered a paper (marked D, and dated September 12) of which it is sufficient for the present purpose to state the concluding passages:

In fine, the present state of the question between the two Governments appears to be this: Great Britain possesses and exercises, in common with the United States, a right of joint occupancy in the Oregon Territory, of which right she can be divested, with respect to any part of that territory, only by an equitable partition of the whole between the two Powers.

It is, for obvious reasons, desirable that such a partition should take place as soon as possible, and the difficulty appears to be in devising a line of demarkation which shall leave to each party that precise portion of the territory best suited to its interest and convenience.

The British Government entertained the hope that by the proposal lately submitted for the consideration of the American Government, that object would have been accomplished. According to the arrangements therein contemplated, the Northern Boundary of the United States west of the Rocky Mountains would, for a considerable distance, be carried along the same parallel of latitude which forms their Northern boundary on the eastern side of those mountains, thus uniting the present Eastern Boundary of the Oregon Territory with the Western Boundary of the United States, from the forty-ninth parallel downwards. From the point where the 49° of latitude intersects the northeastern branch of the Columbia River, called in that part of its course McGillivray's River, the proposed line of boundary would be along the middle of that river till it joins the Columbia, then along the middle of the Columbia to the ocean, the navigation of the river remaining perpetually free to both parties.

In addition Great Britain offers a separate territory on the Pacific, possessing an excellent harbor, with a further understanding that any port or ports, whether on Vancouver's Island or on the Continent, south of the forty-ninth parallel, to which the United States might desire to have access, shall be made free ports.

It is believed that by this arrangement, ample justice would be done to the claims of the United States, on whatever ground advanced, with relation to the Oregon Territory. As regards extent of territory, they would obtain, acre for acre, nearly half of the entire territory to be divided. As relates to the navigation of the principal river, they would enjoy a perfect equality of right with Great Britain; and, with respect to harbors, it will be seen that Great Britain shows every disposition to consult their convenience in that particular.

On the other hand, were Great Britain to abandon the line of the Columbia as a frontier, and to surrender her right to the navigation of that river, the prejudice occasioned to her by such an arrangement would, beyond all proportion, exceed the advantage accruing to the United States from the possession of a few more square miles of territory. It must be obvious to every impartial investigator of the subject that, in adhering to the line of the Columbia, Great Britain is not influenced by motives of ambition with reference to extent of territory, but by considerations of utility, not to say necessity, which cannot be lost sight of, and for which allowance ought to be made in an arrangement professing to be based on considerations of mutual convenience and advantage.

The Undersigned believes that he has now noticed all the arguments advanced by the American Plenipotentiary in order to show that the United States are fairly entitled to the entire region drained by the Columbia River. He sincerely regrets that their views on this subject should differ in so many essential respects.

It remains for him to request that, as the American Plenipotentiary declines the proposal offered on the part of Great Britain, he will have the goodness to state what arrangement he is on the part of the United States prepared to propose for an equitable adjustment of the question ; and more especially, that he will have the goodness to define the nature and extent of the claims which the United States may have to other portions of the territory, to which allusion is made in the concluding part of his statement, as it is obvious that no arrangement can be made with respect to part of the territory in dispute, while a claim is reserved to any portion of the remainder.

The Undersigned, &c.

[vi] *Mr. Calhoun then presented a paper, (dated September 20,) in which he said he had read with attention the counter-statement of the British Plenipotentiary, but without weakening his confidence in the validity of the title of the United States, and, after arguments, concluded thus:

The Undersigned cannot consent to the conclusion to which, on a review of the whole ground, the counter-statement arrives, that the present state of the question is, that Great Britain possesses and exercises, in common with the United States, a right of joint occupancy in the Oregon Territory, of which she can be divested only by an equitable partition of the whole between the two Powers. He claims, and he thinks he has shown, a clear title on the part of the United States to the whole region drained by the Columbia, with the right of being reinstated and considered the party in possession while treating of the title, in which character he must insist on their being considered in conformity with positive Treaty stipulations. He cannot, therefore, consent that they shall be regarded, during the negotiation, merely as occupants in common with Great Britain, nor can he, while thus regarding their rights, present a counter-proposal based on the supposition of a joint occupancy, merely until the question of title to the territory is fully discussed. It is, in his opinion, only after a discussion which shall fully present the titles of the parties respectively to the territory, that their claims to it can be fairly and satisfactorily adjusted. The United States desire only what they may deem themselves justly entitled to, and are unwilling to take less. With their present opinion of their title, the British Plenipotentiary must see that the proposal which he made at the second Conference, and which he more fully sets forth in his counter-statement, falls far short of what they believe themselves justly entitled to.

In reply to the request of the British Plenipotentiary that the Undersigned should define the nature and extent of the claims which the United States have to the other portions of the territory, and to which allusion is made in the concluding part of Statement A, he has the honor to inform him in general terms that they are derived from Spain by the Florida Treaty, and are founded on the discoveries and explorations of her navigators, and which they must regard as giving them a right to the extent to which they can be established, unless a better can be opposed.

In various informal conversations between Mr. Pakenham and Mr. Calhoun, when Mr. Calhoun insisted on the parallel of 49° as the very lowest terms which the United States would accept, Mr. Pakenham told him that, if he wished Her Majesty's Government even to take into consideration a proposal founded on that basis, it must be accompanied by some indications of a desire on the part of the United States Government to make some corresponding sacrifice to accommodate the interest and convenience of Great Britain; that Her Majesty's Government had already gone very far in the way of concession, while the United States Government had as yet shown no disposition to recede from their original proposal. To which Mr. Calhoun replied, on one occasion, that for his part he should have no objection to give up absolutely the free navigation of the Columbia, which had before been offered only conditionally; on another occasion, he said that if Great Britain would consent to the parallel of 49° on the Continent, perhaps the United States might be willing to leave to Great Britain the entire possession of Vancouver's Island, Fuca's Inlet, and the passage northwards from it to the Pacific remaining an open sea to both countries; but he never said that he would be ready to yield both these points. In fact, he said that he was not authorized to make any proposal of the kind, nor should he until he had ascertained that such an arrangement would find favor with the Senate.

1845.

In January, 1845, in answer to a proposal, made by Mr. Pakenham, to submit the question to arbitration, Mr. Calhoun said that, while the President united with Her Majesty's Government in the desire to see the question settled as early as might be practicable, he could not accede to the offer; adding this:

[vii] *Waiving all other reasons for declining it, it is sufficient to state, that he continues to entertain the hope that the question may be settled by the negotiation now pending between the two countries; and that he is of opinion it would be unadvisable to entertain a proposal to resort to any other mode, so long as there is hope of arriving at a satisfactory settlement by negotiation; and especially to one which might rather retard than expedite its final adjustment.

On the 3d of April, Lord Aberdeen addressed to Mr. Pakenham the following dispatch, the tone and contents of which show the seriousness of the position in which the controversy then was, and the determination of Her Majesty's Government to maintain their claims:

APRIL 3, 1845.

SIR: The inaugural speech of President Polk has impressed a very serious character on our actual relations with the United States; and the manner in which he has referred to the Oregon question, so different from the language of his predecessor, leaves little reason to hope for any favorable result of the existing negotiation.

I presume that you will have acted upon my instruction of the 3d of March, and have repeated to the new Secretary of State the proposal of an arbitration, which you were directed to make to his predecessor. If this should be declined by Mr. Polk's Government in the same manner and for the same reason as assigned by Mr. Tyler, namely, the hope that the matter might yet be favorably terminated by negotiation, such a mode of refusal would at least display a friendly spirit, and would not close the door against all further attempts to arrive at such a conclusion. On the other hand, if the proposal should be simply rejected, and the rejection should not be accompanied by any specific proposition on the part of the Government of the United States, we must consider the negotiation as entirely at an end. Indeed, we could scarcely, under such circumstances, take any further step with a due regard to our honor and consistency.

In the event of arbitration being rejected, and the failure of every endeavor to effect a partition of the territory on a principle of mutual concession, you were directed, in my dispatch of the 18th of November, to propose the further extension for a fixed term of years of the existing Convention. This, it is true, would have been an imperfect and unsatisfactory arrangement; but it might have been tolerated in the hope that the prevalence of friendly feelings, and the admitted interest of both parties, would in due time have led to a permanent settlement of an amicable description. The recent declarations of Mr. Polk forbid any such hope; and there is too much reason to believe that the extension of the Convention for a fixed period would be employed in active preparation for future hostility.

You will, therefore, consider this portion of my instructions, to which I have now referred, as canceled.

Judging from the language of Mr. Polk, I presume we must expect that the American Government will renounce the Treaty without delay. In this case, unless the question be speedily settled, a local collision will be liable to take place, which may involve the countries in serious difficulty, and not improbably lead to war itself.

At all events, whatever may be the course of the United States Government, the time is come when we must be prepared for every contingency. Our naval force in the Pacific is amply sufficient to maintain our supremacy in that sea; and Sir George Seymour has been instructed to repair without delay to the coasts of the Oregon Territory.

You will hold a temperate, but firm, language to the members of the Government and to all those with whom you may converse. We are still ready to adhere to the principle of an equitable compromise; but we are perfectly determined to concede nothing to force or menace, and are fully prepared to maintain our rights. This is the spirit in which Her Majesty's Government have declared themselves in Parliament, and to this they will adhere.

I thought it so important that our intentions should be clearly known and understood in the United States without delay, that I detained the last American mail, in order that a correct report of the proceedings in Parliament on the Oregon question might reach Washington as early as possible.

Nothing can be more encouraging and satisfactory than the spirit which has been exhibited on this occasion, both in Parliament and in the country generally; and it is evident that Her Majesty's Government will be warmly supported in whatever measures may be considered really just and necessary.

I am, &c.,

ABERDEEN.

[viii] *Before this dispatch reached Mr. Pakenham, Mr. Buchanan had been appointed Mr. Calhoun's successor in the office of Secretary of State. Mr. Pakenham informed Mr. Buchanan of the instructions which he had received, again to press on the Government of the United States the expediency of arbitration. But Mr. Buchanan said on one occasion that he did not despair of effecting a settlement by negotiation, by adopting (to use his own words) the principle of giving and taking; and on another occasion that settlement by arbitration did not meet with the concurrence of the President and his Cabinet, that they all entertained objections to that course of proceeding, and that they preferred negotiation, hoping, as they did hope, that by negotiation a satisfactory result would at last be attained.

On the 16th July, Mr. Buchanan delivered to Mr. Pakenham a paper (marked J. B.) containing his proposal for settlement. It began thus:

The Undersigned, &c., now proceeds to resume the negotiation on the Oregon question at the point where it was left by his predecessor.

The British Plenipotentiary, in his note to Mr. Calhoun of the 12th September last, requests "that as the American Plenipotentiary declines the proposal offered on the part of Great Britain, he will have the goodness to state what arrangement he is, on the part of the United States, prepared to propose for an equitable adjustment of the question, and more especially that he will have the goodness to define the nature and extent of the claims which the United States may have to other portions of the territory to which allusion is made in the concluding part of his statement, as it is obvious that no arrangement can be made with respect to a part of the territory in dispute, while a claim is reserved to any portion of the remainder."

The Secretary of State will now proceed (reversing the order in which these requests have been made,) in the first place, to present the title of the United States to the territory north of the valley of the Columbia; and will then propose on the part of the President the terms upon which, in his opinion, this long-pending controversy may be justly and equitably terminated between the parties.

The paper (after a lengthened argument) ended thus:

Such being the opinion of the President in regard to the title of the United States, he would not have consented to yield any portion of the Oregon Territory, had he not found himself embarrassed, if not committed, by the acts of his predecessors. They had uniformly proceeded upon the principle of compromise in all their negotiations. Indeed, the first question presented to him, after entering upon the duties of his office was, whether he should abruptly terminate the negotiation which had been commenced and conducted between Mr. Calhoun and Mr. Pakenham on the principle avowed in the first Protocol, not of contending for the whole territory in dispute, but of treating of the respective claims of the Parties, "with the view to establish a permanent boundary between the two countries, westward of the Rocky Mountains."

In view of these facts, the President has determined to pursue the present negotiation to its conclusion, upon the principle of compromise in which it commenced, and to make one more effort to adjust this long-pending controversy. In this determination he trusts that the British Government will recognize his sincere and anxious desire to cultivate the most friendly relations between the two countries, and to manifest to the world that he is actuated by a spirit of moderation. He has, therefore, instructed the Undersigned again to propose to the Government of Great Britain that the Oregon Territory shall be divided between the two countries by the forty-ninth parallel of north latitude from the Rocky Mountains to the Pacific Ocean; offering, at the same time, to make free to Great Britain any port or ports on Vancouver's Island, south of this parallel, which the British Government may desire. He trusts that Great Britain may receive this proposition in the friendly spirit in which it was dictated, and that it may prove the stable foundation of lasting peace and harmony between the two countries. The line proposed will carry out the principle of continuity equally for both parties, by extending the limits both of ancient Louisiana and Canada to the Pacific, along the same parallel of latitude which divides them east of the Rock Mountains, and it will secure to each a sufficient number of commodious harbors on the northwest coast of America.

The Undersigned, &c.

Thereupon, Mr. Pakenham presented a paper, dated 29th July, beginning thus:

[ix] *Notwithstanding the prolix discussion which the subject has already undergone, the Undersigned, &c., feels obliged to place on record a few observations in reply to the statement marked J. B., which he had the honor to receive on the 16th of this month from the hands of the Secretary of State of the United States, terminating with a proposition on the part of the United States for the settlement of the Oregon question.

Mr. Pakenham ended this paper as follows:

After this exposition of the views entertained by the British Government, respecting the relative value and importance of the British and American claims, the American Plenipotentiary will not be surprised to hear that the Undersigned does not feel at liberty to accept the proposal offered by the American Plenipotentiary for the settlement of the question.

This proposal, in fact, offers less than that tendered by the American Plenipotentiaries in the Negotiation of 1826, and declined by the British Government.

On that occasion it was proposed that the navigation of the Columbia should be made free to both parties. On this point nothing is said in the proposal to which the Undersigned has now the honor to reply; while with respect to the proposed freedom of the ports on Vancouver's Island, south of latitude 49°, the facts which have been appealed to in this paper, as giving to Great Britain the strongest claim to the possession of the whole island, would seem to deprive such proposal of any value.

The Undersigned therefore trusts that the American Plenipotentiary will be prepared to offer some further proposal for the settlement of the Oregon question more consistent with fairness and equity, and with the reasonable expectations of the British Government, as defined in the statement marked D, which the Undersigned had the honor to present to the American Plenipotentiary at the early part of the present negotiation.

The Undersigned, &c.

Mr. Pakenham had thus declined to accept the proposal of the United States Government. Mr. Buchanan thereupon delivered another paper, dated 30th August, in which, after further arguments, he withdrew that proposal. The concluding passages of this paper were as follows:

Upon the whole, from the most careful and ample examination which the Undersigned has been able to bestow upon the subject, he is satisfied that the Spanish-American title now held by the United States, embracing the whole territory between the parallel of 42° and 54° 40′, is the best in existence to this entire region, and that the claim of Great Britain to any portion of it has no sufficient foundation.

Notwithstanding that such was, and still is, the opinion of the President, yet, in the spirit of compromise and concession, and in deference to the action of his predecessors, the Undersigned, in obedience to his instructions, proposed to the British Plenipotentiary to settle the controversy by dividing the territory in dispute by the forty-ninth parallel of latitude, offering, at the same time, to make free to Great Britain any port or ports on Vancouver's Island, south of this latitude, which the British Government might desire. The British Plenipotentiary has correctly suggested that the free navigation of the Columbia River was not embraced in this proposal to Great Britain, but, on the other hand, the use of free ports on the southern extremity of this island had not been included in former offers.

Such a proposition as that which has been made, never would have been authorized by the President, had this been a new question.

Upon his accession to office he found the present negotiation pending. It had been instituted in the spirit and upon the principle of compromise. Its object was, as avowed by the negotiators, not to demand the whole territory in dispute for either country; but, in the language of the first Protocol, "to treat of the respective claims of the two countries to the Oregon Territory, with a view to establish a permanent boundary between them, westward of the Rocky Mountains to the Pacific Ocean."

Placed in this position, and considering that Presidents Monroe and Adams had, on former occasions, offered to divide the territory in dispute by extending the forty-ninth parallel of latitude to the Pacific Ocean, he felt it to be his duty not abruptly to arrest the negotiation, but so far to yield his own opinion as once more to make a similar offer.

Not only respect for the conduct of his predecessors, but a sincere and anxious desire to promote peace and harmony between the two countries influenced him to pursue this course. The Oregon question presents the only cloud which intercepts the prospect of a long career of mutual friendship and beneficial commerce between the two nations, and this cloud he desired to remove.

[x] *These are the reasons which actuated the President to offer a proposition so liberal to Great Britain.

And how has the proposition been received by the British Plenipotentiary? It has been rejected without even a reference to his own Government. Nay, more, the British Plenipotentiary, to use his own language, "trusts that the American Plenipotentiary will be prepared to offer some further proposal for the settlement of the Oregon question more consistent with fairness and equity, and with the reasonable expectations of the British Government."

Under such circumstances the Undersigned is instructed by the President to say that he owes it to his own country, and a just appreciation of her title to the Oregon Territory, to withdraw this proposition to the British Government which had been made under his direction, and it is hereby accordingly withdrawn.

In taking this necessary step, the President still cherishes the hope that this long-pending controversy may yet be finally adjusted in such a manner as not to disturb the peace or interrupt the harmony now so happily subsisting between the two countries.

The Undersigned, &c.

1846.

On 9th February, 1846, the House of Representatives, and on 17th April the Senate, of the United States passed a joint resolution authorizing the President to give the requisite year's notice to put an end to the Convention of 1827. The notice was dated the 28th of April; it reached the United States Minister at London on the 15th of May, and was by him sent to Lord Aberdeen on the 20th.

Meantime, on the 18th of May, Lord Aberdeen addressed the following instructions to Mr. Pakenham:

No. 18.] MAY 18, 1846.

SIR: In the critical state of the negotiation for the settlement of the Oregon Boundary, it has become my duty carefully to review the whole course of our proceedings, and to consider what further steps in the present juncture it may be proper to take with the view of removing existing difficulties, and of promoting, if possible, an amicable termination of the question.

I willingly abstain from renewing a discussion, the matter for which is already exhausted, and from repeating arguments with which you have long been familiar; but I think it is not too much to assert that, to any observer looking impartially at the different stages of this negotiation, it will appear that the conduct of Great Britain has throughout been moderate, conciliatory, and just. Can it truly be said that the Government of the United States have advanced to meet us in the path of mutual concession?

The terms of the settlement proposed by the British Plenipotentiaries to Mr. Gallatin in the year 1826, were much more advantageous to the United States than those which had been offered to Mr. Rush in the previous negotiation of 1824; and on your own departure from this country you were authorized still further to augment these advantageous conditions. The United States, on the other hand, have not only recently made, through Mr. Buchanan, a proposal less favorable to Great Britain than that formerly offered by Mr. Gallatin, but, when this was rejected by you, they withdrew it altogether.

In truth, the pretensions of the United States have gradually increased during the progress of these negotiations. Acting in manifest violation of the spirit of the Conventions of 1818 and 1827, it is now formally and officially asserted that the right of the United States to the whole territory in dispute is "clear and unquestionable." The principle, however, of these Conventions plainly recognized the claims of both parties, as indeed was fully admitted by the American Plenipotentiary himself; and it was only on failure of the attempt to effect an equitable partition of the territory that the joint occupancy was established.

Such pretensions, whatever may have been their effect in the United States, cannot in any manner invalidate or diminish our own just claims. With respect to these we have never varied. We have always maintained that we possess the right to establish ourselves in any part of the country not previously occupied; but we have fully acknowledged in the United States the existence of the same right; and we have also at all times been ready, by an equitable compromise and partition, to put an end to a species of occupation which is but too likely to lead to disputes and collision.

Despairing of arriving at any agreement by means of direct negotiation, we [xi] have been urgent in *pressing the reference of the whole matter to an arbitration. We have been willing to submit, either the abstract title of the two parties, or the equitable division of the territory, to the judgment of any Tribunal which could justly inspire confidence, and which might prove agreeable to the United States. All this, however, has been peremptorily refused; the progress of the negotiation has been entirely arrested, and, in fact, it now remains without aay admitted or intelligible basis whatever.

The United States have recently expressed their determination to put an end to the Convention which, for the last thirty years, has regulated the mode of occupation of Oregon by the subjects of both countries; but as this power was reserved to each party by the terms of the Convention, the decision cannot reasonably be questioned. Neither is there anything necessarily unfriendly in the act itself; but, as both parties would thus be replaced in their former position, each retaining all its claims and asserting all its rights, which each would freely exercise, it is obvious that, in proportion as the country became settled, local differences would arise which must speedily lead to the most serious consequences.

In this state of affairs it is matter of some anxiety and doubt what step, with a view to an amicable settlement of the question, may be most consistent with the dignity and the interests of Great Britain. After all the efforts we have made, and the course we have pursued, we might perhaps most naturally pause, and leave to the United States the office of renewing a negotiation which had been interrupted under such circumstances. But Her Majesty's Government would feel themselves to be criminal if they permitted considerations of diplomatic punctilio or etiquette to prevent them from making every proper exertion to avert the danger of calamities which they are unwilling to contemplate, but the magnitude of which scarcely admits of exaggeration.

I think that an opportunity has now arisen when we may reasonably lay aside those formal considerations by which, under ordinary circumstances, we might have been precluded from making any fresh overture or demonstration on this subject.

In complying with the recommendation of the President to terminate the Convention under which the Oregon Territory is at present occupied, the Legislature of the United States have accompanied their decision by resolutions of a pacific and conciliatory character; and have clearly signified to the Executive Government their desire that this step should not lead to the rupture of amicable negotiations for the settlement of the question. I can scarcely doubt that the Government of the United States will be duly influenced by the desire thus unequivocally expressed by Congress; and it is in this hope and belief that I now proceed to instruct you to make another, and, I trust, final proposition to the American Secretary of State for the solution of these long-existing difficulties.

I avail myself of this opportunity the more readily, because, although Her Majesty's Government have strongly pressed a reference of the whole subject to arbitration, they are by no means insensible to the inconvenience attending such a mode of proceeding, and would willingly avoid it if possible. Nothing, indeed, but the apprehension that an amicable settlement by means of direct negotiation was entirely hopeless, would have led them so decidedly to adopt this course; and they are still of opinion that, with such a prospect of failure before them, it would be their duty to adhere as earnestly as ever to this recommendation. Nor can they believe that any Christian Government could ultimately persevere in rejecting a proposal of this nature, whatever might be their objections to its adoption, and in the face of the civilized world deliberately recur to the dreadful alternative of war.

The boundary having been fixed by the Convention of 1818, between the possessions of Great Britain and the United States, and the line of demarkation having been carried along the forty-ninth parallel of latitude for a distance of eight hundred or one thousand miles through an unfrequented and unknown country, from the Lake of the Woods to the Rocky Mountains, it appeared to the Government of the United States that it was a natural and reasonable suggestion that this line should be continued along the same parallel, for about half that distance, and through a country as little known or frequented, from the Rocky Mountains to the sea. And, indeed, with reference to such a country, the extension of any line of boundary already fixed might equally have been suggested, whether it had been carried along the forty-ninth or any other parallel of latitude.

On the other hand, however, it may justly be observed that any division of territory in which both parties possess equal rights ought to proceed on a principle of mutual convenience, rather than on the adherence to an imaginary geographical line; and in this respect it must be confessed that the boundary thus proposed would be manifestly defective. It would exclude us from every commodious and accessible harbor on the coast; it would deprive us of our long-established means of water-communication with the interior for the prosecution of our trade; and it would interfere with the possessions of British colonists resident in a district in which it is believed that scarcely an American citizen, as a settler, has ever set his foot.

[xii] *If, therefore, the forty-ninth parallel of latitude be adopted as the basis of an agreement, it will be incumbent upon us to obviate these objections, which, I trust in great measure, may be successfully accomplished.

You will accordingly propose to the American Secretary of State that the line of demarkation should be continued along the forty-ninth parallel from the Rocky Mountains to the sea-coast; and from thence in a southerly direction through the center of King George's Sound and the Straits of Juan de Fuca, to the Pacific Ocean, leaving the whole of Vancouver's Island, with its ports and harbors, in the possession of Great Britain.

You will also stipulate that from the point at which the forty-ninth parallel of latitude shall intersect the principal northern branch of the Columbia River, called Macgillivray's River in the maps, the navigation shall be free and open to the Hudson's Bay Company, and to the subjects of Great Britain trading with the said Company, until its junction with the Columbia, and from thence to the mouth of the river, with free access into and through the same; British subjects, with their goods, merchandise, and produce, to be dealt with as citizens of the United States; it being always understood, however, that nothing shall interfere to prevent the American Government from making any regulations respecting the navigation of the river, not inconsistent with the terms of the proposed Convention.

In the future appropriation of land, the possessory rights of all British settlers will of course be respected. The Hudson's Bay Company should be confirmed in the occupation of Fort Vancouver, and the adjacent lands of which the Company have been in possession for many years. They would also retain such other stations as were necessary for the convenient transit of their commerce along the line of the Columbia; but all other stations, or trading-posts, connected with their present exclusive rights of hunting and of traffic with the natives, within the territory south of the forty-ninth degree of latitude, would in all probability forthwith be abandoned.

The Puget Sound Agricultural Company have expended considerable sums of money in the cultivation and improvement of land on the north of the Columbia River. They occupy two extensive farms, on which they possess large stocks of cattle and sheep. These parties would also be entitled to be confirmed in the quiet enjoyment of their land; but if the situation of the farms should be of public and political importance, and it should be desired by the Government of the United States, the whole property might be transferred to them at a fair valuation.

I think that these proposals for an adjustment of the whole question at issue would be honorable and advantageous to both parties. It can scarcely be expected that either of them should now acquiesce in conditions less favorable than had been previously offered; and it may reasonably be presumed that each will at the present moment be prepared to make larger concessions than heretofore for the sake of peace. By this settlement, in addition to the terms proposed to us by Mr. Gallatin in 1826, we should obtain the harbors necessary for our commerce, as well as an increased security for our settlers and their possessions; and in lieu of the detached district, with its single harbor, offered by the British Plenipotentiaries on that occasion, the United States would acquire the whole coast, with its various harbors, and all the territory north of the Columbia, as far as the forty-ninth degree of latitude.

I am not disposed to weigh very minutely the precise amount of compensation or equivalent which may be received by either party in the course of this negotiation, but am content to leave such estimate to be made by a reference to higher considerations than the mere balance of territorial loss or gain. We have sought peace in the spirit of peace, and we have acted in the persuasion that it would be cheaply purchased by both countries at the expense of any sacrifice which should not tarnish the honor or affect the essential interests of either.

I have now, therefore, only to instruct you to inform the American Secretary of State that you have been authorized and are prepared to conclude a Convention, without delay, founded on the conditions set forth in this dispatch.

I am, &c.,

ABERDEEN.

On the same day the following dispatch was also addressed to Mr. Pakenham by Lord Aberdeen, inclosing the draught or project of the Treaty:

No. 19.] MAY 18, 1846.

SIR: With reference to my dispatch No. 18 of this date, I transmit to you herewith the draught or project of a Treaty, such, at least in its essential parts, as Her Majesty's

Government are prepared to conclude with the United States for the final settlement of the Oregon question.

That project may be understood to embody all the conditions which are con-
[xiii] sidered by us as *indispensable. The wording of the Articles may be altered as may be deemed expedient, but their substance must be preserved, nor can any essential departure from that substance be admitted on the part of Great Britain.

The preamble may be considered as open to any alteration which may be proposed, and which you may think expedient. In the project which I have sent you, the definition of territory adopted in the Convention of 1827 has been adhered to. That definition appears to be the most suitable and open to the least objection.

If the United States Government should agree to our terms, such or nearly such as they are now proposed, you will do well to hasten as much as possible the conclusion of the Treaty, since the present constitution of the Senate appears to offer a greater chance of acquiescence of that important body in those conditions than might be presented at any future period.

If, on the other hand, the President should decline to accept those terms, and should make any counter-proposition essentially at variance with their substance, you will express regret that you possess no power to admit any such modification, and, without absolutely rejecting whatever proposal may be submitted on the part of the United States, you will refer the whole matter to your Government.

I am, &c.,

ABERDEEN.

The draught or project was, as regards the description of the boundary now in question, identical with the Treaty as ultimately ratified.

On the same day, also, Mr. MacLane, who had before this time succeeded Mr. Everett as the United States Minister at London, addressed a letter to Mr. Buchanan, as follows:

LONDON, *May* 18, 1846.

SIR: I received, late in the day, on the 15th instant, (Friday,) your dispatch No. 27, dated the 28th of April, 1846, transmitting a notice for the abrogation of the Convention of the 6th of August, 1827, between the United States and Great Britain, in accordance with the terms prescribed in the IInd Article, instructing me to deliver the notice to Her Britannic Majesty in person, or to Her Majesty's Principal Secretary of State for Foreign Affairs, as will be most agreeable to Her Majesty's wishes, and at the same time leaving the mode of the delivery of the notice entirely at my own discretion.

I will of course execute your instructions at the earliest practicable moment. As, however, I could only ascertain Her Majesty's wishes, which I am directed to consult, through the Principal Secretary of State for Foreign Affairs, sufficient time has not yet been afforded for that purpose; and, in the midst of the preparation of my dispatches for the steamer of to-morrow, and of my engagements at the Foreign Office connected with one of the topics of this letter, it has not been in my power to give to a subject of so much importance that deliberation which I am sensible a proper exercise of the discretion confided to me requires. To-morrow, however, I propose to seek an interview with Lord Aberdeen for the purpose, and without loss of time finally to execute your instructions in the mode that may be deemed most effectual. I may add, that although it is altogether probable that the presentation of the notice to Her Majesty in person will not be admissible, and that where a Treaty may be annulled upon notice by one party, the mode of delivering the notice need not be dependent upon the assent of the other; yet, in the present instance, I do not apprehend there will be any difficulty in giving and receiving the notice in a mode mutually satisfactory, and in conformity with usage in such cases.

In my last dispatch, (No. 43,) dated on the 3d instant, after an interview with Lord Aberdeen, I informed you that as soon as he received official intelligence of the Senate's vote upon the resolution of notice he would proceed finally to consider the subject of Oregon, and direct Mr. Pakenham to submit a further proposition upon the part of this Government, and also that it was understood that he would not be prevented from taking this course by any disagreement between the two Houses as to the form of the notice.

I have now to acquaint you that, after the receipt of your dispatches on the 15th instant by the Caledonia, I had a lengthened conference with Lord Aberdeen; on which occasion the resumption of the negotiation for an amicable settlement of the Oregon question, and the nature of the propositien he contemplated submitting for that purpose, formed the subject of a full and free conversation.

I have now to state that instructions will be transmitted to Mr. Pakenham by the steamer of to-morrow, to submit a new and further proposition on the part of this Government, for a partition of the territory in dispute.

[xiv] *The proposition, most probably, will offer substantially:

First, to divide the territory by the extension of the line on the parallel of 49 to the sea; that is to say, to the arm of the sea called Birch's Bay, thence by the Canal de Arro and Straits of Fuca to the Ocean, and confirming to the United States what, indeed, they would possess without any special confirmation, the right freely to use and navigate the Strait throughout its extent.

Second, to secure to the British subjects occupying lands, forts, and stations anywhere in the region north of the Columbia and south of the forty-ninth parallel, a perpetual title to all their lands and stations of which they may be in actual occupation; liable, however, in all respects, as I understand, to the jurisdiction and sovereignty of the United States as citizens of the United States. Similar privileges will be offered to be extended to citizens of the United States who may have settlements north of the forty-ninth parallel; though I presume it is pretty well understood that there are no settlements upon which this nominal mutuality could operate, I have no means of accurately ascertaining the extent of the present British settlements between the Columbia and the forty-ninth parallel. They are not believed by Lord Aberdeen to be numerous, however; consisting, as he supposes, of a few private farms and two or three forts and stations. I have already, in a previous dispatch, taken the liberty to remind you that by their Charter the Hudson's Bay Company are prohibited from acquiring title to lands, and that the occupations to be affected by this reservation have been made either by the squatters of that Company, or by the Puget's Sound Land Company, for the purpose of evading the prohibition of the Hudson's Bay Charter.

They are, in point of fact also, according to Captain Wilkes's account, cultivated and used chiefly by the persons employed in the service of the former Company, and as auxiliary to their general business of hunting and trapping, rather than with a view, as it has been generally supposed, of colonizing or of permanent settlement.

Lastly, the proposition will demand for the Hudson's Bay Company the right of freely navigating the Columbia River.

It will, however, as I understand, disclaim the idea of sovereignty or of the right of exercising any jurisdiction or police whatever on the part of this Government or of the Company, and will contemplate only the right of navigating the river upon the same footing and according to the same regulations as may be applicable to the citizens of the United States.

I have already acquainted you that Lord Aberdeen has very positively and explicitly declined to treat of the navigation of the St. Lawrence in connection with that of the Columbia; and that even if it were desirable to us to propose to offer one for the other, he would on no account enter into any negotiation in regard to the St. Lawrence.

From the date of a private letter to the President in August, I have seen no cause to change the opinion that, in any attempt to divide the Oregon territory, the obligation felt by this Government to protect the rights of their subjects which may have been acquired or have grown up during the joint occupation, would most probably interpose the greatest difficulty in the way of an amicable adjustment. And it is now obvious that the proposed reservation of the right to the Hudson's Bay Company of freely navigating the Columbia, and that in favor of the British occupants north of the river, proceed from this source; although it is probable that more or less pride may be felt at giving up now, without what they may deem an adequate equivalent, what has been hitherto tendered by our negotiators.

In fact, except in the surrender to the United States of the title of the lands not occupied by British subjects between the Columbia and the forty-ninth parallel, and also the surrender of the jurisdiction over the river and the country within the same limits, I am afraid it may, with some plausibility, be contended that there is no very material difference between the present proposition and that offered to Mr. Gallatin by Messrs. Addington and Huskisson, the British negotiators in 1827.

It is scarcely necessary for me to state that the proposition, as now submitted, has not received my countenance. Although it has been no easy task, under all the circumstances, to lead to a re-opening of the negotiation by any proposition from this Government, and to induce it to adopt the parallel of forty-nine as the basis of a boundary, nevertheless I hoped it would have been in my power to give the present proposition a less objectionable shape, and I most deeply lament my inability to accomplish it. I have, therefore, felt it my duty to discourage any expectation that it would be accepted by the President; or, if submitted to that body, approved by the Senate.

I do not think there can be much doubt, however, that an impression has been produced here that the Senate would accept the proposition now offered, at least without any material modification, and that the President would not take the responsi-
[xv] bility of rejecting it without consulting the Senate. If *there be any reasonable ground to entertain such an impression, however erroneous, an offer less objectionable, in the first instance at least, could hardly be expected.

It may be considered certain, also, in my opinion, that the offer now to be made is not to be submitted as an ultimatum, and is not intended as such; though I have reason to know that Mr. Pakenham will not be authorized to accept or reject any modification that may be proposed on our part; but that he will, in such case, be instructed to refer the modification to his Government.

It is not to be disguised that, since the President's annual message, and the public discussion that has subsequently taken place in the Senate, it will be difficult, if not impossible, to conduct the negotiation in its future stages without reference to the opinion of Senators, or free from speculation as to the degree of control they may exercise over the result. Whatever, therefore, might be prudent and regular in the ordinary course of things, I think it of the utmost importance, upon the present occasion, if the President should think proper to propose any modification of the offer to be made by Mr. Pakenham, that the modification should be understood as possessing the concurrence of the co-ordinate branch of the Treaty Power.

It is not easy to conjecture, with any certainty, the extent to which this Government might be induced to modify the proposition, even if they should be assured that the Senate, no less than the President, demanded it. It must not escape observation that, during the preceding administration of our Government, the extension of the line on the forty-ninth parallel to the Strait of Fuca, as now proposed by Lord Aberdeen, was actually suggested by my immediate predecessor as one he thought his Government might accept; and that, in regard to those English subjects who would be left within American jurisdiction by adopting that boundary, he considered that the provisions of Article II of Jay's Treaty as a precedent for a convenient mode of dealing with them. By Article II of Jay's Treaty, however, British subjects would not only be secured in the absolute title to all their lands and effects as fully as by Lord Aberdeen's proposition, but would be allowed the option to continue as British subjects, and without any allegiance to the Government of the United States; which, according to Lord Aberdeen's offer, as I understand it, they would not possess. In point of fact, therefore, the substantial points of the present offer, and those which may be expected to be regarded as most objectionable, are little more than the embodiment of the various offers or suggestions which, at different times, have, in some form or other, proceeded from our own negotiators.

I have myself always believed, if the extension of the line of boundary on the forty-ninth parallel by the Strait of Fuca to the sea would be acceptable to our Government, that the demand of a right freely to navigate the Columbia River would be compromised upon a point of time, by conceding it for such period as might be necessary for the trade of the Hudson's Bay Company north or south of the forty-ninth parallel. Entertaining great confidence in that opinion, and deeming it only reasonable, I confess that, from an early period, I have used every argument and persuasion in my power to reconcile Lord Aberdeen to such a limitation, and, although I am quite aware that, with a portion of the British public, an importance which it by no means deserves is attached to the navigation of the Columbia River, and in that of others it is undeservedly regarded as a point of pride, I have been disappointed by the pertinacity with which it has been, at so much risk, insisted upon. Feeling very sure, however, that the present offer is not made or intended as an ultimatum, I think it only reasonable to infer an expectation on the part of those who are offering it, not only that modifications may be suggested, but that they may be reasonably required. And therefore I still entertain the opinion, that although, from a variety of causes--in part, perhaps, from an expectation that in the United States this point may not be absolutely insisted upon, and in part from deference to interests and impressions at home—they could not be induced in the first instance to make an offer with such a qualification; yet, if the adjustment of the question should be found to depend upon this point only, they would yield the demand to the permanent navigation of the river, and be content to accept it for such a number of years as would afford all the substantial advantages to those interests they have particularly in view that could be reasonably desired. If the only question upon which the adjustment of the Oregon question depended should be whether the navigation of the Columbia River should be granted for a period sufficient to subserve all the purposes of British subjects within the disputed territory, or whether the right should be extended indefinitely to a particular class of British subjects, I must believe that no English statesman, in the face of his denial of a similar privilege to American citizens in regard to the St. Lawrence, would take the hazard upon this point alone of disturbing the peace of the world. Indeed, if the same Ministry from whom the present offer proceeds should continue masters of their own proposition by remaining in office until the qualification I am adverting to would have to be dealt with, I should feel entire confidence in the belief I have now expressed.

I regret to say, however, that I have not the least expectation that a less reser-
[xvi] vation than is *proposed in favor of the occupants of land between the Columbia and the forty-ninth parallel would be assented to. I may repeat my conviction, founded upon all the discussions in which I have been engaged here, that in making partition of the Oregon Territory, the protection of those interests which have grown up during the joint occupation is regarded as an indispensable obligation on the score of honor, and as impossible to be neglected. I am quite sure that it was at one time in contemplation to insist upon the free navigation of the Columbia River for

British subjects and British commerce generally, and that it has been ultimately confined to the Hudson's Bay Company, after great resistance, and, in the end, most reluctantly. Being so confined, however, it would be only reasonable to limit the enjoyment of the right to a period beyond which the company might have no great object to use the river for the purposes of their trade. But the interests of the British subjects who have settled upon and are occupying lands north of the forty-ninth, are considered as permanent, and entitled, when passing under a new jurisdiction, to have their possession secured. This, at least, is the view taken of the subject by this Government, and not at all likely, in my opinion, to be changed.

I may add, too, that I have not the least reason to suppose it would be possible to obtain the extension of the forty-ninth parallel to the sea, so as to give the southern cape of Vancouver's Island to the United States.

It may not be amiss, before leaving this subject, to call your attention to the position of the present Ministry. The success of their measures respecting the proposed commercial relaxations is quite certain; and the Corn Bill, having now finally passed the House of Commons, may be expected, at no remote day, to pass the Lords by a majority no less decisive. From that time, however, the tie which has hitherto kept the Whig party in support of Sir Robert Peel will be dissolved; and the determination of the Protectionist party, who suppose themselves to have been betrayed, to drive him from office, has lost none of its vigor or power. Indeed, it is confidently reported, in quarters entitled to great respect, that they have even offered to the leader of the Whig party to select his own time, and that, when he is ready, they will be no less prepared to force Ministers to resign.

I have reason to know that, at present, Ministers themselves believe a change to be inevitable, and are considering only the mode and the time in which it will be most likely to happen. It will not be long, after the success of the measures for the repeal of the Corn Laws, before opportunities enough for the accomplishment of the object will occur. The Factory Bill, regulating the hours of labor, will afford one, and most probably that on which the change will take place. With a knowledge that the change, sooner or later, must be unavoidable, and that the offer has been made to the probable head of a new Ministry to select his own time, may it not be expected that, instead of waiting quietly to allow the Whig leader to select the time of coming in, the present Premier will rather select his own time and mode of going out, and, with his usual sagacity, so regulate his retirement as to leave as few obstacles as possible to his restoration to power? In that case it is not very unlikely he would prefer going out upon the Factory Bill, before taking ground upon more important measures; and, if so, it will not surprise me to witness the coming in of a new Ministry by the end of June, or earlier. With a knowledge of the proposition now to be made, I am not prepared to say that one more objectionable might have been apprehended from a Whig Ministry; unless, indeed, the present Government may be supposed to be prepared to accept qualifications, when proposed by the President, which it was unwilling at first to offer. Upon that supposition, it might be desirable that the modifications should be offered before the coming in of a new Minister, who, finding only the acts of his predecessor, without a knowledge of his intentions, might not be so ready to take the responsibility of assenting to a change.[1] * * * * * *

I have, &c.,

LOUIS MACLANE.

The following was Mr. Pakenham's report after receiving Lord Aberdeen's dispatches of 18th May:

[No. 68.] WASHINGTON, *June* 7, 1846.

MY LORD: Her Majesty's Government will necessarily be anxious to hear as soon as possible the result of my first communications with the United States Government, in pursuance with your Lordship's instructions of the 18th of May, on the subject of Oregon.

[xvii] *I accordingly take advantage of the departure of the Great Britain steamship to acquaint your Lordship that I had yesterday morning a conference, by appointment, with Mr. Buchanan, when the negotiation for the settlement of the Oregon Question was formally resumed.

As the best explanation which I could offer of the motives which had induced Her Majesty's Government to instruct me to make a fresh, and, as your Lordship hoped, a final, proposition for the solution of these long-existing difficulties, I read to Mr. Buchanan an extract from your Lordship's dispatch No. 18, beginning with the words, "In this state of affairs, it is a matter of some anxiety and doubt what steps," &c., to the end of the dispatch. It seemed to me that there was nothing in the observations

[1] The last three paragraphs of this letter are omitted here. They have no relation to the question before the Arbitrator, and they have not (as far as Her Majesty's Government know) been published by the United States Government.

contained in this part of your Lordship's instructions which might not be advantageously made known to the American Government.

Your Lordship's language appeared to make a good deal of impression upon Mr. Buchanan. After I read to him the extract which I had prepared from the dispatch, he requested to be allowed to read it over himself, in my presence, with which request I of course complied. I thought it best not to leave a copy of it in his hands, having in view the possible, although not probable, failure of the negotiation which might render it desirable to deliver to him a copy at length of the dispatch, with a view to its ultimate publication.

I then laid before him a copy of the draught of a Convention which accompanied your Lordship's dispatch No. 19, which Mr. Buchanan said he would immediately submit to the President for his consideration. A minute of what passed between us was then drawn up and signed, with the draught of the proposed Convention formally annexed to it.

Mr. Buchanan frankly told me that, in his opinion, the only part of the proposed arrangement likely to occasion any serious difficulty, was that relating to the navigation of the Columbia, for he said that the strongest objection existed to granting the perpetual freedom of the navigation of that river. I did not fail to point out to him the great difference which existed between a perpetual and general freedom of navigation, and the qualified right of navigation contemplated in your Lordship's proposition. He admitted the force of my observations in this sense, but I collect, from what fell from him on this point, that an attempt will be made to limit the proposed concession to the duration to the existing charter of the Hudson's Bay Company.

At 4 o'clock yesterday evening I again met Mr. Buchanan, by appointment, when he told me that the President had come to the determination to submit our whole proposition to the Senate for their advice, and that it would accordingly be sent to the Senate at an early day with a Message, which Message might, and probably would, suggest some modifications of it. What these modifications might be, Mr. Buchanan said, had not yet been determined; but I imagine they will not involve anything essentially hostile to the adoption of the proposed arrangement, or which may not be overcome by friendly negotiation and explanation between the two Governments.

As relates to the Senate, my Lord, when we consider the moderate and conciliatory spirit in which the entire question of Oregon has been treated by a large majority of that body since the opening of the present session of Congress, I think it may be fairly expected that their advice to the President on the reference which is about to be made to them will rather favor than impede an early and satisfactory termination of the Oregon difficulties.

I should add that, in addition to what Mr. Buchanan said about the navigation of the Columbia, he gave it as his opinion that it would be necessary, and even advisable, with the view to avoid future misunderstanding, to define, or provide for the early definition of, the limits of the farms and lands now in the occupation of the Puget Sound Agricultural Company, and which it is proposed shall be confirmed to the Association in perpetuity. To such a proviso, if conceived in a spirit of liberality and fairness, I imagine that Her Majesty's Government will have no objection. But upon this point, as well as what relates to the navigation of the Columbia, I will act with due caution, and, to the best of my humble judgment and ability, in conformity with the spirit and intention of your Lordship's instructions, as set forth in your Lordship's dispatch No. 19.

I have, &c.,

R. PAKENHAM.

On the 10th of June, the President of the United States sent this Message to the Senate:

I lay before the Senate a proposal, in the form of a Convention, presented to the Secretary of State on the 6th instant, by the Envoy Extraordinary and Minister Plenipotentiary of Her Britannic Majesty, for the adjustment of the Oregon question,
[xviii] together with a protocol of this proceeding. I *submit this proposal to the consideration of the Senate, and request their advice as to the action which, in their judgment, it may be proper to take in reference to it.

In the early periods of the Government, the opinion and advice of the Senate were often taken in advance upon important questions of our foreign policy. General Washington repeatedly consulted the Senate, and asked their previous advice upon pending negotiations with foreign Powers; and the Senate in every instance responded to this call by giving their advice, to which he always conformed his action. This practice, though rarely resorted to in latter times, was, in my judgment, eminently wise, and may, on occasions of great importance, be properly revived. The Senate are a branch of the Treaty-making Power; and by consulting them in advance of his own action upon important measures of foreign policy which may ultimately come before them for their consideration, the President secures harmony of action between that body and himself. The Senate are, moreover, a branch of the war-making Power, and it may be eminently proper for the Executive to take the opinion and advice of that body in advance upon any great question which may involve in its decision the issue of peace or war. On the present occasion, the magnitude of the subject would induce me under any circumstances to desire the previous advice of the Senate; and that desire is increased by the recent debates and proceedings in Congress, which render it, in my judgment, not only respectful to the Senate, but necessary and proper, if not indispensable, to insure harmonious action between that body and the Executive. In conferring on the Executive the authority to give the notice for the abrogation of the Convention of 1827, the Senate acted publicly so large a part, that a decision on the proposal now made by the British Government, without a definite knowledge of the views of that body in reference to it, might render the question still more complicated and difficult of adjustment. For these reasons I invite the consideration of the Senate to the proposal of the British Government for the settlement of the Oregon question, and ask their advice on the subject.

My opinions and my action on the Oregon question were fully made known to Congress in my annual Message of the 2d of December last; and the opinions therein expressed remain unchanged.

Should the Senate, by the constitutional majority required for the ratification of Treaties, advise the acceptance of this proposition, or advise it with such modifications as they may, upon full deliberation, deem proper, I shall conform my action to their advice. Should the Senate, however, decline by such constitutional majority to give such advice, or to express an opinion on the subject, I shall consider it my duty to reject the offer.

I also communicate herewith an extract from a dispatch of the Secretary of State to the Minister of the United States at London, under date of the 28th of April last, directing him, in accordance with the joint resolution of Congress "concerning the Oregon Territory," to deliver the notice to the British Government for the abrogation of the Convention of the 6th of August, 1827; and also a copy of the notice transmitted to him for that purpose, together with extracts from a dispatch of that Minister to the Secretary of State, bearing date on the 18th day of May last.

JAMES K. POLK.

WASHINGTON, *June* 10, 1846.

On the same day the President's Message was considered, and a motion that the Message and documents communicated therewith be referred to the Committee on Foreign Relations was negatived, as was also a motion to postpone the further consideration thereof until 15th June.

On the two next following days the consideration of the Message was continued, and an amendment proposing the addition of a proviso to Article II was moved;[1] but ultimately it was resolved on a division, by 38 votes to 12, that the President should be advised to accept the proposal of the British Government.

On 13th June Mr. Pakenham reported to his Government as follows:

No. 77.] WASHINGTON, *June* 13, 1846.

MY LORD: In conformity with what I had the honor to state in my dispatch No. 68, of the 7th instant, the President sent a Message on Wednesday last to the Senate submitting for the opinion of that body the draught of a Convention for the settle-
[xix] ment of the Oregon question, which I was instructed by your *Lordship's dispatch No. 19, of the 18th of May, to propose for the acceptance of the United States.

After a few hours' deliberation on each of the three days, Wednesday, Thursday, and Friday, the Senate, by a majority of 38 votes to 12, adopted, yesterday evening, a resolution advising the President to accept the terms proposed by Her Majesty's Government. The President did not hesitate to act on this advice, and Mr. Buchanan accordingly sent for me this morning, and informed me that the conditions offered by Her Majesty's Government were accepted by the Government of the United States, without the addition or alteration of a single word.

At the beginning of our conversation, Mr. Buchanan observed to me that the privilege of navigating the Columbia River, which, by the second Article of the Convention, is secured to the Hudson's Bay Company, and to British subjects trading with the same, was understood by the Senate to be limited to the duration of the license under which the Company now carry on their operations in the country west of the Rocky Mountains; to which I replied, that the Article proposed by Her Majesty's Government spoke for itself; that any alteration from the precise wording of that Article which

[1] Appendix No. 5.

the United States Government might wish to introduce would involve the necessity of a reference to England, and consequently, to say the least of it, some delay in the termination of the business. This, he seemed to think, under all the circumstances of the case, had better be avoided, and it was finally agreed that fair copies of the Convention should be prepared, and the signature take place on Monday next.[1]

On Tuesday, probably, the Convention will be submitted to the Senate, where its approval may now be considered as a matter of course, so that the Treaty, with the President's ratification, may be forwarded to England by the Great Western steam-packet, appointed to sail from New York on the 25th of this month.

I have, &c.,

R. PAKENHAM.

On 16th June a further Message was sent by the President to the Senate, stating that, in accordance with the resolution of the Senate, a Convention was concluded and signed on 15th June, and that Convention he then laid before the Senate for their consideration, with a view to its ratification.

On the same day and the two next following days the Message was before the Senate. Mr. Benton's speech was made on the 18th. Ultimately, on a division, by a majority of 41 votes to 14, it was resolved that the Senate advised and consented to the ratification of the Treaty.

Mr. Pakenham then further reported as follows:

No. 79.] WASHINGTON, *June* 23, 1846.

MY LORD: I have the honor herewith to transmit a Convention for the settlement of the Oregon Boundary, which was signed by the United States Secretary of State and myself, on Monday, the 15th of this month. The terms of this Convention, it will be seen, are in the strictest conformity with your Lordship's late instructions.

On Tuesday, the 16th, the Convention was communicated to the Senate, and on Thursday, the 18th, it received the approval of that body by a vote of 41 to 14.

The American counterpart of the Convention, with the President's ratification of it, is forwarded to London by a special messenger, to whose care, with Mr. Buchanan's permission, I commit the present dispatch.

I have, &c.,

R. PAKENHAM.

Lord Aberdeen's dispatch, in answer to Mr. Pakenham's of 13th June, was as follows. It is the document which proves that Mr. MacLane had seen the project of the Treaty:

[xx] *No. 30.] FOREIGN OFFICE, *June* 29, 1846.—*P. S. July* 1, 1846.

SIR: Her Majesty's Government have received this day, with the greatest satisfaction, your dispatch No. 77, of the 13th instant, in which you announce the acceptance by the Senate of the draught of Treaty for the settlement of the Oregon question, which was conveyed to you in my dispatch No. 19, of the 18th of May, and also the intention of the President to proceed forthwith to the completion of the proposed Convention.

In your dispatch you state that Mr. Buchanan had observed to you that the privilege of navigating the Columbia River, which, by the second Article of the Convention, is secured to the Hudson's Bay Company, and to British subjects trading with the same, was understood by the Senate to be limited to the duration of the license under which the Company now carry on their operations in the country west of the Rocky Mountains; to which observation you very properly replied that the Article proposed by Her Majesty's Government spoke for itself.

Nothing, in fact, can well be clearer than the language of that Article. In drawing it up I had not the smallest intention of restricting the British right to navigate the Columbia in the manner supposed, nor can I comprehend how such a supposition could have been entertained by the Senate, for I have reason to know that Mr. MacLane fully and faithfully reported to his Government all that passed between himself and me respecting the navigation of the Columbia. In every conversation that we held on the subject of the proposed Treaty, I not only declared to Mr. MacLane that we must insist on the permanent right being secured to us to navigate the Columbia, but I even showed him the project of the Treaty, and, on his expressing an apprehension that the provision contained in the second Article would not be accepted unless the right of navigation were limited to a term of years, I positively declined to accede to this suggestion.

[1] Appendix No. 5.

I think it right to state these facts, in order to obviate any misapprehension which might possibly hereafter be raised on the construction of the second Article of the Oregon Treaty.

I am, &c.,

ABERDEEN.

P. S. *July* 1.—Since writing this dispatch I have held a conversation with Mr. MacLane, in which he has freely and fully confirmed all that I have stated above with reference to his own understanding of the intent of the second Article of the Oregon Treaty.

A.

Two subsequent dispatches of Mr. Pakenham to Viscount Palmerston (who had succeeded Lord Aberdeen as Her Majesty's Principal Secretary of State for Foreign Affairs) are as follows:

No. 100.] WASHINGTON, *July* 29, 1846.

MY LORD: Owing to one of those irregularities which are not unfrequently witnessed in this country, the President's Message to the Senate, submitting, for the advice and opinion of that body, the proposition lately made by Her Majesty's Government for the settlement of the Oregon Question, and various other papers connected with that transaction, have found their way into the public papers, notwithstanding that the injunction of secrecy has not yet been removed.

Amongst other papers thus published, the collection of which I have the honor to inclose,[1] will be found a dispatch from Mr. MacLane to his Government, reporting what had passed between the Earl of Aberdeen and himself with relation to the proposition which Lord Aberdeen was about to make to this Government, for the partition of the Oregon Territory.

It would appear from this dispatch that Mr. MacLane had no expectation that the terms proposed by Her Majesty's Government would be accepted here; that he discouraged any such expectation on the part of Her Majesty's Government, considering as "erroneous" an impression, which he found had been produced in England, "that the Senate would accept the proposition now offered, at least without any material modification, and that the President would not take the responsibility of rejecting it without consulting the Senate;" and, finally, that he gave it as his opinion to the American Government that the offer then made was not submitted as an "ultimatum," nor intended as such; in short, that some modification of its terms would, without much difficulty, be acceded to by England.

[xxi] *It is most providential, my Lord, that Mr. MacLane's suggestions did not succeed, either in England, in deterring Lord Aberdeen from making his offer, according to his original intention, or here, in inducing the American Government to stand out for some modification of that offer when it was made; for, in either case, all would have been spoiled.

The President's Message, transmitting the proposition of Her Majesty's Government for the consideration of the Senate, is very guarded—upon the whole, rather deprecating than encouraging the acceptance of the offer; but in this course the President ran no risk and incurred no responsibility whatever, for every one in Washington, at all acquainted with the disposition of the Senate, knew that such a proposition would be accepted by that body, by a large majority.

I have, &c.,

R. PAKENHAM.

No. 106.] WASHINGTON, *August* 13, 1846.

MY LORD: The injunction of secrecy having been removed by a resolution of the Senate, I have the honor herewith to transmit three numbers of the Union, official newspaper, containing, in an authentic form, (Union of 7th August,) the papers relative to the conclusion of the Oregon negotiation which I had the honor to transmit in an unauthorized form with my dispatch No. 100, and also (Unions of 8th and 10th August) two Messages from the President to the Senate, the first communicating for approval the Treaty signed here on the 15th of June, the second communicating documents not before communicated to the Senate relative to the Oregon Territory, in answer to a resolution of the Senate of the 17th June last.

Among the papers thus made public, the one which I should most particularly recommend to your Lordship's attention, is a dispatch from Mr. Buchanan to Mr. MacLane, dated the 12th of July, 1845, (Union of 8th August,) setting forth the terms on which the President was willing, at that time, to settle the Oregon question, but evidently with little or no expectation that those terms would be accepted by Great Britain, I might almost say with an expectation scarcely concealed that they would be rejected,

[1] There was inclosed in the dispatch a copy of the Baltimore Sun newspaper of 23d July, 1846.

when, to use Mr. Buchanan's own words, the President would "be relieved from the embarrassment in which he has been involved by the acts, offers, and declarations of his predecessors," and be justified in going to war for the whole territory.

The remarkable thing in this dispatch is the confidence which it betrays that, in the course which the President had made up his mind to follow with reference to the Oregon question, he would receive the countenance and support of the Senate and the country, even to the extremity of a war with England. The result has shown that, in this expectation, he did not do justice either to the wisdom and integrity of the Senate, or to the intelligence and good sense of the American people.

Within a few days after the opening of the late session of Congress it became evident that Mr. Polk's policy respecting Oregon was viewed with no favor by a large majority of the Senate, nor was the war cry raised by the more ardent partisans of the Administration responded to in any part of the country.

In process of time this conclusion forced itself on the mind of the President and his advisers, and hence your Lordship will find in the ulterior dispatches of Mr. Buchanan to Mr. MacLane a far more moderate and subdued tone, until at last they exhibit a positive and conciliatory desire to settle the question by compromise, the title of the United States to "the whole of Oregon" having apparently been forgotten.

If further proof were wanted of the anxiety of this Government to be extricated from the mistaken position in which they had placed themselves, it would be found in the alacrity in which the terms last proposed by Her Majesty's Government for the settlement of the controversy were accepted.

Sufficient time has now elapsed since the promulgation of the Treaty to enable us to judge of the light in which the transaction has been viewed throughout the country, and it is gratifying to say that it has been everywhere received with satisfaction and applause.

No evidence whatever of a contrary feeling has come within my observation, except it be among the disappointed advocates of a war policy, who had staked their political fortune upon the adoption of extreme measures, and even in these quarters, I am bound in truth to say that the irritation is rather against the President and his ministers for having, as they say, deceived and betrayed them, than from any express condemnation of the Treaty itself.

I have, &c.,

R. PAKENHAM.

[xxiii] **Chronological List, showing the Names and Dates of Appointment of the various Principal Secretaries of State for Foreign Affairs in Great Britain, and British Ministers at Washington, and of the various Presidents and Secretaries of State of the United States, and United States Ministers at London, from* 1818 *to* 1872.[1]

GREAT BRITAIN.

British Foreign Secretaries of State.	Period of Office.	British Ministers at Washington.	Dates of Appointment.
Viscount Castlereagh	March 4, 1812, to September 16, 1822	Hon. C. Bagot	July 31, 1815
		Sir S. Canning	July 18, 1820
Mr. Canning	September 16, 1822, to April 30, 1827	Sir S. Canning	
		C. R. Vaughn	May 21, 1825
Viscount Dudley and Ward	April 30, 1827, to June 2, 1828	C. R. Vaughn	
Earl of Aberdeen	June 2, 1828, to November 22, 1830	C. R. Vaughn	
Viscount Palmerston	November 22, 1830, to November 15, 1834	C. R. Vaughn	
Duke of Wellington	November 15, 1834, to April 18, 1835	C. R. Vaughn	
Viscount Palmerston	April 18, 1835, to September 2, 1841	H. S. Fox	Oct. 2, 1835
Earl of Aberdeen	September 2, 1841, to July 6, 1846	H. S. Fox	
		Lord Ashburton, (special mission)	Jan. 18, 1842
		R. Pakenham	Dec. 14, 1843
Viscount Palmerston	July 6, 1846, to December 27, 1851	R. Pakenham	
		Sir H. Bulwer	Apr. 27, 1849
Earl Granville	December 27, 1851, to February 28, 1852	Sir H. Bulwer	
		J. F. Crampton	Jan. 19, 1852
Earl of Malmesbury	February 28 to December 28, 1852	J. F. Crampton	
Lord John Russell	December 28, 1852, to February 21, 1853	J. F. Crampton	
Earl of Clarendon	February 21, 1853, to February 26, 1858	J. F. Crampton	
		Earl of Elgin, (special mission)	May —, 1854
		Vacant	May 28, 1856
		Lord Napier	Jan. 20, 1857
Earl of Malmesbury	February 26, 1858, to June 18, 1859	Lord Lyons	Dec. 13, 1858
Lord John Russell	June 18, 1859, to November 3, 1865	Lord Lyons	
		Sir F. Bruce	Mar. 1, 1865
Earl of Clarendon	November 3, 1865, to July 6, 1866	Sir F. Bruce	
Lord Stanley	July 6, 1866, to December 9, 1868	Sir F. Bruce	
		Sir E. Thornton	Dec. 6, 1867
Earl of Clarendon	December 9, 1868, to July 6, 1870	Sir E. Thornton	
Earl Granville	July 6, 1870, to ——	Sir E. Thornton	

[1] Referred to in the Statement, page 2, note *.

UNITED STATES.

Presidents of the United States.	Period of office.	United States Secretaries of State.	Period of office.	United States Ministers in London.	Period of appointment.
James Monroe	March 4, 1817, to March 4, 1825	John Q. Adams	March 3, 1817, to March 8, 1825	J. Q. Adams R. Rush	December 22, 1817, to April, 1825.
John Q. Adams	March 4, 1825, to March 4, 1829	Henry Clay	March 8, 1825, to March 6, 1829	R. Rush R. King A. Gallatin W. B. Lawrence[1] J. Barbour	 August, 1825, to June, 1826. August, 1826, to October, 1827. December, 1827. July, 1828, to September, 1829.
Andrew Jackson	March 4, 1829, to March 4, 1837	M. Van Buren E. Livingston Louis MacLane John Forsyth	March 6, 1829, to 1831 1831 to March 7, 1833 March 7, 1833, to June 27, 1834 June 27, 1834, to March 5, 1841	J. Barbour L. MacLane M. Van Buren A. Vail A. Stevenson	 Sept. 21, 1829, to June 9, 1831. September, 1831, to March, 1832. March, 1832, to April, 1836. April, 1836, to October, 1841.
Martin Van Buren	March 4, 1837, to March 4, 1841	John Forsyth	....	A. Stevenson	
W. H. Harrison	March 4 to April 4, 1841	Daniel Webster	March 5, 1841, to May 9, 1843	A. Stevenson	
J. Tyler	April 4, 1841, to March 4, 1845	Daniel Webster Hugh S. Legare Abel P. Upshur John Nelson, (acting) John C. Calhoun	.... May 9 to June 24, 1843 June 24, 1843, to Feb. 29, 1844 February 29 to March 6, 1844 March 6, 1844, to March 5, 1845	E. Everett	November, 1841, to August 4, 1845.
J. K. Polk	March 4, 1845, to March 4, 1849	James Buchanan	March 5, 1845, to March 7, 1849	L. MacLane G. Bancroft	August 5, 1845, to Aug. 15, 1846. November 2, 1846, to Aug. 31, 1849.
Z. Taylor	March 4, 1849, to July 9, 1850	John M. Clayton	March 7, 1849, to July 20, 1850	G. Bancroft A. Lawrence	 October 10, 1849, to Sept. 25, 1852.
Millard Fillmore	July 9, 1850, to March 4, 1853	Daniel Webster Edward Everett	July 20, 1850, to 1852 1852 to March 5, 1853	A. Lawrence J. R. Ingersoll	 October 4, 1852, to Aug. 20, 1853.
F. Pierce	March 4, 1853, to March 4, 1857	W. L. Marcy	March 5, 1853, to March 4, 1857	J. R. Ingersoll J. Buchanan G. M. Dallas	 August 22, 1853, to March 14, 1856. March 17, 1856, to May 13, 1861.[2]
J. Buchanan	March 4, 1857, to March 4, 1861	Lewis Cass J. S. Black	March 4, 1857, to Dec. 18, 1860 Dec'ber 18, 1860, to Mar. 4, 1861	G. M. Dallas	
A. Lincoln	March 4, 1861, to April 15, 1865	W. H. Seward	March 4, 1861, to March 4, 1869	G. M. Dallas C. F. Adams	 May 14, 1861, to May 9, 1868.
Andrew Johnson	April 15, 1865, to March 4, 1869	W. H. Seward	....	C. F. Adams R. Johnson	 August 18, 1868, to May 12, 1869.
General Grant	March 4, 1869, to ——	H. Fish	March 4, 1869	R. Johnson J. L. Motley R. C. Schenck	 May 13, 1869, to June, 1871. June 22, 1871.

[1] Chargé d'Affaires.

[2] With vacancy from May, 1856, to January, 1857.

[xxvii] *MEMORANDUM RELATIVE TO THE ORIGIN AND PRIVILEGES OF THE HUDSON'S BAY COMPANY.[1]

In 1669, certain British subjects formed themselves into a Company, for the purpose of undertaking an expedition to Hudson's Bay.

The object of this expedition was twofold:

1. To discover a passage through those parts to the Pacific Ocean, or, as it was then oftener called, the South Sea; and,

2. To establish a trade in furs, minerals, and other things.

For the encouragement of this enterprise a Royal Charter was granted to the Company on the 2d May, 1669. By the terms of this Charter, the Company obtained a Royal Grant of the sole trade and commerce of all the seas, straits, bays, rivers, lakes, creeks, and sounds, in whatsoever latitude they should be, lying within the straits commonly called Hudson's Straits, together with all the lands and territories upon the countries, coasts, and confines of the seas, bays, lakes, &c., aforesaid, that were not already actually possessed by the subjects of any other Christian Prince or State. The territory thus acquired was to be thenceforth reckoned and reputed as one of the British Plantations or Colonies in America, to be called Rupert's Land.

For nearly a century after the formation of the Company, they confined their posts to the ample territory which had been granted to them by the Charter of Charles II, and left the task of procuring furs to the enterprise of native hunters, who brought the produce of their hunting to the established marts of the Company.

The Company continued to enjoy, until 1784, the monopoly of the trade in these territories, when a rival Company was established, called the North-West Company, which had their head-quarters at Montreal. The North-West Company, instead of following the system of trade adopted by the Hudson's Bay Company, dispatched their servants into the very recesses of the wilderness to bargain with the native hunters at their homes. As the nearer hunting-grounds became exhausted, the North-West Company advanced their stations westwardly into regions previously unexplored; and, in 1806, they pushed forward a post across the Rocky Mountains, and formed a trading establishment on a lake, now called Fraser's Lake, situated in 54° north latitude. This would appear to be the first settlement made by civilized men west of the Rocky Mountains.

Other posts were soon after formed amongst the Flat-head and Kootanie tribes on the head-waters or main branch of the Columbia; and Mr. David Thomson, the astronomer of the North-West Company, descended with a party to the mouth of the Columbia in 1811. Mr. Thomson and his followers were, according to Mr. Greenhow, the first white persons who navigated the northern branch of the Columbia, or traversed any part of the country drained by it.

[xxviii] *In consequence of the rivalry existing between the Hudson's

[1] Referred to in the Statement, page 2, note *.

Bay and North-West Companies, which led to frequent conflicts between their respective followers, more particularly with reference to certain settlements formed in the Oregon district by Lord Selkirk, the affairs of the Companies were brought to the notice of Parliament in 1819, and their proceedings were minutely investigated. The Government finally interposed its mediation, and a compromise was effected, by which the North-West Company became merged in the Hudson's Bay Company. Subsequently, and in connection with this arrangement, an "Act for regulating the fur-trade and establishing a criminal and civil jurisdiction in certain parts of North America" was passed in Parliament,[1] containing every provision required to give stability to the Hudson's Bay Company, and efficiency to its operations.

By this act, which was passed in 1821, the Courts of Judicature of Upper Canada were empowered to take cognizance of all causes, civil or criminal, arising in any of the above-mentioned territories, including those previously granted to the Hudson's Bay Company, and in "other parts of America not within the limits of either of the provinces of Upper or Lower Canada, or of any civil Government of the United States."

Shortly before the passing of this act, the Hudson's Bay and North-West Companies were united; and, on the 6th December, 1821, a grant was made by the King to the Company "of the exclusive trade with the Indians of North America."

By this grant the officers in the service of the Company were commissioned as Justices of the Peace for those countries; and the jurisdiction of the Courts of Upper Canada was rendered effective as far as the shores of the Pacific, the only exception made in that respect being with regard to any territory embraced in the grant, situated "within the limits of any civil Government of the United States." This grant was made for twenty-one years, but before the termination of that period a further grant was received from the Crown by the Company.

In the grant of 1821 the following reservations were made in favor of the rights of the Crown, and also of those of subjects of foreign States:

But we do hereby declare that nothing in this our grant contained shall be deemed or construed to authorize the said Governor and Company, or their successors, or any persons in their employ, to claim or exercise any trade with the Indians on the northwest coast of America, to the westward of the Stony Mountains, to the prejudice or exclusion of any of the subjects of any foreign States who, under or by the force of any Convention for the time being between us and such foreign States respectively, may be entitled to or shall be engaged in the same trade. Provided, nevertheless, and we do hereby declare our pleasure to be, that nothing herein contained shall extend or be construed to prevent the establishment by us, our heirs or successors, within the territories aforesaid, or any of them, of any colony or colonies, province or provinces, or from annexing any part of the aforesaid territories to any existing colony or colonies to us in right of our Imperial Crown belonging, or for constituting any such form of civil government, as to us may seem meet, within any such colony or colonies or provinces.

Such were the provisions made by the British Government for the proper government of the territories situated beyond the Rocky Mountains and on the coasts of the Pacific Ocean. The successful result of these measures for extending the trade of the Hudson's Bay Company, and for forming settlements in these territories by Great Britain, is given in the following extract from Mr. Greenhow's History of Oregon and California, in which he says, (page 344:)

The relative positions of the two parties (Great Britain and the United States) as to the occupancy and actual possession of the countries in question had been materially

[1] Act 1 and 2 Geo. IV, cap. 66; July 2, 1821.

> changed since the conclusion of the former Convention (1818) between them. The [xxix] union of the rival British Companies, *and the extension of the jurisdiction of the Courts of Upper Canada over the territories west of the Rocky Mountains, had already proved most advantageous to the Hudson's Bay Company, which had at the same time received the privilege of trading in that country, to the exclusion of all other British subjects. Great efforts were made and vast expenses were incurred by this Company in its efforts to found settlements on the Columbia River, and to acquire influence over the natives of the surrounding country; and so successful have been those efforts that the citizens of the United States were obliged not only to renounce all ideas of renewing their establishments in that part of America, but even to withdraw their vessels from its coasts. Indeed, for more than ten years after the capture of Astoria by the British, scarcely a single American citizen was to be seen in those countries. Trading expeditions were subsequently made from Missouri to the head-waters of the Platte and the Colorado, within the limits of California, and one or two hundred hunters and trappers from the United States were generally roving through that region; but the Americans had no Settlement of any kind, and their Government exercised no jurisdiction whatsoever west of the Rocky Mountains.
>
> Under such favorable circumstances, the Hudson's Bay Company could not fail to prosper. Its resources were no longer wasted in disputes with rivals; its operations were conducted with dispatch and certainty; its posts were extended, and its means of communication were increased, under the assurance that the honor of the British Government and nation were thereby more strongly interested in its behalf. The agents of the Company were seen in every part of the Continent—north and northwest of the United States and Canada, from the Atlantic to the Pacific—hunting, trapping, and trading with the aborigines. Its boats were met on every stream and lake, conveying British goods into the interior, or furs to the great depositories on each ocean, to ship to England in British vessels; and the utmost order and regularity were maintained throughout by the supremacy of British laws. Of the trading-posts many were fortified, and could be defended by their inmates—men inured to hardships and dangers—against all attacks which might be apprehended; and the whole vast expanse of territory above described, including the regions drained by the Columbia, was, in fact, occupied by British forces and governed by British laws, though there was not a single British soldier, technically speaking, within its limits.

The Hudson's Bay Company possessed, in 1844, twenty-two forts or establishments west of the Rocky Mountains, of which several were situated on the coasts.

On the River Columbia were Fort Vancouver, Fort Walla-walla, Fort Okinagan, Fort Colville; on the River Saptin or Lewis, a branch of the Columbia, were Fort Boisé and Fort Hall.

To the south of the Columbia River were Fort George, which occupied the site of the former settlement of Astoria, and Fort Umqua, near the mouth of the Umqua River, which enters the Pacific about one hundred and eighty miles south of the Columbia.

At Puget Sound was Fort Nasqually, near which place also the Company had a large agricultural establishment.

At the entrance of Fraser's River was Fort Langley, and further north were Fort Alexandria, and Fort McLaughlin on the coast.

In 1849, a grant of Vancouver's Island was made to the Company by the Crown, but, in 1859, the island was resumed by the Crown and was made a Colony.

In 1868, the Company surrendered their remaining territorial rights to the Crown, and the territory over which those rights extended, under the title of Rupert's Land, was subsequently admitted into and became part of the Dominion of Canada.

[xxxiii] *APPENDIX.

No. 1.

EXTRACT SHOWING VIEWS OF EARL OF ABERDEEN AND SIR RICHARD PAKENHAM.

Lord John Russell to Lord Lyons, 24th August, 1859; read, and copy given, to United States Secretary of State.

[Extract.]

I have to state to you that the Earl of Aberdeen, to whom I have referred, informs me that he distinctly remembers the general tenor of his conversations with Mr. MacLane on the subject of the Oregon Boundary, and is certain that it was the intention of the Treaty to adopt the mid-channel of the Straits as the line of demarkation, without reference to islands, the position, and, indeed, the very existence of which had hardly at that time been accurately ascertained; and he has no recollection of any mention having been made, during the discussion, of the Canal de Haro, or, indeed, any other channel than those described in the Treaty itself.

I also inclose a Memorandum drawn up by Sir Richard Pakenham, the negotiator of the Treaty of 1846.

[Inclosure in foregoing dispatch.]

Memorandum by Sir R. Pakenham on the Water Boundary under the Oregon Treaty of 1846.

I have examined the papers put into my hand by Mr. Hammond, relating to the line of boundary to be established between the British and United States possessions on the northwest coast of America, and I have endeavored to call to mind any circumstance which might have occurred at the time when the Oregon Treaty was concluded, (June 15, 1846,) of a nature either to strengthen or to invalidate the pretension now put forward by the United States Commissioner to the effect that the boundary contemplated by the Treaty would be a line passing down the middle of the channel, called Canal de Haro, and not, as suggested on the part of Great Britain, along the middle of the channel called Vancouver's or Rosario Strait, neither of which two lines would, as I humbly conceive, exactly fulfill the conditions of the Treaty, which, according to their literal tenor, would require the line to be traced along the middle of the channel (meaning, I presume, the whole intervening space) which separates the Continent from Vancouver's Island. And I think I can safely assert that the Treaty of June 15, 1846, was signed and ratified without any intimation to us whatever on the part of the United States Government as to the particular direction to be given to the line of boundary contemplated by Article I of that Treaty.

All that we knew about it was that it was to run "through the middle of the channel which separates the Continent from Vancouver's Island, and thence southerly through the middle of the said channel and of Fuca's Straits to the Pacific Ocean."

It is true that, in a dispatch from Mr. MacLane, then United States Minister in London, to the American Secretary of State, Mr. Buchanan, dated 18th May, 1846, which dispatch was not, however, made public until after the ratification of the Treaty by the Senate, Mr. MacLane informs his Government that the line of boundary about to be proposed by Her Majesty's Government would "probably be substantially to divide the territory by the extension of the line on the parallel of 49° to the sea; that is to say, to the arm of the sea called Birch's Bay, thence by the Canal de Haro and Straits of Fuca to the ocean."

It is also true that Mr. Senator Benton, one of the ablest and most zealous advocates for the ratification of the Treaty, (relying, no doubt, on the statement furnished by Mr. MacLane,) did, in a speech on the subject, describe the intended line of boundary to be one passing along the middle of the Haro Channel.

But, on the other hand, the Earl of Aberdeen, in his final instructions, dated May 18, 1846, says nothing whatever about the Canal de Haro; but, on the contrary, desires that the line might be drawn "in a southerly direction through the center of King George's Sound and the Straits of Fuca to the Pacific Ocean."

It is my belief that neither Lord Aberdeen, nor Mr. MacLane, nor Mr. Buchanan, possessed at that time a sufficiently accurate knowledge of the geography or hydrography of the region in question to enable them to define more accurately what was the
[xxxiv] intended line of boundary than is expressed in *the words of the Treaty, and
it is certain that Mr. Buchanan signed the Treaty with Mr. MacLane's dispatch before him, and yet that he made no mention whatever of the "Canal de Haro as that through which the line of boundary should run, as understood by the United States Government."

My own dispatches of that period contain no observation whatever of a tendency contrary to what I thus state from memory, and they therefore so far plead in favor of the accuracy of my recollections.

No. 2.

CORRESPONDENCE BETWEEN MR. BANCROFT AND MR. BUCHANAN.

Mr. Bancroft to Mr. Buchanan.[1]

LONDON, *November* 3, 1846.

SIR: * * * * * * * *

While in the Navy Department I caused a traced copy of Wilkes's chart of the Straits of Haro to be made. If not needed in the Navy Department, I request that the President will direct it to be sent to this Legation. It is intimated to me that questions may arise with regard to the islands east of that Strait. I ask your authority to meet any such claim at the threshold by the assertion of the central channel of the Straits of Haro as the main channel intended by the recent Treaty of Washington. Some of the islands I am well informed are of value.

Very respectfully, &c.,

GEORGE BANCROFT.

Hon. JAMES BUCHANAN,
Secretary of State.

Mr. Buchanan to Mr. Bancroft.[1]

DEPARTMENT OF STATE,
Washington, December 28, 1846.

SIR: I have obtained from the Navy Department, and now transmit to you, in accordance with the request contained in your dispatch No. 1, (November 3,) the traced copy of Wilkes's chart of the Straits of Haro. This will enable you to act understandingly upon any question which may hereafter arise between the two Governments in respect to the sovereignty of the islands situate between the Continent and Vancouver's Island. It is not probable, however, that any claim of this character

---

[1] As officially printed in the United States.

will be seriously preferred on the part of Her Britannic Majesty's Government to any island lying to the eastward of the Canal of Arro, as marked in Captain Wilkes's Map of the Oregon Territory. This, I have no doubt, is the channel which Lord Aberdeen had in view when, in a conversation with Mr. MacLane about the middle of May last, on the subject of the resumption of the negotiation for an amicable settlement of the Oregon question, his Lordship explained the character of the proposition he intended to submit through Mr. Pakenham. As understood by Mr. MacLane, and by him communicated to this Department in his dispatch of the 18th of the same month, it was: "First, to divide the territory by the extension of the line on the parallel of 49° to the sea; that is to say, to the arm of the sea called Birch's Bay, thence by the *Canal de Haro* and Straits of Fuca to the ocean," &c.

I am, &c.,

JAMES BUCHANAN.

GEORGE BANCROFT, Esq., *&c., &c., &c.*

[Inclosure: Chart of the Straits of Juan de Fuca, Puget Sound, &c. By the United States Ex. Ex., 1841.]

No. 3.

LETTERS OF MR. CRAMPTON SHOWING MR. BUCHANAN'S OPINIONS.

Mr. Crampton to Viscount Palmerston.

No. 2.] WASHINGTON, *January* 13, 1848.

MY LORD: On the receipt of your Lordship's dispatch No. 21, of the 17th ultimo, by which I am instructed to communicate with the United States Government with a view to the adoption of early measures for laying down such parts of the line of boundary between the British and United States territory in North America, described in the Convention of the 15th June, 1846, as the two Governments may, upon mutual consultation, deem it advisable to determine, I waited upon Mr. Buchanan for the purpose of putting him in possession of the views of Her Majesty's Government upon the subject.

After having read to him your Lordship's dispatch, together with the draught of instructions to the two Commissioners to be appointed in case the views of Her Majesty's Government were coincided in by the Government of the United States, I proceeded to inquire of Mr. Buchanan whether the manner suggested by your Lordship of bringing the matter under the consideration of the President of the United States, by reading to him your Lordship's dispatch and presenting to him a copy of the proposed draught of instructions, would be admissible.

[xxxv] *To this course Mr. Buchanan objected, as being informal, and contrary to the practice of the United States Government, which coincided, he added, in that respect, with that of the Government of Great Britain, and he requested me, in case your Lordship's instructions did not preclude me from so doing, to communicate to him in writing the present proposal of Her Majesty's Government, together with the considerations upon which it is founded, as explained in your Lordship's dispatch. He might otherwise, he said, find it difficult to convey to the President and to his colleagues in the Cabinet as clear an exposition as he could wish of the views of Her Majesty's Government upon

the subject, adding that these appeared to him to be so fair and unobjectionable that he could conceive no possible case in which any inconvenience to either Government would result from an unreserved communication of them in writing.

I trust that your Lordship will not disapprove of my having, under these circumstances, so far departed from the course pointed out by your Lordship's instructions as to comply with Mr. Buchanan's request by addressing to him the note of which I have the honor to inclose a copy, and in which I have embodied the substance of your Lordship's dispatch.

With respect to the expediency of laying down that part of the boundary line suggested by your Lordship's dispatch, Mr. Buchanan said that he coincided in opinion with Her Majesty's Government, but he added that it was his own "impression," although he had not examined the subject with sufficient attention to enable him yet to say that it was his "opinion," that it would be desirable to go further, and to proceed to mark out on the ground, without unnecessary delay, the boundary line from the point where the forty-ninth parallel of latitude meets the shore of the Gulf of Georgia, eastward to where it strikes the Columbia River, (the portions for which an estimate is made in the third section of Colonel Estcourt's Memorandum,) and this appeared to him to be advisable from the reports he had lately received of the rapid manner in which colonists from the United States are spreading in that direction.

Speaking of the word "channel," as employed in the Convention of June, 1846, Mr. Buchanan said that he himself, and he presumed Mr. Pakenham, in negotiating and signing that Convention, had always conceived "channel" to mean the "main navigable channel," wherever situated, but he admitted that he had never himself examined, nor did he even recollect ever to have seen, Vancouver's chart; and although he did not seem prepared to contest the probability of the channel marked with soundings by Vancouver in that chart being, in fact, "the main navigable channel," he evidently hesitated to adopt that opinion without further geographical evidence, throwing out a suggestion that it would perhaps be better that such instructions should be given to the naval officers to be employed as Joint Commissioners, as would enable them both to determine which of the channels was, in fact, the main navigable channel, and to mark the boundary down the middle of that channel so soon as ascertained.

The subject, Mr. Buchanan assured me, should receive the immediate attention of the United States Government, with every disposition to avoid delay or difficulty in the accomplishment of an object which he felt to be extremely desirable for both Governments.

I have, &c.,

JOHN F. CRAMPTON.

Mr. Crampton to Mr. Marcy.

WASHINGTON, *February* 9, 1856.

SIR: I have been instructed by Her Majesty's Government to call the serious attention of the Government of the United States to the unsatisfactory and hazardous state of things which continues to exist on the boundary which divides the Territory of Washington from the British Possessions occupied by the Hudson's Bay Company; and Her Majesty's Government direct me to express their regret that their repeated remonstrances have not led to any measures which seem to have succeeded in restraining the acts of the authorities of that Territory.

I have already had the honor of addressing your Department (in a note to Mr. Hunter on the 27th July last) respecting the depredations upon the property of the Hudson's Bay Company on the Island of San Juan, by Mr. Ellis Barnes, Sheriff of Watcom County, of the Territory of Washington, in virtue of an alleged claim for taxes due to the authorities of the Territory; and I have now the honor to inclose the copy of a further letter from the Governor of the Hudson's Bay Company, together with its accompanying documents, in regard to the same matter, from which it appears that no reparation whatever has been made to the Company for the very heavy losses which they incurred on that occasion.

You will at once perceive, Sir, that the occurrence in question has arisen out of the conflicting claims of the authorities of Vancouver's Island and of Washington Territory to the jurisdiction of the Island of San Juan, as appertaining, under the provisions of the Treaty between Great Britain and the United States of 1846, to the dominions of their respective Governments.

San Juan is one of the small islands lying in the Gulf of Georgia, between Vancouver's Island and the main-land; and the question which has arisen between the parties regards the position of the channel through the middle of which, by the provision of the Treaty of 1846, the boundary line is to be run.

In the early part of the year 1848, I had the honor, by the instruction of Her Majesty's Government, to propose to the Government of the United States to name a Joint Commission for the purpose of marking out the northwest boundary; and more particularly that part of it in the neighborhood of Vancouver's Island, in regard to which, as you will perceive from a reference to my note of the 13th January of that year to the Honorable James Buchanan, the Secretary of State of the United States, Her Majesty's Government already foresaw the
[xxxvi] possibility of the occurrence of misunder*standing between the settlers of the respective nations; and Her Majesty's Government, moreover, then proposed, in order at once to preclude such misunderstandings, that before instructing their respective Commissioners, the two Governments should agree to adopt as the "channel" designated by the Treaty, that marked by Vancouver in his charts as the navigable channel, and laid down with soundings by that navigator.

Mr. Buchanan entirely concurring in the expediency of losing no time in determining the position of the boundary line, nevertheless felt some objection to adopting the channel marked by Vancouver as the "channel" designated by the Treaty, in the absence of more accurate geographical information, and he suggested that the Joint Commissioners, when appointed, should be in the first place instructed to survey the region in question, for the purpose of ascertaining whether the channel marked by Vancouver, or some other channel, as yet unexplored, between the numerous islands of the Gulf of Georgia, should be adopted as the channel designated by the Treaty, or, in other words, should be found to be the main channel, through the middle of which, according to the generally admitted principle, the boundary line should be run.

To this suggestion Her Majesty's Government, in the hope that immediate measures would be taken by the Government of the United States to name Commissioners to proceed to the spot with those already designated by the British Government, made no objection.

It has been a subject of regret to Her Majesty's Government that, from causes upon which it is unnecessary to dwell, no appointment of Commissioners has, up to the present time, been made by the Government of the United States; and I am now instructed again to press this matter on their earnest attention.

Should it appear possible, however, that this proposal cannot be met by the Government of the United States without further difficulty or delay, I would again suggest the expediency of the adoption by both Governments of the channel marked as the only known navigable channel by Vancouver, as that designated by the Treaty. It is true that the Island of San Juan, and perhaps some others of the group of small islands by which the Gulf of Georgia is studded, would thus be included within British territory; on the other hand, it is to be considered that the islands in question are of very small value, and that the existence of another navigable channel, broader and deeper than that laid down by Vancouver, by the adoption of which some of those islands might possibly fall within the jurisdiction of the United States, is, according to the reports of the most recent navigators in that region extremely improbable; while, on the other hand, the continued existence of a question of doubtful jurisdiction in a country so situated as Washington Territory and Vancouver's Island, is likely to give rise to a recurrence of acts of a similar nature to those to which I have had the honor of calling your attention, and which I have no doubt would not be less deplored by the Government of the United States than by that of Great Britain.

I am, &c.,

JOHN F. CRAMPTON.

No. 4.

CONVERSATION AND CORRESPONDENCE BETWEEN MR. BANCROFT AND VISCOUNT PALMERSTON.

Mr. Bancroft to Mr. Buchanan.[1]

UNITED STATES LEGATION,
London, August 4, 1848.

SIR: * * * * *

The Hudson's Bay Company have been trying to get a grant of Vancouver's Island. I inquired, from mere curosity, about it. Lord Palmerston replied that it was an affair that belonged exclusively to the Colonial Office, and he did not know the intentions of Lord Grey. He then told me, what I had not known before, that he had made a proposition at Washington for marking the boundaries in the northwest by setting up a landmark on the point of land where the forty-ninth parallel touches the sea, and for ascertaining the division line in the channel by noting the bearings of certain objects. I observed that on the main-land a few simple astronomical observations were all that were requisite; that the water in the Channel of Haro did not require to be divided, since the navigation was free to both parties; though, of course, the islands east of the center of the Channel of Haro were ours. He had no good chart of the Oregon waters, and asked me to let him see the traced copy of Wilkes's chart. He spoke of the propriety of settling

---

[1] As officially printed in the United States.

definitively the ownership of the several islands, in order that settlements might not be begun by one party on what properly belongs to the other. On returning home I sent him my traced copy of Wilkes's chart, with the note, of which I inclose a copy.

I am, &c.,

GEORGE BANCROFT.

Mr. Bancroft to Viscount Palmerston.[1]

90 EATON SQUARE, *July* 31, 1848.

MY DEAR LORD: As your Lordship desired, I send for your inspection a traced copy, made for me at the Navy Department, of Wilkes's Chart of the Straits of Juan de Fuca, Puget's Sound, &c., &c. Unluckily, this copy does not extend quite so far north as the parallel of 49°; though it contains the wide entrance into the Straits of Arro, the channel through the middle of which the Boundary is to be continued.

The upper part of the Straits of Arro is laid down, though
[xxxvii] not on a large scale, in Wilkes's map of *the Oregon Territory,
of which I am sorry to say I have not a copy, but which may be found in the Atlas to the Narrative of the United States Exploring Expedition.

I remain, &c.,

GEORGE BANCROFT.

Viscount Palmerston to Mr. Bancroft.

FOREIGN OFFICE, *August* 24, 1848.

Viscount Palmerston presents his compliments to Mr. Bancroft, and has the honor to return to him herewith, with his best thanks, the traced copy of Wilkes's Chart of the Straits of Juan de Fuca, &c., which Mr. Bancroft so obligingly sent to Lord Palmerston on the 31st ultimo.

Mr. Bancroft to Viscount Palmerston.

108 EATON SQUARE, *November* 3, 1848.

MY LORD: I did not forget your Lordship's desire to see the United States surveys of the waters of Puget's Sound, and those dividing Vancouver's Island from our territory.

These surveys have been reduced, and have just been published in three parts; and I transmit, for your Lordship's acceptance, the first copy which I have received.

The surveys extend to the line of 49°; and by combining two of the charts, your Lordship will readily trace the whole course of the channel of Arro, through the middle of which our boundary line passes. I think you will esteem the work done in a manner very creditable to the young navy officers concerned in it.

I have, &c.,

GEORGE BANCROFT.

---

[1] Inclosure in last foregoing letter.

Viscount Palmerston to Mr. Bancroft.

FOREIGN OFFICE, *November* 7, 1848.

SIR: I beg leave to return you my best thanks for the surveys of Puget's Sound, and of the Gulf of Georgia, which accompanied your letter of the 3d instant.

The information as to soundings contained in these charts will, no doubt, be of great service to the Commissioners who are to be appointed under the Treaty of the 15th of June, 1846, by assisting them in determining where the line of boundary described in the first Article of that Treaty ought to run.

I have, &c.,

PALMERSTON.

No. 5.

PROPOSED AMENDMENT OF ARTICLE II OF TREATY.

The following was moved in the Senate of the United States, on 12th June, 1846, as an addition to the Resolution advising the President to accept the proposal:

With the following proviso at the end of the second Article of the proposed Convention, to wit:

"*Provided*, That the right of navigating the Columbia River secured to the Hudson's Bay Company, and to all British subjects trading with the same, be limited to the year A. D. 1863, when it shall cease and determine."

Mr. Buchanan to Mr. MacLane.

No. 34.] DEPARTMENT OF STATE, *Washington, June* 13, 1846.

SIR: The President communicated to the Senate, on the 10th instant, a confidential message, of which I transmit you a copy, asking their previous advice in regard to the Projet of a Convention for the adjustment of the Oregon question delivered to me by Mr. Pakenham on the 6th instant.

On yesterday the Senate adopted the following resolution:

Resolved, (two-thirds of the Senators present concurring,) That the President of the United States be, and he is hereby, advised to accept the proposal of the British Government accompanying his message to the Senate dated 10th June, 1846, for a Convention to settle boundaries, &c., between the United States and Great Britain, west of the Rocky or Stony Mountains.

The vote of the Senate stood 37[1] to 12.

[xxxviii] I have learned from the best sources that the Senate gave this advice under the conviction that, by * the true construction of the second Article of the Projet, the right of the Hudson's Bay Company to navigate the Columbia would expire with the termination of their present license to trade with the Indians, &c., on the northwest coast of America on the 30th May, 1859. In a conversation with Mr. Pakenham to-day I communicated this fact to him, and requested him to state it in his dispatch to Lord Aberdeen.

---

[1] So, in the letter as officially printed in the United States.

The Treaty will be signed and sent to the Senate on Monday next; and it is more than probable that they will, in some form or other, place upon their records their understanding of its true construction in this particular.

I have, &c.

JAMES BUCHANAN.

V

CORRESPONDENCE.

CORRESPONDENCE.

No. 1.

Mr. Fish to Mr. Bancroft.

No. 351.] DEPARTMENT OF STATE,
Washington, July 18, 1871.

SIR: I transmit to you herewith the draught of a note which, in conjunction with the representative of Her Britannic Majesty, you will present to the Government of the Emperor of Germany, in pursuance of the thirty-fourth article of a treaty signed at Washington on the 8th of May, 1871, of which a copy is herewith sent, requesting that His Imperial Majesty will be pleased to act as Arbitrator in a question which has arisen between the Governments of the United States and of Great Britain, in regard to a line of boundary between the territories of the United States and those of Her Britannic Majesty, under the first article of the treaty concluded at Washington on the 15th of June, 1846, a copy of which is also sent to you. You will accordingly arrange with your British colleague for the simultaneous presentation of your respective notes.

Draught of note to be presented to Emperor of Germany inviting him to act as arbitrator.

I am, &c.,

HAMILTON FISH.

[Inclosure No. 1.]

Draught of note to be presented to the Government of the Emperor of Germany.

The Government of the United States and the Government of Her Britannic Majesty having agreed, by a treaty signed at Washington on the 8th of May, 1871, of which a copy is hereunto annexed, together with a copy of the previous treaty of June 15, 1846, herein referred to, to submit to the arbitration and award of His Majesty the Emperor of Germany the decision of the question set forth in the thirty-fourth article of the first-named treaty, in the following words: "Whereas it was stipulated by Article I of the treaty concluded at Washington on the 15th of June, 1846, between Her Britannic Majesty and the United States, that the line of boundary between the territories of the United States and those of Her Britannic Majesty, from the point on the forty-ninth parallel of north latitude up to which it had already been ascertained, should be continued westward along the said parallel of north latitude to the middle of the channel which separates the continent from Vancouver's Island, and thence southerly through the middle of the said channel and of Fuca Straits to the Pacific Ocean; and whereas the commissioners appointed by the two high contracting parties to determine that portion of the boundary which runs southerly through the middle of the channel aforesaid were unable to agree upon the same; and whereas the Government of Her Britannic Majesty claims that such boundary-line should, under the terms of the treaty above recited, be run through the Rosario Straits, and the Government of the United States claims that it should be run through the Canal de Haro, it is agreed that the respective claims of the Government of the United States and of the Government of Her Britannic Majesty shall be submitted to the arbitration and award of His Majesty the Emperor of Germany, who, having regard to the above-mentioned article of the said treaty, shall decide thereupon finally, and without appeal, which of those claims is most in accordance with the true interpretation of the treaty of June 15, 1846;" and the high contracting parties reposing entire confidence in the spirit of justice and impartiality which distinguishes His Imperial Majesty, the common friend of the two states, having agreed, in pursuance of the said treaty, to address themselves to His Imperial Majesty, and having further mutually engaged, in the event of His Imperial Majesty being willing to afford his good offices as arbitrator on this occasion, to consider the award of His Majesty as absolutely final and conclusive, and to give effect to the same without any objection, evasion, or delay whatsoever, the undersigned has received the orders of his Government to communicate to His Imperial Majesty the treaty which has thus been made on the part of the Government of the United States, and to express the President's earnest desire that His Imperial Majesty will be pleased to take upon him the office of arbitrator in the question. The undersigned has the honor to request His Serene Highness the Prince Bismarck to lay this communication before His Majesty the Emperor of Germany, and to be pleased to make known to the undersigned His Imperial Majesty's determination with regard to his acceptance of the desired arbitration.

[Inclosure No. 2.]

Extract from the treaty between the United States and Great Britain of June 15, 1846.

ARTICLE I.

From the point on the forty-ninth parallel of north latitude, where the boundary laid down in existing treaties and conventions between the United States and Great Britain terminates, the line of boundary between the territories of the United States and those of Her Britannic Majesty shall be continued westward along the said forty-ninth parallel of north latitude to the middle of the channel which separates the continent from Vancouver's Island, and thence southerly through the middle of the said channel, and of Fuca's Straits, to the Pacific Ocean: *Provided, however,* That the navigation of the whole of the said channel and straits south of the forty-ninth parallel of north latitude remain free and open to both parties.

[Inclosure No. 3.]

Extract from the Treaty of Washington of May 8, 1871.

ARTICLE XXXIV.

Whereas it was stipulated by Article I of the treaty concluded at Washington on the 15th of June, 1846, between the United States and Her Britannic Majesty, that the line of boundary between the territories of the United States and those of Her Britannic Majesty, from the point on the forty-ninth parallel of north latitude up to which it had already been ascertained, should be continued westward along the said parallel of north latitude "to the middle of the channel which separates the continent from Vancouver's Island, and thence southerly, through the middle of the said channel and of Fuca Straits, to the Pacific Ocean;" and whereas the commissioners appointed by the two high contracting parties to determine that portion of the boundary which runs southerly through the middle of the channel aforesaid were unable to agree upon the same; and whereas the Government of Her Britannic Majesty claims that such boundary-line should, under the terms of the treaty above recited, be run through the Rosario Straits, and the Government of the United States claims that it should be run through the Canal de Haro, it is agreed that the respective claims of the Government of the United States and of the Government of Her Britannic Majesty shall be submitted to the arbitration and award of His Majesty the Emperor of Germany, who, having regard to the above-mentioned article of the said treaty, shall decide thereupon, finally and without appeal, which of those claims is most in accordance with the true interpretation of the treaty of June 15, 1846.

No. 2.

Mr. Bancroft to Mr. Fish.

[Extract.]

No. 249.] AMERICAN LEGATION,
Berlin, July 29, 1871. (Received August 18.)

SIR: This day, at a quarter before 1, I took the British chargé in my carriage to the Foreign Office, where we delivered simultaneously formal notes, identical in terms, addressed to Prince Bismarck, chancellor of the empire, requesting the German Emperor to accept the office of Arbiter on the northwestern boundary question, under the treaty of Washington. I annex a copy of the note.

Joint notes presented to the German Government.

* * * * * * *

I remain, &c.,

GEO. BANCROFT.

Mr Bancroft to Prince Bismarck.

AMERICAN LEGATION,
Berlin, July 29, 1871.

The Government of the United States of America and the Government of Her Britannic Majesty having agreed, by a Treaty signed at Washington the 8th of May, 1871, of which a copy is hereunto annexed, together with a copy of the previous treaty of June 15, 1846, herein referred to, to submit to the arbitration and award of His Majesty the Emperor of Germany the decision of the question set forth in the thirty-fourth article of the first-named treaty, in the following words: [Here follows verbatim the entire article thirty-fourth, of the first-mentioned treaty.] And the high contracting parties reposing entire confidence in the spirit of justice and impartiality which distinguishes His Imperial Majesty, the common friend of the two states, having agreed in pursuance of the said treaty to address themselves to His Imperial Majesty; and having further mutually engaged, in the event of His Imperial Majesty being willing to afford his good offices as Arbitrator on this occasion, to consider the award of His Imperial Majesty as absolutely final and conclusive, and to give effect to the same without any objection, evasion, or delay whatsoever, the undersigned has received the order of his Government to communicate to His Imperial Majesty the treaty which has thus been made on the part of the United States, and to express the earnest desire of the President of the United States that His Imperial Majesty will be pleased to take upon him the office of Arbitrator in the question.

The undersigned has the honor to request His Serene Highness the Prince Bismarck to lay this communication before His Majesty the Emperor of Germany, and to be pleased to make known to the undersigned His Imperial Majesty's determination with regard to his acceptance of the desired arbitration. The undersigned seizes this opportunity to renew to His Serene Highness Prince Bismarck the assurances of his highest consideration.

GEO. BANCROFT.

No. 3.

Mr. Bancroft to Mr. Fish.

No. 253.] AMERICAN LEGATION,
Berlin, August 21, 1871. (Received September 7.)

SIR: The German Secretary of State has notified to me and to the British Legation that the Emperor of Germany accepts the office of Arbitrator on our northwestern boundary question. I suppose I am acting entirely in harmony with your wishes in proposing to the British Legation a very early attention to the

Emperor of Germany accepts the office of Arbitrator.

subject, in the hope that we may speedily bring the matter to a conclusion and an award. Should any delay occur, I will take care that the fault shall not be on our side. I venture to expect an award in our favor. I have watched for a quarter of a century the course of this negotiation. In all that time the present Administration is the first that has taken the subject in hand from a right point of view, and if a favorable award is obtained it will be mainly due to the form of arbitration which you established by the Treaty of Washington.

I remain, &c.,

GEO. BANCROFT.

No. 4.

Mr. Bancroft to Mr. Fish.

No. 255.] AMERICAN LEGATION,
Berlin, September 1, 1871. (Received September 20.)

Formal acceptance by the Emperor of Germany of the office of Arbitrator.

SIR: I inclose a copy of the note which I have received this day from the German Secretary of State, notifying me formally that the Emperor of Germany has accepted the office of arbitrator in the controversy on the northwestern boundary between the United States and Great Britain.

I remain, &c.,

GEO. BANCROFT.

Mr. Von Thile to Mr. Bancroft.

[Translation.]

BERLIN, *September* 1, 1871.

The undersigned has had the honor to receive the esteemed note of Mr. Bancroft, Envoy Extraordinary and Minister Plenipotentiary of the United States of America, of the 29th of July last, wherein he, in the name of his High Government, has made the request that His Majesty the Emperor and King would accept the office of arbitrator, referrd to in the thirty-fourth article of the treaty dated Washington, May 8, 1871, in the present boundary question between the United States and Great Britain. The undersigned has not failed to obtain His Majesty's decision with regard to his acceptance of this office, and has the honor most respectfully to announce that His Imperial and Royal Majesty has most graciously been pleased to accept the said office of arbitrator.

While the undersigned most respectfully adds that the Royal Chargé d'Affaires of Great Britain at this capital made a similar request on the 29th of July last, and has this day received an answer by note, he avails himself of this occasion to renew to His Excellency the Envoy the assurance of his most distinguished consideration.

V. THILE.

No. 5.

Mr. Davis to Mr. Bancroft.

No. 379.] DEPARTMENT OF STATE,
Washington, September 28, 1871.

The President expresses his grateful acknowledgments for the action of the Emperor.

SIR: With reference to your dispatch of the 1st instant, No. 255, and to the note of Mr. Von Thile, a copy of which accompanied it, announcing the consent of His Majesty the Emperor of Germany and King of Prussia to act as the arbitrator between this Government and that of Great Britain, in determining the controversy respecting the boundary between the two countries, in the manner provided in the thirty-fourth article of the Treaty of Washington of May 8, 1871, the President desires that you will convey to the Secretary of State for the German Empire, with a request that they may be communicated to His Majesty, his grateful acknowledgments for the promptness with which His Majesty has been graciously pleased to accede to the wishes of the two Governments.

I am, &c.,

J. C. B. DAVIS,
Acting Secretary.

No. 6.

Mr. Bancroft to Mr. Fish.

No. 307.] AMERICAN LEGATION,
Berlin, December 12, 1871. (Received Jan. 3.)

SIR: I this day left with Mr. Von Abeken, who, during the illness of the Chancellor of the Empire and of the Secretary of State, takes charge of the Foreign Office, the memorial of the United States on the Canal de Haro as their northwestern boundary, to be delivered through Prince Bismarck into the hands of the Emperor. At the same time I left at the British Embassy in Berlin not only the copy required by the treaty, but several extra copies of the memorial and evidence.

Has delivered the memorial.

I annex a copy of the letter addressed to Mr. Petre. I hope you will approve my offer to join in bringing this boundary question to a speedy issue.

Up to late last night the representative of Her Britannic Majesty at Berlin had not received from his government any instructions on the subject.

I remain, &c.,

GEO. BANCROFT.

[Inclosure.]

Mr. Bancroft to Mr. Petre.

AMERICAN LEGATION,
Berlin, December 12, 1871.

The limit of time allowed by the Treaty of Washington of May 16, 1871, for presenting the Case of the United States on the disputed boundary question which has been referred to the German Emperor for arbitration, being close at hand, the undersigned is constrained this day, through His Serene Highness Prince Bismarck, Chancellor of the German Empire, to lay before His Majesty the German Emperor the printed Case of the United States, accompanied by the evidence offered in support of the same.

In conformity with the Treaty of Washington, ratified June 17, 1871, the undersigned has the honor likewise to communicate a copy of the Case and evidence to the Hon. Mr. Petre, as the representative of Her Britannic Majesty at Berlin.

It will give the undersigned great satisfaction to join with the representative of Her Britannic Majesty in bringing this long-contested question to a decision at the earliest possible moment. The undersigned gladly seizes this opportunity of renewing to Mr. Petre, Her Britannic Majesty's representative at Berlin, his assurances of highest respect and consideration.

GEO. BANCROFT.

No. 7.

Mr. Bancroft to Mr. Fish.

(Extract.)

No. 308.] AMERICAN LEGATION,
Berlin, December 15, 1871. (Received Jan. 3.)

SIR: * * * * * * *

British Case and evidence delivered.

Admiral Prevost, formerly British commissioner for running the northwestern boundary, arrived here this morning and delivered the British Case and evidence, of which I am promised a copy this evening. I will lose no time in sending you a copy and reporting to you the aspect of the case.

I remain, &c.,

GEO. BANCROFT.

No. 8.

Mr. Bancroft to Mr. Fish.

No. 314.] AMERICAN LEGATION,
Berlin, December 28, 1871. (Received Jan. 16.)

Receipt of memorial acknowledged.

SIR: Herewith I inclose a translation of a letter received from the Chancellor of the German Empire, acknowledging the receipt of the American memorial on the northwest boundary question, and informing me that he was on the point of laying it before the Emperor.

I remain, &c.,

GEO. BANCROFT.

Mr. Von Philipsborn to Mr. Bancroft.

[Inclosure.—Translation.]

BERLIN, *December* 20, 1871.

The undersigned has the honor to acknowledge the receipt from the Envoy Extraordinary and Minister Plenipotentiary of the United States of America, Mr. Bancroft, in reply to his note of the 12th instant, respecting the boundary dispute between the United States and Great Britain, the memorial and proof which were therewith transmitted. The undersigned is on the point of submitting these documents, as well as those communicated by the Royal Chargé d'Affaires of Great Britain on the 13th and 15th instant, to His Majesty the Emperor and King. The undersigned avails himself of this further occasion to renew to the Minister Plenipotentiary the assurance of his most distinguished consideration.

For the Chancellor of the Empire.

VON PHILIPSBORN.

No. 9.

Mr. Bancroft to Mr. Fish.

No. 369.] AMERICAN LEGATION,
Berlin, June 11, 1872. (Received June 27.)

Replies of the United States and Great Britain delivered.

SIR: Admiral Prevost arrived yesterday from London with the second and definitive statement of the British Government on our boundary question, which Mr. Odo Russell, the British Embassador at Berlin, transmitted to the Foreign Office yesterday, furnishing me with a copy of it late last evening. I have at once this morning presented the American reply to the Prince of Bismarck, and have furnished the British Embassador with copies of it.

Admiral Prevost tells me that he intends to remain here until the Imperial Arbitrator shall have rendered his decision.

The mail of to-morrow from Hamburg will take to you a copy of this second British statement, as well as copies of the paper which I have submitted in behalf of the United States.

I remain, &c.,

GEO. BANCROFT.

No. 10.

Mr. Bancroft to Mr. Fish.

No. 373.] AMERICAN LEGATION,
Berlin, June 17, 1872. (Received July 3.)

SIR: I send you by the Hamburg packet of the 19th instant three bound copies of the English version of our reply to the British argument on the San Juan question; ten copies of the same with maps, and fifteen without maps; ten copies of the German with maps, and fifteen without maps. A bound copy of the English second and definitive statement is also inclosed in one of the parcels. I annex copies of the correspondence that attended the delivery of the reply.

Transmits copies of the replies and of the correspondence attending their delivery.

I remain, &c.,

GEO. BANCROFT.

[Inclosure No. 1.]

Mr. Odo Russell to Mr. Bancroft.

BRITISH EMBASSY,
Berlin, June 10, 1872.

SIR: The undersigned, Her Britannic Majesty's Embassador Extraordinary and Plenipotentiary to His Imperial Majesty the Emperor of Germany, has the honor to transmit to Mr. Bancroft, Envoy Extraordinary and Minister Plenipotentiary of the United States to the Court of Berlin, in pursuance of the provisions of the thirty-sixth Article of the Treaty of Washington, of the 8th of May, 1871, copies, in duplicate, of the second and definitive statement of the British Government in the matter of the line of Boundary between the Territories of Her Majesty the Queen of the United Kingdom of Great Britain and Ireland and those of the United States, which the undersigned has this day delivered to His Serene Highness Prince Bismarck to be laid before His Imperial Majesty the Emperor of Germany. The undersigned will have the honor of furnishing Mr. Bancroft with additional copies of this statement if he should desire them.

The undersigned, &c.,

ODO RUSSELL.

[Inclosure No. 2.]

Mr. Bancroft to Mr. Odo Russell.

AMERICAN LEGATION,
Berlin, June 11, 1872.

SIR: The undersigned, Envoy Extraordinary and Minister Plenipotentiary of the United States of America to the Emperor of Germany, has the honor to acknowledge the receipt of the note of Mr. Odo Russell, British Embassador at Berlin, of last evening, and copies in duplicate of the second and definitive statement of the British Government according to the provisions of the Treaty of Washington of the 8th of May, 1871.

Mr. Odo Russell having already delivered this statement to his Serene Highness the Prince of Bismarck to be laid before His Imperial Majesty the Emperor of Germany, the undersigned expresses the hope that this long-continued controversy may be brought very speedily to an end through the friendly intervention of the Imperial Arbitrator.

The undersigned, &c.,

GEO. BANCROFT.

[Inclosure No. 3.]

Mr. Bancroft to the Prince Bismarck.

AMERICAN LEGATION,
Berlin, June 11, 1872.

The undersigned, Envoy Extraordinary and Minister Plenipotentiary of the United States of America, takes leave in the name of his Government, through His Serene Highness the Prince of Bismarck, Chancellor of the German Empire, to lay before His Imperial Majesty the Emperor of Germany the accompanying definitive reply of the United States to the Case of the Government of Her Britannic Majesty of the 13th of December, 1871.

The undersigned has communicated a copy of this definitive reply to the representative of Her Britannic Majesty at Berlin.

The undersigned has received from the British Embassador at Berlin a copy of the second and definitive statement on behalf of the Government of Her Britannic Majesty, together with notice that the same was yesterday submitted through his Serene Highness the Prince of Bismarck to His Majesty the Emperor of Germany.

Nothing remains for the undersigned but to express his hope that, now that each party has presented its last word, an early decision may soon remove the cloud of difference that has so long existed on this subject between the Government of the United States and the Government of Her Britannic Majesty.

The undersigned, &c.,

GEO. BANCROFT.

[Inclosure No. 4.]

Mr Bancroft to Mr. Odo Russell.

AMERICAN LEGATION,
Berlin, June 11, 1872.

SIR: The undersigned, Envoy Extraordinary and Minister Plenipotentiary of the United States of America to the Emperor of Germany, has the honor to transmit to Mr. Odo Russell, Her Britannic Majesty's Embassador at Berlin, in pursuance of the thirty-sixth article of the Treaty of Washington of the 8th of May, 1871, copies in duplicate of the definitive reply of the Government of the United States to the Case of the Government of Her Britannic Majesty of December 13, 1871, which the undersigned has this day delivered to His Serene Highness the Prince of Bismarck, to be laid before His Imperial Majesty the Emperor of Germany.

The undersigned will have the honor of furnishing Mr. Odo Russell with an additional copy of this statement, together with other copies, if he should desire them, and avails himself of this opportunity to renew, &c.

GEO. BANCROFT.

[Inclosure No. 5.]

Mr. Odo Russell to Mr. Bancroft.

BRITISH EMBASSY,
Berlin, June 11, 1872.

SIR: The undersigned, Her Britannic Majesty's Embassador Extraordinary and Plenipotentiary to His Majesty the Emperor of Germany, has the honor to acknowledge the receipt of Mr. Bancroft's letter of this day's date, informing him that he had submitted to His Majesty the Emperor of Germany, through Prince Bismarck, the second and definitive reply of the Government of the United States on the disputed boundary question, and at the same time inclosing copies of it for Mr. Russell's use and information.

In thanking Mr. Bancroft for this communication, and cordially reciprocating His Excellency's wish expressed in his even-dated note that this long-continued controversy may, through the friendly arbitration of the Emperor, be brought very speedily to a close, the undersigned, &c.

ODO RUSSELL.

No. 11.

Mr. Bancroft to Mr. Fish.

[Extract.]

No. 377.] AMERICAN LEGATION,
Berlin, June 24, 1872. (Received July 13.)

SIR: * * * * * * *

I transmit a translation of the acknowledgment that the definitive statements of both parties are already in the hands of the Imperial Arbitrator.

Receipts of definitive statements by the Imperial Arbitrator acknowledged.

I remain, &c.,

GEO. BANCROFT.

[Inclosure.]

Mr. Von Thile to Mr. Bancroft.

[Translation.]

BERLIN, *June* 18, 1872.

The undersigned has the honor most respectfully to acknowledge the receipt from Mr. Bancroft, Envoy Extraordinary and Minister Plenipotentiary of the United States of America, of the obliging note of the 11th instant respecting the boundary dispute between the United States and Great Britain, together with the accompanying reply. The undersigned has not failed to lay before His Majesty the Emperor and King this reply, as well as that delivered on the 10th of this month by the Embassador of Great Britain at this Court.

At the same time the undersigned, &c.

VON THILE.

No. 12.

Mr. Bancroft to Mr. Fish.

No. 379.] AMERICAN LEGATION,
Berlin, June 28, 1872. (Received July 15.)

SIR: I am officially informed that the names of the gentlemen who will be requested to examine and report upon the Haro boundary question will be forwarded to the Imperial Arbitrator to-day for his approval. This approval will follow as a matter of course, and if the gentlemen designated accept the appointment, the consideration of the case will go forward without delay. I am assured that everything which is proper will be done to accelerate a decision.

Appointment of gentlemen to examine Haro boundary question.

I remain, &c.,

GEO. BANCROFT.

No. 13.

Mr. Bancroft to Mr. Fish.

[Extract.]

No. 401.] AMERICAN LEGATION,
Berlin, September 30, 1872. (Received October 16.)

SIR: I am assured, on the best authority, that the decision respecting our northwest boundary approaches its solution, and I have heard nothing from any quarter that does not confirm me in the opinion that the decision will be in our favor.

Decision approaches its solution.

The writers of telegrams, who run a race with one another, are already making the public familiar with this view of the subject. I shall telegraph the decision to you so soon as it becomes known to me in an authentic form. * * * *

On the 3d day of October, Mr. v. Thile, who has had the charge of the Foreign Office in Berlin since I have been here, retires, and his place is to be supplied by Mr. de Balan, now German Minister in Brussels. Mr. de Balan will retain for the present his diplomatic rank and appointments, until the German Diet comes together, when it will be proposed to make the place which he is to fill equal to that of a Minister of State.

Mr. v. Thile goes out of office with the unanimous and unqualified esteem of all who have transacted business with him. He is a man of honor, integrity, and thorough and most various culture.

I remain, &c.,

GEO. BANCROFT.

No. 14.

Mr. Bancroft to Mr. Fish.

[Extract.]

No. 410.] AMERICAN LEGATION,
Berlin, October 4, 1872. (Received November 7.)

SIR: The papers relating to our Arbitration were completely finished last week and forwarded to the Emperor at Baden for his final action and signature. Just as they arrived, the death of his youngest brother was announced to him by telegraph, and he hastened to Berlin before declaring his opinion.

Announcement of award delayed by death of Prince Albrecht.

His deceased brother, Prince Albrecht, more than twelve years younger than himself, was buried on Saturday with the honors paid to a field-marshal, a rank which he had received from the Emperor of Russia only a few hours before he was struck down by apoplexy.

We are daily, I might almost say hourly, expecting to be summoned to receive the award. I have taken measures—I hope they will prove sufficient—to give you the decision by telegraph twenty-four hours before it is made known to the telegraphic bureau in this city.

* * * * * * *

I remain, &c.,

GEO. BANCROFT.

No. 15.

Mr. Bancroft to Mr. Fish.

[Telegram.]

BERLIN, *October* 23, 1872. (Received October 23.)

The three Experts to whom the American Memorial on the Canal de Haro and the British Case were referred, have made, each for himself, a very elaborate report on the question, supporting their opinions by reasons stated with technical precision and exactness. The Emperor has also, with the highest sense of official duty, given his personal attention to the subject, and after the most careful study and deliberation, he has arrived at the conclusion satisfactory to his own sense of justice.

Claim of the United States of America most in accordance with the true interpretation of the Treaty.

The reports of the Experts, with reasons, have not been communicated to us. The decree of the Imperial Arbitrator which has been communicated has the form not so much of a decree in council as of a cabinet order. It does not enter into any elaborate exposition of the decision, but, without diverging in the least from the point presented for arbitration, decrees that the claim of the United States of America is most in accordance with the true interpretation of the Treaty of June 15, 1846. I shall forward the official copy of the decree by a special messenger.

BANCROFT.

No. 16.

Mr. Fish to Mr. Bancroft.

[Telegram.]

WASHINGTON, *October* 24, 1872.

Congratulations on the award. The President directs thanks, in which I concur, for your able management of the case.

FISH.

No. 17.

Mr. Bancroft to Mr. Fish.

No. 413.] AMERICAN LEGATION,
Berlin, October 24, 1872. (Received November 14.)

SIR: At four minutes before 10 o'clock last evening I received the award of the Emperor on the question of boundary submitted by the Government of the United States of America and the Government of Her Britannic Majesty to his arbitration.

Award received and forwarded.

I send the award by Mr. Frank Austin Scott, as special messenger. He will sail by the first German steamer, the Main, which leaves Bremen on Saturday, the 26th instant.

I inclose also a translation of the award, and a copy and translation of the note of Mr. Von Balan relating to it.

I congratulate you most heartily on this result, which is so greatly due to your own wisdom and forethought: first, in selecting as arbitrator a man of excellent judgment and an inflexible love of justice; next, in having defined with the utmost precision the question for arbitration; and lastly, in having brought together every document and book that could be of use in elucidating and establishing the rights of the United States.

I have this day, as by order of the President, in the name of the people of the United States expressed to His Majesty, the German Emperor, their thanks for the great pains and attention which His Imperial Majesty has devoted to the question submitted to him for adjudication. A copy of this letter is also annexed.

Thanks of President expressed to Emperor.

I remain, &c.,

GEO. BANCROFT.

[Inclosure No. 1.]

Award of His Majesty the Emperor of Germany on the San Juan boundary question.

Wir Wilhelm, von Gottes Gnaden, Deutscher Kaiser, König von Preussen, &c., &c., &c.

Nach Einsicht des zwischen den Regierungen Ihrer Britischen Majestät und der Vereinigten Staaten von Amerika geschlossenen Vertrages de dato Washington den 6ten* Mai, 1871, Inhalts dessen die gedachten Regierungen die unter ihnen streitige Frage: ob die Grenzlinie, welche nach dem Vertrage de dato Washington den 15ten Juni, 1846, nachdem sie gegen Westen längs des 49ten Grades Nördlicher Breite bis zur Mitte des Kanals, welcher das Festland von der Vancouver Insel trennt, gezogen worden, südlich durch die Mitte des gedachten Kanals und der Fuca-Meerenge bis zum Stillen Ocean gezogen werden soll, durch den Rosario-Kanal, wie die Regierung Ihrer Britischen Majestät beansprucht, oder durch den Haro-Kanal, wie die Regierung der Vereinigten Staaten beansprucht, zu ziehen sei, Unserem Schiedsspruche unterbreitet haben, damit Wir endgültig und ohne Berufung entscheiden, welcher dieser Ansprüche mit der richtigen Auslegung des Vertrages vom 15ten Juni, 1846, am meisten im Einklange stehe;

Nach Anhörung des Uns von den durch Uns berufenen Sach- und Rechtskundigen über den Inhalt der gewechselten Denkschriften und deren Anlagen erstatteten Vortrages,

Haben den nachstehenden Schiedsspruch gefällt—

Mit der richtigen Auslegung des zwischen den Regierungen Ihrer Britischen Majestät und der Vereinigten Staaten von Amerika geschlossenen Vertrages de dato Washington den 15ten Juni, 1846, steht der Anspruch der Regierung der Vereinigten Staaten am meisten im Einklange, dass die Grenzlinie zwischen den Gebieten Ihrer Britischen Majestät und den Vereinigten Staaten durch den Haro-Kanal gezogen werde.

Urkundlich unter Unserer Höchsteigenhändigen Unterschrift und beigedrucktem Kaiserlichen Insiegel.

Gegeben Berlin den 21ten October, 1872.

[L. S.] WILHELM.

[Inclosure No. 2.—Translation.]

We, William, by the grace of God, German Emperor, King of Prussia, &c., &c., &c.

After examination of the treaty concluded at Washington on the 6th* of May, 1871, between the Governments of Her Britannic Majesty and

* Sic in original, May 8th.

of the United States of America, according to which the said Governments have submitted to our arbitrament the question at issue between them, whether the boundary-line which, according to the Treaty of Washington of June 15, 1846, after being carried westward along the forty-ninth parallel of northern latitude to the middle of the channel which separates the continent from Vancouver's Island is thence to be drawn southerly through the middle of the said channel and of the Fuca Straits to the Pacific Ocean, should be drawn through the Rosario Channel as the Government of Her Britannic Majesty claims, or through the Haro Channel as the Government of the United States claims; to the end that we may finally and without appeal decide which of these claims is most in accordance with the true interpretation of the treaty of June 15, 1846.

After hearing the report made to us by the experts and jurists summoned by us upon the contents of the interchanged memorials and their appendices—

Have decreed the following award:

Most in accordance with the true interpretations of the treaty concluded on the 15th of June, 1846, between the Governments of Her Britannic Majesty and of the United States of America, is the claim of the Government of the United States that the boundary-line between the territories of Her Britannic Majesty and the United States should be drawn through the Haro Channel.

Authenticated by our autographic signature and the impression of the imperial great seal.

Given at Berlin, October the 21st, 1872.

[L. S.] WILLIAM.

[Inclosure No. 3.—Translation.]

Mr. Von Balan to Mr. Bancroft.

BERLIN, *October* 23, 1872.

His Majesty the Emperor and King, having made the award in the Arbitration referred to him by the Treaty of Washington, May 6, [8,] 1871, in the Boundary Dispute between the United States and Great Britain, the undersigned has the honor to transmit herewith a copy of this award with the remark that he sends to the Royal Embassador of Great Britain at this Court a like copy.

At the same time the undersigned avails himself of this further opportunity to renew to the Envoy of the United States, Mr. Bancroft, the assurance of his most distinguished consideration.

VON BALAN.

[Inclosure No. 4.]

Mr. Bancroft to Mr. Von Balan.

AMERICAN LEGATION,
Berlin, October 24, 1872.

MR. SECRETARY OF STATE FOR FOREIGN AFFAIRS: I have communicated to my Government the Award of the Imperial Arbitrator, received last evening, relating to the northwestern boundary of the United States of America. In return the President of the United States has charged me, in the name of the people of the United States, to express to His Majesty the German Emperor their thanks for the great pains and attention which His Imperial Majesty has devoted to the question submitted to him for adjudication.

The definitive, friendly settlement of the difference has a peculiar interest and importance. It is now exactly ninety years since the King of Great Britain first formally recognized the existence of the United States of America as an independent State, and from that time to the present controversy regarding the boundaries of their respective possessions in America has never ceased even for a single day. During this period the two countries have been repeatedly on the verge of war, growing out of their opposing claims to jurisdiction. After an unrelenting strife of ninety years, the award of His Majesty the Emperor of Germany closes the long and unintermitted, and often very dangerous, series of disputes on the extent of their respective territories, and so for the first time in their history opens to the two countries the unobstructed way to agreement, good understanding, and peace.

I gladly seize this occasion, &c.,

GEO. BANCROFT.

No. 18.

Mr. Bancroft to Mr. Fish.

No. 415.] AMERICAN LEGATION,
Berlin, October 24, 1872. (Received November 14.)

SIR: The importance of the award of the German Emperor is known in England as well as on our own Pacific coast. It establishes us in the equal possession of the Channel of Haro and in the exclusive possession of all the other channels leading north from Fuca Straits and Washington Sound.

Importance of the award.

The award was a grievous disappointment to Admiral Prevost, the very amiable high officer of the British Navy, who had for twenty-one years participated in the management of the case. Up to the last moment he confidently expected a decision in his favor.

The conduct of the present British Embassador at this Court, throughout the whole period of the discussions, has been exactly what could have been wished. We have during the whole time preserved intimate friendly relations. This morning he was so good as to call on me, and while it could not be expected of him to be gratified by the award, he did express, and as I believe most sincerely, the greatest satisfaction that all strife between the two Governments, respecting boundaries, had found its end, and that there is no longer an obstacle to the uninterrupted reciprocity of good feeling between the two countries. I met his friendly expressions with perfect cordiality. While a decree could not be on both sides, I pointed out to him that since George III acknowledged our independence in the late summer of 1782 to the present time, the strife about boundaries between the two Governments had known no intermission; now at last there remained no further differences; that therefore the definite friendly settlement effected by the award of the German Emperor opened the way to a new career of reciprocal good feeling between the two countries.

Conduct of the British Embassador.

I remain, &c.,

GEO. BANCROFT.

No. 19.

Mr. Nicholas Fish to Mr. Fish.

No. 421.] AMERICAN LEGATION,
Berlin, November 2, 1872. (Received November 19.)

SIR: I annex a copy and translation of a note from the Secretary of State for Foreign Affairs, in reply to Mr. Bancroft's of the 21st ultimo, in regard to the costs and expenses of this Government in the Northwest Boundary arbitration.

Re-imbursements of costs and expenses of the Arbitration declined.

The German Government decline to accept payment for their expenses in the matter.

In order that I may know the more fully the wish of the Department as to the course of acknowledging this friendly act, I delay answering Mr. Von Balan's note until I receive a reply to the telegram I sent you, which ran as follows: "Fish, Secretary, Washington: German Government decline compensation for expenses of arbitration. (Signed.) Fish, Chargé."

I have, &c.,

NICHOLAS FISH,
Chargé d'Affaires ad interim.

[Inclosure.—Translation.]

Mr. Von Balan to Mr. Fish.

BERLIN, *November* 1, 1872.

The Minister of the United States of America, in a note dated October 21, 1872, has been pleased to request to be advised what costs and expenses have been incurred by this Government in the boundary question between the United States and Great Britain.

In reply to this inquiry, the undersigned, while expressing his thanks for the offer of re-imbursement, which it has been deemed proper to make, has the honor to inform the American Chargé d'Affaires, Mr. Fish, that there are no costs or expenses to be charged by this Government in the matter.

The undersigned avails himself of the occasion to renew to the Chargé d'Affaires the assurance of his distinguished consideration.

VON BALAN.

No. 20.

Mr. Fish to Mr. Bancroft.

[Extract.]

No. 529.] WASHINGTON, *November* 27, 1872.

SIR: I have to acknowledge the receipt of a dispatch of the 2d instant, No. 421, from Mr. Nicholas Fish, Chargé d'Affaires *ad interim*, inclosing a copy of a note addressed to him by the Secretary of State for Foreign Affairs, stating that the German Government decline to accept payment for expenses incurred in the arbitration of the boundary question between the United States and Great Britain.

Friendly act of German Government highly appreciated.

The President, highly appreciating this friendly act, has instructed me to convey, through the Legation, to the Imperial Government, an expression of his thanks for the courtesy thus extended to the Government of the United States. * * * * * * *

I am, &c.,

HAMILTON FISH.

No. 21.

Sir E. Thornton to Mr. Fish.

WASHINGTON, *November* 21, 1872. (Received November 21.)

Effect to be given to the award without delay.

SIR: In compliance with an instruction which I have received from Earl Granville, I have the honor to inform you that on the 7th and 8th instant His Lordship caused letters to be addressed to the Colonial Office and to the Admiralty, inclosing copies of the award of the Emperor of Germany on the San Juan Water-Boundary, and requesting that effect may be given to it with as little delay as possible by the withdrawal of the detachment of Royal Marines from the Island of San Juan, and the due notification of the award to the proper Colonial Authorities.

Measures to this end.

In accordance with the tenor of these letters a copy of the award will be forwarded to the Governor-General of the Dominion of Canada and to the Lieutenant-Governor of British Columbia, with a request that proper notification of it may be made and effect given to it.

The Admiralty will also communicate a copy of the award, with as little delay as possible, to the Admiral in command of the Pacific Station or to the Chief Naval Officers at Vancouver's Island, with the instructions that, in accordance therewith, the detachment of royal marines now stationed at the Island of San Juan should be at once withdrawn. The Admiral or Chief Naval Officer will also be requested to convey to the officer in command of the detachment, and to the men under his orders, the appreciation of Her Majesty's Government of the harmonious manner in which the joint occupation has been conducted, which reflects the greatest credit on the officers and men of the occupying force of both countries.

Boundary-line through the Haro Channel.

Earl Granville has further instructed me to propose to the Government of the United States that the work of the Boundary Commission, which was interrupted in 1859, should be resumed and completed by the preparation of a map or chart showing the exact position of the boundary-line from the Gulf of Georgia through the Haro Channel to the ocean, under the Treaty of 1846 and the award of the Emperor of Germany.

Her Majesty's Government considers that, in compliance with the Thirty-fifth Article of the Treaty of Washington, this should be done with as little delay as possible in order to give effect to the Emperor's award. It presumes that the surveys which have already been made will render it unnecessary for another commission to meet on the spot, but it leaves the details of the arrangement to be made for the completion of the work of the commission for further consideration.

I have, &c.,

EDW'D THORNTON.

No. 22.

Sir E. Thornton to Mr. Fish.

BRITISH LEGATION,
Washington, November 23, 1872.

San Juan evacuated by British.

MY DEAR MR. FISH: I have just received a telegram from Lord Granville in the following words:

Admiralty have received a telegram repeating that the detachment of Royal Marines has evacuated San Juan.

Believe me, very truly, yours,

EDW'D THORNTON.

No. 23.

Mr. Fish to Sir E. Thornton.

DEPARTMENT OF STATE,
Washington, November 25, 1872.

MY DEAR SIR EDWARD: Thanks for your note of Saturday giving me copy of Lord Granville's telegram.

Action of British Government highly appreciated.

The spontaneous action of the British Government in accepting the award is highly appreciated.

Believe me, as ever, very truly, yours,

HAMILTON FISH.

○

CHARTS WHICH ACCOMPANIED THE CASE OF THE GOVERNMENT OF HER BRITANNIC MAJESTY.

No. I.

Carta Esférica de los Reconocimientos hechos en la Costa N. O. de America, en 1791 y 1792, por las goletas Sutil y Mexicana, y otros buques de Su Magestad. (Published at Madrid, 1802.)

No. II.

A chart showing part of the coast of Northwest America, with the tracks of His Majesty's sloop Discovery, and armed tender Chatham, commanded by George Vancouver, esq., and prepared under his immediate inspection by Lieutenant Joseph Baker, in which the continental shore has been traced and determined from latitude 50° 30′ north and longitude 236° 12′ east to latitude 52° 15′ north and longitude 232° 40′ east at the different periods shown by the tracks. (Published at London in 1798.)

No. III.

North America, west coast.—Haro and Rosario Straits, surveyed by Captain G. H. Richards and the officers of Her Majesty's ship Plumper, 1858–'59; and the shores of Juan de Fuca Strait to Admiralty Inlet. (From Captain H. Kellett's survey, 1847.)

No. IV.

America, northwest coast.—Strait of Juan de Fuca, surveyed by Captain Henry Kellett, R. N., 1847; Haro and Rosario Straits, by Captain G. H. Richards, R. N., 1858; Admiralty Inlet and Puget Sound, by the United States exploring expedition, 1841; south coast of Cape Flattery, by the same, in 1853.

No. V.

Map of Oregon and Upper California, from the surveys of John Charles Frémont and other authorities. (Drawn by Charles Preuss, under the orders of the Senate of the United States. Washington City, 1848.)

www.ingramcontent.com/pod-product-compliance
Lightning Source LLC
LaVergne TN
LVHW010213110826
845151LV00004B/1073